Exile & Embrace

NORTHEASTERN UNIVERSITY PRESS) *Boston*)

Exile & Embrace

Contemporary Religious Discourse on the Death Penalty

ANTHONY SANTORO

Northeastern University Press
An imprint of University Press of New England
www.upne.com
© 2013 Anthony Santoro
All rights reserved
Manufactured in the United States of America
Designed by Eric M. Brooks
Typeset in Arnhem and Egyptian Slate
by A. W. Bennett, Inc.

Hardcover ISBN: 978-1-55553-816-3
Paperback ISBN: 978-1-55553-817-0
Ebook ISBN: 978-1-55553-818-7

University Press of New England is a member of the Green Press Initiative. The paper used in this book meets their minimum requirement for recycled paper.

For permission to reproduce any of the material in this book, contact Permissions, University Press of New England, One Court Street, Suite 250, Lebanon NH 03766; or visit www.upne.com

Library of Congress Cataloging-in-Publication Data are available upon request.

5 4 3 2 1

Except where otherwise noted, all biblical citations are from the New Revised Standard Version Bible, copyright © 1989 National Council of the Churches of Christ in the United States of America. Used by permission. All rights reserved.

A version of chapter 2 originally appeared as "Between Moral Certainty and Morally Certain: The Religious Debate over the Death Penalty in the United States," in Volker Depkat and Jürgen Martschukat, eds. *Religion and Politics in Europe and the United States: Transnational Historical Approaches.* © 2013 by the Woodrow Wilson International Center for Scholars. Reprinted with permission of The Johns Hopkins University Press.

(For my family)

I can remember how when I was young
I believed death to be a phenomenon of the
body; now I know it to be merely a function
of the mind—and that of the minds of the
ones who suffer the bereavement.
> (WILLIAM FAULKNER,
> *As I Lay Dying*

Contents

Preface   xi

Acknowledgments   xv

List of Abbreviations   xix

1) Introduction   1

2) Between Moral Certainty and Morally Certain *The Churches Discuss the Death Penalty*   26

3) Between the Innocent Man and Osama bin Laden *The Believer and the Death Penalty, as Viewed from the Pew*   47

4) The Exile *Instantiated and Revealed*   81

5) The Bloggers' Exegesis *From the Death Penalty to Taxonomies of the Executive*   121

6) Death, Difference, and Conscience   147

7) Opening the Space *From Exile to Embrace*   177

8) Conclusion   207

Appendix   213

Notes   215

Bibliography   267

Index   297

Preface

About fifteen years ago, watching a hockey game, I was asked, apropos of nothing, whether I supported the death penalty.

This may sound like an unusual question in an unusual context, but it makes perfect sense if you knew Marie Deans.

By then I did oppose the death penalty, though it wasn't something to which I gave a lot of thought. My opposition was by no means the result of a deliberative process; it was far more reflexive than reflective. I was nineteen or so, in college, and trying to figure out more directly personally relevant issues.

I hadn't always opposed capital punishment, either. I can remember arguing for a radical expansion of the death penalty in high school government classes. But, again, this was reflexive, not something I had actually thought about.

That question, and my realization, led ultimately to this book. I set out to answer as best I could a question of my own: what *is* the death penalty? What is it, when we really think about it? And that's what brings me back to my realization that I had opposed and supported something I had never particularly thought about.

Have we ever really thought about it? As a nation, as a people, as a society? The question sounds gratuitous. I can see where it would sound either insulting or superior, though I do not mean it to be either. And yet I have to ask, have we ever really thought about what it means to arrogate to ourselves the authority and power to take human life?

I am, as I have said, an abolitionist, though I like to think that my opposition to the death penalty is better founded than it was when Marie first inquired. About ten years ago, I went to work for Marie at a nonprofit she had founded, the Virginia Mitigation Project (VMP). The primary goal of the Project was to help defense counsel provide indigent defendants — of which there are no shortage within the capital punishment system — with a comprehensive mitigation defense. This involved extensive background investigation, many hours of interviews, and confronting the reality of what it means to oppose the death penalty. I represented VMP in coalition-building efforts with other activist groups, and there, and at other public events dealing with capital punishment, I began to appreciate the extent to which religious belief seemed to influence people on both sides of the argument. I also ran VMP's monitoring project, which is an elevated way to say that I sat with piles upon piles of newspaper clippings spanning well over a decade and tried to tally up the total number of murders, capital-eligible murders, and murders charged as capital in Virginia over that period. It may not sound like much, but reading hundreds of different newspaper articles and confronting the horrible facts of these cases does make things more real.

Our timing wasn't great—we were working in the aftermath of 9/11, and raising funds for this kind of work was particularly difficult. I went to grad school several years later and began work on the dissertation that ultimately became this book. Like many such projects, this one started somewhere else entirely before evolving over a series of complex and not altogether related steps into a version of this book. It wasn't until I was well into the research that I figured out that what I was doing was trying to answer that question, the question that had apparently lodged somewhere in my brain during my work with VMP and never been dislodged: what *is* the death penalty, and have we really thought about it?

In many ways, this book begins and ends with a pair of protests on June 25, 2008, one in Richmond, Virginia, outside the executive office building, and one in Greensville County, Virginia, a little ways down the interstate. A pair of events occurred that day. The Supreme Court decided *Kennedy v. Louisiana* (128 S.Ct. 2641 [2008]), which held it unconstitutional to execute persons who rape children but neither kill nor intend to kill their victims. That evening, Virginia executed Robert Stacy Yarbrough, the state's one hundredth execution in the modern era (i.e., since the Supreme Court's 1976 decision in *Gregg v. Georgia*).

Executions in Virginia are scheduled to take place at 9 p.m., which benefits protestors in a strange way: we have ample time to protest on the sidewalk outside the executive office building right through the afternoon rush hour and then head down to the field outside the state prison, where we're permitted to renew our protest and vigil.

This "milestone" vigil remains the largest vigil I have ever attended. Representatives from out-of-state organizations joined "the usual suspects" in Richmond or Greensville or both. I renewed acquaintances with people I'd met years earlier while with VMP, including relatives of death row inmates. I describe the Greensville portion some in my conclusion, but what I remember most about the Richmond protest was the feeling of relative anonymity. As we stood on the sidewalk on a dazzlingly sunny (and, as I recall, fairly hot) summer afternoon beside a traffic-clogged street at rush hour, people didn't seem particularly to notice. There were a few ambivalent honks, a few less ambiguous signs of support and, well, not, and a great deal of studious ignoring—windows up, radio on, rapt attention to some vague spot in front of the driver or their cell phone conversation. For some we were actively there; for others we were a passive, albeit loud, bit of background.

This vigil also had a more visible media presence than others I've participated in, which is to say, it *had* a media presence. What it lacked—the subject of much speculation—was a hearse. Typically, the vehicles bearing the executed body away from the prison drive out the gates and up the road adjacent to the field. We waited long past the "normal" time, and waited still past the time when even botched executions are typically done. No vehicles at all. Camera crews and protesters alike drove away into the night.

I got home from this vigil and the others I attended that summer in time to catch some late local news, and each time I saw a clergyman—I don't recall any clergywomen—solemnly speaking to the biblical rightness of the death penalty as a necessary way to respond to heinous crimes—that ubiquitous adjective, "heinous"—and as a way God has told us to honor and preserve life.

In this as in so many other things, both sides say exactly the same thing, for almost the same reasons, but to very different ends. Abolitionists and retentionists—death penalty opponents and proponents alike—use death to witness to life. The following is my exploration of the meaning and act of this witnessing as told and as done by people thinking about it in contemporary America.

Justice Thurgood Marshall believed, or perhaps hoped, that if Americans ever took the time to learn about how capital punishment really worked and what it really did, we would turn against it. I am not persuaded of this. I *am* persuaded that we need to spend more time thinking about what it really means to use death to witness to life. This book's cover image speaks eloquently on this point. Have we really thought about this? Have we really thought about this in terms of our professed values and beliefs? Have we really thought about what it means to kill, and to sanction and even rejoice in killing? Have we really thought about what *else* that means?

If we haven't, we should.

(*Preface* (xiii

Acknowledgments

No project like this is or can ever be the product of one person's effort. I would like to thank the following individuals for their help and contributions.

First, I would like to thank Marie Deans, who, the first time we met, asked me whether or not I supported the death penalty. It was perhaps the first time I ever seriously considered it, and may have indirectly set this project in motion.

My heartfelt thanks also to Richard Pult and everyone at Northeastern University Press for making this process much easier than I suspect it could have been. Thank you also to Christi Stanforth for her hard work in improving this book.

The fieldwork and archival research undertaken for this project were generously supported by a doctoral fellowship from the German Historical Institute (GHI) in Washington, DC, and by grants from the Soheyl Ghaemian Travel Fund for Scholars and the Graduiertenakademie of Heidelberg University. Without this support, I would not have been able to conduct that research. My thanks also to BASF for funding the doctoral fellowship that helped support me for most of this period.

I would like to thank all of the people who granted me interviews for taking the time to do so. I am also deeply grateful to the diocesan/synod/convention staffs that helped me notify their respective clergy about my project and solicit interest in helping me put together the statewide Bible study survey. A large number of people helped me get the word out over the summer of 2008, which translated into an excellent series of studies, without which the project could not have worked as it did. Thank you. Of course, I am also very grateful to the pastors, priests, and lay leaders who arranged and hosted these studies, as well as to everyone who attended and participated in the sessions. Not all of you were overjoyed to have me there, and not everyone fully trusted my intentions, but you were candid and open with me regardless, and for that, I thank you.

Special thanks to Rev. Joseph M. Vought and Diane Bayer. Joe and I had a number of great conversations over good beer, and Joe gave me his copy of Miroslav Volf's *Exclusion and Embrace*. It's safe to say that this had a significant impact on the book—thanks, Joe. Diane, thank you for the study Bible—my Oxford NRSV has seen better days, and the commentary in the New Interpreter's is excellent.

The research staffs at the National Death Penalty Archive and the American Friends Service Committee archives were invaluable, particularly Donald Davis, Brian Keough, and Mary Osielski. Marie Deans, Father Jim Griffin, and Joe Vought allowed me to boost some of their personal file collections, to be returned at a later date. I'm reasonably certain you each got everything back.

In order to have a better understanding of the intricacies of the death penalty as it operates, as well as to clarify any number of legal questions I had, I spoke with a number of attorneys and legal scholars. Jennifer Givens, Rob Lee, and Laura Thornton of the Virginia Capital Representation Resource Center; David Bruck of the Virginia Capital Case Clearinghouse; and William Bowers, Tripp Chalkley, William Funk, and Mark Stichel all answered my questions patiently and were informative and helpful. Daniel Ritson and David Tabakin each read the entire manuscript in various stages from a legal point of view and offered helpful comments. Nicholas Kennedy went well above and beyond in generously helping me track down vital materials. I am indebted to all of you.

Thanks also to Detlef Junker, Wilfried Mausbach, and the Heidelberg Center for American Studies for all of their support over the past several years. Thanks also to Philipp Gassert. Uta Balbier, my supervisor during my GHI fellowship, has been a great friend and collaborator from our very first panel together as we continue to work together on various projects. A number of other colleagues helped me refine my thinking and presentation. Volker Depkat and Jürgen Martschukat's comments on an early draft of chapter 2 wound up significantly impacting the remainder of the book. Ron Granieri, Stewart Hoover, Mark Rozell, and Steven Whitfield gave me great comments at conference presentations and helped me refine some of my ideas. Kelly J. Baker, William Bowers, Jennifer Green, Robert Jewett, Charles Mathewes, Sean McCloud, Austin Sarat, and Chad Uran took the time to help me out at various other stages of this process. Jacob Heil and Anja Milde were among those who had the generally thankless job of reading my drafts and helping me sharpen and shorten. And special thanks of course to the other two-thirds of the "Totemic Triad," Sebastian Emling and Katja Rakow, who have been a tremendous source of support, intellectual stimulation, and fun over these last several years.

I am of course deeply grateful to my doctoral supervisor, Manfred Berg, and my second reader, Inken Prohl. Both of them provided a tremendous amount of support throughout that process and have continued to support my work. Thank you. I am also particularly thankful to John D. Bessler and Susan F. Sharp, my manuscript reviewers, whose thoughtful and engaged comments and suggestions were of immense value in refining this book. Any errors or shortcomings are, of course, my own fault.

Thanks also and particularly to my family. Frank and Linda, my parents, and Brenna and Jeremy, my siblings, have provided immeasurable support over the years.

Lastly, and most importantly of all, thank you and all my love to my girls. To my wife, Iris, without whom this book could not and would not have been completed, thank you. To my daughters, Lilja and Eyja, you made even the worst days better and are sources of incomparable joy. I love you all.

Abbreviations

ABC) American Baptist Churches (USA)
AFSC) American Friends Service Committee
AOG) Assemblies of God
CWU) Church Women United
ELCA) Evangelical Lutheran Church in America
LCMS) Lutheran Church—Missouri Synod
LDS) Church of Jesus Christ of Latter-day Saints
MICC) Michigan Catholic Conference
NAE) National Association of Evangelicals
NCADP) National Coalition to Abolish the Death Penalty
NDPA) National Death Penalty Archive
NIV) Holy Bible, New International Version
NRSV) Holy Bible, New Revised Standard Version
PCUSA) Presbyterian Church (USA)
SBC) Southern Baptist Convention
TEV) Holy Bible, Today's English Version
UCC) United Church of Christ
UMC) United Methodist Church
USCC) United States Catholic Conference
USCCB) United States Conference of Catholic Bishops
VAUMC) Virginia Conference of the United Methodist Church
VCC) Virginia Council of Churches
VICPP) Virginia Interfaith Center for Public Policy
VIS) Victim Impact Statements

1

> We all carry within us our places of exile, our crimes and our ravages. But our task is not to unleash them on the world; it is to fight them in ourselves and others.
>
> (ALBERT CAMUS, *The Rebel: An Essay on Man in Revolt*

> To speak of a disaster as "tragic," then, may seem to be a scoundrel's recourse, at least if it is supposed somehow to justify an unwillingness to address suffering. It is far more in accord with our democratic sensibility to accept the responsibility for doing something to remedy the situation.
>
> (KEVIN CROTTY, "Democracy, Tragedy, and Responsibility"

Introduction

In 1972, when Marie Deans was thirty-two and pregnant with her second child, her mother-in-law, Penny, was murdered. Penny's husband, Jabo, had died a year before, and when Marie became pregnant, "it was like a new life . . . for all of us." Penny drove from her home in Charleston, South Carolina, to visit Jabo's family in North Carolina and tell them about the baby. Sometime during her return drive a man began following her. When she arrived home, he entered the house behind her, fatally shooting her twice. Marie and her husband were prevented from entering the home when they arrived at the scene; they found out that Penny had been killed by asking police at the scene about an ambulance they had passed en route, an ambulance with no lights on. That ambulance, they were told, was bringing Penny to the hospital for an autopsy.[1]

Deans had had an inclination toward abolitionism before Penny's death, but said that it was fairer to say that she was not for the death penalty than that she was in favor of abolishing it. The way her mother-in-law's murder was handled, however, changed that. When Deans and her husband decided that they did not want the death penalty sought, police and prosecutors marginalized and disregarded them. They later learned that Penny's killer had escaped from a Maine prison. During the escape he had killed another woman and stolen her car. After the man's sister turned him in, Deans and her husband told prosecutors that they would do everything in their power to fight extradition to South Carolina. In the end, Penny's killer received a life sentence in Maine, and Deans had embarked on a lifelong career of abolitionism.

Deans eventually moved from South Carolina to Richmond, Virginia, where she founded the Virginia Coalition on Jails and Prisons. Affiliated with the Southern Coalition on Jails and Prisons, the Virginia Coalition was dedicated to stopping the expanding prison-industrial complex, seeking new approaches to criminal justice, and opposing the death penalty, which she described as "something that is destroying the soul of our people." Deans corralled lawyers for indigent defendants and visited some of the men on death row, where she shared a last meal with Richard Whitley, who was executed on July 6, 1987. Whitley "wanted ice tea and he wanted tea for everybody, so they brought a jug of ice tea. I am sitting near the bars close to Richard and they put the jug down and it says on the side, 'Cider Vinegar' and without thinking I said, 'Oh my God. And our Lord thirsted and they gave him vinegar.'"[2]

Patricia Streeter's daughter, Sarah, was raped and murdered twelve days before her eighteenth birthday. When Streeter first saw the man who killed her daughter, she was surprised. She "thought he would look like a monster, but he didn't." For two years, since the police had arrived at her home at 6:45 a.m. to confirm that Sarah was her daughter, Streeter had survived, hounded by the media, waiting for the trial to begin. There she sat in the same room with her daughter's killer, hearing the details of the crime repeatedly over the course of the proceedings. Streeter was satisfied when the man was sentenced to death; anything less, she said, would have "carried the message that [her] daughter's life was of little value." She acknowledges the arguments against taking life in retribution for crimes, but she sees the problem from the other side. What about self-defense, she wonders? What about war? If taking life is acceptable in those situations, then perhaps capital punishment is also justified. After all, the murderer made a choice to kill, and we are left to deal with that choice.[3]

Jane M. May agrees with Streeter. May served on the jury that sentenced Bobby Lee Ramdass to death for murdering a convenience store clerk in Fairfax County, Virginia. During the trial, May and the other jurors learned about Ramdass's childhood. He suffered such abuse that May conceded that "with [his] dismal and abused life, this young man obviously was not grounded in the principles of right and wrong." Nevertheless, while this poor childhood — which also included a parent tutoring Ramdass in the finer points of committing crimes — may have contributed to his offense, May refused to see it as an excuse for Ramdass's actions: "Each of us is held responsible for our behavior and for our mistakes." Conservative columnist Cal Thomas said much the same while voicing his disgust that Zacarias Moussaoui escaped a death sentence. Moussaoui, the alleged twentieth hijacker on September 11, 2001, was sentenced to life in prison by a Virginia court. He may have had an unstable childhood and a dysfunctional family life, Thomas allowed, but "there are plenty of people with similar 'dysfunctional' backgrounds, [and] they do not plot to assassinate innocent civilians." The punishment should fit the offense, Thomas wrote, which means it should fit the offender, and the most salient characteristic of the offender is not any trauma they may have suffered but the fact that they chose to commit their crime.[4]

Danny King is one of those who chose to commit his crime. He was executed in 1998 for the 1990 murder of Carolyn Rogers. During his time on death row, King had a "Damascus Road" moment, where he realized who he had become and where he had led himself, and set about to repair his life as best he could. He also began to write poetry, some of which reflected his self-awakening and his growing realization of the broader implications of his situation:

> If the world were a story book subject
> would you choose it for your children to read
> Could you answer the questions that they may ask
> about the Sorrow, the Pain and the Greed
>
> Or would you seek to gently mask it
> with words slightly less than true
> As you looked at the trust in the eyes of your child
> would you wonder just what you should do
>
> These questions I ask not to shame you
> but in the hope they will lead you to see
> The acts of the parent decide for the child
> what the shape of their future will be

> Is this world you have built one of beauty
> or a curse that you choose to pass on
> Will your children remember the victories
> or the failures left behind when you're gone[5]

This book addresses a question that can be phrased deceptively simply: What is the death penalty? It is certainly, as Christian Boulanger and Austin Sarat have said, "legally administered state killing, used as a punishment in response to a crime." This is precisely what capital punishment is, but this brief definition leaves too much unsaid. We can refine the definition somewhat using David Garland's definition of punishment. Punishment, Garland says, is more than specific punishments meted out in response to specific crimes. Punishment "is a social institution embodying and 'condensing' a range of purposes and a stored-up depth of historical meaning" and has condemnatory, ritualistic, and communicative purposes and effects. Possible punishments for given crimes are decided upon and fixed prior to the specific offense, which then is judged accordingly. A single voice dominates throughout, that of the *we*. *We* respond. *We* exact justice and react justly, or *we* fail to discharge our obligation in this regard. Initially, and finally, we are compelled to recognize that the death penalty is about death.[6]

This *we* is doubly noteworthy. Not only is the United States the last remaining Western country to execute its offenders, but it is also, by all measures, the most religious of its Western peers. In pointing this out, I am not arguing for a consideration of the death penalty as an exercise in American exceptionalism—such seems to me entirely beside the point. Rather, I wish to call attention to the importance of considering religion when trying to understand the cultural vitality of capital punishment in contemporary America. At root, as Supreme Court Justice William Brennan noted,[7] the death penalty is a moral question, and it is one that the churches and religiously motivated activists on both broad sides of the debate have long contested. Understanding how religion and punishment interact here gives us a fuller picture of how the death penalty has survived and continues to thrive in portions of the country.

It can be deceptively easy to structure a study on the death penalty. Comparative studies benefit from a dizzying array of information available on innumerable data points and metrics, while local studies permit detailed analyses of representative phenomena and practices. This book—part meditation on capital punishment, part analysis of the interaction between religion and the death penalty in contemporary America—draws on elements of each broad category. This is a national story told in parts through a local study. The national story is the United States in the modern era, that is, the period since the Supreme Court's 1976 decision in *Gregg v. Georgia*, which overturned 1972's *Furman v. Georgia* and restored the death penalty to constitutional legitimacy.[8] The local study focuses on Virginia in the same time span. By using the religious discourse to locate and deconstruct the modern death penalty, and by shifting between these two focal points to highlight the continuity and commensurability of the local and national debates, I explore the continued institutional and mythic salience and vitality of the American death penalty.

I make three arguments in this book. First, the death penalty has far less to do with either the offender or the offense than it does with us. This is due to the confluence of the "state of exception" with the Real in the capital murder event. In making this claim, I begin with two assumptions. First, the death penalty is more culturally legible if we begin from the position that in the context of the various "wars" America is waging—against drugs, against crime, against terror—the contemporary political state is one of a constant state of exception, one of heightened urgency that legitimates granting exceptional power to sovereign persons and institutions in the defense of innocent life. Within this state of exception, "the care of life coincides with the fight against the enemy."[9] Second, the transgressive event—in this case, the murder (as distinct from the capital murder)—is the reality, while our response to it is the Real. We must first determine whether the offense demands that we consider the life-and-death question; we must then decide whether or not to seek death to protect other lives. Inasmuch as the debate over capital punishment is one over death, it is simultaneously a debate over life—over whence the "right to life" derives, whether and when that right can be revoked or considered forfeit, whether death is legitimate, and, the converse of this last, whether we have the requisite authority to impose death. Given all of these needs, the death penalty cannot be exclusively, or even primarily, about the offender; it must be, and is, about us. This is a point on which Deans, Streeter, May, and Thomas all agree.

The second argument, a corollary to the first, is that the retentionist and abolitionist discourses are virtually identical in their essential Cartesian humanism.[10] They are also strikingly similar in their appropriations of the "normal" and its deployment in the respective conceptions of exile and embrace, as the following chapters show. The difference between the two discourses boils down to the difference between event and process. Fundamentally, the difference is that the event-based retentionist point of view is characterized by a move to embrace in order to exile, while the process-based abolitionist point of view is characterized by a move to exile in order to leave open the possibility of later embrace and in some cases to actively seek out this embrace.

Though both exile and embrace will be developed in the following chapters, it may be helpful to sketch both concepts briefly here. Exile is a differentiation, a declaration that the other is more *not like us* than *like us*. That said, the other cannot be exclusively *not like us*—they must, somewhat paradoxically, remain enough *like us* to be clearly *not like us*, for reasons that will be made clear. Exile is a declaration that the other is beyond a point of no return, or, in some cases, beyond a point of meaningful return. Embrace, on the other hand, is a declaration that the other is or could be more *like us* than not.

Third, in both discourses, the defining feature of the exile is necessary guilt combined with adequate culpability. This is the case regardless of the discursive context; if there is anything like a universal in the broad death penalty debates and discourses, it is this point. The American death penalty would lose all symbolic resonance and, I argue, would lose its legitimacy totally—even within the retentionist discourse—without this element of guilt, which is most clearly visible in the presumed identity of legal guilt and actual guilt. My characterization of the exile differs from two tropes widely seen in the broad discourse over the death penalty. The first of these is the other as the "monster" that Streeter expected. If the other is conceived as an individual who is fundamentally *not like us*, then I would argue that this other has a very limited role in the discourse. If, however, we understand the other as Austin Sarat and Susan F. Sharp do[11]—as someone who is more *not like us* than *like us*, or is *not like us* in a crucial element—then this other plays a much greater role in the discourse. The exile is very near this other, though the method of instantiating otherness is the crucial determinant. The retentionist discourse argues that the exile is created by their offense, while the abolitionist discourse tends to argue that the exile is revealed by the offense. These different understandings of how we should understand the offense colors how each discourse depicts the exile relative to how much they are *like us* as opposed to *not like us*. Thus, though my concept of the exile differs from the popular image of the other, Streeter's monster or Thomas's "Islamofascist," for example, it is in line with and allows for the subsequent dehumanization of the other that comprises a significant portion of the broader death penalty discourse.[12]

In this introduction, I want to do four things. First, I will briefly locate the United States within a broader worldwide perspective on the death penalty. Second, I will provide a short overview of the history of the American death penalty as relevant to our exploration. Third, I will explain how the death penalty currently works by looking at a representative case study. Finally, I outline the remainder of the book.

Situating the American Death Penalty Globally

According to Amnesty International, 141 countries are currently "abolitionist in law or practice," while 57 retain capital punishment for ordinary crimes. In 1965, in the middle of the period when the American churches were turning against the death penalty, 25 countries were abolitionist. Eleven of these had abolished the death penalty for all crimes, while the remaining 14 "had abolished it for ordinary crimes in peacetime." By 1988, 35 countries had completely abolished, with 17 more abolishing for ordinary peacetime crime. By 2001, those numbers were 75 and 14, respectively, and as of August 2012, 97 countries were completely abolitionist, 8 had abolished for ordinary peacetime crime, and 36 more were categorized as de facto abolitionist, having carried out no known executions for at least ten years. All of Europe except Belarus; a majority of African countries; most of Oceania; and most of North, Central, and South America is abolitionist either by law or by practice. Much of Asia, including all of the Middle East except Israel and Turkey; a minority of African countries; and much of the Caribbean join the United States as the world's retentionist nations.[13]

The United States is a world leader in both executions and number of death sentences pronounced. In 2010, the United States ranked fifth in number of known executions, behind China, Iran, North Korea, and Yemen. In the same year, American juries imposed over one hundred death sentences, good for seventh among the countries for which that information is available, behind Pakistan, Iraq, Egypt, Nigeria, Algeria, and Malaysia. These numbers underscore the American uniqueness with regard to capital punishment, which thrives in the United States despite being counterindicated three different ways. Carsten Anckar's study of factors that determine support for the death penalty found both type of government and the predominant religion can be used to predict the use of capital punishment. Authoritarian states and states that merge religion and law frequently support the death penalty, while democracies and disestablished states do not. Majority Islamic and Buddhist countries support and use the death penalty, while majority Christian countries tend to reject it; majority Hindu countries are split, and Israel has abolished. The older and more stable a democracy is, the more likely it is to reject the death penalty. Democracies, as Michael J. Perry notes, predicate themselves on a fundamental respect for human rights, which they typically enshrine in their constitutions. This enshrinement of basic human rights advances a twofold claim: "*Each and every human being has equal and inherent dignity*," and we "*should live our lives in accord with the fact that every human being has inherent dignity*." As we will see in the chapters that follow, abolitionists and retentionists each advance both claims from their respective positions, though they necessarily draw different conclusions about how we should act in order to protect fundamental human dignity.[14]

The dominant pattern would predict that the democratic, majority Christian United States would be abolitionist, and yet it is among the world leaders in executions and death sentences. As Harold Hongju Koh has remarked, *"No other civilized, democratic government that has our commitment to human rights resorts to the death penalty in the way we do."* One reason the United States may be unique in this regard is its particular federalist political structure, with power divided among national, state, and local governments. Peter A. Ozanne, for example, has argued that this divided structure makes the relevant jurisdictions much more receptive to the popular will than is the case in our peer nations. We need not go as far as Ozanne does to note that in Western Europe, for example, the death penalty was abolished nondemocratically in democratic states; political elites abolished capital punishment over the popular will. Ozanne's argument is compelling and helps explain much of why the American death penalty persists; it is, as David Garland has noted, an eminently local phenomenon, as the contemporary and historical debates have always shown. The presence and activity of organized religions is another reason that capital punishment has endured where it has and been done away with elsewhere. When we look at these debates, as we will throughout this book, we will see that institutional religion has always influenced how the public thinks about and legislates capital punishment from the colonial era to the present.[15]

The Death Penalty in America
From the Colonial Era to the Modern Era

Capital punishment has been a constant in American history. It has varied in form and frequency, but it has always been present. This means that we can work quickly from the colonial to the modern era by looking briefly at the history of challenges to the status quo. Like the death penalty itself, challenges to capital punishment have been relatively constant, if discontinuous, and they offer a useful way to guide us from the colonial era to the modern era.

Early colonial criminal codes were based on biblical and ecclesiastical laws mixed with laws enacted to promote the individual colony's stability, order, and success. Virginia's first legal code, Sir Thomas Dale's 1611 "Lawes Divine, Morall, and Martial," was a draconian code that prescribed a variety of punishments for an assortment of crimes. Designed to restore civil order and to increase the profitability of the Virginia Company's venture, punishments included burning, breaking on the wheel, impalement, and being lashed to a tree and left to starve to death. Offenses that could be punished with death included "blasphemy, the uttering of 'traitorous words' or 'unseemly, and unfitting speeches' against the colonial government, failing to honor the Sabbath, bartering with Indians, stealing roots, herbs, grapes, corn, or livestock, perjury, robbery, sodomy, adultery, rape, and murder."[16]

Laws in Massachusetts and New York were similar. Massachusetts's first criminal code, the *Body of Liberties*, was enacted in 1641—eleven years after the colony's first execution—and generally tracked with Mosaic law. Idolatry, blasphemy, bearing false witness, and assaulting one's parents were all capital offenses, though executions were generally reserved for criminals whose offenses "threatened the religious and moral purity of the Holy Commonwealth": murder, witchcraft, and sexual crimes. New York's "Duke Laws," passed in 1665, made such acts as blasphemy, striking one's parents, and several different varieties of murder and sexual offenses capital crimes.[17]

From the late 1600s to the revolution, the colonies came further under the direct influence of the British crown and British penal norms. England's "Bloody Code" developed in this period; the roster of capital offenses in England quadrupled, from around fifty to over two hundred, by the end of the eighteenth century. Lists of capital crimes expanded in the colonies as well, from several dozen to "hundreds" in the mid-1700s in colonies like Virginia. Somewhat mitigating this expansion was the continued use of alternative punishments, such as corporal punishments, banishments, mock hangings, benefit of clergy, and jury nullification, where juries would either decline to convict or convict defendants of a lesser crime if they deemed capital punishment disproportionate to the offense. In fact, despite the variety of crimes for which one could be put to death in the colonies, executions were comparatively infrequent and most often befell outsiders and "incorrigible[s]," or repeat offenders. Benefit of clergy, a protection that originally developed in England to relegate offenses involving clergy to trial in ecclesiastical courts, gradually expanded in England and the colonies until, by the mid-1700s, claiming benefit of clergy after conviction was a way to avoid punishment for many first-time offenders. These offenders were generally branded on the hand to show that they had received this benefit, leading to the modern custom of raising a hand when swearing an oath; originally, this gesture was a formal inspection of the hand for the mark of a prior conviction.[18]

Americans began seriously to question the utility and value of capital punishment in the 1760s and '70s, and extensive debate over its propriety emerged by the 1780s and '90s. Prominent political leaders such as George Clinton, Benjamin Franklin, Thomas Jefferson, and James Madison all favored radical restrictions on capital punishment, which, by the revolution, had become decoupled from theological purposes and had been turned toward punishing murder, property crime, and slave crime. After the revolution, the new states widely restricted the death penalty, the better, state legislatures thought, to reflect the Enlightenment values of the new republic. In so doing, they joined the traditional peace churches like the Quakers, who had begun agitating to restrict or abolish capital punishment a century earlier but whose numbers were never sufficient to force a wide debate on the issue. Franklin's famous rhetorical question aptly sums up the mood of this era: "If I am not myself so barbarous, so bloody-minded and revengeful, as to kill a fellow creature for stealing from me fourteen shillings, how can I approve of a law that does it?"[19]

European Enlightenment thought also drove the move to restrict the death penalty in this period. No influence was greater than that of Cesare Beccaria's treatise *On Crimes and Punishments*, which electrified the colonial intelligentsia on arrival. Newspapers advertised the book and published it serially. Publishing houses in cities up and down the eastern seaboard pumped out English translations. The nation's first three presidents, George Washington, John Adams, and Thomas Jefferson, were avid readers and proponents of Beccaria's idea, and Enlightenment thought formed the intellectual basis from which American thinkers such as Jefferson and Dr. Benjamin Rush advocated restricting and abolishing capital punishment, respectively. Jefferson agreed with Beccaria that it was the certainty of punishment, not its severity, that had the greatest deterrent and practical effect: "The principle of Beccaria is sound. Let the legislators be merciful but the executors of law inexorable." Dr. Benjamin Rush, one of the first American abolitionists for whom "the death penalty . . . was inseparable from religion," attacked the death penalty as "a usurpation of 'the prerogative of heaven . . . whether it be inflicted by a single person, or by a whole community.'" The combination of these influences within this cultural ethos is best reflected in a 1786 Pennsylvania penal reform statute reducing the number of crimes subject to the death penalty: this statute stated, "It is the wish of every good government to reclaim rather than destroy."[20]

These factors combined to generate a wave of states—Pennsylvania (1794); New Jersey, New York, and Virginia (1796); and Kentucky (1798)—enacting graduated murder statutes, the first such statutes in any jurisdiction deriving from the English legal tradition. A wave of state abolitions followed between the 1830s and 1850s. This period was defined by a belief in the capacity of penal institutions to reform wayward individuals, which, combined with an emphasis on the power of the penitentiary to act according to its name and bring about the offender's internally driven reformation, led to a moment in which the death penalty was hotly debated in many northern states, limited in others, and abolished outright in three. The most prominent partisans on each side of these abolition debates tended to be clergy, a pattern that that has largely continued into the present. Death penalty opponents scored an early victory in Maine. In 1835, over ten thousand Mainers witnessed a public hanging that, as was so often the case at such events, erupted into drunken violence and had to be controlled by police. In response, the Maine legislature passed a law in 1837 barring executions for at least one full year from the date of the conviction; executions would be permitted to proceed only when the governor explicitly authorized them. Maine did not have another execution for nearly thirty years.[21]

Between 1835 and 1837, Maine's churches were active in urging this kind of reform effort, "challeng[ing] the notion that Christian scripture required the execution of murderers [and] noting that some of the greatest human tragedies had taken place in man's mistaken zeal in following God's law." In 1846, Michigan became the first English-speaking jurisdiction to abolish capital punishment, followed by Rhode Island (1852) and Wisconsin (1853). True to form, religion figured prominently in these abolitions. In Michigan, for example, a house select committee issued a report in 1844 urging repeal of the death penalty on the basis of the fact that "no man hath a power to destroy life but by commission from God, the author of it," and disputing that the Bible supported capital punishment; the report also expressed concern over wrongful — and irremediable — executions.[22]

Following the disruptions caused by the Civil War and Reconstruction, the abolitionist wave swelled again from the late nineteenth century to World War I. Abolitionism in this period was marked by the emphasis on "scientific" or "rational" corrections; mistrust of the electric chair, then being touted by proponents as a more humane, error-free method of execution; and the emergence of the Social Gospel, an actively socially conscious expression of Christianity. Abolitionists compared the electric chair to burning at the stake, a comparison made as late as 1985 by Supreme Court Justice William Brennan, and argued "that capital punishment was 'out of harmony' with Christian traditions" and that it "violate[d] the sacredness of human life," as abolitionists in Minnesota and North Dakota argued. Proponents, meanwhile, pointed to the era's lynching and vigilantist violence and claimed that the death penalty was necessary to deter both crime and such displays of mob justice. The abolitionists temporarily won arguments in the ten states that abolished in this era — Colorado (1897), Kansas (1907), Minnesota (1911), Washington (1913), Oregon (1914), North Dakota (1915), South Dakota (1915), Tennessee (1915), Arizona (1916), and Missouri (1917) — but these gains were short-lived; with the exceptions of Minnesota and North Dakota, all of these states reenacted death penalty statutes in the coming years.[23]

The next major changes came during the next big abolitionist period, from the 1950s until the *Furman* decision in 1972. Several factors drove the rise in abolitionism in this period. The first was probably a residual shock from the Holocaust.[24] Great Britain's Royal Commission on Capital Punishment report (1953) also stimulated American abolitionism. The report found that the death penalty in Britain had by that point been so restricted that it would be unrealistic to pare away more categories of capital-eligible crimes; the only reasonable question, it concluded, was whether capital punishment should be retained at all. This report had two effects in the United States. First, it provided American abolitionists with an important resource in their struggle against capital punishment. Second, abolitionists pointed to the report as evidence that modern, civilized democracies were having the conversation and that Americans needed to revisit the debate as well. Abolitionists also approvingly noted Supreme Court Justice Felix Frankfurter's 1950 testimony before the commission on behalf of his own opposition to the death penalty.[25]

Several widely publicized cases brought capital punishment before the public in new ways. Two defendants in particular—Barbara Graham and Caryl Chessman—became celebrities. Graham, executed in 1955 despite her protestations of innocence, raised the issue of the propriety of executing women, and her case became the basis for a best-selling book and a popular movie, which garnered Susan Hayward an Oscar for best actress. Chessman's best-selling books publicized his case and raised the issue of whether it was justifiable to execute someone who never committed a murder. His ultimate execution provoked widespread protests both in the United States and abroad. The furor surrounding the Chessman execution highlighted the two principal elements of the abolitionist efforts in this period, namely, a belief in rehabilitation rather than retribution and a belief in the ability of and need for offenders to reform themselves.[26]

This era also saw the fights over the death penalty head into the courtroom in two significant ways. First, as Stuart Banner points out, criminal appeals "skyrocketed" in this period. The rate of executions declined in concert: appeals of murder convictions, less than 2 percent of court caseloads in the late 1930s, just after the peak years of executions in America, climbed to 6 percent in 1965. From 1945 to 1960, appeals made up roughly 15 percent of state supreme court dockets; they represented more than a quarter of the courts' caseloads between 1965 and 1970. Petitions for a writ of habeas corpus, "the vehicle by which state prisoners can ask federal courts to review their convictions," increased fourfold between 1952 and 1962. At the same time, groups including the NAACP's Legal Defense Fund (LDF) used the courts to challenge the constitutionality of capital punishment in cases of rape, given the extraordinary racial bias inherent in such proceedings. In 1965, the LDF broadened their focus to mounting constitutional challenges to the death penalty per se. When Supreme Court Justices Arthur Goldberg, William O. Douglas, and William Brennan signaled their willingness to consider the constitutionality of the death penalty in their dissent from *Rudolph v. Alabama*, the LDF devised a method of constitutional attack on capital punishment that in 1972 saw the death penalty declared unconstitutional as applied.[27]

Most importantly, this period saw the churches begin to turn against the death penalty en masse. Over two decades beginning in the mid-1950s, this watershed saw most of the denominational bodies in the United States declare their opposition to the death penalty. In 1956, the Methodist Church revised its earlier position calling for study of capital punishment to declare that it "deplore[d] the use of capital punishment." The Methodists were quickly followed by the "American Baptists (1958), [the] Union of American Hebrew Congregations (1959), the American Ethical Union (1960)[,] . . . the United Church of Christ (1962), the Reformed Church in America (1965), and the Lutheran Church in America (1966)." In 1974, "the U.S. Catholic Conference [went] on record in opposition to capital punishment," presaging a development in Catholic doctrine culminating in the changes to the Catholic catechism, as we will discuss in the next chapter.[28]

In 1972 the Supreme Court decided *Furman*, ruling that the death penalty was unconstitutional as applied. The states rushed to amend their laws to craft new death penalties that would pass constitutional muster, and in 1976 the Court reversed itself in *Gregg*, declaring that these new statutes met *Furman*'s standards. The death penalty was back. *Gregg* inaugurated the modern era, an era in which the courts began to close themselves off to capital punishment. This period of "deregulating death," as Robert Weisberg termed it, saw the Supreme Court make an abrupt about-face: in late 1982, after ruling in favor of fourteen of the first fifteen capital defendants whose cases it heard following *Gregg*, the Court "essentially announced that it was going out of the business of telling the states how to administer the death penalty phase of capital murder trials."[29]

In *Barefoot v. Estelle*, which began this turn, the Court held that federal circuit courts are not compelled to grant stays or grant inmates full hearings on the basis of claims that their habeas corpus rights were improperly denied.[30] In *California v. Ramos*, the Court upheld a state provision requiring that capital juries be informed that the governor had the power to reduce a life sentence, meaning that life imprisonment was never completely certain.[31] In *Wainwright v. Goode* and *Barclay v. Florida*, the Justices upheld death sentences in cases where the aggravating factors were neither specified in the state law nor clearly based "in either the facts of the case or [the state's] . . . capital-sentencing law," respectively.[32] *Pulley v. Harris* rejected an inmate's claim of discrimination based on an unclear pattern of sentencing in cases with similar facts, while *Wainwright v. Witt* expanded prosecutors' abilities to strike potential jurors who have moral qualms about capital punishment.[33] The Court made it easier "to impose death sentences on accomplices who neither killed nor intended to kill during the crime,"[34] while making it harder for inmates to raise claims of ineffective trial counsel.[35] After twice ruling that victim impact statements (VIS), statements describing the emotional damage suffered by families of murder victims, were inadmissible as evidence, the Court reversed itself and permitted them.[36] Although it had declared mandatory death penalty statutes unconstitutional, the Court nevertheless upheld state laws mandating death sentences if juries found at least one aggravating circumstance but no mitigating circumstance, despite the apparent contradiction.[37] The Court also upheld the constitutionality of executing mentally retarded and juvenile offenders, while declining to address the racially biased application of the death penalty, even as it acknowledged that bias.[38] Finally, in a roundly criticized decision, the Supreme Court ruled that the Constitution does not guarantee inmates a hearing to consider evidence of actual innocence, even if this evidence was not available during the original trial.[39]

This rash of defeats and narrowing of the opportunities for offenders to seek legal relief did not end litigation; in fact, both *Stanford* and *Penry* were subsequently overturned. The progressive closing of the litigatory avenue forced abolitionists to turn their attention away from specific issues and toward individual defendants and narrow classes of defendants. Attempts to attack capital punishment in court morphed into attempts to attack capital punishment in the court of public opinion. This development is ultimately what led to the peculiar creation and utilization of the exile in the contemporary abolitionist discourse, which can only be understood when the limits of the scapegoat are properly seen as the threshold beyond which a new category of offender is created: the exile.

The Death Penalty in Virginia
Current Procedures and Death Row

Virginia's death penalty is representative of the various retentionist states' processes. When capital-eligible murders occur, local prosecutors decide whether to pursue capital charges. The prosecutor presents a bill of indictment to a grand jury, which determines whether there is enough evidence to prosecute. If so, they will return a "true bill," at which point the prosecutor can proceed with the capital charge. Opponents have stoutly criticized the extent of prosecutorial discretion and the arbitrariness to which it leads. The American Civil Liberties Union's (ACLU) 2003 report on Virginia's capital system, for example, points out that whether an individual is charged with capital murder depends greatly on a variety of nonlegal factors, such as geography—where the crime was committed—and race: "the probability of being charged with capital murder increases if the victim is white and/or the perpetrator is black."[40]

The capital murder trial consists of three phases. The first of these is jury selection. A jury is impaneled to hear both the guilt and the sentencing phases of the trial through a process called voir dire. This jury must be "death-qualified," which means that all jurors must profess to be capable of choosing either a life or a death sentence, as determined by their judgment based on the evidence presented in court. Critics charge that this process demonstrably biases juries in favor of conviction while depriving the defendant of their right to a trial by a fair and impartial jury, an issue that will be dealt with at length in chapter 6.[41]

Once voir dire is complete and the jury impaneled, the trial moves into the guilt phase. At this stage the jury determines whether to find the defendant guilty of capital murder. If the jury returns a guilty verdict, then the trial moves into the sentencing phase. At this point, the prosecution is charged with proving one of two statutory aggravators in order to convince the jury to impose a death sentence — they must prove that the defendant would "constitute a continuing serious threat to society or that his . . . offense . . . was outrageously or wantonly vile, horrible or inhuman." The defense, on the other hand, may present any manner of mitigating evidence to try to convince the jury to render a life verdict, including, but explicitly not limited to, the lack of a prior criminal record, temporary insanity, victim consent, impaired conduct, age, or mental illness or developmental issues.[42]

Defendants are afforded three rounds of appeals after juries recommend a death sentence. Once the trial court certifies the verdict, the Supreme Court of Virginia (SCVA) reviews the proceedings on direct appeal. During this mandatory appeal, the SCVA reviews the complete court record and briefs submitted by the defense and the state to determine whether the trial court committed any errors; whether the sentence of death was imposed prejudicially or was driven by passion, rather than the legal process; or whether the death sentence is disproportionate to the crime. The SCVA "can affirm the death sentence, commute the sentence from death to life imprisonment, or remand the case back to the circuit court for a new sentencing hearing."[43]

Once the SCVA affirms, a number of procedural rules limit the number of subsequent claims that the defendant may raise. The most important of these is procedural default. At trial, attorneys are expected to object to anything that disadvantages their clients. When they do, the objection is recorded and is "preserved," meaning that it can be raised on appeal. If they do not, the claim is defaulted and cannot be raised. Most death penalty states have a "plain-error review" standard, which means that when a lawyer's failure to object was clearly wrong and substantially harmful to their client, the courts will review the claim even if it has been defaulted. Virginia courts, however, "do not follow the plain-error doctrine. Virginia Supreme Court Rule 5:25 establishes a different test — for good cause shown or to attain the ends of justice — and the court has *never* invoked this exception during the modern death penalty era." In fact, the SCVA has overturned proportionally the fewest number of death penalty cases of any state in the modern era. A second limiting rule is Virginia's 21-Day Rule, which holds that courts cannot consider evidence — even evidence of innocence — discovered or presented more than twenty-one days after sentencing. An exception was added in 2001 for biological evidence, but this remains the most restrictive such rule in the country.[44]

If the defendant fails on direct appeal, they may file a habeas corpus petition in state courts. The criminal process is over at this point; habeas petitions are civil actions. Petitioners sue on the grounds that they are being held in violation of their constitutional rights. The type of evidence that state courts can hear at habeas is further limited, as it is at the next phase of the process, federal habeas. Again, the claims that can be raised at federal habeas are narrower and fewer than at state habeas. Moreover, federal habeas petitions have long been the target of conservative "law and order" politicians and have been gradually eroded throughout the modern era, even though — or, more precisely, because — roughly two-thirds of capital cases were overturned at habeas. Petitioners may also appeal directly to the Supreme Court at the conclusion of each stage in this process.[45]

Virginia's death penalty is both exceptional and fully representative of all state death penalties. Virginia is exceptional in its history, current usage, and "reliability" of sentences. The first permanent English settlement in Virginia, the Jamestown colony, was founded in 1607; the first execution was carried out in Virginia in 1608. Over the past four centuries, Virginia has put nearly fourteen hundred men, women, and children to death, a total that includes the first woman executed in the colonies and the youngest child on record — a slave boy named Clem, age twelve. In the modern era, Virginia has put 109 men and women to death, including three who committed their crimes as juveniles, two just four days apart; both numbers rank the state second nationally, trailing only Texas in both categories. Virginia's death penalty is also unusually "reliable" — the SCVA and the federal Fourth Circuit Court of Appeals are both statistically the least likely among their peers to overturn death sentences, giving Virginia juries power unmatched nationally. At the same time, however, Virginia is bound by the same federal case law as every other death penalty state. Like all southern states, and like the United States generally, Virginia's execution history is skewed sharply toward black defendants. Nor has it escaped controversy on other fronts — in addition to racial bias, Virginia has dealt with cases of actual innocence, alleged innocence, and the propriety of executing juveniles, women, the mentally retarded, and foreign nationals.

Finally, as is the case in the United States generally, the leading voices on both sides of the debate are religious organizations.[46]

In Virginia and nationally, debates over the death penalty characteristically focus on six major issues: deterrence, or the lack thereof; cost; retribution; race; innocence; and morality. Deterrence, long a justification for capital punishment, remains part of the popular discourse, though it is increasingly clear that whether executions are a better deterrent than life in prison cannot be demonstrated using any known method of analysis.[47] Cost-based arguments in favor of the death penalty likewise seem to be diminishing, not only due to moral concerns, as will be discussed in subsequent chapters, but also as the general public becomes better acquainted with the fact that capital punishment costs more than incarceration.[48]

Deterrence and cost arguments are broadly based on a question of effect versus impact: if we do this, what will be the result? Two other issues — racial disparity and the problem of innocence — are questions of the process itself, and whether it can ever be made fair enough and perfect enough to be justifiable. Bias and innocence are also more visible — one can see the photographs and news footage detailing crimes, trials, executions, and exonerations; it is impossible to see would-be offenders deterred or, ordinarily, the death penalty's impact on state and local budgets. It is easy to see, for instance, that African Americans make up slightly fewer than 42 percent of inmates on death row, a percentage that virtually equals that of white offenders (44.4 percent). It is easy to see that in the modern era, 35 percent of executed offenders have been black, while 77 percent of the victims in crimes resulting in executions have been white. We can see that there have been 253 executions for crimes involving an African American killing a white person, but only sixteen cases of whites being executed for killing an African American. That application of the death penalty is racially biased is incontrovertible. To paraphrase prominent Virginia lawyer and later Supreme Court Justice Lewis Powell in *McCleskey v. Kemp*, at the least we can see that there is a "discrepancy" in application that "correlate[s] with race." According to *McCleskey*, however, the question is not whether there is *systemic* discrimination in application, but whether there was *individual* discrimination in application—whether the specific defendant was discriminated against based on his or her race.[49]

Innocence is another prominent issue in the public debates over the death penalty, particularly when extraordinary circumstances arise, such as former Illinois governor George Ryan's 2003 blanket commutation of all 167 people on Illinois's death row. Ryan declared a moratorium on March 9, 2000, and directed a commission to investigate Illinois's death penalty system and recommend ways to repair it. Unsatisfied, Ryan pardoned four inmates outright on January 10, 2003, having become convinced of their innocence, and issued his commutation the next day.[50] The importance of innocence, and of innocents, underscores the importance of guilt and of culpability and further underscores the contest over the preservation of life.

Whatever the systemic problems, those on death rows face conditions that can best be described as inhumane. Virginia's death row is divided into three pods—A, B, and C pods—each of which contains two twelve-cell units.[51] A control room overlooks each pod. The pods themselves are designed to minimize any blind spots and permit maximum visibility. Inmates are allowed to interact only with those inmates on their pod, not with those from other pods. Guards can enter the individual cells at any time for any reason. During these "shakedowns," the inmates are handcuffed and/or shackled and strip-searched, frequently including cavity searches, while their meager possessions and living space are ransacked looking for "contraband." Inmates have been left naked and cold for days at a time following shakedowns; in some cases, prison officials have actively worked to prevent inmates from contacting their attorneys—if they had counsel at all—to complain about these humiliations.[52]

Cells on Virginia's death row are 6'10" by 7'6". They contain a steel bunk welded to the wall and adorned with a one-and-a-half-inch-thick mattress, a metal box for storage or writing, a sink, and a toilet. Cells have windows that can be cracked using a crank handle, though security bars and metal mesh shield the far side of the window. Cell doors are stainless steel with a window (3" by 36") and a food slot through which food and medicines can be passed into the cell. In order to take a shower, inmates must extend their arms through the slot to be handcuffed before the cell door will be opened. Typically, Virginia death row inmates will spend nineteen hours a day in their cell, with some time out for recreation (pacing around a small cage in the prison yard, singly—never in groups) or playing cards or chatting with the other men in the pod in the dayroom, where they may sometimes be permitted to take their meals. There is no air-conditioning, and the basic construction of the building—accounting for security concerns and the need to be able to seal off as much of the building as redundantly as possible—means that air circulation is poor at best. Deans described Virginia's death row in summer as "a combination sensory deprivation chamber and oven."[53] Inmates are permitted to purchase fans from the prison commissary, though prison officials frequently target fans for confiscation on grounds that the inmates are disassembling them and weaponizing the fans' parts. The typical five daily hours that inmates are permitted out of their cells can be reduced—or eliminated—at prison officials' discretion. As Thomas crowed in his column lamenting that

Moussaoui escaped a death sentence, death row inmates have been known to lose their minds in similar circumstances.

This dehumanization, these conditions, are all about control, which is to say, about power. Various forms of power collectively form a solid red line connecting all portions of the public discourse on capital punishment. Power is also one of many topics on which the retentionist and abolitionist discourses agree, even if they disagree on what power signifies. Both sides agree that society must reexert its power in the wake of horrific crimes, but whereas the abolitionist discourse balks at subjecting even capital murderers to these conditions, the retentionist discourse sees these conditions as willfully chosen, foreseeable (and thus foreseen) consequences, and thus perfectly acceptable:

> At one extreme is the position best articulated by Sister Helen Prejean: no matter the offense, prisoners retain their basic humanity and are better than their worst acts.... At the other extreme is an attitude ... [that] if an individual commits a crime ... then the prison conditions that accompany the term of incarceration are part of the punishment ... the risks inherent in incarceration—mediocre medical care, substandard food, harsh living conditions, a lack of vocational and educational training, and sexual or physical violence perpetrated by other inmates and guards—are the price one pays for committing a criminal act.... "If you don't want to be raped in prison, then don't break the law."[54]

Todd Peppers and Laura Anderson note that the takeaway from the above is that most people believe "some criminals are inhuman and disposable, thus deserving of inhumane conditions."[55] I think the basis for this response is more complicated than that. The above does not show that the horrific conditions to which inmates are subjected are justified on the basis of their inhumanity. Rather, these conditions are perceived as justified because of the offender's choice. In order for the death penalty to retain its symbolic legitimacy, the offender *must* be capable of rationally choosing to commit the criminal act *and* be capable of rationally making this choice in light of the full range of consequences that would result from the act, including incarceration in inhuman conditions. When the offender is *not* capable of making this choice, the death penalty's legitimacy disappears, both in the discourse and in the law.

If the exile is not the typical other, neither is it the typical scapegoat, the second dominant figure in the broad death penalty discourse. Indeed, virtually everything about the death penalty, from the arbitrariness with which victims are selected to the ritual of the execution itself, roughly corresponds with René Girard's articulation of the scapegoat, a correspondence with which many who have worked intimately with capital punishment are familiar. As

Rev. Joseph M. Vought, a former death row chaplain, told me, "Girard has been helpful, really helpful. . . . I was blown away when I read it. A friend of mine, a fellow pastor, said, 'You've got to read [it] if you're doing death penalty work.'"[56]

A death-driven but life-focused discourse in the context of the political state of exception, the capital punishment discourse posits two basic questions: do they deserve to die, and do we have the right to kill them? In asking these questions, the discourse takes as given four basic conditions: (1) in response to a crisis, (2) real victims are selected and real acts of violence performed on them, (3) not because of their crimes, but because of our recognition of them as victims, and (4) our intention in perpetrating the violence against these victims is to resolve the crisis.[57]

The explanatory capacity of this model is apparent. As I will show, the capital punishment discourse is, at its core, a debate over the best means to preserve and validate life. This being the case, the broad mainstream of the debate acknowledges the need to reserve executions for the "worst of the worst." In this reduction in intended scope we can see immediately Giorgio Agamben's politics of fear, as well as the real victims generating and responsible for the real crisis posited by Girard.[58] On the one hand, the abolitionist position might point to the number of executions—over 1,300 since 1976 as of August 1, 2012—and question whether we truly are executing the worst of the worst, and whether the various elements of our "war on crime' are bearing any positive fruit. The retentionist argument, on the other hand, might point to the nearly 600,000 recorded murders from 1976 to 2005 compared with under 1,100 executions in the same period. This means that around one-fifth of 1 percent of murders result in an execution. Surely, they argue, this shows that we do reserve the death penalty for the exceptions, for the worst of the worst, and do not utilize it either capriciously or arbitrarily.[59]

When these arguments arise within a context where questions of morality and justice arise, then the scapegoat appears complete. As I will show, however, the scapegoat is inadequate to explain the continued strength of the death penalty in the United States, because both the abolitionist and retentionist discourses demand that the victim be not simply real, but also both guilty and culpable. Neither retributive justice, now taken as the norm by the American criminal justice system, nor restorative justice can be satisfied without guilt and culpability. As we will see, guilt is less the point of contestation between the religious retentionist and abolitionist discourses than is culpability. As noted, Girard's readings are passed around and appreciated by people intimately involved with the American death penalty. Taking Girard's theories of mimetic rivalry and the scapegoat seriously, reading them critically, and applying them to the American death penalty gets us most of the way to an explanation of the continued power of capital punishment in the United States, but we need to modify them to get us the rest of the way there, as I show in subsequent chapters. I hope to offer this clarification not only to other scholars in the field, but also to those directly engaged with the process.[60]

Outline

This book focuses on the religious discourse on the death penalty in the modern era, since executions resumed in 1976. The continued vitality of religion in the United States hardly needs introduction. According to data from a 2006 report, "85–90 percent of Americans routinely respond 'yes' when asked 'Do you, personally, believe in God?' Eighty-two percent of Americans are Christians. . . . Nearly three fourths of Americans (71.5 percent) pray at least once a week and almost half (49.2 percent) attend church at least once a month." Mindful of Catherine Albanese's observation that it might be more helpful to think of religion less in terms of definition and more in terms of description, I elaborate on my understanding of "religion" and "religious discourse" in the next chapter, as well as, in different contexts, chapters 3 and 6. Here it will suffice to say that I treat religion as a transcendent discourse that informs practices designed to bring about either a proper human world or proper human subjects. Religion, as a response to the particular conditions of modernity, which is to say, of "living-in-the-world," is a way of conceiving and clarifying our obligations—to the divine, the political and social order, and to each other—in response to these conditions of modernity.[61] Religious discourses, then, are discourses that derive from or deliberately orient themselves relative to religion.

The present study alternates between a state-specific focus and a national focus. Given Virginia's extensive execution history, the particularities exclusive to the state, and the robustness of the religious discourse on the death penalty in the state, it is an ideal case study. As Mark Costanzo points out, Virginia is likely to be "among the last states to allow the practice of killing to die out."[62] That said, Virginia is also part of a broader national discourse, which means that the debates in Virginia can be taken as representative of the broader national debates. Where the death penalty is concerned, what happens in Virginia does not stay in Virginia.

In asking the question that provoked this study—What *is* the death penalty?—and in offering exile and embrace as models that explain the continued relevance and resonance of the death penalty in contemporary American Christianity and culture,[63] I employ historical, anthropological, and religious studies methods. I utilize a number of institutional and private archives and draw on many hours of recorded interviews with clergy, bloggers, death row chaplains, and activists on both sides of the debate. I also employ participant observation, particularly in regard to the statewide Bible study survey that forms the basis for chapter 3. In some cases, I was able to engage in a variant of multisited ethnography. In other cases, where I was more observer than participant, I relied on links between this method and the "cultural lives" approach, pursuing a discourse analysis of the discussions and texts, particularly with regard to questions of what support for or opposition to capital punishment does for the identity of the individual practitioner and what that support or opposition does for the individual's concepts of God, the state, and the role of the believer within the state.[64] In all cases, however, the in-person observation and interaction helped clarify the issues at stake. This fieldwork was indispensable in seeing how individuals grapple with the questions and how they come to and explain their positions.[65] Perhaps most importantly, these methods and sources helped me to approach the problem of the "Repugnant Cultural Other"[66] — in this case, both support for the death penalty and the death penalty itself — such that while my own abolitionist bias will no doubt be evident in what follows, this book nevertheless deals fairly and critically with both sides of a contentious moral debate.

Both the retentionist and abolitionist debates create, simultaneously and sequentially, the *we* and the *they* — the offender and the law-abiding, in one set of phrasing. My focus lies here, at the creation and employment of the *we* and the *they* in the discourse. This focus comes largely at the expense of other elements, such as the questions of technological development, both in terms of the technology employed and the question of technologies of power,[67] as well as, for the most part, the legal, procedural, or other cultural articulations of the *what* of capital punishment. I focus on the notions of *we* and *they* that are created by and drive the religious discourse on the death penalty. In this sense, this book begins and ends with the question of *who* and *whom*. The death penalty is a violent societal employment of power designed to either mask or correct a societal problem involving violence. But *who* puts *whom* to death? I argue that while the offenders, the *they*, are indispensable, they are ultimately far less meaningful than the *we*. The death penalty is not a question of offenders and their violence. It is a question of the society that employs it. It is about *our* violence.

Chapter 2 foregrounds the subsequent chapters by establishing the basic parameters of the discussion. Broaching the related questions of what it means to be morally certain that the state has the right to take life and whether and how we can declare a particular individual deserving of death with the requisite degree of moral certainty, I explore the operative conceptions of the right to life at work in the capital punishment discourse and the operative conceptions of the death penalty as an event versus a process. I also clarify further what I mean by "religion" and thus religious discourse. The chapter begins to model exile and embrace as they arise in the discourse by addressing forward- and backward-looking approaches to the death penalty using doctrinal and social statements prepared by churches at the denominational, synod, or congregational/parish levels. These statements are the "result of a long and careful process of study" that produces "well-considered and definitive statement[s]" on an issue "represent[ing] a deliberate and informed consensus"[68] and are thus indispensable resources in a consideration of the broader religious discourse on the death penalty.

Chapter 3 reverses direction. Taking up a challenge issued by the churches to bring the message from the pulpit to the pew, this chapter reports on and details the results of a statewide Bible study survey. In the fall and winter of 2008–9, churches from several different denominations hosted sessions in which participants discussed and debated the death penalty. These most often took the form of Bible studies, sessions in which a group of participants read aloud and discuss and interpret a particular biblical passage or narrative. Treating these sessions as liturgical and reconciliatory practices, I report on the discussions and what they show about conceptions of forgiveness and the identity of the self relative to the other, especially with regard to questions of conversion and exile. The chapter also continues differentiating process- from event-based understandings of capital punishment.

Chapter 4 develops the exile as it appears in the retentionist and abolitionist discourses. I use Girard's conceptions of the scapegoat and mimetic rivalry to ground the discussion before turning to the related questions of guilt and culpability. While Girard's scapegoat *may* be guilty of the transgression for which it is being punished, I argue that in the American discourse on capital punishment, with few exceptions, the offender *must* be (legally) guilty. I detail the five characteristics of the exile and examine the uses to which it is put in the current retributive climate, primarily with regard to the question of how best to honor and preserve life. I argue that while legal guilt is vital, the exile's defining most important characteristic is culpability, or the lack thereof, and show how this impacts the broader discourse.

Chapter 5 takes a different approach to the question of how the religious discourse on capital punishment reveals our own conceptions of identity by exploring the religious discourse on the death penalty in an explicitly political context, the 2005 Virginia gubernatorial campaign, which pitted the eventual winner, Roman Catholic abolitionist Democrat Timothy M. Kaine, against Baptist retentionist Republican Jerry Kilgore. The chapter focuses on the religious debates in the political blogosphere and details the bloggers' and their readers' biblical exegesis on the rightness of the death penalty. I show that they were concerned less with the death penalty itself and more with proper political order and legitimacy and the executive's proper role in our democracy.

Chapter 6 continues by examining tropes of exile and embrace in the criminal and legal process by exploring two related questions: *whom* do we execute, and *who* is the *we* that proclaims the death sentence?[69] Two legal norms guide this exploration: the notions that death is different and that the jury represents and acts as the conscience of the community. Using litigant and amicus curiae briefs, the chapter uses the exile to test whether death truly is different before turning to the problem of conscience. Working through the idea of the jury as the community's conscience, I conclude by arguing that the death penalty may be, as James McBride argues, an establishment of religion,[70] and suggest an alternative approach that may relieve this tension.

Chapter 7 details the exile's counterpart, embrace. Taking my lead from Miroslav Volf, I work through his idea of *exclusion*, showing the ways in which it, like Girard's scapegoat, is a near-fit with the American death penalty discourse, and showing too the ways in which the fit is inexact and the concept needs to be modified. I then turn to his idea of embrace, which I use to address the question of sovereignty relative to the offender and society.[71] Drawing primarily on interviews with and writings by current and former death row chaplains, as well as on sermons, liturgies for execution vigils, and interfaith service programs, I show that exile and embrace are not opposites, but parts of the same response to transgression. I also show how that the idea of embrace can enhance our ability to see our own violence in the death penalty before turning to some concluding remarks.

Two final notes are in order. First, this is not a theoretical work in the sense of trying to take a new approach to religion per se. I generally deal with religion via religious traditions and the understanding of the participants themselves. When I deal theoretically with religion per se, I do so explicitly. Some readers may object that I spend a disproportionate amount of time focusing on belief and discourse, rather than practices. This is a deliberate choice, one I made with David Morgan's observation that belief is a form of practice fully in mind.[72] Moreover, the discourses I examine generally arise in contexts where they are acts, not mere speech. Sermons are practices as well as discourses, as are congregational Bible studies and exegetical debates carried out in public during an electoral campaign. In what follows, then, I treat discourse as a category of practice.

Second, for the sake of clarity, I use the first-person plural ("we") forms while presenting or explicating viewpoints or arguments; I hope that this has helped me present a richer, more nuanced description of each side's arguments rather than signaling endorsement of the same. I have also opted to use masculine pronouns throughout when discussing offenders generally. This is not only for purposes of clarity and ease of reading, but also because the death penalty is almost exclusively used against males. Of the 1,301 offenders executed in the modern era, 12—fewer than 1 percent—were women. Of the current death row population of roughly 3,250 nationwide, 58 are women.[73]

2

> The Bible recognizes in capital punishment . . . a deterrent character and an expiatory character, in addition to its retributive character. . . . The Bible also teaches explicitly that capital punishment is the just punishment for murder, in order to atone for the pollution of the land. . . . Yet the [O]ld Testament teaching of justice is tempered by mercy. "But if the wicked turn from all his sins . . . he shall surely live, he shall not die."
>
> (REV. D. DE SOLA POOL,
>   *Capital Punishment among the Jews*

> As I read the New Testament, I don't see anywhere in there that killing bad people is a very high calling for Christians. I see an awful lot about redemption and forgiveness.
>
> (JAMES W. L. PARK, former execution officer, San Quentin, California

Between Moral Certainty and Morally Certain
The Churches Discuss the Death Penalty

Virginia's 2005 gubernatorial election pitted Democratic lieutenant governor Timothy Kaine against Republican attorney general Jerry Kilgore in an election that featured a new wrinkle: for the first time in the modern era, an individual personally opposed to the death penalty had won his party's nomination for governor. Conventional wisdom held that this was a political kiss of death in a state where the majority of voters support the death penalty. This is not abstract support or poll-tested support—Virginia is home to the nation's second-busiest death chamber; only Texas has carried out more executions in the modern era.

Kilgore repeatedly attacked Kaine on capital punishment. Kilgore stressed his belief that the death penalty is just and necessary to protect citizens and help prevent crime. Kaine just as frequently stressed that his Catholic faith taught him that the death penalty is morally wrong, but that he would carry out the duties of his office if elected. The immediate context of the debate was local, but partisans in each camp made it clear that the debate was anything but. Stephen Neill, a spokesman for the Catholic Diocese of Richmond, acknowledged the long-standing debate among Catholics as they struggle with church teaching that life is sacred from womb to tomb. Robert F. Drinan, SJ, a vocal death penalty opponent, validated Kaine's position from the Catholic perspective, reiterating that upholding the law over and against one's personal, religious opposition is legitimate, indirectly linking Kaine to former president John F. Kennedy. Rev. Donald Runion, Kilgore's pastor, argued that Kilgore was right, that "the death penalty is biblically permissible as part of the state's role of keeping order in society." Nevertheless, Runion agreed with Neill that capital punishment is an issue of conscience, one that believers should decide within the context of their faith tradition and its teachings. This state-level debate brought the death penalty into the open and gave voters and believers a chance to evaluate their beliefs and the positions of their religious traditions on capital punishment.[1]

The continued salience of religious viewpoints in the contemporary debate over capital punishment is indisputable. During the 2005 campaign, a majority of respondents polled stated that while they disagreed with Kaine's stance, they accepted that his was a sincerely held religious belief and took him at his word when he pledged to carry out his duties as governor. Kaine's persuasive articulation of his religious beliefs thus mitigated what could have been a serious political liability. Similarly, a 2004 Zogby International poll found that, for the first time, a minority of Catholic respondents (48 percent) supported capital punishment. Prior polling had found that Catholics supported capital punishment in roughly the same proportion as Americans in general, averaging around 70 percent over the last several decades. Respondents credited church teachings as the primary reason for the decline in support.[2]

Nor is religion meaningful only in the abstract: "It is clear that throughout the history of penal practice religion has been a major force in shaping the ways in which offenders are dealt with." Scholars are divided over the precise extent to which religion influences the death penalty in contemporary America, but some basic patterns have emerged. Several studies have found that religion is perhaps as important as race and gender in predicting how jurors will vote in a death penalty case. Some commentators argue that the dominance of evangelical Christianity within the South is one of the primary explanations for the pronounced geographic disparity in American executions. The death penalty is largely a southern institution: as of August 1, 2012, 1,301 executions had been carried out in the United States since 1976. Of these executions, 1,066 — nearly 82 percent — were in the South; Texas and Virginia, the two states with the most executions, accounted for 592 together, or slightly less than half of all American executions in the modern era. Dr. Barrett Duke, vice president for public policy and research for the Southern Baptist Convention's Ethics and Religious Liberty Commission, surmises that the higher proportion of evangelical Christians directly translates into increased support for capital punishment. A quick look at the dominant religious groups in various regions of the country provides some measure of correlation for this claim. Of the ten states with the highest execution totals — Texas, Virginia, Oklahoma, Florida, Missouri, Alabama, Georgia, Ohio, North Carolina, and South Carolina, in descending order — only Ohio lies outside of the South. According to the 2010 US Religious Census, the Southern Baptist Convention (SBC) is the largest reporting denomination in terms of number of adherents in the region, sometimes by a wide margin. By contrast, in the Northeast and the Upper Midwest, home to the majority of states that have abolished the death penalty, the Catholic Church and the Evangelical Lutheran Church in America, two abolitionist denominations, are the dominant church bodies.[3]

The churches' doctrinal and social statements on capital punishment show the major theological differences between retentionist and abolitionist churches. These differences essentially break down to two related questions: how is the Bible to be read and understood, and what is the relationship between the teachings of Jesus of Nazareth and those contained in the Old Testament? Should the believer read the Bible literally, to look for the letter of the law, as the SBC's statement indicates, or should the believer try to seek out the spirit of the law, as the United Church of Christ (UCC) suggests? Does the message of love, mercy, and forgiveness preached by Jesus counter Old Testament teachings, or is there nothing in the New Testament that contradicts what is contained in the Old? We will consider these questions in subsequent chapters, but it is important to acknowledge them here before turning to the issues at the core of the contemporary debate. At its core, the question is the contest over the understood structure of the political state, its duties, and the means by which these duties may legitimately be discharged.[4]

Jean Bethke Elshtain has remarked that the death penalty tempts us to view the state as an idol, giving it ultimate power of life and death. We see this idea in the Church Women United (CWU) statement decrying the false promise of the death penalty and hear echoes of it in assertions that murderers can "forfeit their right to life." Formulations like these displace the right to take life from the deity to the state, usurping what is otherwise broadly held by Christians to be a prerogative of God alone. At the same time, however, Elshtain admits that taking seriously the inherent dignity and worth of every individual conflicts with this opposition, particularly in cases where the "moral certainty of the guilt of a person for a particularly horrific crime" is not in question. This is the "if it were my family" response, an acknowledgment of the distance between what we desire, or believe we would desire, and what we believe is just, or what we would like to think we would see as just.[5]

This tension between retribution, atonement, and vengeance — and the mechanisms that we invest with the authority to seek these in our names — and questions of the inherent value and dignity of the individual remain at the center of the religious debate over capital punishment in the United States. We can reduce most of the expansive debate to questions of protection — of how we can best protect ourselves, others, our future, our society, our values, human dignity, human rights, justice and the systems that we invest with the authority and power to seek justice, and so on. As I hope will be clear as we proceed, none of these questions are as simple as they may appear. This expansive debate is dominated by two sincerely held needs that we will explore in this chapter: the need to be morally certain, and the need for moral certainty. The first is a question with regard to the state, the second with regard to individual defendants. Tracing these two lines of argument clarifies the grounds on which the respective religious bodies support or oppose capital punishment in the contemporary political state. Following these arguments also helps us see the respective bodies' understandings of the nature of crime and punishment generally.[6]

Punishment and Religion

Although I have largely confined this book to the modern era and contemporary debates, it is worth pausing over the basic question suggested by the chapter title, that being the question of morality and the idea of the moral. Briefly defining both religion and punishment will help clarify this. As David Garland explains, punishment is "the legal process whereby violators of the criminal law are condemned and sanctioned in accordance with specified legal categories and procedures." Condemnation, categorizing an offense as a particular crime subject to a defined range of sanctions, ritually imposing punishment — these are all part of the social institution of punishment. As I show, the churches' statements generally agree that punishment expresses and communicates our understandings of morality in the modern moment, in response to the particular conditions of "living-in-the-world."[7]

Religion, too, is concerned with the particular conditions of living-in-the-world. As Bruce Lincoln clarifies, religion is minimally characterized by a transcendent discourse that informs practices designed to bring about either a proper human world or proper human subjects, which in turn gives rise to a community that identifies itself with regard to these discourses and practices, as well as an institution capable of and charged with regulating these discourses and practices, modifying them where necessary while preserving their transcendent validity. The basic question of human living, then, can be variously phrased as *What am I to do* and *Who are we to be?* This is to say, religion as a source of morality—of discourses and actions capable of guiding and helping create the proper world or proper subjects—is a question of the identification of our rights and duties, relative to the divine, to the human social order, and to each other, pursuant to trying to answer and live up to the questions of what we are to do and to be.[8]

Here, then, religion and punishment exist synergistically. Religion provides one basis for punishment, not in the sense that punishment is or should be designed to carry out religious dicta, but in the sense that punishment is an expression of and communicates our common, shared morality, as the churches articulate. The links between religion and law are seldom so clear as in issues of transgression, sanction, and punishment. As Winnifred Fallers Sullivan argues, "Modern secular law is not . . . indifferent to religion. . . . It is replete with ideas and structures that . . . parallel . . . ideas and structures in religious traditions: crime, sin, and so forth." For the churches, the basic moral question of who we are to be and what we are to do provides a basis for justifying as well as limiting punishment. In the discourses and debates over the death penalty, the need to be morally certain that the state has the right to punish with death and the need to achieve moral certainty regarding an individual's guilt are overlapping procedural and ethical needs. If punishment is in part an expression of our collective morality, then the procedural problems attendant in perfectly expressing that morality—such as racially, geographically, or economically biased application, poor quality of counsel, evidentiary concerns, or procedural barriers to postconviction relief—are cause for concern.[9]

At the same time, understanding punishment as this expression demands continual reexamination of that morality. This reexamination is at the heart of the most basic element of the religious debate over capital punishment: are human life and dignity best honored and protected by taking the life of those who kill? The need for moral certainty and the need to be morally certain are expressions of this ethical tension as it arises via living-in-the-world.

Let's take a moment to differentiate these two ideas, which I use throughout the remainder of this book. *Morally certain* pertains to the state and the authorities and powers attributed to it. We need to be morally certain that the state has the right to take life as punishment for certain offenses. If we can be *morally certain* that this is so, then we broach a second question: can we ever possess *moral certainty* that a particular defendant is guilty of the particular crime for which he stands accused? As Barbara J. Shapiro shows, "moral certainty" has long been an expression of the need to be sure of a defendant's guilt beyond a reasonable doubt, to use a widely recognized phrase. To achieve "moral certainty" means to prove a proposition sufficiently that it "command[s] universal assent," as we can see from a nineteenth-century case that clearly defines the term:

> the circumstances taken together should be . . . conclusive . . . producing in effect a reasonable and moral certainty, that the accused, and no one else, committed the offense charged. . . . It is not sufficient to establish a probability . . . that the fact charged is more likely to be true than the contrary, but the evidence must establish the truth of the fact to a reasonable and moral certainty; a certainty that convinces and directs the understanding, and satisfies the reason and judgment, of those who are bound to act conscientiously upon it.

Former Oklahoma governor Frank H. Keating also used this phrasing, though he noted that he thought that "there should be a 'moral certainty standard,' that is, even an even higher standard *above* what 'proof beyond a reasonable doubt demands.'"[10]

In the churches' official statements and the debates, the need for moral certainty is a need to be sure, beyond a reasonable doubt, that the accused is truly guilty of the crime for which they can be sentenced to death. Focusing on the criminal justice system, this is a need to be sure that the system is or can be made sufficiently error-free in its application that the requisite level of certainty can be attained. The need to be morally certain, on the other hand, speaks to perceptions of the state, of its rights, responsibilities, and limitations. Does the state have the right to take the lives of its citizens as punishment for certain crimes? Within this debate over the question of moral certainty are two other debates that define the perceived role of the state from the perspective of the religious body or individual in question. The first of these is the question of the relationship between limitations on individual and on state action. The second is the question of the constitution of government itself, and where it stands relative to the individual citizen believer.

Detached and Derivative Views of Capital Punishment

Because these two debates provide the context for all of the issues discussed in relation to the death penalty, it will be helpful to outline the three broad camps within which the various religious bodies fall.[11] The first contains churches and religious organizations that believe the state lacks the right to punish with death. This group cites the system's failures—the racial, geographic, economic, and social inequalities in application and the chance of wrongful executions—and uses awareness of these failings to argue against the state's right to execute. So long as "where a crime is committed, the race of the victim and offender, and the quality and costs of defense" are as disproportionately determinative, so long as the nation's death rows are filled disproportionately with "Blacks, Hispanics, and Native Americans" as well as the "poor . . . and educationally deprived," then the death penalty has no legitimacy. As long as this is the case, the abolitionist churches argue, they must oppose executions. These churches also reject the notion that the system can ever be perfected sufficiently to never execute an innocent. Though the question of whether and how recently innocents have been executed remains contested, the church statements back the process up one step, noting the significant number of wrongful convictions in capital cases. They treat wrongful convictions as morally equivalent to wrongful executions, in a sense, because each condemns the system to obvious fallibility.[12]

As compellingly as the churches explain these systemic failures, they give no indication that these problems form the basis for their opposition. This opposition, derived from their faith traditions, is based on the idea that all life is sacred and that it is God's right alone to take life. As the Episcopal Church declared, for example, "the taking of . . . human life falls within the providence of Almighty God and not within the right of man." Even if the system were perfectible, the abolitionist churches indicate that they would still oppose executions in deference to the sacredness of human life. Because "the life of an individual is of infinite worth in the sight of Almighty God," "the value of God-given life" cannot be overstated. Executions "violat[e] the *sacredness* of human life," while "abolition [would be] further testimony to our conviction . . . that God is indeed the Lord of Life." The American Ethical Union, echoing the churches, phrased the matter most succinctly: "The willful taking of human life . . . violates our belief in the intrinsic worth of every human being." This is an expression of what Ronald Dworkin calls a *detached* view of life. According to this detached view, capital punishment "is wrong in principle because it disregards and insults the intrinsic value, the sacred character . . . of human life"; this view is "detached" because "it does not depend on or presuppose any particular rights or interests."[13]

A second group of churches believes that the death penalty is permissible and that the state should utilize it. In contrast to the detached objection, these churches argue in favor of a *derivative* right to execute murderers. Whereas the detached viewpoint treats life as worth protecting in and of itself, the derivative viewpoint proceeds less from the nature of life and more from a notion of individual rights. Though the term does not explicitly arise in these statements, it is very much present when the denominations describe their positions. As Barrett Duke, vice president for public policy and research for the SBC's Ethics and Religious Liberty Commission, described the Southern Baptist position on the death penalty at a Pew forum, "it would . . . be appropriate to say that Southern Baptists believe that all people are conceived with the right to life. Some forfeit that right by their own actions." According to Dworkin, the derivative position stems from "rights and interests that it assumes all human beings . . . have." The retentionist position, insofar as it claims that one can forfeit one's right to life through one's actions, implies that this right is conferred by, and can be revoked by, the state. This is a derivative view of the right to life. The SBC's position statement includes a bill of particulars detailing the biblical requirements without which, presumably, capital punishment cannot be justly imposed. These include "proof of guilt" and requirements that the "civil magistrate . . . judge all people equally under the law, regardless of class or status" and "without reference to the race, class, or status of the guilty." The emphasis paced on "profound respect for the *rights* of individuals" as a justification for the death penalty is what identifies this position, and those like it, as derivative.[14]

I don't claim that these two approaches must work in opposition to each other, nor even that they can. Indeed, in defining the two categories, Dworkin noted that "if government has both a detached and a derivative responsibility to protect human life, then its ordinary laws against murder serve them both at once—protecting the rights and interests of particular victims, and also recognizing and respecting the intrinsic value of human life." The denominational statements bear out this speculation. The retentionist SBC is concerned primarily with rights, to the point that life is treated as a right that can be forfeit, but it also opens its statement by acknowledging, "The Bible teaches that every human life has sacred value." At the same time, although the primary focus of abolitionist statements is the question of the intrinsic value and dignity of all human life, they also include questions of rights within their considerations.[15]

Examples of this dual concern can be found in statements from the two largest groups that make up the third category, those churches who believe that the death penalty is not per se prohibited, but is unnecessary and thus impermissible in the current political and social moment. According to the Roman Catholic Church and the Evangelical Lutheran Church in America (ELCA), if there were no other way to protect human life or to protect society than to execute offenders, then it would be permissible. This is not the situation in the United States, they argue, and because the state can protect itself and its citizens via less-than-lethal measures, it is obligated to do so. Both churches also include derivative elements in their statements of opposition: the ELCA notes that "God entrusts the state with the power to take human life when failure to do so constitutes a clear danger to society," and Pope John Paul II's *Evangelium Vitae* declares that the purpose of punishment is to "redress the violation of personal and social rights by imposing on the offender an adequate punishment for the crime." The preservation of rights exists alongside, but ultimately subordinate to, the preservation of the intrinsic value of life.[16]

As Christian Brugger has shown, this change in the Catholic position is a recent development, not in the sense of a change of doctrine but rather in the sense of a "deepened ... application [of doctrine] in the context of present-day historical circumstances." The 1997 *editio typica*—authoritative version—of the *Catechism of the Catholic Church* included changes to sections 2263–67, which deal with legitimate defense. The death penalty, according to section 2267, is not absolutely prohibited, but is permitted only "if this is the only possible way of effectively defending human lives against the unjust aggressor." Vitally, Brugger notes, the catechism treats the death penalty not as a legal punishment but rather as "an act of collective self-defense by the community against a dangerous internal aggressor." This means that capital punishment, like any other form of legitimate killing, is subject to the doctrine of double effect, in which the primary intended consequence cannot be a sin. For killings to be legitimate, the lethal consequences of an action may be foreseen but not intended. Because there is no way for capital punishment not to intend the death of the offender, it is thus prohibited in favor of less-than-lethal measures of community defense. Thus the Catholic Church, like the ELCA, allows in theory what it prohibits in practice.[17]

Morally Certain

Cataloging these differences in the churches' approaches to the question of whether the state has the right to take life also helps us see how they move from problems of being morally certain to problems of moral certainty. The churches agree across the board on several issues. The sanctity and dignity of human life are unquestioned, as is the notion that the current system is insufficiently capable of ensuring that no wrongful executions or other miscarriages of justice can occur. The churches agree that racial, social, and economic factors play too great a role in deciding who lives and who dies, though they respond to this situation in different ways. Whereas the abolitionist churches highlight these problems, retentionist churches background them by "urg[ing] that [death penalty] legislation ... include safeguards to eliminate any inequities." The churches agree on the need for reform, either to bring the system closer to infallibility or to resolve specific problems en route to eventual abolition. Finally, there is no question that one of the state's primary responsibilities is to protect the lives of its citizens. The dispute is over the conclusions to which these principles lead.[18]

All of these concerns speak to specific cases and to the application of capital punishment generally, but they do not deal with the question of whether one can be morally certain that the state possesses the right to execute in response to certain crimes. The essential question here, and the primary point of departure between the abolitionist and retentionist churches, can be phrased simply: what is capital punishment? It is not necessary here to delve into theories of punishment or penology; for our purposes, it is enough to consider two major differences in the way the churches approach this question. Abolitionist and retentionist churches divide on the question of the morality of punishment and over what punishment communicates about responsibility.

With regard to the former, the churches actively question whether punishment is an intrinsic good or an intrinsic evil. Their opinions fall along a continuum running between two poles that treat punishment as necessary and intrinsically good versus as inherently evil and always in need of justification. The National Association of Evangelicals (NAE) argues that crime cannot be considered violative unless the punishment imposed in response is reciprocally harsh. Punishment is thus a necessary good. From this viewpoint, it makes no sense to cavil about the incidence of heinous crimes, or any infractions, when the proposed remedy falls short of reciprocity. This view goes beyond justifying capital punishment—it demands it. To punish the murderer with less than death is to communicate to criminals and the public alike that the inherent value and dignity of human life is diminished. Arguments like this defend retribution as necessary and proper and cite it as the dominant rationale for supporting capital punishment.[19]

The abolitionist churches advance the opposite claim: "Punishment, since it involves the deliberate infliction of evil on another, is always in need of justification." While generally not denying the state the right to imprison or otherwise sequester dangerous individuals, they demand that "punishment [where possible] be determined with a view to the reformation of the criminal and his reintegration into society." They reject retribution as a valid rationale for punishment, particularly when that punishment involves taking life. Indeed, the abolitionist churches, in rejecting the validity of retribution as a penal aim, denounce it as incompatible with justice and lament that the Supreme Court legitimated retribution as a valid penal aim.[20]

If the question of retribution is rephrased as a question of the legitimacy of state-sanctioned vengeance, then the disagreement stands in starker relief and highlights the different conceptions of capital punishment per se. Retentionist denominations, such as the Lutheran Church—Missouri Synod (LCMS), hold that the death penalty is not revenge, while the SBC notes that although God denies humans the right to take personal vengeance, he nevertheless gave the magistrate—the state—the power to take life in response to crime. The Assemblies of God (AOG) aver that both the Old and New Testaments deny the legitimacy of personal vengeance, while the Christian Church (Disciples of Christ) maintains that "Holy Scriptures clearly mandate that we are not to . . . render evil for evil, and . . . are not to seek retribution with vengeance for the evil done to us." Finally, as the ELCA states, "People often respond to violent crime as though it were exclusively a matter of the criminal's individual failure. The death penalty exacts and symbolizes the ultimate personal retribution."[21]

This brings up the second disagreement between abolitionist and retentionist churches, that of what crime and punishment communicate about responsibility and who bears it. Posing this question raises many others, including questions of forward- versus backward-looking approaches to crime, punishment, and criminals; of the responsibility of the individual nonoffender, and how the death penalty communicates this; the nature of evil as contagion; and how and from what vantage point we view the crime itself. These questions, and their relevance to conceptions of exile and embrace, will be addressed later in the book; for now, we will focus on the immediate, broad-strokes question of responsibility.

As a rule, retentionist denominations treat the matter of responsibility as beginning and ending with the offender. They also argue for a division between the citizen and their government in questions pertaining to life, paralleling the division between "God's kingdom of grace and His rule in power." An important point to note is the implicit distance between heaven and earth, even when it seems that the two are most closely allied, as in the following statement: "God has vested in the civil magistrate the responsibility of protecting the innocent and punishing the guilty." At the very least, this statement accepts a God who has withdrawn from the temporal adjudication of human crimes. The God of the Old Testament, who intervened personally or via prophets and signs to confront Cain, Moses, and David for their murders, has been replaced by the God of the New Testament, who uses a combination of miracles and human intermediaries to bring about the conversion of the murderer Saul and then, via the newly rechristened Paul, gives to the state, the magistrate, the authority to execute vengeance upon wrongdoers.[22]

Supreme Court Justice Antonin Scalia makes this point as well, stating that the death penalty "is undoubtedly wrong unless one accords to the state a scope of moral action that goes beyond what is permitted to the individual." Under this theory—a viewpoint echoed in the retentionist statements—the idea that governmental morality and individual morality have the same scope is a fallacy. The difference in moralities reflects the different roles and responsibilities of individuals and states. Individuals are forbidden to kill, except in narrowly prescribed circumstances, such as self-defense or just war. Governments, on the other hand, "[do] not bear the sword in vain."[23] Charged with protecting their citizens, governments may under certain circumstances legitimately take the lives of those who have committed murder. This upholds the sacredness and dignity of human life and communicates to citizens and any would-be murderers both the value with which life is held and the penalty to be levied for violating the image of God, the *imago dei*.[24] This is not to say that Scalia justifies the death penalty based on his faith, but that he believes that his faith—which he believes sanctions the death penalty, despite the changes to the most recent catechism—does not bar him from participating in the process that wields the sword.[25]

From this viewpoint, the state differs from citizens and believers in its recourse to violence.[26] For individuals, killing is a choice; for the state, it is an obligation. In this view, the state must punish murder by taking the lives of those who kill. The element of individual choice is implied even when it is not directly stated, as in the LCMS statement. The more frequent imposition of the death penalty on the poor and on minorities, the statement holds, is the result of a greater number of "crimes against person," including murder, arising from those within "subculture[s] of violence" within the inner cities. Leaving aside the factual infelicity—capital crimes committed in inner cities are punished with the death penalty far less frequently than those committed in the suburbs and exurbs—the description of *subcultures* of violence implies an element of willful belonging, which aggravates rather than mitigates the abstract murder in question.[27]

The abolitionist denominations express a different conception of the distance between believers/citizens and the state. They minimize this distance, particularly where life is concerned. They grant that the state has powers and rights that individuals do not have; they do not tend to argue against incarceration on the grounds that it represents a power greater than that enjoyed by the individual, for example. At the same time, however, abolitionist denominations draw up short on the question of life. In matters of life and death, the state's rights and responsibilities are equivalent to the individual's, and it is here that the perceived distance between the individual and the state closes. These churches argue that capital punishment necessarily forecloses any possibility of rehabilitation, reconciliation, and redemption, and devalues the "God-given dignity of every human life, even those who do great harm." This devaluation has several consequences. First, they argue, it further devalues the victim, whose memory is defined even more fully by violence and death. Second, it communicates contradictory lessons: that we can protect life by taking life; that we can teach that killing is wrong by killing.[28]

For this lesson to be contradictory, the churches must accept the "fallacy" that the permitted moral scope of action for individuals and states must match in this context. The abolitionist statements do just this. These statements argue that humans have the capacity and authority to govern their actions and to punish crimes against the social order up to, but not including, the taking of life. On this point, the distance previously accepted between the individual and the state, in terms of imprisonment, levying fines, and so on, is dismissed. Neither the individual nor the state has the right to usurp God's sovereignty over life. The Presbyterian Church (USA) (PCUSA) makes this argument most directly. Even the two abolitionist bodies that grant that the state does possess the right to punish with death, the Catholic Church and the ELCA, limit that to cases of absolute necessity, when no other options are available. The distance is thus simultaneously granted in the abstract but denied in the current social and political situation. Because "modern society has the means of protecting itself, without definitively denying criminals the chance to reform," the state is limited to "incapacitat[ing] offenders in a manner that limits violence, and hold[s] open the possibility of conversion and restoration."[29]

Though the state has the power to act in ways that the individual cannot, it lacks the authority to do so when it need not; it need do so only in cases that are most analogous to individual self-defense. Importantly, the abolitionist churches do not differentiate the criminal from the law-abiding as the retentionists do. The abolitionist churches do not question the matter of choice and the personal responsibility that follows from actions voluntarily undertaken; on this the two sides agree. They differ, however, on how to understand these actions in their broader societal context. Whereas the retentionists begin and end with the crime itself, the abolitionists seek to place it into a broader picture, which leads to different understandings of moral certainty.

Two Understandings of Moral Certainty

In their considerations of whether we can be morally certain that the state has the right to execute convicted criminals, the abolitionist churches bemoan two consequences that attend the devaluation of life that they see in the death penalty. These are further devaluing the murder victim by linking them to yet another death and communicating contradictory lessons about the utility of killing to demonstrate our abhorrence of killing. We can add a third to these, one that follows from and conflicts with the commitment to seek the offender's redemption. This is the distortive effect that this devaluation has on our approach to crime more generally. Despite being morally certain that the state has no right to take life as punishment, the abolitionist bodies approach the issues surrounding moral certainty more thoroughly than the retentionists do. As the history of the death penalty shows, "its application has been discriminating with respect to the disadvantaged, the indigent and the socially impoverished." The American Baptist Churches (ABC) note that the majority of people on death row are "poor, powerless, and educationally deprived," while roughly half of those on death row belong to a minority group. The UCC goes further, stating that the death penalty has demonstrably been discriminatorily applied to "Blacks, Hispanics, and Native Americans." This concern persists: the PCUSA opens its 2000 statement calling for a moratorium with a lengthy argument that the death penalty remains racist in its application, focusing on the Supreme Court's 1987 decision in *McCleskey v. Kemp*, in which the Court "refused to act on data demonstrating the continuing reality of racial bias."[30]

Accompanying observations that the death penalty continues to be administered in a racially biased way are various twists on the truism that "capital punishment means that them without the capital get the punishment." Both the ABC and the Fellowship of Reconciliation note the preponderance of indigents among those ultimately receiving the death penalty, and the National Council of the Churches of Christ in the USA made the economic injustices inherent in the application of the death penalty a plank in its original declaration of opposition to capital punishment. Alongside arguments regarding racial and economic bias are observations that the execution of an innocent remains an ever-present threat: the PCUSA cites a study suggesting that as many as 8 percent of death row inmates are innocent of the crimes for which they were convicted. When former Illinois governor George Ryan emptied his state's death row, the primary reason that he gave was the disproportionate number of innocents found there; at the time that Ryan declared first a moratorium and then a blanket commutation, Illinois had executed twelve people since 1976, while thirteen had been exonerated in that same span.[31]

Retentionists express the same worry that an innocent person may be executed, but their response to this possibility points to a different understanding of moral certainty than that held by the abolitionist churches. The solution to the possibility that an innocent person might be executed is to call for death sentences to be handed down "only when the pursuit of truth and justice result in clear and overwhelming evidence of guilt." By focusing their attention on the question of whether or not one can possess moral certainty that the defendant sitting before them is guilty of the crime with which they have been charged, retentionists render questions of unfairness of application less relevant from their perspective and demonstrate a more narrow understanding of moral certainty. If the guilt of the defendant in question can be ascertained with moral certainty, and if it is morally certain that the state may legitimately impose a death sentence, then any inherent bias in the system—racial, socioeconomic, or otherwise—is irrelevant. Moral certainty, for retentionist churches, extends only to specific cases, to specific defendants; the question of whether defendants who have committed similar crimes are punished commensurately, reliably, is either a separate issue or simply beside the point.[32]

Abolitionists, on the other hand, approach the question of moral certainty from a broader understanding of its demands; abolitionists demand to know whether *this* defendant—however certain his guilt—is particularly noteworthy among a class of similar defendants. Although abolitionist churches are morally certain that the state does not possess the authority to execute, they nevertheless invest far more energy in dealing with the question of moral certainty than the retentionists do, and to a different end: to compound the argument against the state's right to take life. The state does not have the right to execute, they argue. Even if the state *did* have that right, the fallibilities of the individual human beings charged with implementing the legal, juridical, and penal systems culminating in executions would ensure that the application of the death penalty would always be part of a flawed process and thus an unjust application of power. When the ELCA states that they "increasingly question whether the death penalty has been and can be administered justly," they give every indication that they believe it cannot, for the reasons discussed above. Justice is better served, they argue—indeed, can only be considered justice—when it is directed toward rehabilitative and restorative ends, and their statement against vengeance makes the reason clear: "People often respond to violent crime *as though it were exclusively a matter of the criminal's individual failure*." Such a response, seeing only individual failure, is misleading and harmful, they argue, since it ignores the failures of the greater community and its corporate responsibility.[33]

The idea of corporate responsibility for crime is driven in part by the nature of the response: "The use of the death penalty in a representative democracy places citizens in the role of the executioner." The "fallacy" that Scalia mentioned is displayed here. Individual and governmental morality are not distinguished one from another, nor is there any asserted distance between the state and the citizen; the citizen and the state are essentially interchangeable here. This is, of course, the meaning of the phrasing within the legal system, the reason that criminal cases are the people of the jurisdiction versus the defendant. Indeed, current governing Supreme Court case law takes seriously the notion of the jury as the "conscience of the community," which we will explore in chapter 6. The very phrasing that communicates that the state is also a victim of the transgression makes all citizens responsible for the punishment. The abolitionist denominations accept the consequence of this and fit it into their theological framework, expressing their understanding of the culpability borne by the society at large. This is what the PCUSA means when it states that Christians cannot isolate themselves from the "corporate responsibility" that they bear both for victims and for executions. Expressions of this sense of corporate responsibility can take the form of more personalized expressions of regret for shortcomings, as in the Mennonite Church and Mennonite General Conference statements acknowledging that they have fallen short in their Christian duties in preventing crime and restoring from its effects. It can also find expression in arguments that the death penalty, because it "ignores corporate and community guilt" and "exacts and symbolizes the ultimate in personal retribution," is an illegitimate and unfair response to social problems that we have failed to adequately address or work to solve.[34]

Toward the Exile

Punishment levied in response to violent crime is always characterized by a strong exilic element, in which the offender is removed from society forcibly and either detained in a temporary or permanent state of exile, via incarceration, or exiled from society permanently, via execution. There is a long history of literally exilic punishments in America from the colonial period forward. From the establishment of the colonies until the Revolutionary War, banishment, or "transportation," was a criminal justice tool deployed by the British Crown as an alternative to capital punishment. A series of ad hoc arrangements for the transportation of prisoners to the colonies gave way to a systematized model via the Transportation Act of 1718. This act set the terms of banishments—some offenses required banishment for a period of years, others for life—while also giving the courts the power to arrange for transportation. These transportations were rationalized and paid for out of public funds, imposing order on what had been a loose process.[35]

Such punishments were by no means confined to the mother country dumping its undesirables on its colonies, however—the American colonies and states, too, frequently used variants of exilic punishments. Criminals were subject to banishment from colonial or state borders for certain offenses, as were slaves. English criminals were subject to banishment as well—Massachusetts and Virginia made prolific use of this practice to protest the English practice while foisting the banished on other colonies. Nor were banishments restricted to criminals: a variety of "civil" banishments were perpetrated against religious minorities, such as the Quakers, and other civil undesirables; Victor Navasky cites religious dissident Anne Hutchinson, banished from the Massachusetts Bay Colony for her religious views, as an early, perhaps the earliest, example of such punishments. Minorities too were subject to expulsion from communities. Expulsions were used against Native Americans and free blacks in states like Virginia, where an 1806 law mandated that free blacks leave the state within one year or risk reenslavement.[36]

In our time, exilic punishments take the form not only of prison sentences but also of residency restrictions imposed on gang members and sex offenders. In Georgia, for example, certain kinds of offenders can be banished from 158 of the state's 159 counties. Other jurisdictions have laws banning gang members from city and county limits on pain of imprisonment, and as of 2007, "as many as ten states have allowed some form of banishment as a condition of probation or replacement for imprisonment." As I will show over succeeding chapters, exilic punishments create a category of persons—the exile—that is defined relative to us, that defines us, and that determines and is determined by our conceptions of who has the responsibility and ability to freely choose their actions.[37]

Neither retentionist nor abolitionist churches dispute society's right to exile dangerous individuals. What they disagree about is whether that right to exile extends to taking life. This dispute is not merely over whether or not the state has the right to kill as punishment, though that question has been directly answered by a majority of faith groups, most often in the negative. The debate ultimately is over the interpellation of the criminal as the other and when and how that happens.

In the statements issued by retentionist denominations, when the offender chooses to commit the crime for which he can be sentenced to death, his actions, voluntarily taken, cause him to become the other, someone recognizably different from the remainder of the populace. At that point, the offender has chosen an action that can, and should, lead to exile from (and for the protection of) society via his death at the hands of the state. The state, in turn, is constrained to act but has the ability to take its retribution in ways forbidden to individuals. Abolitionists, on the other hand, reject this scheme of dual responsibilities, arguing instead for a rough equivalence of moral responsibility. If individuals are prohibited from killing except in cases of absolute necessity, then so too is the state. These churches take this to mean that because contemporary society can protect itself without taking life, then it is bound to engage less violent means of protection in place of more violent or lethal means.

That said, however, the criminal is an other for abolitionists too, though the commission of the crime is more the signal of the existence of that otherness than the signal event. The inclusive and embracing rhetoric and vision of justice tempered by mercy—justice turned toward rehabilitation and reconciliation so that, when possible, the errant can be returned to society—reveal an understanding of that criminal as also alien, as "not like us." In addressing the questions of whether one can be morally certain that the state has the right to kill, and whether one can possess moral certainty that a particular defendant especially merits execution, both sides trade in concepts of exile, though for different reasons and to different ends. This process of creating the exile consists of two essential, mirrored movements, movements that categorize the offender as "like us" or "not like us." These movements are the same but are made in reverse order: retentionists move offenders conceptually from "like us" to "not like us," while abolitionists make the opposite move, from "not like us" to (provisionally) "like us."[38]

Finally, the resolution of these questions produces different communicative effects. Retentionists intend the death penalty to stand as a sign of what society absolutely cannot and will not tolerate, even if it means destroying humans made in the image of God in order to achieve that. The essential directive of the death penalty, according to these statements, is to legitimize combating evil in society by any means necessary, even if that means that the saints are forced to take the life of the evildoers. Abolitionists reject the notion of protecting society "by making killers of all of us because one of us kills." Nor are abolitionist groups comfortable with the implications of giving the state the power over life. Echoing Elshtain's observation that the death penalty tempts us to see the state as an idol, the CWU's statement on the death penalty decries the "false confidence" in capital punishment as a solution to violent crime, which is, "in part, a reminder of the human failure to ensure justice for all members of society." Lastly, retentionists argue that individuals can forfeit their right to live by their actions, thus declaring in favor of a derivative view of rights, in which even the right to life can be said to derive from the state. Abolitionists, by denying the state the authority to take life as a punishment, can plausibly claim to hold and communicate a natural rights—or a detached—view of life. In sum, this difference regarding the nature and construction of the state in the current political moment, and our rights and obligations in relation to it, underlies the divergence of opinion over the death penalty in the churches.[39]

From the National to the Local
Bringing the Discussion Indoors

The fact that these discussions and statements have been examined in the national context should not be taken to mean that the state-level organizations are not also active. Although state-level discussions often include specific details or crimes to put a recognizable face on what may otherwise be an abstract issue, these discussions tend generally to replicate the national conversations. The Texas Catholic Conference, for example, rejects the death penalty "because of its moral incongruity in today's world," holding that capital punishment leads away from "the compassionate example of Christ," which "calls us to respect the God-given image found even in hardened criminals"; the statement notes further that "the race of the victim has been proven to be the determining factor in deciding whether to prosecute capital cases." The Texas Conference of Churches, an ecumenical group composed of representatives of Catholic, Protestant, and Orthodox traditions, decried the leveling effect of the death penalty. Consistent with the abolitionist viewpoint, the statement focuses on the idea of the proper distance between the individual and the state, asking "all judicatories, churches, members and caring citizens [to] *acknowledge our complicity in the continuing use and support of the death penalty*." The conference goes on to add their understanding of the basics of biblical justice: though "the Bible does authorize every government to 'bear the sword' (Rom. 13:4) . . . the governments and nations of this world are also called upon to care for 'the least of these brothers and sisters' of Christ (Matt. 25:40)." In Iowa, meanwhile, a state where the churches rally against periodic attempts to reinstate the death penalty, the Iowa Catholic Conference urged its members to oppose extending the cycle of violence and to recall that each individual is created in the likeness of God; believers are bound, the conference argues, to seek life instead of death and to "follow the example of Jesus, who both taught and practiced the forgiveness of injustice."[40]

Virginia's churches and denominations have also been active in exhorting their members and congregations to take action against capital punishment. The UMC's Virginia Annual Conference and the ELCA's Virginia Synod both issued statements supporting the national organization's positions, as did the Abingdon Convocation of the Episcopal Church. The Episcopal Diocese of Virginia cited former attorney general William G. Broaddus and former Christian Coalition president Pat Robertson, both of whom support a moratorium on executions in Virginia, in declaring its intention to forward copies of its resolution to the governor, lieutenant governor, attorney general, and general assembly. The Episcopal Diocese of Southern Virginia went one step further, reminding its members of God's ability to redeem even the worst among us while urging its members to contribute to abolitionist groups and to urge ecumenical groups such as the Virginia Interfaith Center for Public Policy (VICPP) to work toward abolition. Several individual parishes and congregations also passed resolutions calling for a moratorium or outright abolition, as did two counties. The First Unitarian Church of Richmond's resolution is exemplary in its scope and clarity. This statement attacks the racial and economic bias in the application of the death penalty, as well as the progressive curtailing of rights of appeal, while reminding congregants of the need to pursue "justice, equity and compassion in human relations" because of the "inherent worth and dignity of every person."[41]

The question that needs to be addressed, however, is how these views are reflected in or make their way into the views emerging from the pews, from the congregants themselves. To put it another way, if Thomas Jefferson was right in asserting that "it is in our lives and not our words that our religion must be read," then it is reasonable to ask what the churches are doing to communicate their message to their adherents and how they seek to bring their members to oppose in action what the churches oppose in word. The Iowa Catholic Conference, for its part, "challenge[d] the people of Iowa . . . to examine the issue of capital punishment in the light of basic moral and religious values," noting that their own review led them to "speak more strongly than ever against the death penalty." The statement shows that the Iowa Conference recognized both a need and an opportunity—a need to move beyond discourse and an opportunity to reaffirm the faithful's opposition and defeat attempts to reinstate the death penalty in Iowa.[42]

This need/opportunity dynamic interests more than the churches themselves; abolitionists sometimes view churches with impatience. Henry Schwarzchild, founder of the National Coalition to Abolish the Death Penalty (NCADP), once complained that the churches "have certainly not exercised any sustained or visible moral force on what is essentially a moral issue." Kathy Lancaster, a Presbyterian minister who has spent several decades working on social justice issues, including capital punishment, lamented the churches' lack of "energy, ability, or single focus to be able . . . to carry [their opposition] back to their denominations in a way that would take." Indeed, a survey conducted by the PCUSA found that roughly three-fourths of their clergy opposed the death penalty, but the same ration of their congregants supported it. This was the largest split they had observed on any social issue.[43]

Materials produced by and for Virginia's churches replicate this national pattern. In its "Death Penalty Study Packet," the Virginia Council of Churches (VCC) included statements in opposition to the death penalty from national church bodies alongside summaries of judicatory statements from three of the largest reporting denominations in the state: the Catholic Church, the Episcopal Church, and the UMC. In the fall of 2003, the Virginia Conference of the UMC (VAUMC) held a death penalty workshop designed to bring together clergy, lay activists, academics, and penal professionals. One impetus for organizing the workshop was a "Call for Moving Forward with Study and Action on the Death Penalty." Adopted by the VAUMC in 2002, the call issued a challenge to move from word to deed, at least insofar as bringing the issue up for discussion and offering congregants and parishioners the opportunity to engage the issue from within the context of their faith tradition. Commending members of the Virginia General Assembly who had recently introduced or supported legislation that would have curtailed the death penalty, particularly by removing juveniles and the mentally retarded from the classes of eligible defendants, the call summoned members to participate at various levels: district superintendents, for example, were charged with emphasizing the denomination's opposition to the death penalty at an event within the following twelve months. More pertinently, the call requested that every local church "undertake . . . a study of the death penalty and Christian responsibility through one or more groups such as an adult class . . . or a Bible study group."[44] The next chapter will present the findings from a statewide series of Bible studies and will begin to detail how the other—the exile—functions relative to the death penalty as a process versus the death penalty as an event.

Cain said to his brother Abel, "Let us go out to the field."
And when they were in the field, Cain rose up against his
brother Abel, and killed him. Then the Lord said to Cain,
"Where is your brother Abel?" He said, "I do not know; am
I my brother's keeper?" And the Lord said, "What have you
done? Listen; your brother's blood is crying out to me from
the ground!"

(GENESIS 4:8–10

One day, after Moses had grown up, he went out to his people
and saw their forced labor. He saw an Egyptian beating a
Hebrew, one of his kinsfolk. He looked this way and that, and
seeing no one he killed the Egyptian and hid him in the sand.
. . . When Pharaoh heard of it, he sought to kill Moses. But
Moses fled from Pharaoh.

(EXODUS 2:11–12, 15

Then David's anger was greatly kindled against the man. He
said to Nathan, "As the Lord lives, the man who has done this
deserves to die . . . because he had no pity." Nathan said to
David, "You are the man!" . . . David said to Nathan, "I have
sinned against the Lord." Nathan said to David, "Now the
Lord has put away your sin; you shall not die."

(2 SAMUEL 12:5–7, 13

Then they dragged [Stephen] out of the city and began to
stone him; and the witnesses laid their coats at the feet of a
young man named Saul. While they were stoning Stephen,
he . . . knelt down and cried out in a loud voice, "Lord, do not
hold this sin against them." When he had said this, he died.
    And Saul approved of their killing him. . . . Saul was
ravaging the church by entering house after house; dragging
off both men and women, he committed them to prison.

(ACTS 7:58–8:1, 8:3

Between the Innocent Man and Osama bin Laden
The Believer and the Death Penalty, as Viewed from the Pew

It is probably safe to suggest that for most Christians the overriding conception of the foundational biblical characters is that they were generally good and holy men chosen by God for a specific purpose. As James, a federal judge, put it, "Very few people who were chosen by God . . . are also killers, murderers." Yet as we can see from this chapter's epigraphs, these foundational figures can indeed be killers, can be "people who un-make life" themselves or by proxy. Cain, certainly, is a well-known killer, but the remainder of his life is less well known—Genesis records that he came down in the lineages as the founder of the first city. Moses, the prophet who led the Chosen People out of slavery and into the Promised Land, fled Egypt as a young man to escape punishment for a homicide he committed. David, greatest of the Israelite kings, was condemned by God for his sin: David sent Uriah the Hittite into battle with the express purpose of having him killed so that he could claim Bathsheba, Uriah's wife, whom David had impregnated. Saul of Tarsus, who later converted and changed his name to Paul and became the greatest of the apostles, participated in the stoning of Stephen the Martyr and persecuted early Christians with legendary zeal.[1]

Understanding these figures and their actions in the context of the Bible study is a humanizing experience. Participants see the spectrum of human behavior in these figures, who were capable of acts of violence, including murder, and acts of great compassion; who possessed overwhelming faith and crushing doubt. The studies turn these figures from legends into people from whom we can learn valuable and applicable lessons. By considering the need for reconciliation with God, and the points at which that happens or fails to happen in the narratives, participants work through questions of sin and reconciliation and faith and doubt in their own terms and as relevant to their own lives. In these sessions, individuals work through the ways that they feel the need to try to reconcile themselves to and with God and with those around them—including, sometimes, murderers and the families and friends of their victims.

This chapter presents the findings of a series of Bible studies hosted by Virginia churches considering the death penalty, either directly in the form of a topical discussion or series of discussions or as part of a larger, liturgically driven series. Over the course of the Bible studies, it became clear that while most of the participants clearly either support or oppose capital punishment, very few did so unquestioningly. Most had some doubt, something that troubled them. Individuals professing abolitionist beliefs were troubled by cases in which they could understand if not condone executions. Retentionists frequently voiced lingering doubts as to whether we can always manage to avoid the unthinkable, the execution of an innocent. As one member of a Methodist church in central Virginia suggested, in order to come to our opinions and understand what we think about the issue, we need to look between the two extremes. We need to look, he said, between the innocent man and a captured Osama bin Laden, for him the paradigmatic extremes at which notional support or opposition break down. He suggested that even the staunchest opponents would be willing to justify executing some individuals and that even the most strident proponents would pause long enough to question seriously whether innocent persons are sentenced to death.[2]

Rocky, a deacon at a Catholic church in the Shenandoah Valley, carried this idea further. We tend to go through two stages of reaction to violent crimes like murder, he said. First comes the instinctual reaction, then the just. This does not necessarily mean that the two reactions will differ; a proponent of the death penalty is as likely to find that the instinctual reaction is the just one as an opponent is to find the opposite. The inference is that, even for those not immediately affected by violent crimes, responding to those crimes is a two-stage process rather than simply a reaction and result. How, though, do we know how to react? How are we guided in coming to terms with the crime and its aftermath? Without a frame of reference, without a context within which to work through our reactions and feelings, how are we to understand what happened? How are we to empathize with victims — or their violators? These questions are found at the center of the process of trying to determine what one's faith tradition teaches about how to act in the here and now and were topics to which the various conversations repeatedly returned.[3]

In this chapter, I explore conceptions of exile and embrace as they arose during the Bible studies. I begin by offering a way to understand the Bible studies as practices and as engagements before turning to look at materials prepared for topical Bible studies focusing on capital punishment. These materials include both those produced by local congregations for their own use and those published for the respective denomination for use in all churches, as well as ecumenical guides intended for a broad audience. We will examine them for what they reveal about the typical issues confronting a congregation and for patterns in what is deemed sufficiently important from a communicative perspective as to merit inclusion in the session/course materials. We will look at both biblical content and "real-world" information and scenarios against which participants can discuss and analyze their impulses and reactions. We will focus primarily on the related conceptions of distance and reconciliation as the guides present them with regard both to instruction and introspection. Moreover, I will show how these concepts of distance and reconciliation — between the individual and God and between the individual and others — are problematized and located relative to the respective denomination's position on the death penalty and related issues.[4]

I then turn to the conversations themselves. Over the fall and winter of 2008–9, I worked with churches across the state that were willing to host a session or series of sessions considering capital punishment and related issues. These sessions took several forms. Most commonly, the session was a variant on a roundtable discussion facilitated most often by a minister, deacon, or other lay leader. Many of these roundtable sessions were Bible studies in the strict sense of the term. Participants knew ahead of time what text would be read during the session and could prepare as they saw fit. After reading the texts aloud, participants analyzed the story and tried to relate it to their lives and experiences. Other formats included guest speakers, including lawyers and academics, and more personal, non-text-based discussions. Sessions were held in cities, suburbs, and rural areas, and over four hundred participants in total attended the twenty sessions.

I treat these Bible studies as exercises in liturgical reading and as reconciliatory practices. This reading is helpful for several reasons. First, understanding the Bible studies in light of both of these types of practice brings the death penalty and its symbolic resonances more clearly into view. Second, viewing the studies as these related types of practice reinforces the tension between justice and mercy that resides at the core of Christianity and considerations over the legitimacy of capital punishment. Further, this pairing allows us to see more deeply into the collocations and associations that arise in these conversations, showing in greater detail how the participants conceptualize and locate the concepts and ideas with which they are working. Finally, examining these sessions as reconciliatory practices and as exercises in liturgical reading enables us to begin to see the concepts of the other at work, and how they differ. When we explore these concepts of the other in this way, we can clearly distinguish between two related but inverted pairings of exile and embrace: the ways in which what is desired contrasts with what is needed. When we parse the conversations, we see that proponents and opponents generally have a clear idea of where they stand on the issue, including knowing what makes them uncomfortable or less certain in their position. What also becomes clear, however, is the extent to which perceived necessities—what the believer, society, or church "needs"—differ from the ends that they espouse.[5]

Liturgical Reading and Reconciliatory Practices

Describing Bible studies as liturgical reading acknowledges the ritual character of the activity. Studies typically begin and close with an invocation, solemnifying the time between the two prayers as work dedicated to developing the believer's faith, in the sense both of education (what does the scripture say?) and interpretation (what does it mean?). The study session involves a complex, continually shifting locus of attention, alternately within the text, within the imagined world of that text, within the world of the believer, and, connecting the two, within the contested idea that is "God's will" in both the world of the text and the world of the believer. The Bible study is a ritual reading in which the chosen text is read, interpreted, and understood in light both of context, immediate and ancient, and, perhaps more importantly, of memory, predicated on the reading of both the text and the action.[6]

The act of reading liberates the text from its context and treats it as a connected but discrete piece to be considered on its own merits and in relation to the greater whole. This removal disrupts the normal rhythms of the greater narrative within which the selection is located and requires participants to interrupt and interrogate their previously held understandings of the text, both in itself and within the broader narrative. The story of Moses's murder of the Egyptian, which we will discuss below, is a stark example of this. Reading this story is potentially disruptive in at least three ways. First, pulling that piece out disrupts the greater narrative of Moses's life, forcing it into a more episodic format than may be the case in the greater narrative. Second, and directly related to the first, understanding the killing requires reintegrating that story into the greater whole, possibly further disrupting the greater biographical narrative and demanding that the reader continue to interrogate and cross-examine that reintegrated narrative. These two disruptions color the third, the reader's interrogation and cross-examination of themselves and of God in seeking to discern God's wishes. This disruption, which results in questions variously phrased in terms of the nature of God's will and the meaning of the story in the here and now, signifies the process by which believers permit themselves "to be cross-examined, challenged, and remade by the Scripture." Reintegrating the reintegrated narrative into the individuals' understandings of their faith traditions and of themselves in light of those traditions furthers the desired end of transforming believers via continual repetition and engagement.[7]

The liturgical reading invites the reader to ask questions such as "What does this writer want me to see? What of my own story am I being invited to retell or recast in the light of the way the text presents the story of God's action in Jesus Christ?" It is a way to dislocate, reconstruct, and reintegrate one's identity more fully in keeping with what it means to be a believer. This dislocation and reconstruction occurs in "the interpretative zone between current events and biblical imagery," traversing the distance from Word to life and back. In this way, Bible studies are "pew-based" analogues of sermons, which negotiate the same distance to the same end, albeit from the pulpit out to the pews. What makes Bible studies—indeed, all forms of liturgical reading—communal speech acts, or collective performances, is the intent to inform, both in the sense of imparting information and in the sense of impacting belief and behavior. If the aim of liturgical reading, including Bible studies, is to help believers "develo[p] moral sensibilities, hermeneutical skills, and powers of discernment that enable the reader to negotiate God's world," then "reading Scripture works to convert, transform the reader." Without this, liturgical reading would be an exercise in aesthetics, rather than communication; because of this, liturgical reading is Eucharistic.[8]

If liturgical reading, including Bible studies, is Eucharistic, then it is a reconciliatory activity. John Berkman argues that the Eucharist is "the primary context for reconciliation . . . in the Christian life." Berkman notes that tradition has long held it necessary for believers to reconcile with their fellows before bringing themselves before God to be reconciled with him. The biblical basis for this argument is found in Matthew 5:23–24: "when you are offering your gift at the altar, if you remember that your brother or sister has something against you, leave your gift there before the altar and go; first be reconciled to your brother or sister, and then come and offer your gift." Nor is this idea remote from contemporary discussions, as we will see.[9]

Liturgical reading is a reconciliatory practice in three distinct ways. First, the readings reconcile the texts with believers and their world. Second, the practice of reading reconciles the text and the believer with God, however incompletely; and third, this reading reconciles the text and believer with the specific chains of memory that impact the occasion. These include the experience that the individual brings to the table, the local institutional memory of the minister or other leaders conducting or participating in the session, and the larger institutional memory of church teachings and tradition. This understanding of Bible studies as liturgical, reconciliatory reading practices takes on a different dimension when the discussions center on capital punishment from the point of view of the respective faith tradition. As one participating minister put it, "The particular form of [Jesus's] execution has become the principal symbol for Christians worldwide. . . . We have capital punishment, in a sense, at the very center of our faith." How, then, is this central idea dealt with in a Bible study setting?[10]

"What Does God Want?"

Genesis 1 to Genesis 8 covers considerable narrative and theological ground. Reading from creation to the disembarkation of Noah's family from the ark following the flood, and pausing there to reflect on what is being said about humanity at each end of that block of text, the reader may be struck with two apparently contradictory ideas. In the Genesis 1 creation narrative, humankind is created on the sixth day and given dominion over the world; at this point, humans and beasts alike are consigned to a vegetarian diet, the better, presumably, to honor and preserve life. Father Jim Griffin, a former death row chaplain, cites Genesis 1 as the basis for that ministry: "God looked at what God had made . . . and said that it was good. . . . And even if it's been belittled by . . . the murderer, that doesn't belittle God's relationship with him. . . . [That's] the basic reason for death row or any . . . social justice-type ministry. . . . That's the bottom line."[11]

Seven chapters later, however, the presentation of humankind has altered significantly. When Noah and his family disembark, Noah immediately sacrifices one of each clean animal and bird, making burnt offerings of them. God's comment to this is a resolution nevermore to destroy the world in order to destroy humans, "for the inclination of the human heart is evil from youth." Noah's transgression, the impetus for God permitting humans to shift from a vegetarian to an omnivorous diet, is all the more noteworthy in the context of Genesis 6, which explains what it was that caused God to destroy the world in a flood in the first place: "'I have determined to make an end of all flesh, for the earth is filled with *violence* because of them.'"[12]

Here, then, are the horns of the dilemma. As discussed in chapter 2, retentionist and abolitionist churches agree that life is not only good but sacred and to be protected from violation. They agree on the need to restore individuals to God. Facilitating this reconciliation is an act of love, and to act out of love is the central commandment guiding interpersonal relations. The question is how to act, which act of love is God's desire. Is the death penalty, as one minister argued, an act of love?

> What would be the most loving for that person? I think it would be this: He needs to consider the afterlife and where he's going, because the tack that he's on is showing every indication that he's headed for eternal judgment, which is Hell. That's a real thing. Jesus spoke more about Hell than he did Heaven. Jesus spoke more about Hell than any other person in the Bible. So if you believe in Jesus, you have to believe in eternal punishment. . . . There is no motivation greater than saying, "On July 29, at 4 o'clock in the afternoon, you're going to enter eternity. Guaranteed. Because we're going to make you enter eternity." . . . So he's got a chance—and that's a luxury, to know when exactly you're going to die. So he's got a chance to sit and think about, "Wow, I'm not going to be here." . . . And if he wants to consider his ways, then that's what it's all about. . . . If that man repents, and it's a genuine, true repentance, then his soul is definitely going to be with God. If he doesn't, then he knows exactly where he's going, and God's been as fair with him as possible. . . . In that sense, actually, it's helping this man, or this woman, to see exactly what they've turned into. . . . Very few people, I think, look at it and try to study it as, "Why is the death penalty an act of love?" And I think it really is.[13]

Is it? Or is it an act that destroys another life? What does God *want*—what does God want us to do with criminals, with murderers?

To ask that question in the Bible study setting is to engage in the re-creative practice described above. Taking that question seriously and attempting to answer it draws the object of the question—God's will, as it can be known—into the interpretative zone prescribed by the action of liturgical reading. As the VCC noted in its "Death Penalty Study Packet," "Christians . . . owe it to ourselves, to society, to those who wait on Death Row and, above all, to our Lord, to examine ourselves carefully in regard to the death penalty." The study guides surveyed cover a wide array of scriptural citation and narrative references. They also differ in scope — single or multiple sessions — and whether the desired impact is limited to the individual believer or whether the study is designed to lead to organized abolitionist action. What they have in common, however, is a method for coming to theological conclusions utilizing scripture, reason, tradition, and experience. The "moral obligation [for] all serious Christians to become informed about the Church's position opposing the death penalty" can be supported by producing and providing guides that "enable . . . Christians to examine their denomination's and judicatory's positions on the death penalty," that is, tradition. Assertions that the churches need to increase awareness of the injustices inherent in the death penalty and the way it cheapens life are based on reason and experience. So too are calls for churches to educate their members about alternatives to capital punishment and ways that they can advocate for "a more just and humane way of dealing with society's worst offenders." Arguments citing biblical text engage scripture. While all of these studies use these four elements as pillars, none does so as succinctly as the United Presbyterian Church's "Capital Punishment Study Resource":

[This guide] seeks to help . . . a group achieve four basic objectives:
- to reflect on their emotions and attitudes toward capital punishment in light of the gospel
- to study the current situation regarding capital punishment and the human dimensions involved
- to study the denomination's position on capital punishment
- to identify possibilities for action[14]

Limitations, Reconciliation, Forgiveness

What God wants, these studies argue, is a combination of limitations, reconciliation, and forgiveness, which the studies treat as processes, not events. They employ several noteworthy biblical passages to this end, not as elements of an argument but as orienting themes. One modular study, designed to be used for age groups running from elementary school to adults, orients itself around Ezekiel 33:11's call for reconciliation. Another uses a passage from John to rebut retentionist claims that the death penalty is biblically sanctioned, arguing that those who kill in God's name have known neither God nor Jesus — neither the Judge nor the Redeemer. Another study pulls all three elements together to discuss God's plan for the offender, combining verses arguing for limitations on actions and violence with those calling for forgiveness and reconciliation.[15]

We need to limit violence for two main reasons. First, limiting our own violence enables us to get past the instinctive reaction and work toward the just. Second, we need to accept a limit on violence before either forgiveness or reconciliation can occur. The progressive development of limits on acceptable violence is evident over the course of the Old Testament. One such limitation arises in the Noah narrative. Though God gave Noah the right to eat of the flesh of the beasts, God withheld the right to the blood, to the life. Animal consumption and sacrifice were permitted to channel humanity's violent, destructive impulses, yet God retained dominion over life. This may seem a minor detail, but it is a meaningful caveat in the midst of a debate over whether someone can forfeit their right to life.[16]

The progressive limits on justified violence enter familiar territory when we return to the Cain and Abel narrative and move forward to the law of retribution. Rather than exact revenge or permit others to do so, God marked Cain, preserving his life. We can see this principle carried further in the Mosaic Law. The *lex talionis*, the "eye for an eye," so frequently if incorrectly cited as a justification for capital punishment, is not merely an imposed limit, though it is that. It should be viewed not as an event—a discrete imposition of a limit—but as part of an ongoing process. By limiting the right of response, the *lex talionis* created an alternative to other extant legal codes, which allowed or called for disproportionate response against families, tribes, or villages. The Mosaic law also allowed for cities of refuge, where certain classes of killers could flee until disputes could be settled, which we can see as an ancient analogue of our system of degrees of murder.[17]

Further developments in the rabbinic tradition moved this process from legal to procedural limitations, instituting procedures that made it virtually impossible to carry out a death sentence, further limiting vengeance and violence. Two limitations in particular are noteworthy. Execution methods were consistently modified to lessen the physical damage to the body while taking life. The operative principle here was to act out of love: "The verse saith, But thou shalt love thy neighbor as thyself, [which implies:] choose an easy death for him." The second limitation was a series of procedural and evidentiary restrictions at every stage of the process that made "legal capital punishment impossible of practical application." The most notable of these may be the way criminal intent was to be determined: "All those under sentence of death according to the Torah are to be executed only . . . after . . . warning, and provided the warners have let them know that they are liable to a death sentence. . . . The warners must also inform them of the kind of death they would suffer [and failing that, they are not to be executed]." Without this specific warning and affirmative response from the prospective murderer that they intend to commit their crime anyway, criminal intent may not be provable. This is but one of the procedural restrictions on capital punishment that made it practically impossible to carry out in this period.[18]

The New Testament continues this process, repudiating any manner of vengeance and "mov[ing] us from the Old Testament perspective of limited retaliation to nonretaliation and active love." "Vengeance," John Howard Yoder remarks, "does not need to be commanded; it happens." Understanding this, these guides go beyond advocating imposing limits on violence. They argue instead that Christians are to understand the progression of limits by which violence and vengeance are to be ever more restricted. These limits are not discontinuous events occurring in succession over a period of millennia but, rather, part of a continuous, ongoing process.[19]

These study guides challenge the common understanding that the Old Testament is Law and the New Testament is Grace. Mercy, they note, is a common Old Testament theme. Equally important, even the clearest manifestations of mercy and forgiveness in the New Testament retain the law. Forgiveness is incumbent upon the believer, and it is to be a habit, a learned practice. Anticipating the objection that will follow from too much emphasis on forgiving offenders, the studies declare that forgiveness and letting people "run rampant," as one participant put it, are two different things before elaborating on that response in two ways. First, they point out the distance between human emotions and God's will, turning to both the Old and New Testaments to make this point. In Ezekiel, one guide shows, we can see another iteration of the idea expressed at 33:11, that "if the wicked turn away from all their sins that they have committed . . . they shall surely live; they shall not die." Despite this, the people protest: "Yet you say, 'The way of the Lord is unfair.'" The answer that follows shows the process of which forgiveness is a part: "Repent and turn away from all your transgressions. . . . Cast away from you all the transgressions that you have committed against me, and get yourselves a new heart and a new spirit!" The guides also point out that though Jesus forgave and "extended mercy and a loving gentleness to the offender," he nevertheless "firmly condemn[ed] sinful behavior" and challenged sinners to reform and fulfill his command in John 8 to go and sin no more.[20] Forgiveness is thus tied with the process of repentance and reform, which, as we will see, is one of the most powerful arguments against the death penalty. Moreover, forgiveness is one of the necessary pieces of the process of restorative justice, an end toward which several of the guides are dedicated. The question, given the apparent rejection of the idea of forgiveness above, and given Rocky's bipartite explanation of how we react to crimes, is whether and how the information and messages contained in the study guides, particularly the emphasis on process at the expense of event, work their way into the discussions themselves.[21]

"What I'm concerned about is . . ."

"I'd like to begin with what may sound like a simple question: How many here think that Moses should have been put to death for killing that Egyptian?"[22]

As conversation starters go, this was a dud. It was intended to be provocative and to jar participants in this session into getting past their own preconceptions more quickly. Bludgeoning people with facts doesn't always have this effect, though, and early on Sunday morning, coffee was sipped and the moderator had to expand on his question before anyone was willing to dig in and hazard an answer. Further prodding brought out a series of answers that collectively came down somewhere in the area of yes, legally, he probably should have, but no, of course Moses should not have been put to death. It was a bit of an unfair way to ask the question, James continued, because of the plan that God had for Moses, and the fact that "only Moses . . . had the skill and the life experiences" to fulfill this plan. We remember Moses in a variety of ways, not all of them biblical. We remember, of course, Charlton Heston and the various comedic and dramatic depictions of Moses returning from Sinai with the stone tablets. We remember the staff turning to a snake, the parting of the Red Sea, the delivery of the slaves, the rigors of the Exodus. As far as who Moses was, we remember him in an equally impressive variety of ways. He was the foremost of the prophets, the lawgiver, the conduit by which the people were redeemed from bondage.[23]

One thing that we're not entirely clear on is whether Moses *killed* the Egyptian or *murdered* him. Part of this may be a symptom of the same unease with which we read "Thou shalt not kill"—or is it "Thou shalt not murder"? Murder, after all, requires malice aforethought—as the Code of Virginia says, murder is "willful, deliberate, and premeditated killing." The killing of the Egyptian does not clearly fit this description, though we do note that Moses "looked this way and that" before killing the Egyptian—after seeing no potential witnesses. Does that suffice to make the killing willful, deliberate, and premeditated? Participants' collective ambivalence on this was clear in the lack of consistency with which they described the homicide, which they called a "murder" and a "killing" without really differentiating or clarifying which they felt was which.[24]

Another thing that we're not entirely clear on is when Moses learned that he was a Hebrew, not an Egyptian. The narrative is unclear: verse 11 refers to the Hebrews as Moses's "people" and his "kinfolk," while verse 19 refers to him as "an Egyptian." Some participants argued that he always knew he was a Hebrew, others that he found out just before the killing. This question is not a matter of idle speculation. Once broached, it swiftly leads to practical concerns and apologetics. Did Moses need Aaron to speak for him because Moses did not speak Hebrew? If Moses believed himself to be Egyptian, was he a particularly compassionate Egyptian who saw human value in the slaves and acted accordingly? That would explain why he fled—after all, how would Moses, adopted son of the Pharaoh's daughter, answer questions about why he killed a fellow Egyptian in defense of a Hebrew slave? If Moses was a member of the dominant class, rather than the dominated, we understand his flight.[25]

If he knew that he was a Hebrew, though, our consensus is that the killing was clearly justified. We may quibble over whether he would have been justified in killing the Egyptian if there were no mortal danger to the slave, though this problem seemed untroubling to most participants. Moses the Hebrew acted in defense of his brethren, and can we in any case fault him for defending the oppressed, even to the point of using lethal violence? And why, for that matter, was the Egyptian beating the slave? Perhaps this was an extraordinary case, an overseer abusing the slave for the sheer pleasure of it. Did Moses only try to stop the Egyptian killing the slave, not try to kill him? That would make it a killing, not a murder, and how we understand that would hinge on how we understand the sixth commandment, for most Protestant and Jewish groups, or the fifth, for Catholics and Lutherans. Are we forbidden to kill, or to murder? Maybe Moses had only recently discovered his true lineage and was conflicted—over his own identity, over how he could reconcile his life with that identity. Perhaps the killing was a blind rage inspired by the complex emotions he would have been feeling then; perhaps it was an expression of remorse. After all, but for what he had learned a short time previously, perhaps he could have joined that Egyptian in beating the slave—or maybe he had been that Egyptian before, and hated what he saw in the moment, and in himself, so much that he could only strike out violently.[26]

There's not much question that Moses knew that he had done something wrong—he fled, after all, and "the guilty flee, that's not a truism." Given this, what should we make of the incident that immediately precipitates his flight in the narrative? Moses breaks up a fight between two Hebrews, admonishing the one who was at fault, though how this is ascertained is left open in the story: Moses does not see the fight begin; he happens upon it. In response, the admonished Hebrew turns to Moses and wonders how it is that he presumes to judge them and whether Moses means to kill him as he had the Egyptian. Moses's realization—"Surely the thing is known"—coincides with a realization and further complication of the narrative. The Hebrew asked how Moses decided to take it upon himself to judge. This question could only have been asked of a fellow Hebrew, not an Egyptian. Was Moses a collaborator, a member of the oppressed class aiding in that oppression? Was Moses, one participant wondered as we discussed the session on the way to the parking lot, the ancient equivalent of a black overseer in the antebellum South?[27]

No, someone responded: Moses is more analogous to a conductor on the Underground Railroad, or one of "the Dutchmen [who] tried to hide the Jews" during the Second World War. Continuing the World War II comparisons, Rocky noted that Moses reminded him of Dietrich Bonhoeffer, a reluctant leader prodded into action against his wishes who, rather than turn his back on his people, tries to save them at great personal risk. Whatever triggered the flight, the consensus among participants was that Moses knew he had done wrong. That's why it was such an act of personal courage to answer God's call and to return to the scene of his crime, there to face down his conscience, which we tend to believe has been troubling him throughout the intervening years; to face the law that would have him executed for his crime; to face the trials that come with being a leader. Perhaps we should consider the murder in this light, as Pastor Frazier suggested. Maybe the killing of the Egyptian was the act of sacrifice necessary for Moses to become the leader he was destined to be. Here we can use René Girard's theory of ritual violence to clarify this element of the narrative: Moses broke taboo — a member of the master class killing another member of the master class in defense of a member of the slave class — and broke the law, imperiling himself and necessitating his exile from the community until he later returned to assume leadership over that community.[28]

When Moses kills, we need to know why. We need to know the motive; we need to go "where the courts want to go." The variety of opinions and questions detailed above testify to this need to resolve the moral and biographical ambiguities in the Moses narrative. Perhaps, to paraphrase Joseph, who led the Hebrews into Egypt in better times, Moses meant it for evil, but God meant it for good. After all, Moses's flight carried him into the land of Midian, where he learned the desert survival skills that doubtless were beneficial during the Exodus. We're also interested in why Cain killed Abel, but that's not as ambiguous as Moses slaying the Egyptian. We feel as though we have Cain figured out: he felt rejected by God, was deeply envious of his brother Abel, and could not handle those emotions. They overwhelmed him and he succumbed to his urge to lure his brother out into the field and kill him. There is no apologia for Cain the way there is for Moses; in fact, study participants were keenly aware that Cain was not redeemed into a later calling, as Moses was. Nor, in fact, do we see that Cain ever repents. The closest he comes is protesting against his punishment, griping that it is too much to bear, a complaint with which we have little sympathy. Cain is selfish, ego-driven, too dedicated to himself to have his heart right with God, and when confronted by God, he does not face up to his sin, but stands defiant. He, like Moses, knows that he did wrong, but whereas Moses fled, Cain stands before God brazen and unrepentant.[29]

All the same, many participants identified with Cain, to the point of being ready, in some cases, to castigate God as "a stupid parent" for so openly favoring one child over another and thus opening the door to the instinctual reaction: sibling rivalry. As Pastor Frazier argued, however, this is more than normal sibling rivalry: God's poor parenting opens the door to *mimetic rivalry*, the desire to possess what the other possesses, which Girard argues is at the root of all conflict. The scriptures, Pastor Frazier commented, "[tell] us a lot about who we are as human beings"; we are, he noted, people instinctually driven to this mimetic rivalry, which dominates Genesis. We see it in the Cain and Abel narrative; in the Isaac/Ishmael conflict; in Jacob's conflict with Esau; and in Joseph's conflict with his brothers, which led the Hebrews into Egypt and, later, into slavery. A number of foundational events in the early biblical histories break down to this mimetic rivalry and the violence that it sows. Moreover, as individuals, we can easily identify with this rivalry. As Andrew, a career law enforcement officer, put it, "We all look for recognition; we all want to be tops in whatever we do, and it's hard when someone as close as your brother . . . gets the recognition and you don't." Emmett, a financial planner, agreed: "[Cain] could have been any of us." If law is the only thing that keeps us from killing each other whenever we feel provoked, as one participant asked, can we really claim to be any better than Cain?[30]

Were it any of us, had we made the choice that he made, we would likewise bear the mark of Cain. We too would wear the orange jumpsuit. Were we Cain, had we acted as he did, we would be the exile, the prisoner, two terms describing Cain that most often arose during discussions. We would likewise have to live with our consciences and the consequences of our action, though it is unclear whether we consider Cain of sound mind. Perhaps, as one participant suggested, this story is an indication that mental illness has entered the world. After all, as another participant picked up the point, look at what a meager provocation that was. Abel offered of the firstlings of his flock, by definition the very best, and Cain offered just some of the produce of his fields. Participants readily agreed that Abel's offering was preferable to Cain's and that it was Cain's responsibility to have made a better offering had he wished God's favor. Because he was in part responsible for the situation, and because the provocation is seen as relatively minor compared with the result, study participants saw little moral ambiguity in Cain and his situation, far less than with Moses. They nevertheless saw something of themselves in Cain, or rather something of Cain in themselves, an important distinction to which we will return.[31]

Participants weren't willing to let Abel off the hook, though. Carol, director of Christian formation at her church, wanted to know why Abel did not help Cain. Emmett commented on the "Am I my brother's keeper?" portion of the narrative, turning that around onto Abel. What kind of brother, he wondered, doesn't try to help his brother when he needs it? Surely Abel saw that Cain was not right with God, and he presumably knew why, yet he did not help. Andrew echoed the same sentiment:

> ANDREW: Maybe Abel should have said something to his brother. Maybe [he] should have come to him and said, "Hey, you want to be good with God, here's what you do."
> JAMES: Maybe. Does that suggest, though, that Abel had it coming? . . .
> ANDREW: The story doesn't give any great detail. It doesn't say whether there was any great animosity between the two brothers, whether there was ongoing arguments, or strife, or anything. It just says this, this, this. We don't know what Cain was like at this time.
> JAMES: So this is basically the sound-bite version?
> ANDREW: Yeah, basically.

Yet "God doesn't take a life for a life." As Andrew, a death penalty proponent, observed, "It sounds like no one can do any death other than God." The takeaway from this story, it seems, is a rejection of revenge, both that of vigilantism and of retribution. A sentiment repeatedly expressed in the sessions is that this is not ours to do. Maybe, as one participant suggested, banishing Cain kept him alive in our memories longer. Were his punishment simply death, maybe we would have forgotten the lesson. Cain does not repent yet, much to our consternation, still lives, perhaps to come home to himself and repent at a later date, to reconcile himself with God down the road. Maybe, participants mused, this is why God leaves a way to mitigate his punishments. Perhaps that is the significance of the mark, which, as Pastor Frazier noted, bears a resemblance to the mark on our foreheads on Ash Wednesday and the mark we receive at baptism. Maybe it is a mark of the fugitive from the sight of God — or perhaps the mark is a promise of forgiveness, of pending repentance.[32]

The Problem of Forgiveness

As participants discussed Cain's narrative, they tended to agree that forgiveness and repentance are not easily to be sought or offered. Rather, they are moral skills, something that we have to practice. We, like Cain, will have to repent, but unlike Cain, we will have to practice doing the right thing, practice forgiving, in order to avoid his mistake. Without practice in making the right decision — in forgiving those who harm us and forgiving ourselves when need be — how can we know we will be able to make the right decision when we are tested?

This question arose frequently in discussions, often accompanied by concrete examples of exemplary forgiveness, the most prominent of which centered around the 2006 Nickel Mines school shooting. On October 2, 2006, Charles Carl Roberts IV entered the schoolhouse in Nickel Mines, a small Amish community in Bart Township, Pennsylvania, armed with a variety of weapons. Roberts sent the men and boys away, along with a pregnant woman and several infants, then bound the girls and lined them up against a wall. He told them that he could not cope with his hatred of God and needed to "punish some Christian girls to get even with him." Marian Fisher, thirteen, told Roberts to shoot her first, trying to protect the younger girls; Roberts complied. He shot ten girls before turning the gun on himself as police tried to break into the school. Fisher and Naomi Rose Ebersol, nine, died instantly. Anna May Stoltzfus, twelve, was pronounced dead on arrival at Lancaster General Hospital. The Miller sisters, Lena Zook and Mary Liz, ages eight and seven, died the next day. Esther King (thirteen), Sarah Ann and Rachel Ann Stoltzfus (twelve and eight), Barbie Fisher (eleven), and Rosanna King (six) survived their severe injuries, though King remains confined to a wheelchair with severe brain damage from the shooting.[33]

As the community reeled from the horrific attack and local residents tried to protect the families' privacy by physically obstructing media vans, details spread out through the national and world media. As the scale of the tragedy became clear, the community and the nation tried to respond and come to terms with yet another school massacre. Gifts and messages of condolences poured in from across the country, requiring hundreds of volunteer manhours to sort and deliver. The Amish, consistent with their beliefs, do not carry health insurance; funds were established to cover the victims' medical expenses, raising over $3.2 million for those purposes by late November. The community started a separate fund to help Roberts's widow, Marie, and their three children. And, to the shock of most observers, the community moved to forgive Roberts and reach out to his family. Grieving parents contacted Roberts's family and met with his parents, offering condolences for their loss, sharing their mutual heartbreak, and offering solace and forgiveness. The community opened its arms to Roberts's family, inviting his widow and children to the children's funerals and attending Roberts's funeral; by one account, half of the mourners at Roberts's funeral were members of the community, including the families of the children he had murdered. The ties lasted; Roberts's mother, Terri, remained in touch with the families and regularly visits Rosanna King, the youngest victim, to read and sing to her.[34]

Not everyone was impressed by the community's quick offer of forgiveness. The negative responses ranged from declarations that Roberts was beyond the pale of forgiveness to declarations that we should never aspire to be someone who could forgive such an atrocity to declarations that the families reacted immorally in not only forgiving their children's killer but also failing to lament the fact that he committed suicide and thus deprived us of the opportunity to execute him. Forgiveness offered to such an individual under such circumstances, this argument went, disrespected the dead and left the rest of us having to hold the moral line in the families' stead.[35]

For the most part, however, the community's forgiveness was seen as a noble, if bewildering, gesture. One op-ed in particular summed up many of the responses to this "incomprehensible" act of forgiveness. David Weaver-Zercher, who teaches American religious history at Messiah College (PA) and has written several books on the Amish in America, was "moved by the Amish ability to extend words of grace to the killer's family." Yet he was troubled, he wrote, by the realization that this forgiveness was so out of character with mainstream American values and capacity to forgive that it seemed radical by comparison. The community professed to be puzzled by the strength of the response to their forgiving Roberts; they were simply doing as Jesus had done for them and commanded them to do, they said. It wasn't easy, but they had their faith and their families to draw on; they had a community that practiced forgiveness as a matter of daily communal life and that both forgave communally and helped each other to practice the forgiveness that they were commanded. They recognized that this tragedy could lock them beyond a point of no return, could make them "prisoners of the past. . . . Forgiveness brings freedom," they said. They cited Matthew 18:21–22, which commands believers to forgive those who sin against them "seventy times seven" times, and acknowledged that it remains difficult, that it remains a process. As one father said, "Every morning when I get up, I have to start all over again with forgiveness."[36]

Still, for all that we marveled or disapproved of the community's response, blame had to be assigned; all parties directed blame somewhere. People opposed to extending forgiveness to this killer blamed those who forgave for abetting this kind of evil. People who marveled at the forgiveness blamed a society that cannot practice forgiveness or deal with this kind of evil and blamed the churches for not teaching us any better. Roberts properly received the majority of that blame, even as details emerged about him. He left multiple suicide notes for his wife, one mentioning his guilt over sexually abus-

(*Between the Innocent Man and Osama bin Laden*   (63

ing two relatives—claims that were not substantiated. They mentioned his rage toward and hatred of both himself and God. He had gone to the school that day armed not just with several weapons but also with a variety of sexual lubricants, apparently intending to sexually abuse the girls as well. Despite all of the revelations about the crime, one detail that the community made clear to the world was that Roberts was, like them, a sinner in need of grace. If the families of the victims knew that they, like Roberts, were sinners in need of grace, he, like they, was a grieving parent. In 1997, Marie Roberts gave birth to a baby girl; the child died in twenty minutes. Roberts, it seems, never recovered. The mass murderer was also a grieving father whose last words to his other children on the morning of the murders were reportedly, "Remember, Daddy loves you."[37]

For the families, though, remembrance goes hand in hand with continuing to forgive. Every day they have to start again. In this, their story of tragedy and forgiveness mirrors that of others who have been able to forgive people who killed their loved ones. SueZann Bosler saw her father, Rev. Billy Bosler, murdered in front of her. An assailant broke into his church and stabbed him twenty-four times. She was stabbed in the back of the head and survived by pretending to be dead, but saw as the assailant ransacked the building and watched as her father took his last breath. She then spent over a decade fighting to have her father's killer sentenced to life rather than death, at one point threatened by the trial judge with six months in jail on contempt charges if she so much as mentioned her opposition to the death penalty on the stand. Bosler described the trial process and aftermath as a scab, one that kept being opened and hurting afresh. Each time the scab was opened, each day that the Nickel Mines families wake up without their children, the offense and pain are new, and, as they have said in their stories, they have to forgive again. Saying that forgiveness is a process recognizes that the single offense can be a recurring offense. This is the second half of the "seventy times seven" comment from the Amish families—they have to forgive so often because they are injured so often.[38]

Appropriately, the Nickel Mines shootings arose in conversations in connection with the Cain and Abel narrative—in the context, that is, of how we should think about an unrepentant killer. Without living forgiveness as the Amish do, participants wondered, how can we be sure that we'll forgive someone who harms us, as they did? Can we take comfort in the hope that these stories offer of forgiveness for those of us who are "just trying to get it right along the way" even if we cannot live up to Jesus's command to forgive as we are forgiven? And what about Moses? If Moses was not ready for his calling when he was young, if he had to learn from his sin and his subsequent experience in order to become the prophet he was to become, how are we to react to "some kid who's in the inner city and he kills somebody in a crack cocaine deal and he's nineteen years old . . . or how about if he's twelve?"[39]

What these conversations reveal is the extent to which we see the stories of Moses and Cain as processes, rather than as defined by single events. Cain is largely defined by a single event — slaying his brother — but even that strong identification resides within at least an enduring process: God marking Cain and exiling him. The story does not end with the murder, and whatever moral clarity participants saw in the story of the murder, the marking and exile was significantly more morally complex. Nor does Moses's story end with the homicide. In fact, Moses's story can be said to begin with the killing before continuing over much of the next four books. We are generally willing, in other words, to give Moses, and to a lesser extent Cain, the benefit of the doubt. There are several reasons for this. First of all, it is easy to see the whole story — we need only read on a bit further. All of the salient details are available to us, at least as determined by the ancient scribes or by their divine inspiration, depending on how one reads the Bible. Participants also felt they could rely on God's judgment, which is explicitly recorded in both instances. It is not for us to judge either Cain or Moses because God has already done so. We have a "moral norm," a "right" response against which to measure our reactions without the obligation to judge. Relieved of this burden, participants found it easier to interpret these narratives and decide how they apply to our lives — in other words, to dislocate, reorient, and reintegrate.

We are not always so willing, as a visiting former death row chaplain urged one congregation, to "read beyond the headlines." To do so would be to involve ourselves in understanding the process, the sequence of events, both before and after the crime. This need not mean that we become less willing to support capital punishment, though it does make it more likely that support will wane, for several noteworthy reasons. First, bearing in mind Rocky's observation about the instinctual reaction, our inclination is to identify with the victims, which means that we are less likely to identify with the perpetrator. This sounds simple enough, and a glance at public reaction to any high-profile crime supports Rocky's assertion that this is part of our first, instinctual reaction. When we engage the process rather than the event, however — when we learn more about the story behind the headline — we run the risk of finding something in the defendant with which we can identify. One lawyer, a commonwealth's attorney and former capital defender, spoke to this from his professional experience: "Everybody on that jury knows somebody who didn't grow up as well as they did, or, unfortunately, they didn't grow up well themselves. If they identify," if they meet the defendants "in all [of their] complication[s] and contradiction[s]," then jurors may withhold a death sentence.[40]

On the other side, as Jesse, a staunch proponent of the death penalty, worried, "What I'm concerned about is, does this lead to the thought that there is redemption in killers and murderers?" When we see more of the story than is contained in the headlines and sound bites, when we look at examples and relate them to our own experience, what do we see? How do we view offenders in light of our varied understandings of the death penalty as either an event or a process? And what does it mean to think in terms of event and process?[41]

Process versus Event

To differentiate between event and process in terms of the death penalty is not to deny that the death penalty is itself a process, or, if we limit our gaze simply to the execution itself, the culmination of a process. It is instead to think in terms of categories of response, in terms of a narrower versus a broader narrative or a less restrictive alternative rather than a more restrictive alternative. As we saw in chapter 2, some view all questions regarding the death penalty as beginning and ending with the murder in question. This is an event-based perspective, and this perspective corresponds with a ritualistic, event-based perspective on the death penalty itself. The process-based viewpoint sees both the murder and the punishment in terms of a longer continuum of events and corresponds to a markedly different perspective on capital punishment. The difference is that between forward- and backward-looking conceptions of the individual and of the rightness of punishment.

The event-based perspective corresponds with the retentionist position and with retentionist theology. This theology holds that civil society is the second divinely invested institution, following the family and preceding the church, and that it is invested with the authority to demand justice. Both the institution of civil society and the ordination to justice arise in contexts that retentionists interpret as supporting capital punishment. The institution of civil society, according to this interpretation, occurs in Genesis 9. Following Noah's sacrifice, God lays down a set of guidelines for how humans are to interact with each other. Among these guidelines is the following piece of chiastic verse:

> Whoever sheds the blood of a human,
> by a human shall that person's blood be shed
> for in his own image
> God made humankind.[42]

Civil society is thus instituted alongside, and perhaps contingent upon, a command to dispense lethal justice in response to murders, though we should perhaps add a caveat in here. This verse is an instance where the particular Bible one reads can make a meaningful difference in what the plain text means. Some translations, such as the King James Bible and all versions and commentaries using that version, and Today's English Bible, render Genesis 9:6 prose. Other versions, including the New American Bible, New International Version, and New Revised Standard Version, more properly render the verse a poem. The difference between prose and poem is the difference between law and proverb. If Genesis 9:6 is a poem, it cannot be a law: as the Christian Reformed Church in North America noted in their capital punishment position statement, there are no instances in the Bible where a divine command is rendered in verse; all such laws are prose. Because Genesis 9:6 is a poem in the original, the statement continues, it must be considered a proverb, not a law.[43]

The rights and responsibilities of the state are likewise granted in another passage retentionists believe endorses capital punishment, which has its own linguistic difficulties, as we will discuss in chapter 5:

> Do you wish to have no fear of the authority? Then do what is good, and you will receive its approval; for it is God's servant for your good. But if you do what is wrong, you should be afraid, for the authority does not bear the sword in vain! It is the servant of God to execute wrath on the wrongdoer.[44]

So long as guilt is clear, the transgression determines the punishment. There is no need to justify the death penalty on any deterrence grounds. Indeed, *The Liberty Bible Commentary*, for example, explicitly rejects the relevance of deterrence to this conception of divinely ordained justice. Where advocates do argue for deterrence, though, they do so consistent with this event-based perspective: since the goal of an execution is to prevent murders, the execution itself acts as an event that causes the cessation of a fraction of the greater process at which it is aimed—evil. Evil, like vengeance, simply *is*, but it is to be confronted and overcome. No compromises can be made; the line between "good" and "evil" is fixed and bright, and the two poles themselves are fixed and absolute. To know "good," we need only look to the scripture, which tells us what "good" is: "based on the fact that we are reading his word every day. . . . That's how we get to know him, we will know that this is God's action. . . . He is not a god of confusion." As one avowedly retentionist participant opined, had people like Nat Turner and Adolf Hitler—"who believed that he was actually doing God's work"—bothered to read the Bible carefully, they would have realized that they were taking God's word out of context and that they were doing evil.[45]

If the crime is the defining event, and the execution a consequential event following therefrom, it stands to reason that "we're not putting these people to death. They're putting themselves to death. . . . They know what the outcome is going to be if they go out and commit these murders." Salvation, in this view, is likewise an event rather than a process. It is we, not God, who bar the door to redemption; we need only repent to receive grace. In response to the idea that executing an offender cuts off their chance at redemption, this viewpoint says "No! Tell them, on this day, you're going to die; if you want to repent, repent before that time." Repentance is the desired goal, but it does not change anything about the earthly situation. Any discussion over whether the person being executed is the same as the person that committed the crime, a concern that recurs frequently in abolitionist discourse, is irrelevant.[46]

Karla Faye Tucker may be the perfect example of this kind of debate. Tucker was executed in 1998 for a 1983 double murder. She and her boyfriend, Danny Garrett, broke into Jerry Dean's apartment to "whip [his] ass." Dean and Tucker knew and despised each other, and the last straw apparently came when Dean spilled oil on Tucker's carpet as he repaired his motorcycle. Dean, a manual laborer, left his tools on the floor near his bed, including the three-foot pickax that Tucker and Garrett used to kill him. The pair took turns hacking Dean with the ax before turning it on his companion, Deborah Thornton. Thornton had been having problems with her marriage and had gone home with Dean after meeting him that evening at a party; she had no connection with either Garrett or Tucker. Tucker boasted that she'd had an orgasm with each stroke of the ax, a boast that certainly did her no favors in the jury's eyes. She and Garrett both received death sentences for the murders, though Garrett died in prison of liver disease in 1993.[47]

Tucker's execution was the subject of political controversy in 1998 and again a year later, when conservative commentator Tucker Carlson revealed that he had been shocked when then-governor George W. Bush mocked Tucker's please for mercy in an interview discussing the execution controversy. Much of the controversy in early 1998 centered on the legitimacy of Tucker's conversion experience and what that meant for her as an individual. Deborah Thornton's husband, Richard, and their daughter, Katy, rejected Tucker's sincerity and said that she was trying to manipulate the situation in her favor. Reading the conversion's meaning backward, they stated that no one who had been born again would have been capable of such a crime in the first place, an argument that seems to come close to rejecting the idea of conversion altogether. Ron Carlson, Thornton's brother, said that he accepted his sister's killer's conversion as genuine and had forgiven her, not because of her conversion but because, in language reminiscent of the Nickel Mines families, Jesus said he should, so he did.[48]

For her part, Tucker said that the old Karla, the Karla who had committed those murders, was gone; "God," she said, "reached down inside of [her] and just literally uprooted all that stuff and took it out." Jerry Falwell and Pat Robertson, two conservative stalwarts who would never be described as "soft on crime," were among the most prominent of those arguing that her conversion was real and should have meaningful consequences in the here and now. Speaking on Fox News Channel's *Hannity and Colmes*, Falwell acknowledged that he had no way to know for sure that her conversion was real, but that he had looked into her eyes and judged her "truly repentant, truly rehabilitated," and capable of offering "something positive." The majority of cases, he said, demanded consequences even after God forgave the offender, but this woman was special and deserved mercy. Robertson concurred, saying that this woman was not the same person who had committed those murders and that there was nothing to gain from her death; her execution, he said, was not justice — it was vengeance. "If I were the governor," Robertson said, "I would say she has paid a price and God forgives her and so do I."[49]

We can see the difference between event- and process-based viewpoints in the way Tucker's conversion is understood. Because the event-based perspective is backward-looking, the newly redeemed believer remains defined in terms of their previous actions, a fact of which, were their conversion sincere, they would be cognizant. This backward-looking perspective thus is not only morally reaffirming, but also serves as a shibboleth, a metric by which the faith of the death row convert can be gauged. Anyone who converts in prison and seeks to have their death sentence set aside, even to have it commuted to life without parole, is thus viewed with skepticism, as a snake-oil salesman, rather than as a true believer, who would know that consequences are not lifted and that blood must be redeemed. Thus for Falwell, "99 percent of the time . . . there's a debt to pay to society, even after you are forgiven by the Lord." Thus for the author of a letter to the editor of the *Houston Chronicle*, insisting that a born-again experience should factor at all in clemency decisions reveals that person to be "a calculating, deceptive phony."[50]

Texas capital defense attorney David Dow tells a similar story about a chaplain who ministered to his clients on Texas's death row. The chaplain "told them if they repented, Jesus would forgive them, but if they fought, they would burn in hell. In his universe, pursuing legal appeals was a form of fighting." Because repentance involves taking account of one's sins and accepting responsibility for them as a sinner, and because this viewpoint views legal action against a duly imposed sentence as a means of shirking responsibility, pursuing legal appeals indicates a lack of repentance. Dow admits, though, that there is clearly something attractive about this argument — the chaplain had succeeded in talking several of his clients into dropping their appeals and becoming "volunteers." Still, Dow says, the chaplain had reached these men in a way that no one else ever had, and in a way that "could have saved lives, if someone had cared enough to find it sooner."[51]

The process-based viewpoint opposes the event-based viewpoint on all of these points and may be characterized as a "responsibilist" position, following Victor Anderson. This perspective should be understood from the three points at which it most strongly attacks the event-based perspective: deterrence, innocence, and redemption and the question of God's will. From this perspective, we should determine God's will based on what we see of God's own actions. This is why these study guides repeatedly cite passages such as Ezekiel 33; Matthew 5, the Sermon on the Mount; and Luke 6, the Sermon on the Plain, passages that emphasize forgiveness and returning to God, rather than retribution, however just. Redemption is the overriding goal, but whereas the event-based approach sees redemption in terms of an action—an event that can be time-limited—the process-based approach sees redemption as a process that cannot, and should not, have a limit artificially imposed on it.[52]

The distinction between the event- and process-based views of redemption is best captured in an exchange between two participants at a session at an LCMS church. After Jesse proposed his idea of presenting the execution date as a sort of "redeem-by" date, Natalie was unsure: "You could say, you have one week to repent. Well, maybe you're not ready, maybe it will take you longer than one week. Is it our right to say, well, you only have one week . . . so repent now? . . . Maybe it takes them a month, for example." Several participants brought this back to Moses and wondered how many times we have missed calls to repent, how many burning bushes we've walked past, "maybe every day"; if we have, what must we assume of the offenders? This view holds that punishment is to be redemptive in a way that Jesse's closed-ended idea does not permit. The biblical reference that arose in discussion here was that of Saul of Tarsus, struck blind on the road to Damascus; when he regained his sight, he repented of his sins and eventually became the greatest of the apostles.[53]

Further, this viewpoint calls for an explicit distinction to be made between the instinctual—the "God-given"—reaction and the just reaction, the reaction that "transcend[s] the instinctual." Trying to move from "a God-given response [to] a Christian response" means attempting to behave in accordance with the "fitting response to God's acts of grace, forgiveness, salvation, and mercy toward us." Carol referenced the 1996 film *Eye for an Eye*, in which a mother whose daughter is raped and murdered trains to kill her daughter's killer after he is freed on a legal technicality. Describing what she believed her reaction to the murder of one of her children would be, Carol said:

> I would like to see Jesus in someone else who helps me to not do that. . . . I look at Pastor Frazier, and all of those people he worked with on death row and how he helped them to find who they were. Too bad he couldn't have been there in their fit of rage. I think that's what I mean when I say we have Jesus. We have Christian

friends, we have values that Christ taught us. I would hope that there would be someone there who would stop me so I wouldn't do that act of violence.[54]

Thinking of redemption in this way brings us back to viewing forgiveness as a process. Abundant literature testifies to how important it is for victims to find a way to forgive their transgressors, including "survivor stories" written by people who have lost loved ones to murder. Bible study participants tended to understand this, but also tended to push the question of forgiveness back to themselves and their own continuing faith development. Because forgiveness is viewed as a process, and because Christians are commanded to forgive as they are forgiven, it is a continuous process, rather than an episodic action. This idea arose in discussions via the Nickel Mines killings and the admiration—and bewilderment—that participants had for the parents who were able to forgive, the recognition that this act was the product of a process of acting and living forgiveness, a process that would continue and that did not culminate with one single remarkable act of forgiveness. This underlies Rocky's pronouncement that he himself is "still mad at Cain," who, he pointed out, had not *yet* repented. This argument, that not only vengeance is God's but so too are life and the right to "[throw] the switch," is broadly persuasive to many who would otherwise support capital punishment. In three separate sessions, participants admitted that this argument was the one that pushed them into the abolitionist camp, while several other participants, though affirming their support for capital punishment, also admitted that this idea caused them more doubt and equivocation than any other abolitionist argument.[55]

This is a question of authority—who has it and who acts despite lacking it—and is another expression of the difference between detached and derivative rights. If we do not have the authority to take life in response to crime, then one of the abolitionists' stock queries—why do we kill to show that killing is wrong?—takes on a new meaning. If both vengeance and life belong to God, as this viewpoint holds, then usurping God's authority not only violates the principle of acting in concert with the progressively greater limits imposed on retributive violence, but also acts in defiance of the Christian idea of conversion. Executing unrepentant offenders before they can convert is seen as rejecting the possibility of conversion, which, one participant noted, "I as a Christian have to take seriously." Once the subject of conversions is broached, the discussions turn to whether or not conversion only affects the hereafter, as Beatrice suggested, or whether it affects the here and now, as one study guide suggested, drawing on Ezekiel 18: "*even the criminal convicted of a capital crime will be freed from execution, if he repents.*"[56]

This is not to suggest that those holding this point of view advocate turning offenders out onto the street once they have converted—in fact, they almost universally reject that idea—but to point out the difference between forward- and backward-looking views of conversion. The backward-looking view resolves the dilemma posed by conversion by arguing that it changes nothing, that it is an event that now defines a person, even a new person, but does not absolve that person of their past transgressions. This view says, "We may rejoice that Karla Faye Tucker has made her peace with God, but this does not mean that she is exempt from Caesar's laws." The forward-looking view sees the issue of conversion as a further obstacle to execution, wondering whether we can justly execute someone if they are now a fundamentally different person than they were when they committed the crime. One guide quotes Augustine to make this point: "'Man' and 'sinner' are two different things. God made man; man made himself sinner. So, destroy what man made but save what God made. . . . Do not take away his life; leave him the possibility of repentance. Do not kill him so that he can correct himself."[57]

Demystifying the Ritual

A second issue that troubled many of the participants is the question of innocence, a question that is newer, having largely developed with the advent of DNA-matching technologies. Where before defendants and prisoners could be found not guilty, now, in cases where biological evidence is left and properly preserved, the defendant or prisoner can be found innocent. This is a meaningful distinction. Previously, in cases where the defendant could not be proven to have committed the crime, this lack of proof did not remove the possibility that they had committed the offense. The rise of DNA-matching technologies changed this, removing the need to disprove a negative from the equation and making it possible to categorically declare an individual innocent of a crime.[58]

This change, along with well-publicized instances of wrongful convictions in capital cases, has led to innocence becoming definitive within the capital punishment debate now in ways it could not have before. If we know that innocents have been and continue to be convicted, the discussion in the sessions went, we cannot continue to take the chance that we will make a mistake and fail to rectify it in time. We don't want to see too many cases of wrongful imprisonment, but, as one participant pointed out, this is a question where evidence of innocence in capital cases is somewhat irrelevant, since we would want all convictions to be based on a correct determination of actual guilt. Wrongful imprisonments, however, can be rectified and compensation made when they are discovered. Some parishioners who struggled with their church's teachings on capital punishment before the advent of actual innocence found themselves changing their views when it became clear that it was not only possible, but perhaps probable—or even certain—that innocents have been executed. The recent executions of Cameron Todd Willingham by Texas and Troy Anthony Davis by Georgia, both of whom presented widely believed claims of actual innocence, have only furthered these discussions.[59]

Questions of innocence do not remain abstract for long, however; they quickly draw toward the concrete, toward the legal process. Referring to Northwestern University's School of Journalism's Medill Innocence Project, whose efforts led to the exoneration of five men then on Illinois's death row, one mother wondered how it is that university students are able to prove the innocence of someone who has been duly convicted and sentenced. How is it, one participant wondered, that the system—the investigators, prosecutors, trial judge, jury, and appellate judges—managed to get it wrong with all of the resources available to them, but journalism students could ferret out the correct story? Participants were concerned with questions about the inequality and arbitrariness that they see built into the capital punishment system, from racial and economic to geographic and counsel-related inequalities in application. They were concerned that prosecutors, whether appointed or elected, are, as James, a federal judge, phrased it, "political animals." They were concerned about the lack of resources, including time, available to public defenders. Participants and study guides alike focused on the problem of accomplice and "snitch" testimony, and participants were concerned with the lack of experience and knowledge that the jury has in weighing the evidence before them. As Caroline, a retired schoolteacher and former juror in a non-capital case recalled from her experience, "The jurors don't know a whole lot, and we a couple of times came back with questions, and the judge just said, 'Go back and read your instructions.'" In the end, participants agreed that the system is human, and thus fallible and somewhere between liable and prone to making mistakes. All of this, however, leaves the question unresolved: can we truly achieve a sufficient level of moral certainty as to know that the defendant in question is not only truly guilty, but truly noteworthy among a class of similar offenders and thus particularly deserving of death?[60]

Questions over wrongful convictions and procedural problems endemic to the system accompanied discussions about the nature and reality of deterrence. Deterrence makes four basic assumptions: that all behavior is rationally undertaken following a cost-benefit analysis; that people expect to suffer negative consequences for their actions; that potential consequences are understood and taken into account prior to and at the time of the action; and that potential offenders are able to identify with others being punished. Proponents and opponents alike questioned or disregarded deterrence based on any of these assumptions. Some, including those with experience dealing with death row inmates, flatly dismissed the first criterion. Others cited external evidence, such as a nationwide survey of police chiefs, which ranked expanding the death penalty last on a list of crime-control measures, or by pointing out that abolitionist states have lower murder rates than retentionist states. Even strong proponents of the death penalty rejected deterrence for various reasons: "These criminals out there know that the chances of getting the death penalty even if they're caught are very, very slim, so how could it be a deterrent? [Deterrence] ... doesn't exist." Whether it is simple common sense that the death penalty must deter at least some potential killers or a rejection of the idea, deterrence invites us to see the death penalty for what it really is: a ritual sacrifice.[61]

Consider the four broad categories corresponding to positions on deterrence and on the morality of the death penalty itself. A pro–death penalty, pro-deterrence perspective endorses a utilitarian conception of retributive justice, which holds that an execution is a communicative act that positively prevents other murders from taking place. From this perspective, the execution balances the moral books and is a substitutionary positive good. A pro–death penalty position that disregards deterrence, or considers it ancillary or irrelevant, likewise regards the execution as the sacrifice necessary to restore moral equilibrium. We see the former position in Andrew's assertion that murderers execute themselves by committing their crime in the first place, while the latter is analogous to Beatrice's assertions that if we are not going to defeat evil, we may as well disband the police. Both incline toward the event, the ritual, at the expense of process; articulating a belief that God has given us the power to police ourselves even to the point of taking life, or has given us free will in order to know when to make exceptions to the "Thou shalt not kill" commandment, reinforces the religious nature of the ritual. From each of these viewpoints, the execution ritual is a *derivative* religious practice, an event "where social actors expand their notions of religious significance and make their nonreligious practices conform to religious rules by committing acts which are believed to please the powers ... or by avoiding acts that are believed to anger the powers." If it is God's will that offenders be punished in this manner—if we are to understand texts such as Genesis 9 as "giving [us] all the authority to ... let me use the word *police* here—he's saying, 'Police yourselves,'" the derivative character of the execution is clear.[62]

The two positions that reject the death penalty, meanwhile, reject the ritual in favor of the process. The position that opposes capital punishment but acknowledges deterrence rejects the practice because of its specific result, despite its general result. That is, if the penalty is morally or authoritatively prohibited, then the ritual, though perhaps efficacious, must be dispensed with in favor of less-than-lethal options. The fourth position, which opposes capital punishment and rejects deterrence, rejects both the event and its ritual justification. These positions, based on a recognition of the process inherent in God's will, predicated on notions of repentance, redemption, and forgiveness, are essentially *discursive* practices, "linguistic exchanges among social actors about the nature of superhuman powers [and] appropriate ways of interacting with them."[63]

Procedural concerns—due process concerns—are more important to this point of view than to the event-based perspective. The event-based viewpoint argues that the relevant question is whether or not we are morally certain of *this* defendant's guilt, and though it acknowledges that there are serious procedural problems within the system, anything short of the execution of an innocent is cause for reform, not rejection. The process-based viewpoint sees the moral and authoritative issues compounded by failures of due process and inequities in application—failures of the process itself—which leads to a recognition of the inability of the ritual to discharge its function properly. Rather than balancing the moral books, in this view, the ritual is akin to a religious sacrifice. This sacrifice is designed not to correct a moral imbalance or rectify the effects of violent crime, but to discharge our general aggressions onto specific, and perhaps undeserving, victims. In other words, the ritual uses a scapegoat to bear the anger and violent, retributive emotions of society and to achieve a different sort of deterrence: preventing us from becoming vigilantes.[64]

The Vigilante and the Scapegoat

One Sunday in late September I participated in a Bible study at an Episcopal church in western Virginia. I'd arranged everything with the minister and a lay leader, and we shook hands over coffee after the early morning service. We had spoken on the phone but had never met, and spent a few minutes figuring out how few degrees of separation we had, passing along greetings to and from various mutual friends and acquaintances and commenting on the beautiful morning, which at that time of year means sunny and sticky. The minister introduced me to some of his congregants and lay leaders and talked about being an abolitionist minister in an abolitionist denomination with a retentionist congregation drawn from a retentionist area. When he introduced the session, he made a point of repeating this and thanked me for giving them the opportunity to convene this discussion and providing them with an opportunity to talk about their experiences in light of their faith tradition. The subtext wasn't hard to miss—this graceful gesture was genuine, but it was also a conferral of legitimacy. By thanking me, the minister sanctioned the event and my presence, an imprimatur that may have made it easier for any discussants suspicious either of the undertaking or my motives to relax and be more candid in the discussion.[65]

Trust is a vital commodity in this kind of research. It is also vital to the public discourse on the death penalty — do we trust the state to get it right enough to satisfy us that we can be morally certain of the propriety of executions in general and possess moral certainty regarding specific executions? Where trust is important, mistrust is equally so. One perspective, puzzlingly, seldom arises in these discussions. Despite Americans' deep ambivalence about the proper range and limits of governmental authority, objections to the death penalty based solely on mistrust of government are relatively rare. This particular Sunday, Jerry, an accountant, made that objection: "I have a personal opinion that says that I don't want to give the right to a group of people . . . an abstract group, which is called the government, to choose who lives and who dies. I have a major problem with that." Why doesn't this argument arise more in these discussions?[66]

The answer, Franklin Zimring argues, lies in the vigilante tradition. This tradition of extralegal "justice" has been a running theme throughout American history, and not only, as Zimring argues, could it help account for the southernization of the death penalty, but, when expanded to encompass all extralegal "mob justice," it is also a defining feature of the death penalty as scapegoating ritual. Based on this description, the event-based perspective identifies with the vigilante tradition and correlates it with the need for and efficacy of capital punishment, while the process-based perspective rejects this tradition. In each case, acceptance or rejection mirrors the reasons each discourse accepts or rejects the death penalty as a ritual. The vigilante tradition is the ultimate celebration of event over process, of the ritual disgorging of society's violent urges against capriciously selected victims defined as guilty by a procedurally flawed legal system.[67]

Beatrice makes the provigilantist argument best, incorporating and embellishing on similar arguments made by other participants. Evil, she says, is an unquestioned reality, and one that must be combated at all costs. Christians, because they are saved and thus different from others (the "saints"), are required to pay any price to confront and destroy evil, a responsibility that is likewise incumbent on society at large; why else would we have police, she wonders, if we're not trying to defeat evil? The forward-looking process that is redemptive love is subsumed and destroyed by the backward-looking process of redemptive wrath, those acts of legitimated violence that redeem the community at the expense of the offender. There is a point of no return beyond which an offender cannot be temporally redeemed, according to this view, and just consequences can never be taken away, not even by spiritual redemption. These consequences are the bedrock of our freedom and prosperity — other former peer nations have fallen into second-rate status because they have lost sight of consequences, according to Beatrice — and if transgressions or crimes are left uncorrected, the result is a viral progression of sin. Cycling back, this sin, refigured as a communicable infection, can only be stopped if Christians uphold their sacred duty by any means necessary: *"whatever you can do to stop the spread of evil is appropriate*, and that's where the death penalty comes in."[68]

Two elements stand out from an otherwise fairly standard account of the saints' battle against evil. The first is the need to make evil even more evil, to render evil particularly heinous and vile. Beatrice's apologia on Moses's behalf is an example of this. Speaking of an explicitly master/slave society, Beatrice makes the reasonable assumption that Moses witnessed the Egyptian masters administering to the Hebrew slaves' "beatings every day all the time." Perhaps this instance was different, though: "Maybe that Egyptian was just killing this person just out of sheer pleasure." This comment—which considers the wanton, sadistic abuse of slaves a more justifiable provocation to murder than the more "banal" evil of slavery—brings to light the second element, the blurring between law as necessary and law as right, and between law as necessary and law as sufficient. It also strongly conveys an idea of an exceptional state of affairs. The idea of law as right leads Jesse and Andrew to agree that, according to law, Moses should have been put to death, while Beatrice and others return to the refrain of necessary consequences following transgression, to law as right and necessary. Their process-minded counterparts agree with both of these and likewise confront the tension between law as right and law as necessary, though they tend to focus on instances where law existed but was wrong. On this point they cite Paul and the various mobs described at the crucifixion and the martyrdom of Stephen; Jim Crow; and *Roe v. Wade*, and they have a different conception of the necessary results of law as necessary.[69]

The tension between law as necessary and law as sufficient is most visible in the fight over the idea of appeals and due process. Understandably, event-based perspectives tend to reject the idea of appeals outright, or express a belief that they should be bundled into a single court action capable of deciding all claims. The defendant has already been judged and found guilty by a jury of his peers, and this is the most important issue in the process. The simple fact of legal guilt precludes any meaningful consideration of due process concerns; if the offender is legally guilty, then any mistakes, biases, injustices, or other problems in the execution of the law are simply irrelevant. The decision of the jury—of the offender's peers, called and impaneled as a representative cross-section of the community, and so the bearer of community values—has been spoken, and that word is to be final. The jury's decision compels the universal assent that follows from moral certainty. The event-based viewpoint thus subsumes a portion of our system of due process to the service of a form of vigilantism. The community cannot be wrong, and its wishes must be carried out, even to the exclusion of legal processes.[70]

Intriguingly, in these sessions, the ire of those bewildered by and unaware of the value of the appeals process was directed not at the lawyers, the presumptive target, but at the process itself. Lawyers are generally recognized as doing their job and acting in the best interests of their clients. At their best, death penalty proponents acknowledged, these trial lawyers "are good for society . . . and they come up with something to make you say, 'Hey, wait a minute' . . . But." The "but" is the view that lawyers are not just trying to do everything possible on behalf of their client, but are trying to dismantle the system. The need to carry out the community's wishes in defiance of the continued legal process therefore extends the vigilantist idea of event-based justice into—and at the expense of—the supremacy of process inherent in the criminal justice system. Attorneys engaging in "frivolous" appeals and delay tactics thus threaten the efficacy of what we might call "double deterrence." Under this idea of double deterrence, society reaps the benefit of whatever general or marginal deterrence accompanies executions. At the same time, because society is sufficiently comfortable with the protective functions of the legal and criminal justice system's ability to deal with horrific crimes, the vigilantist impulse is restrained, and vigilantism is deterred. Otherwise, as Beatrice said, "what's going to happen is you're eventually going to cause vigilantism, because the government that's supposed to protect us is not doing its job."[71]

The vigilante brings us back to the division between the instinctual and the just and the resolution of that problem. A vigilantist conception of the criminal justice system that demands immediate action following an incomplete legal process is attractive to those who feel threatened by violent crime and, critically, who view the problem of crime and punishment as essentially stable. This backward-looking approach sees things as they purportedly are, not as they could become, and acts accordingly. The vigilante is attractive because it is an active expression of this backward focus, although there remains some ambiguity about the idea of vigilantism. The vigilante idea works the best when it is an expression of community values, of commonsense right, and when the vigilante is someone or something else. As Marcie put it, "I can see myself. . . . I think, 'Gee, I wish I could shoot a gun or do things like that so I could go after him.' . . . I can see a justification, but I don't want to go to hell, I don't want to suffer for it." As Jesse phrased it in an inadvertently ironic retort to an offhand remark that we do not want vigilantism, "Can we take a vote on that?" The event-based perspective also sees evil as an infective force that needs to be dealt with at whatever cost. As Diana, director of Christian education for her church's school, declared, "It's not about salvation. . . . It's checks and balances"—the check of violence to balance violence and communicable evil. It is this perspective that is at work when the answer to the perennial question "What did Jesus write when he bent to write in the sand?" is that "He was writing out the law," the Mosaic law demanding that adulterers be put to death. For some participants, this tells us that the mob was brought to see themselves as fellow sinners in need of forgiveness, thus sapping their righteous indignation. For others, this idea disarms the mob not because they see themselves as sinners in need of forgiveness, but because they see themselves as sinners subject to the same punishment: "[When] they all went away, my first thought was, 'Gee, they've all had relations with her.'"[72]

The process-based approach rejects vigilantism. This view accepts the proverbial release of one hundred guilty to save one innocent and questions the basic fairness of a process that results in laws that are demonstrably applied according to wealth, race, class, and other factors. This perspective sees problems less at the guilt phase of the capital trial and more at the sentencing phase. The process-based perspective sees all humans as sinners liable to divine judgment. While it agrees with the need to punish violent criminals, it declines to arrogate to humanity the power to dispense with life as an act of criminal justice. It is concerned with the integrity of the process in two ways. It is concerned that the various disparities in the system—racial, economic, geographic, and so on—have reduced its integrity to the point where its judgments must be considered suspect and analyzed accordingly. It is also concerned that the process remain integral and whole—that the systemic failures and disparities not be hidden by removing vital protections for defendants and convicted offenders appealing their sentences; we will see this in detail in chapter 6.

This perspective contests the "good guys/saints versus bad guys/sinners" narrative. It acknowledges that Cain could be anyone, and that while we may like to think we would have stood up to the mobs at the stoning of Stephen and the crucifixion, we would have been there throwing the stones and chanting for his death. This perspective acknowledges that we do not execute people, we execute fears—the fears to which we are vulnerable: "We cannot banish dangers, but we can banish fears." Following a session at a Catholic church in the Richmond area, a particularly outspoken individual who proclaimed herself deeply committed to the sacredness of all life quietly told me that despite her sincere, faith-formed opposition to capital punishment, she nevertheless felt "genuinely relieved" and "safer" following the executions of Linwood and James Briley, who masterminded the largest death row escape in American history, and Timothy Spencer, the "Southside Strangler." Her fears were banished via the execution, and given her beliefs she had to struggle with the relief that the executions brought her.[73]

The process-based perspective recognizes our vulnerability to peer pressure and to emotion while highlighting our capacity to make poor decisions, even fatally poor decisions. As Pastor Frazier said,

> This is valuable stuff . . . [thinking about] our own complicity, grace, violence, the animal instincts that reside in us, human sin, [and] the capacity for grace and forgiveness and redemption. It's our story. . . . That's the thing that hit me again and again — there but for the grace of God go I. . . . I mean, given the right circumstances, I will tell you, I could be there. I know, given the right set of circumstances, I would be on row. And I happen to believe that it's a human — it's the human condition.

This is the perspective that sees hope in the redemption of the thief on the cross and in the other biblical narratives of murder and redemption, in the tales of Cain, Moses, David, and Paul, that wonders how we know when to forgive. It is also the perspective that forces us to face the fact that our instinctive reaction may not correspond with what we believe is the just. This in turn compels us to see more of the offender in us than we may be comfortable with — it compels us, in other words, to embrace them, to see them as *like us*.[74]

Despite the differences between the two approaches, they have two prominent similarities. Both reconcile the tension between following divine versus human law in favor of the divine, though to different ends. Either God mandates retribution or he mandates ceasing retribution to allow for reform; in either case, the dilemma is not understanding which law is paramount, but living up to it despite ourselves. In both cases, our covenantal obligations are clear. Second, both sides acknowledge and utilize the scapegoat. The event-based perspective uses the scapegoat to discharge societal violence, while the process-based perspective uses the scapegoat to prevent that discharge. More properly, both sides reconceive the scapegoat as the *exile* and make this a central trope in their discourses.

4

The Lord said to Cain, "Why are you angry, and why has your countenance fallen? If you do well, will you not be accepted? And if you do not do well, sin is lurking at the door; its desire is for you, but you must master it."

(GENESIS 4:6–7

Deeply ingrained in our legal tradition is the idea that the more purposeful is the criminal conduct, the more serious is the offense, and therefore, the more severely it ought to be punished.

(*Tison v. Arizona*, 1987

The Exile
Instantiated and Revealed

"Are you familiar with the work of René Girard?"

Rev. Joseph Vought asked me that question over a beer while we were talking about his ministry, particularly his death row ministry, which I will talk about more in chapter 7. We had spent the previous hour discussing the walks he's made with men to the death chamber, the way his prison ministry has impacted his church ministry, and the various pro/con arguments on the death penalty going on all around us. We had talked about the scapegoating and the distance that is a part of the death row process, about perceptions of the execution versus the reality of what and how much of us goes into that chamber with the men. Our authority? Our power? Our ideals? Our understandings of ourselves—individual, collective, societal, moral, religious? Are these men our evil counterparts, wholly unlike us? Or are they more like us, and we like they, than we would be comfortable admitting? Discussing executions in theological language, we talked about whether these men are executed for their sins only, or whether they bear some of our sins with them as well.

"Girard has been helpful, really helpful, in terms of the mimetic theory and scapegoating.... I was blown away.... A friend of mine, a fellow pastor, said, 'You've got to read [it] if you're doing death penalty work.'"[1]

The Bible study participants I discussed in the previous chapter frequently expressed a deep ambivalence about how closely they could identify with the biblical killers we discussed, an ambivalence that ran through the way they related these narratives to their own lives and experiences. The Girardian scapegoat is, quietly, a common component of these discussions, as we will see later in this chapter. For now, we can set the table by looking at some common elements of the scapegoat in responses to the Karla Faye Tucker execution. Some commentators claimed that Tucker was executed for our crimes as well as hers, as a way to hide the damage that we as a society have done to people like her. Others contended that she was the "worst of the worst" and killed herself by her own actions. Both assessments showcase the idea of the scapegoat as it occurs in the American death penalty debate. The scapegoat is clear in assertions that she died for our crimes as well as hers. Claims that she was the "worst of the worst" beg the question of whether she remained so or whether she had fundamentally changed. More directly, the "worst of the worst" language begs a second question: why was this defendant selected to bear our wrath when so many others are spared?[2]

I make three connected arguments in this chapter. First, the Girardian scapegoat is helpful in understanding how the death penalty works in contemporary America. But it doesn't get us all the way there—there is something missing from the scapegoat that is central to the American death penalty: guilt. Guilt—legal guilt—is the keystone of the American death penalty, as both the retentionist and abolitionist discourses are acutely aware. This is my second claim: taking the four elements of Girard's scapegoat and adding a fifth—legal guilt—we arrive at the exile, the figure at the center of both broad discourses and the vehicle by which they advance their arguments and articulate their understandings. Third, to apply an inexact metaphor, the retentionist and abolitionist exiles are electrons to each other's protons—they are identified and rhetorically used in opposite ways, but are generally bound together as part of a larger whole. I'll begin by using some examples to show how Girard's conceptions of how mimesis and scapegoating operate before turning to a detailed analysis of the scapegoat and its role in death penalty activism on both sides. This analysis will help us move from the scapegoat to the exile. Once we have identified the exile, we can see how this figure relates to the "normal individual" and what this perceived relationship implies about how we understand ourselves and our roles and capacities in responding to violent crime.

Mimetic Rivalry in Law

Girard's scapegoat theory advances two principal claims. The first is that mimetic rivalries generate violence that threatens to overwhelm society unless it is discharged. During these periods of sacrificial crisis, the scapegoat is the chosen recipient of this violence, thus relieving the tension and hopefully, from the perspective of the participants, restoring order. The second is that the crimes for which the scapegoat is punished, whether or not he is actually guilty, are those that undermine and destroy the differences within society. These are crimes that break taboos, including murder, and that force undifferentiation on the society in place of differentiation. These crimes, in other words, produce a negative leveling effect: *anyone* is a potential victim. Crimes capable of provoking a sacrificial crisis are those that threaten the very basic structure of society, that remove distinctions between individuals or groups of people. This is the leveling effect — all people are potential victims, regardless of social distinctions — and this effect provides much of the scapegoat's power.

We can see this leveling in two key concepts at work in the current moment: *senseless* and *deterrence*. As Girard tells us, the sacrificial crisis is characterized by a lack of distinction between impure and purifying violence. At first blush, the term "senseless" implies precisely this distinction. Senseless violence, including murder, is by definition illegitimate, impure; it is the kind of violence that breeds rather than halts violence. If capital punishment were not so openly and, so far as law is concerned, irreparably capricious and arbitrary, then the distinction between senseless and purposeful violence would be stronger. If the distinction were stronger, then the sacrificial mechanism would remain intact and indicate that the crisis had not yet arisen. Attacks on the death penalty based on that capriciousness, though, show that the scapegoating mechanism has been exposed. Comments made by Justice Scalia in *In re. Troy Anthony Davis* show this:

> This court has *never* held that the Constitution forbids the execution of a convicted defendant who has had a full and fair trial but is later able to convince a habeas

court that he is "actually" innocent. Quite to the contrary, we have repeatedly left that question unresolved, while expressing considerable doubt that any claim based on alleged "actual innocence" is constitutionally cognizable.[3]

If innocence in fact is not constitutionally cognizable, then the system is inherently capricious, which invalidates the pure scapegoating mechanism. Once exposed, the formerly pure sacrificial violence becomes ambiguous, at a cost of no longer discharging society's pent-up violence.[4] Although we remain able to describe illegitimate violence in terms such as "senseless" and that label can retain its previous meaning, the sacrificial mechanism has been shorn of its claims to purification. This has serious implications with regard to conceptions of redemptive violence.

As I discuss below, abolitionists seize on this claim and focus it on questions of fairness, fallibility, and culpability to turn the exposure of the scapegoating mechanism into a means toward abolition. It is important to note, however, that the ambiguity surrounding the nature of the death penalty's violence is not restricted to the abolitionist discourse. Retentionists too note the injustices in the system and bemoan the lack of deterrence. A good example of this is Derrick, whose comments at a Bible study reported in the previous chapter are worth examining in greater detail:

> It'd be interesting to look at [statistics] to see how many people that are convicted get off with life versus the number of people that are convicted and are sentenced to [death]. . . . I think when you see that comparison, it's going to be so alarmingly spread apart, that you're going to have the answer as to why the death penalty is not a deterrent. . . . Look at these small numbers and compare it to the number of violent crimes. . . . These criminals out there know that the chances of getting the death penalty even if they're caught are very, very slim, so how could it be a deterrent? [Deterrence] . . . doesn't exist.[5]

If we accept the idea of deterrence, then we accept the idea of the rational, calculating murderer, and vice versa—the "cold-blooded killer" of popular imagination *must* be capable of being deterred.[6] At the same time, however, the retentionist discourse bemoans the way insufficiently vigorous use of capital punishment undercuts reasonable general deterrence. However legitimate these state killings are, they are also recognized as somehow senseless. Executions cannot provide sufficient deterrence to break or demonstrably lessen the violence that precipitated the crisis in the first place. They cannot, in other words, be shown to contribute to general deterrence and thus, however morally or legally legitimate they may be, are not wholly pure; they are to some degree senseless.

We can see mimetic rivalry at work in legal codes, both secular and religious.

The Ten Commandments and Virginia's statute defining capital punishment can both be read to center on two problems: mimetic rivalry and questions of differentiation and undifferentiation. As Girard points out, the sixth through ninth commandments — thou shalt not murder, commit adultery, steal, or bear false witness — all prohibit crimes reflecting mimetic desire, while the tenth prohibits that desire itself: "You shall not covet your neighbor's house; you shall not covet your neighbor's wife, . . . or anything that belongs to your neighbor." These restrictions on mimetic desire and rivalry are paralleled in the Virginia statute in the clauses that permit capital charges to be brought in instances of murders committed during armed robberies; murders connected to the trafficking of Schedule I or II controlled substances; murders committed as part of an ongoing criminal enterprise; murder for hire; or abduction for pecuniary gain.[7]

We can see mimetic rivalry in the first five commandments, too, which we can subsume under the heading of "proper partnership." The injunction to have no other gods defines the parties, while the other commandments impose limits on human behavior — specifically, limits on godly mimesis. The prohibition against taking God's name in vain is a prohibition against trying to invoke the power in that name to our own ends; that power inheres in God and is not for our use. The injunction to keep the Sabbath holy is likewise a limit on our capacity to act, and a further calling toward an acceptable, limited mimesis. To use language that we will revisit in chapter 7, these commandments define some of the parameters of the role each partner is to play.

We should also note that these commandments declare certain social differentiations. These differentiations create a basis for order, and crimes that undermine that order by destroying these differentiations are, according to Girard, the most serious and the most likely to provoke a sacrificial crisis. We can see this same concern over proper differentiations reflected in Virginia's capital statute. The murder of a child under age fourteen by someone over age twenty-one and the murder of a woman calculated to end the pregnancy without a live birth both seek to protect a class of individuals — children — who are specifically protected by a wide variety of civil and criminal laws. Murder committed during rape or other sexual assault or during an abduction planned to culminate in any sexual assault represents the extreme of differentiation, turning an individual into an "it," an object. Other capital-eligible offenses, including murder for hire or murder committed in the furtherance of drug or criminal enterprises, confront the idea of evil as a contagion that will spread if left unchecked; rampant, indiscriminate evil clearly presents problems if we are to maintain proper differentiations among elements of society.[8]

The remaining crimes eligible for a death sentence relate to two other elements of the problem of differentiation. Our capacity to respond to violence is undermined when our responses are attacked, as by the murder of law enforcement personnel in the line of duty, of judges, of witnesses that have been subpoenaed in a criminal proceeding, or in cases of murders committed by inmates in a state correctional institution. This set is a subset of the last category, indiscriminate victimization. Undermining our capacity to respond to violence necessarily expands the scope of potential victims. Crimes such as multiple murders in the same transaction, multiple murders committed within a three-year period, or acts of terrorism or attempted terrorism resulting in the loss of life victimize indiscriminately, whether deliberately, as in the case of terrorism, or by implication, as in the two instances involving multiple homicides.[9]

We can see these processes at work in other contexts as well, such as the explanations for the September 11 attacks offered by the American media and political elites. Both basic explanations — "they hate us for our freedoms" and "they hate us because we have done and continue to do harm to them" — imply mimetic rivalry and impose it on the terrorists as their basic motive. We can see this without evaluating the respective merits or demerits of either statement. To say that "they hate us for our freedoms" bases itself on the purported mimetic desire of the terrorists and/or of those on whose behalf the terrorists claim to be acting. Our freedoms, this explanation goes, are light against the terrorists' darkness, progress against their backwardness. Our way of life poses a threat to their ideals because those for whom the terrorists speak yearn more for our lifestyle than for theirs. This explanation thus stands or falls on the explicit understanding that mimetic desire is at work and that acts of terror are undertaken to lessen or destroy that desire. This is so when the "war on terror" is depicted as the civilized world allied with those who wish to join that world but are held back by local tyrants versus those tyrants and their protégés, their ideological peers, or their proxies. It is also so when we simply acknowledge, as this explanation demands, that terrorism can make a victim of anyone at any time or place, without warning. We all are potential victims, and we all must stand or fall together; from there, it's a short step to former president George W. Bush's appropriative distortion of Matthew 12:30: You're either with us (lack of differentiation) or with the terrorists (lack of differentiation).[10]

The alternative explanation — they hate us because we do harm to them and theirs — likewise is predicated on mimetic desire. In this instance, the desire is that of a victim against an aggressor. Whereas the aggressor enjoys peace, stability, and wealth, the victim perceives these as coming at their expense, and thus tries to imitate the desire of the aggressor for these things, coming to desire them for themselves. The victim sees the desire — that which the aggressor desires — and utilizes any means necessary to achieve it, including lethal violence. In each case, the recognition of mimetic desire leads to the identification of the self and the reciprocal other.

If this were not clear in the boilerplate response summations above, it becomes clear when remedial measures are proposed. Discussions focused on any sort of policy change acknowledge both mimetic desire and the standing of the other as the reciprocal other. Returning to the death penalty Bible studies to make this point more fully, the reciprocal other is acknowledged in the opposed assertions that we are empowered to combat evil via any means necessary and that we need to beware of our own response, lest we become the very thing that we seek to combat. The reciprocal other lies at, and between, Beatrice's assertion that anything that hinders the spread of evil is permitted and James's reminder that we need to be on guard against our own reactions, so that we do not become "so driven to prevent another 9/11 that we compromise our fundamental values and become as bad as the enemy."[11]

The problem of differentiation and undifferentiation recurs here, which we can see in the multiple and reciprocal processes at work in retentionist and abolitionist discourse. In one of the sessions, Beatrice, recalling a prison break some years earlier, recounted her reaction to the news:

> Well, you know, what's going to happen is, and I know we've done this, when we were in Washington state, three people broke out of prison. We were in Washington state, they were in Texas, and I said, "Hey, if they all use the bathroom a couple of times, they can make it up to Washington state." So we bought a gun.[12]

There are several problems of differentiation and undifferentiation in this statement, all of which operate on multiple levels and connect with the broader discourse. To take the most obvious and most important, there is no differentiation between different types of offenders, nor is there any consideration with regard to differentiation among victims. We may suspect, as Beatrice did, that these were violent offenders. There is no apparent recognition of the possibility that the escapees may have been white-collar criminals, sentenced perhaps for embezzlement or for insurance fraud. The escapees, by virtue of being (presumably) incarcerated violent felons as well as escapees, undifferentiate the pool of potential future victims. This is so because of the logic of "senselessness" and because of the effects of crimes that strike at the heart of our ability to protect ourselves, as discussed above. Prison escape is certainly a crime that undermines our confidence in the state's ability to protect its citizens, while the logic of senselessness means that anyone could become a victim at any time — even from fifteen hundred miles away. Because all are potential victims of senseless crime, because violent crime imposes undifferentiation on society, the sensible reaction to such undifferentiation is to prepare for preemptive, legitimate violence: to purchase a gun and pre-

(*The Exile* (87

pare to become a vigilante, because "the government isn't doing its job." This phenomenon also leads committed abolitionists into tension between their ideals and their reactions to executions, which can be occasions for relief, as some abolitionist Bible study participants admitted. They oppose and are saddened by the process, but they would feel dishonest not admitting that when some killers are put to death, they feel personally relieved, personally safer. Their fears have been put to death via the execution of the offender.[13]

This same pairing also features prominently in discussion of the "natural" reaction, either alone or contrasted with the "just" reaction. Speaking about the instinctive, natural, or God-given reaction aptly describes our reaction to violent crime: we immediately correlate all crimes and criminals and all victims into distinct groups, imposing an undifferentiation on each set and defining them relative to each other. The objection to what retentionists refer to as the "bad childhood" defense operates in the same way. This objection sees both commonality and difference between innocent victims—and innocent jurors—and those convicted of murder. This defense is objectionable because "there's a lot of people who have [risen] above that situation":[14]

> Especially in today's society, no one grew up in a perfect home, no one had a great upbringing, everyone's seen things and done things that they wish they had never seen or done or whatever. How long do you use that as your excuse and say, "That's what I know," instead of saying, "It's my responsibility to change that, and if I know that that's what I know, then I guess I need to change that for the better"?[15]

The two statements quoted above, both of which came from conflicted supporters of capital punishment, underscore the first way of differentiating between "us" and "them." The sentiment appears also in discussions with jurors. Speaking about the defendant in a California case resulting in a death sentence, one of the jurors said, "The testimony . . . was heartbreaking, it brought tears to my eyes. But, you know, his crime wasn't caused by that blow, he never had a job, he resorted to robbing for a livelihood."[16] *We* overcome our common bond, our imperfect upbringing; *they* do not. *We* find a way to move forward, to deal constructively with the hardship that life dishes out, and *we* refrain from making the choices that *they* make. Vitally, this differentiation, between those who make the choice to kill and those who do not, is foregrounded by an undifferentiation, a declaration that all face the same choice and all are sufficiently alike as to have similar grounds from which to compare and, when it comes to that point, to condemn.

The same dynamic is at work in unconflicted abolitionist and retentionist statements on the same issue. We cannot simply say, as Pastor Frazier acknowledged, "that people that had horrific things happen to them are bound and determined to do horrible things, commit crimes, but there is an overwhelming tendency to go there." This statement should be heard alongside his other comment—that were his circumstances a little bit different, he "would be on [death] row." Angela, director of religious education for her parish, agreed, pointing out that "not everyone that is abused chooses to [kill]. . . . I'm not disagreeing with you that society has failed these people." The sequential dynamic is the same as above—recognition followed by distinction—but the pattern is subtly different because of the conclusions that the individuals have come to on the issue itself.[17]

The committed retentionist position is the outlier in this way. It is the outlier not because of how it operates, since it shares the dynamic of recognition followed by distinction. It is distinguished by how it responds when the victim is discussed: "One of the things that is just appalling to me . . . is when a person . . . on trial gets up and says, 'Oh, poor me, I went through a tough life.' . . . You never get to hear the horror that the victim went through in being murdered." Where elsewhere Jesse was concerned that the moral lesson of the Moses narrative would be to undermine the process of differentiation—"What I'm concerned about is, does this lead to the thought that there is redemption in killers and murderers?"[18]—he here draws a different distinction between the offender and the victim. The way the idea is expressed falls into the same pattern discussed above, where both the offender and the victim become undifferentiated categories, classes of individuals, rather than specific individuals. Our ultimate reaction—the "just" response—is determined by the ways we continue these processes of differentiation and undifferentiation, and it is here, in and via these continuing processes, that we reach the limits of the scapegoat.

From the Scapegoat to the Exile Five Markers

In 1993, representatives from more than a dozen churches and church organizations signed on to a joint statement titled "From Fear to Hope: Statement of Religious Leaders in Virginia on Public Safety and the Death Penalty." The statement distills the situation facing people of faith in America engaging the death penalty into its four most important elements:

> Our religious traditions impel us to be concerned about public safety and to evaluate the death penalty from a moral perspective.
>
> We understand the fears of the general public regarding crime. We share these fears. Drug trafficking and murder are terrible scourges that cry out for effective remedies. We must encourage personal responsibility, basic moral values and a respect for human life. At the same time we must call upon society as a whole to remedy the social circumstances that contribute to hopelessness, despair, and a breakdown in respect for the value of life. . . . Despite our fears, we are called to look with

honesty, courage and moral conviction at how our Commonwealth is attempting to stem the tide of violence. We can understand how fear and frustration may tempt us to find simple solutions. We are convinced that the escalating imposition of the death penalty is a misguided attempt to improve public safety.[19]

The four necessary elements are clear here. First, there is a real crisis, in this case, a crisis that could be variously phrased as a lack of respect for human life or of proliferating violence or evil. Second, our response, at least in some cases, is to inflict death for death. Third, these real acts of violence are directed at specific victims with the intent, fourth, to resolve the crisis. This resolution can come at the societal level, in the form of general or marginal deterrence, or at the individual level, in the form of closure for the victims.[20] The retentionist and abolitionist discourses disagree over the relative validity of each of these criteria as well as what each criterion means. These disagreements form the basis for the differences in the way each discourse creates and uses the exile.

If Girard's scapegoat is defined by these four features — (1) in response to a real crisis, (2) real acts of violence are committed (3) against specific victims, (4) for the purposes of resolving the crisis[21] — we are left to address the question of guilt. It may seem self-evident that the guilt of the executed should not be in question. Indeed, this tension is the starting point for differentiating the scapegoat, which belongs more properly to problems of persecution, from the exile, which belongs more properly to problems of prosecution. Whatever one believes about the legitimacy of a particular punishment, legal guilt is the minimal necessary component of any legitimate system of punishment. Without the moral certainty that legal guilt creates and provides, the system becomes illegitimate. At the same time, a system that has such gross discrepancies when evaluated with regard to race and economic status can only claim legitimacy if those convicted are themselves actually guilty and not just legally so; moral certainty legitimates those particular cases, leaving systemic questions to the side, questions over the noncognizability of actual innocence notwithstanding.[22]

There is a practical as well as philosophical question tied in to the basic question of guilt. If our system wrongfully punishes innocents, then it must let at least an equivalent number of guilty go free and unpunished. Punishing innocents is thus doubly illegitimate: innocents are punished while the guilty are left unpunished and free to victimize again. Revelations of innocents on death row, then, can and do cut both ways, depending on how they are understood. We can view such revelations as indications that the system is at least procedurally illegitimate, even if not philosophically so. This was George Ryan's reaction in 2000 when he declared the moratorium in Illinois. We can also, however, view revelations of innocents on death row as indications that the system is intact and functioning properly. Were it otherwise, this argument goes, innocence would be discovered after the execution, not before.[23]

If it is illegitimate to execute innocents, then the sacrificial act in and of itself is insufficient to restore social order. There must be an additional component that effects this restoration, and there is, which we can see when we look at executions via the kind of deterrence that the system accepts as valid. The presence of guilt is not in itself sufficient to delegitimize the ritual. If it were, then a perfect system perfectly executed could be expected to produce perfect deterrence, which is an unsupportable hypothesis. The system has repudiated the scapegoating ritual not through any civilizing process, but through a change in intent, the redirecting of the system's efforts toward retributive justice — that is, by reorienting itself to revenge. This reorientation is a consequence of an incomplete dismantling of the scapegoating mechanism. While the system repudiates the mechanism insofar as it considers the execution of innocents illegitimate, this repudiation itself "unmask[s]" and thereby exposes the true legitimizing force behind state killing: revenge.[24]

The coupling of revenge and guilt highlights the fact that there is a variety of general deterrence widely accepted as legitimate: deterring private citizens from seeking revenge. When she opined that the government needed to do its job and execute killers to prevent people from becoming vigilantes, Beatrice was echoing what Justice Potter Stewart stated in his opinion in *Furman*: "When people begin to believe that organized society is unwilling or unable to impose upon criminal offenders the punishment they 'deserve,' then there are sown the seeds of anarchy — of self-help, vigilante justice and lynch law." Justice William Brennan made a similar point in *Furman*, arguing that not only does the death penalty "exert [a] widespread moralizing influence upon community values, it also satisfies the popular demand for grievous condemnation of abhorrent crimes and so prevents disorder, lynching, and attempts by private citizens to take the law into their own hands." When the Supreme Court restored capital punishment in *Gregg*, it also noted that "there is no convincing empirical evidence either supporting or refuting" general deterrence, the moralizing, restoring effect that Brennan spoke of in *Furman*.[25] This left vengeance and the prevention of vigilantism, with the former used to forestall the latter.

The Court's 1991 decision in *Payne v. Tennessee* formalized the legitimacy of revenge in capital proceedings while signaling that the Court had no intention of further interference with state death penalty laws. At issue in *Payne* was the admissibility of victim impact statements (VISs) as evidence. These statements are declarations of the harm the murder caused the victims or victims' surviving family members. Overturning two prior cases that had held that this type of evidence was irrelevant and inadmissible, *Payne* found that VISs were a valid and necessary part of the capital trial process. In so doing, the Court accepted a shift in the rationale behind capital punishment, effectively declaring revenge the fundamental justification for capital punishment.[26]

Payne concerned the murder of twenty-eight-year-old Charisse Christopher and her two-year-old daughter and the attempted murder of her three-year-old son Nicholas. In a famous passage from the prosecutor's summary at trial:

> Nicholas was alive. And Nicholas was in the same room [as his mother and sister]. Nicholas was still conscious. His eyes were open. He responded to the paramedics. He was able to follow their directions. He was able to hold his intestines in as he was carried to the ambulance. So he knew what happened to his mother and baby sister.
>
> There is nothing you can do to ease the pain of any of the families involved in this case. There is nothing you can do to ease the pain of Bernice or Carl Payne, and that's a tragedy. . . . They will have to live with it the rest of their lives. There is obviously nothing you can do for Charisse and Lacie Jo. But there is something that you can do for Nicholas.
>
> Somewhere down the road Nicholas is going to grow up, hopefully. He's going to want to know what happened. And he is going to know what happened to his baby sister and his mother. He is going to want to know what type of justice was done. He is going to want to know what happened. With your verdict, you will provide the answer.[27]

Franklin Zimring calls this the "degovernmentalization" of the death penalty, the process of turning it from a state function into a service provided on behalf of the victims' relatives. The fact that "the prosecutor in *Payne* presents himself as *Nicholas's* lawyer instead of *the state's* lawyer" makes clear the "provision of service" intent. We can hear it also in former California Attorney General Dan Lungren's description of the execution of Robert Alton Harris as "a solemn act that showed the state's ability to 'respond to the true needs and concerns of victims.'" This coincides with Justice Stewart's concern that victims be punished to prevent vigilantism, as well as with demands that the government "do its job" and execute offenders in order to prevent mob justice. If the state is an agent acting on behalf of the victims rather than on its own behalf, it cannot pretend to any legitimacy apart from base vengeance.[28]

We can see this in a proposed change to Virginia law that would have permitted victims' family members to witness executions. The bill's proponents hailed it as a measure of fairness aimed at helping families deal with their loss, while opponents decried it as an act of barbarism. State senator and future attorney general Mark L. Earley, admitting that the bill "ha[d] nothing to do with being tough on crime," defended it as a provision ensuring fairness, a provision that would allow families to deal with their emotions by allowing them to witness the execution. The rest of us, he pointedly remarked, are not qualified to "sit in judgment" on these emotions, and thus also presumably not on the bill. Opponents immediately contested the state-service element by proposing amendments to the bill that would permit the families to decide on the method of execution or to throw the switch. More seriously, the bill's opponents recognized its promotion of base vengeance and declared that its passage "would revert the state 'to medieval times'" and that "the state might as well stuff 'a Red Delicious apple in [the offender's] mouth.'"[29]

This turn toward victim service is a relatively recent addition to discussions of the legitimacy of state killing. As James noted in one Bible study:

> I will tell you positively . . . there is nothing, absolutely nothing in the legal history of this country, or the legal history of England . . . there's not even a concept of "victims' rights" until you hit the political pundits of the last twenty-five years saying, you know, "Well, what about the victims?" . . . But there has always been the idea that the state can extract retribution on behalf of its citizens.[30]

Retributive justice, James notes, has a long lineage of legitimacy, but he differentiates between action on behalf of the populace at large and action on behalf of specific victims.

However we assess the impact of the various victims' rights organizations, it is important not to overlook what is arguably their greatest contribution to the discourse: the exaggeration of the power of the individual defendant and of the threat they pose. This is not to minimize or diminish the scope of individual crimes; that must be acknowledged. At the same time, however, we cannot overlook the fact that the system, predicated on retributive models of justice, and, after *Payne*, directed toward advocacy on behalf of individuals and toward remedying individual rather than societal wrongs, is predisposed toward inflating the power and danger individual defendants pose.

A presentation made at one participating church illustrates this well.[31] Russell E. "Rusty" McGuire, Deputy Commonwealth's Attorney in Louisa County, Virginia, spoke about the death penalty from his professional experience. Arguing for or against the death penalty from a moral or biblical point of view was not his prerogative, he said. Instead, he discussed the process by which prosecutors decide to bring capital charges against defendants. In a fluid and expansive presentation, McGuire detailed the common-law history of the death penalty as it developed in America as well as its gradual restriction to specific categories of murder. As he came to the question of what constitutes a capital crime, he asked the crowd whether it is a capital offense to shoot your neighbor because you dislike them and want to kill them. Is it a capital offense to rape a family member, or to rape a child? What about killing a police officer

(*The Exile* (93

while trying to escape arrest? In each of these cases, he pointed out, the nodding and shaking of heads corresponded with the correct answer: no, no, no, and yes, respectively, though the third question elicited a more ambivalent response than the others. The point, he said, is that when we discuss capital punishment, we are by definition discussing limited circumstances; we are no longer speaking of rape unless the victim was also murdered, nor are we speaking about all murders. We are discussing murder with an underlying felony. In other words, he said, we are discussing the "worst of the worst"—we are discussing exceptions. In order for a jury to impose a death sentence at the sentencing proceeding, they must find either that the defendant "would constitute a continuing serious threat to society" or that his offense was "outrageously or wantonly vile, horrible, or inhuman."[32]

To illustrate this, McGuire related the story of a case he had worked in early 2008, which is worth quoting at length:

> Let me tell you about Janice Adams. Janice Adams was a single mother. She was raising a fourteen-year-old daughter. . . . She had been in an abusive relationship. She had told—she had decided that Timothy Gray was no longer going to live with them. She wanted him out. She packed his things, and she put them on the bed. Timothy Gray came home that night, with her, because he didn't drive. She picked him up . . . drove to the house and said, you know, "You need to go." He didn't like that answer. She was upstairs in the bathroom, getting ready to go out that night. She'd found a new man, she'd moved on. These two had been separated for some time; it was time he finally got all his things out of the house. He decided to go down to the kitchen—and I'm sorry that I have to get graphic, but I have to, so you understand what I'm about to talk about. He grabbed a knife out of the chock block there in the kitchen. He went upstairs, and brutality and torture is the only way I can explain to you what happened that day. He stabbed her thirty-six times. He cut a major vein in her throat. She could not hold it with her left hand because of cuts going across it; these are called defensive wounds. She reached over with her right hand. The medical examiner testified at the trial that applying pressure that way, she would have lived for maybe twenty to thirty minutes. She died with her right hand, holding that, asking him for help. He just walked out the door. . . . When the officers get there to the scene—and you can imagine, there's blood everywhere, she's dead on arrival—her earring, that was in her ear, with a chunk of her ear, is on the floor. Hair is in the sink. The glass area of the bathtub is broken, where her body is found. Death penalty or not? No, that is not. This is why I like to explain death penalty law, because I think when we all think about the death penalty . . . we think every murder case is a death penalty case. No, they're not. . . . I was very naive before I started practicing law, thinking that any type of death is capital punishment. No. It's reserved for people who do significantly heinous crimes, and then we

look at it and make sure this person has some sort of future dangerousness that we can't guarantee that they're not going to harm others, or if the crime was *so vile*. . . . Those are the types of cases that we look at. . . . I would never try to persuade anyone to believe in the death penalty. That's something that each of you has to come to your own conclusion. But as a prosecutor, what I do . . . In every case, we also focus on the victims. I had to look Janice Adams's daughter in the face, and her family, and let them know that justice occurred in that courtroom. . . . I've got to look at the family that no longer has a loved one, that has to live the rest of their life knowing that their sister, mother, father, or daughter was brutally tortured, and every day they think about the person that did it to them.[33]

We cannot dispute McGuire's characterization of this murder as brutal and torturous. The brutality of the killing, however, is only part of the reason the story packs the emotional punch that it does. The second blow lands just behind the first: not only was this a particularly brutal slaying; it is also a case of a victim killed for doing what we would recognize as the right thing. Adams was moving on from an abusive relationship, working, taking care of her daughter, and had even helped her killer out, picking him up and bringing him back to the house to retrieve his belongings. The phrasing of the summation leads inexorably toward a conclusion, that Janice Adams was murdered for doing the right thing and for putting her life back together in a way that did not involve Timothy Gray. This second element of the emotional content of the story rests on its element of undifferentiation. The senselessness of this killing helps us empathize with the victim, eliciting the sort of "there but for the grace of God go I" response that commonly follows crimes where the victim was simply in the wrong place at the wrong time, doing things that anyone could be doing on any given day, such as paying for gasoline or making an ATM withdrawal.[34]

This, we are told, is not a death penalty crime. The inescapable implication is, if not this, then what? McGuire's anecdote is an example of the propensity to inflate the power of the murderer and to reinforce one of the requisite elements of the exile. If any of us could be Janice Adams, senselessly and brutally murdered, then anyone else could be Timothy Gray; the murderer looms large as "an omnipresent danger . . . on the streets." "Dangerousness" is central to this process; indeed, for a jury to find a sentence of death warranted in a capital case in Virginia, they must find that the defendant poses a continuing danger to society—must find future dangerousness. A striking feature of the retentionist discourse is that future dangerousness is knowable, and is knowable exclusively based on prior actions. As one Bible study participant encapsulated the idea, "We're all at risk, and why should innocents be made to suffer because of someone that cannot be controlled? . . . I can-

(*The Exile* (95

not see releasing people into society *that are going to continue to go and do as they have*." Recidivism is assumed, and future dangerousness is posited from past actions, though these assumptions are not borne out by the statistical evidence, which suggests that murderers have lower rates of recidivism than other offenders. Recently, the Supreme Court halted the execution of Texas inmate Duane Buck. At Buck's trial, a psychologist testifying for the prosecution informed the jury that Buck is predisposed to violent crime because he is black.[35] Establishing future dangerousness may not be an exact science, but arguments regarding dangerousness cannot descend to the level of vulgar race-baiting.

By this point in the legal process, whatever else previously characterized such defendants, they have now become the "other." Whatever else they may have been, those convicted of capital murder become the killer writ large. In a very real sense, this turn to identifying the offender as a "killer" makes the question of future dangerousness much easier to answer: a killer kills, and we must presume that he will kill again. Individual murderers become symbols of "the public's fears of criminal victimization, smoldering indignation at youthful violent offenders, and frustration over the apparent failure of government to do anything about either." As that redoubtable bastion of culture wars combativeness Pat Buchanan argued, the question is one of traditional morality, "a religious concept of man as rational being, possessed of a God-given knowledge of right and wrong, and of a free will to choose either," versus what he ironically terms a progressive morality. For Buchanan, the traditional view correctly understands that choices are independently made, are not contingent on any external influence, and render one accountable to both God and the law. If the government fails to prosecute wrongdoers, then it risks losing its moral legitimacy. With the loss of moral legitimacy comes the risk of vigilantism, which would be legitimate if rendered necessary by the state's failure to fulfill its obligations to punish the evildoer.[36]

"If we don't enforce the death penalty, others will," intoned William Tucker, then a media fellow at Stanford University's Hoover Institution. Tucker's op-ed urged readers to remind Mario Cuomo, who at the time was New York's governor, and Justice Brennan that if they and their offices fail to enforce the death penalty, others will, and will do so without concern for such frivolities as public mandate or the bother of due process. It's difficult to read the piece and not hear an endorsement of this sort of aimless vigilantism coupled with an attitude that would blame Cuomo, Brennan, and those of like mind for any such action. A letter to the editor of the *Fresno Bee* recalled one such crime, a lynching that occurred sixty years earlier: a group of enraged students hanged two men accused of kidnapping and murdering a classmate. The letter writer opined that "the times and the events dictated the only way for a very hostile community to vent off its steam. Yes . . . the action was justifiable. At a very minimal cost."[37]

The cost—the lives and the damage to due process and the rule of law—is deemed minimal because of the nature of the crisis we face. The community's only recourse is to select a victim on whom to visit its collective frustrations, to "vent its steam" in a single violent outburst that will enable order to be restored, at least for a time. These victims will be chosen not at random, but based on a determination of their guilt, which in turn depends on intrinsic and sometimes irrelevant characteristics, leading to capricious sentencing. If the criminal justice system selects these victims for us based on the recommendations of the juries in those cases, then so much the better, but if not, the community fairly openly reserves its right to assess guilt and impose punishment on its own. Even if the sporadic release of violence is contained within the legal system, guilt is the most important factor, not because it makes any one defendant particularly more culpable or deserving of the ultimate punishment than any other equally guilty defendant, but because legal guilt separates the "we" from the "they."

Once legal guilt is established, factors that death penalty opponents argue lessen a particular defendant's culpability are irrelevant. Indeed, to credit these factors sincerely, to consider seriously whether these factors in any way mitigate the defendant's guilt, is posited as disrespectful and degrading to the defendant from the retentionist point of view, because it robs him of his human dignity. The question of whether capital punishment is humane hinges not on the mechanism of punishment, but on the question of approach. As Sharon Keller, an outspoken death penalty advocate and current presiding judge on the Texas Court of Criminal Appeals, summarized this position, "The ability to make moral decisions—to choose our behavior—is a characteristic that distinguishes human beings from animals. We impose the death penalty because the criminal is responsible for his act. . . . To fail to hold a person responsible for his choice would be to treat him inhumanely."[38]

From this perspective, society's obligations in responding to violent crime are entirely congruent, and this congruence forms the basic pattern by which the retentionist discourse creates its exile. This is because of the peculiar way that retribution as a justification for punishment and the scapegoating impulse reinforce each other. As Stuart Banner notes, in the decades following *Furman* retribution has gone from being dismissed as an illegitimate rationale for punishment to being the dominant expression of the need for and aims of punishment.[39] Because of what retribution demands, and the way it demands it, the scapegoat is never far behind:

We have been taught that the idea of retribution, the idea of seeking a method of punishment to satisfy a community's needs to see an offender punished is a primitive notion that no longer has a place in our society. I suggest to you, from my own experience, and in my own judgment, that that notion is wrong. The idea that the punishment must fit the crime is something more than the idea that we have to find a way to isolate the offender and to try to rehabilitate him, the idea that somehow we ought to try to discourage others from committing crimes by imposing prison sentences and other forms of punishment. But, that is not enough. Somehow society needs to feel that when a criminal act has been committed, its interests have been vindicated.[40]

No longer dismissed as mere vengeance, as something that is beneath or behind us, retribution has been restored to intellectual legitimacy and is treated as a social cohesive. A criminal law based on the principle of retribution "remind[s] us of the moral order by which alone we can live as *human* beings, and in our day the only punishment that can do this is capital punishment." We utilize—or even simply support—the death penalty because it is the best safeguard and recognition of humanity, both ours, as the victimized, and the offender's, as the victimizer. Moreover, capital punishment provides "a grammar of social symbols. . . . The criminal trial is a 'miracle play' . . . in which we carry out our inarticulate beliefs about crime and criminals within the reassuring formal structure of disinterested due process."[41] One may legitimately wonder whether acting on inarticulate beliefs not subject to examination in the trial process, which has been described as the crucible of truth, can ever form the basis for a system of justice empowered to take a person's life.

The retentionist exile originates in this recognition, that the crime was a choice willfully made by an individual existentially capable of making that choice. The choice is all that matters, and once that choice is made, we owe it to the victims, to ourselves, and even to the offender to recognize our common humanity and rationality by moving decisively to exile the offender from our midst. In so doing, we give vent to our collective rages and frustrations, exorcising them while heaping them onto a victim designated for that purpose by their actions, and use that exilic moment as a social cohesive. It is cohesive rather than divisive because we pursue moral certainty via procedural certainty, as discussed in chapter 2. Here another element of Weisberg's critique comes to the fore. If the offender generates himself or herself as offender by committing the crime, then the legal process re-creates the offender as a *killer*. If the exilic moment of the ritual execution is insufficient in and of itself to restore order, as is indicated by the failure of any general deterrence, it remains sufficient at least to restore a sense of commonality. This restored sense of commonality, from the retentionist perspective, mitigates some of the offender's power. By exiling the offender, we uphold the value of human life; by acting to uphold the value of human life, we reclaim some of the power that the offender had acquired by their action. We may not have been able to resolve the crisis broadly, but this specific act of violence directed at this specific victim in response to the crisis has had some result.

From the Retentionist to the Abolitionist Exile
The "Normal Person"

The preceding argument is tight with a tension that derives in part from two elements that characterize it. The first of these is the apparent failure to recognize that while the offender's power over us emerges from the enormity of their actions and the consequences of those actions, it is also conferred upon him by the processes described above. This power in turn determines the process by which the offender is exiled. The second characteristic is the curious fact that what we claim to fear most—the cold-blooded killer—is what we emulate when it comes time to dispense justice. Indeed, in rejecting vigilantism in favor of the criminal justice process, we reject the notion of executing justice in a burst of passion in favor of a methodical, planned homicide. If our laws pertaining to murder are an accurate indication of the threats we perceive from different types of actions, then the action that we consider less threatening as an offense—the crime of passion—is the very action we consider intrinsically threatening to our system—the retributive passion of the lynch mob. As David Garland has shown, the contemporary American execution is the mirror opposite of the classic lynching—a cold, methodical homicide replicating in mirror reverse the hot passion of the lynch mob.[42]

The abolitionist discourse is likewise fraught with tension that results from two defining characteristics of that discourse and of the exile as created by and situated within that discourse. The distinction between the two should be drawn on the basis of the difference between what Stephen L. Carter identified as *bilateral individualism* and what we might call *multilateral individualism*. Bilateral individualism, Carter explains, is a construction of victimhood that "awards the status of victim to someone who loses something—property, physical safety—because of the predation of someone else." Victims are created by real, identifiable transgressions perpetrated by real, identifiable offenders. The response should be to counter these transgressions by imposing punishments that may deter future transgressions. Civil society is obligated to punish in order to counter these acts of victimization and demonstrate that the forces of law and order have not lost control. This last is vital, because if it is not or seems not to be the case, people will protect themselves from evil by whatever means necessary.[43]

This bilateral individualism tracks well with the retentionist exile. Both respond to a real crisis with real acts of violence perpetrated against real victims, in response to which real acts of violence are (or should be) committed against real transgressors. Both also demand a necessary component of legitimacy, without which neither the exile nor the bilateral individualist structure stands. Despite their similarities, however, the retentionist exile and the bilateral individualist model differ in a subtle but critical aspect. Both models are predicated on differentiations between "them" and "us," which, as categorical approaches, appear in the abstract to be more solid with bilateral individualism than with the exile. The distance between "us" and "them" is thus greater with bilateral individualism than with the exile, which gives "us" greater latitude in framing our response to "them." As Carter explains, while bilateral individualism stipulates that the guilty must be punished, it also holds that the jury is authorized to decide on and impose punishment, within the bounds prescribed by law, in response to these transgressions.[44] The retentionist exile, on the other hand, leaves the jury no such choice.

We might object that this is simply an articulation of the theory of retributive justice and that in reality a jury operating under the auspices of bilateral individualism would decide the same way. This is true in many cases, but recall Andrew, who observed that we are not responsible for executing criminals—they execute themselves via their actions. In this formulation, prevalent in the retentionist discourse, we lack the choice that bilateral individualism presupposes. According to this view, the fact that we have a death penalty gives us the right and the duty to utilize it. The difference between the two models—the retentionist exile and bilateral individualism—comes down to the element of choice. Although we can plausibly understand bilateral individualism to "demand" specific punishments in response to certain crimes, it nevertheless leaves the decision open. The exile, however, leaves us no option; our necessary response is determined by the offense. We, the victims, are victimized further by having our ability to choose how to respond removed from us. Whereas bilateral individualism seeks to rationalize our need to respond to violence with violence, the exile permits and requires no such rationalization. The retentionist exile is in fact more unilateral in conception than bilateral. The difference is in the distance. If offenders are *not like us*, then we must decide how to deal with them, must rationalize our reprisal. If, however, offenders are *like us* by virtue of "that ability which separates us from the beasts—the ability to choose"—then our choice is predetermined by their choice, and is thus no choice at all.[45]

The abolitionist exile is similar to the retentionist exile and to the offender posited by bilateral individualism. Like the retentionist exile, the abolitionist exile views the ability to make a choice as indispensable. At the same time, the abolitionist resembles the bilateral individualist in arguing that the distance between "us" and "them" is greater than the retentionist exile would admit. Moreover, the abolitionist concept of exile denies that the offense determines how we *must* respond to crime; it is closer to the bilateral individualist idea that we choose how we respond. Rather than ceding power to the offender, the abolitionist conception of exile diminishes the offender's power while arguing for greater power—and greater responsibility—on the part of society. It does this by operating within the restraints imposed by the court and by an ideologically retributivist political system, attacking the concept of the "normal" criminal where it is weakest and attempting to turn the question from guilt to culpability.

As Jennifer Culbert shows, in the modern era, the basic set of criteria by which juries determine whether to impose death sentences "hinges on moral norms instead of formal principles." Culbert derives her idea of the "normal person" from legal philosopher H. L. A. Hart, who argued that punishment is morally acceptable only if it is applied to the perpetrators of particular crimes and if the severity of the punishment corresponds with the offender's intention in committing the crime:

> A good reason for administering a less severe penalty is made out if the situation or mental state of the convicted criminal is such that he was exposed to an unusual or specially great temptation, or his ability to control his actions is thought to have been impaired or weakened otherwise than by his action, so that conformity to the law which he has broken was a matter of special difficulty for him as compared with normal persons normally placed.[46]

Implicit in this is the idea that the best way to define the "normal person" is as "an autonomous, rational, self-determining agent" who is "in full possession of their faculties and who act[s] only as they intend."[47]

This supports the retentionist conception of the normal exile being granted so much power and limiting our power to respond to offenses. The idea of necessary consequences, expressed as some variant on "they knew the consequences of their actions," utilizes a social contract approach to make this point. In making this point, it returns to the definition of the "normal person" from which it proceeded. If we start with the idea that the defining feature of humanity is the ability to choose, then the social contract demands both that individuals be held accountable for their choices and that we hold them accountable. Consequences must be objectively foreseeable and intended, since to hold otherwise—to hold consequences as less than inevitable or as incidental to the offense—would be to minimize the choice itself and enervate the defining characteristic of humankind. We must always proceed as though the consequences were intended, because to act otherwise would be to respond to transgression as if it were simply an action, simply an occurrence, rather than a choice. Here we return to the rational agent who, having freely chosen to commit an offense which they and we know to be prohibited under the rules governing our society, must be punished as a rational agent having freely chosen to undertake that action and generate the consequences, which are both identifiable and foreseeable. At this level, the ability to make the choice and concerns over treating the offender with dignity, as a rational human being, far outweigh any mitigating factors that may lessen culpability to the point that they are rejected out of hand, as in the instinctive reaction against the "poor childhood" defense. We all have mitigating circumstances that could lessen our culpability, the argument goes, but if we do not treat ourselves and others as fully rational, then we forfeit the ground from which to punish transgression at all.

The difference between the retentionist and abolitionist exiles can be seen in the difference between them and the Foucauldian ideas that each somewhat resembles. The retentionist exile resembles the Foucauldian "dangerous person," the individual who "of his own free will [has] chosen evil rather than good." The individual who has chosen freely to commit a sufficiently evil deed to require a sentence of death is by definition a dangerous individual in this sense, though the retentionist exile differs from the Foucauldian "dangerous person" in that the exile must be guilty, whereas the dangerous person need merely be culpable. Nevertheless, this intrinsically dangerous person simultaneously provokes and obviates the need to deliberate future dangerousness rather than impute it from past action.[48]

To continue with Beatrice's example above, it is this concept of the intrinsically dangerous individual that necessitates an immediate assumption — however reasonable or founded in experience — that any prison break is a violent prisoner bent on further violence against us. This contrasts with the abolitionist exile, which, as we will see below, resembles Foucault's delinquent, the "criminal type whose biography, character, and environment mark him or her off as different from the non-delinquent." Whereas Foucault's delinquent is fabricated rather than discovered by the prison system, however, the abolitionist exile, bearing the outward signs of the delinquent, is discovered, not fabricated. This is not to deny the importance of prison-abetted recidivism in contributing either to future offenses or to the abolitionist discourse, but to argue that the abolitionist reads the exile backward, treating the offense as the sign of exile, rather than the moment of instantiation.[49]

The Abolitionist Exile
Differentiating from the "Normal"

The legal and political developments of the modern era progressively closed off avenues by which the various abolitionist groups could assault the death penalty head-on. Instead, these groups found themselves restricted to working to save individual lives in the face of a criminal justice system that would not admit any challenges based on classes of individuals, even when generally racially discriminatory application was demonstrated. In the second half of this period, abolitionists changed tactics, shifting toward attacks at the edges and trying to progressively limit the classes of individuals subject to capital punishment. They based these attacks largely on issues of culpability, winning a succession of cases and in the process creating their own version of the exile, and thus of the normal, which they pitted against the dominant retentionist understanding. The two most important such cases were *Atkins v. Virginia* and *Roper v. Simmons*, which banned executions of the mentally retarded and juveniles, respectively.[50]

In 1987, the National Coalition to Abolish the Death Penalty (NCADP), one of the largest national abolitionist organizations, decided that while it would be impossible to pursue total abolition, it would be worthwhile to pursue means of limiting the application of death sentences. The NCADP began by putting two categories of offenders on its target list: juveniles and the mentally retarded. This conference was the first to hold workshops on how to address these categories of offenders. In 1988, the organization announced that it would begin working with other national, state, and local organizations on legislative campaigns against executions of juveniles and the mentally retarded.[51]

One such organization working toward this end was the Virginia Interfaith Center for Public Policy (VICPP). Formed in 1982, the VICPP is an association of people of faith dedicated to fostering religious values in the processes of government "by means of programs of legislative information, General Assembly seminars, and advocacy" on such matters as "legislative process and ethics; human services; children and youth needs; discrimination; criminal justice; environmental protection; [and] church-state relations." The VICPP's legislative guides not only show that the churches constantly agitated on the issue, but also indicate how their articulations of their positions evolved. In 1983, for example, the VICPP opposed legislation that would have permitted juvenile court judges to commit troubled children to the Department of Corrections. This was part of a general position opposing incarceration at the expense of less costly, more effective alternatives. The 1984 agenda continued to oppose detaining children in adult jails as part of a package of positions supporting a separate support system to help troubled youth without incarcerating them alongside adults. By 1987, this position had shifted slightly; the VICPP argued that the state needed "a separate Department of Youth Services" because "special and distinct programs directed at youth in trouble are appropriately lodged apart from Adult Corrections," positions repeated in the 1988 agenda.[52]

Alongside these agenda points were calls for the abolition of the death penalty and opposition to any attempts to expand its use, as well as calls for the expansion of mental health treatment for prisoners. Throughout the 1980s, the VICPP tried to contain and oppose the death penalty where it was while trying to limit its reach by working to remove two particularly questionable classes of offenders — children and the mentally ill/retarded — from the pool of death-eligible offenders. This commonsense approach, while not novel, is based on the notion of the "normal person" and should be seen as the basis for an expanding, and ultimately somewhat successful, abolitionist effort and discourse throughout the remainder of the modern era.[53]

Children, the mentally ill, and the mentally handicapped are considered especially vulnerable because they do not fit the conception of the "normal person." Until the Supreme Court's 2005 decision in *Roper*, which held it unconstitutional to execute anyone who committed their crime before turning eighteen, and its 2002 decision in *Atkins*, which held it unconstitutional to execute the mentally retarded, Virginia law allowed the execution of "juveniles as young as 16 . . . the mentally retarded, the severely brain damaged, and the mentally ill." Prior to *Roper*, Virginia abolitionists had failed in several attempts to achieve a state ban on juvenile executions. The controversy over the juvenile death penalty (JDP) was especially relevant in Virginia, "one of the few states that ha[d] actually executed juveniles" in the contemporary era, including two within a four-day span in January 2000. From the first recorded execution of a juvenile in the colonies in 1642, at least 366 juvenile offenders were executed in the United States, roughly 10 percent of them in Virginia. The JDP was one area in which Virginia's abolitionists could demonstrate a wide range of support. Virginia People of Faith against the Death Penalty, Virginians for Alternatives to the Death Penalty, and the ACLU of Virginia were actively fighting the JDP, while nearly forty different religious leaders signed resolutions in opposition to the JDP.[54]

We can see that the broad opposition to the JDP broke down essentially to three categories of opposition. The first of these was based on brain development, with various statements and publications citing research showing that the brain continues to develop into one's twenties. Specifically, they noted, the portions of the brain that control judgment, reasoning, and impulse control continue developing into the twenties, leading juveniles to rely more on the parts of the brain responsible for impulses, rather than foresight and rational planning of actions relative to consequences. The VICPP and the Virginia Council of Churches (VCC) drew two conclusions from this research. First, they noted that laws allowing for the execution of juvenile offenders were out of step with other laws protecting or restricting juveniles. As mentioned above, Virginia code treats juveniles as a protected class by making the murder of a child under fourteen by someone over twenty-one a capital-eligible offense. Moreover, as the VICPP noted,

> In most other societal circumstances [children and the mentally retarded] are considered to be incapable of mature judgment and full adult responsibility: e.g., legal contracts, purchase of alcoholic beverages, consensual sexual acts. Both are regarded as vulnerable populations and should receive a higher degree of protection than that afforded responsible adults.[55]

The retentionist discourse is founded on the idea that the offender made a calculated, reasoned choice to kill. If, however, children are more vulnerable and cannot reasonably be expected to make a mature, rational judgment, to make a genuine choice to kill, then they are not sufficiently normal to be reasonably treated as a normal individual in the sense that Hart and Culbert explain. They are more *not like us* than *like us*. This is the second broad objection to the JDP: because children are more unlike us than like us, we have less warrant to punish than we would if they were like us. If, as Charles Colson argues, justice demands getting what we deserve because "we did in fact know better," the same cannot be said of children or the mentally retarded.[56] The issue is not guilt—it's culpability.

The mentally ill belong to the class of more vulnerable/less culpable offenders, and here the media helps demonstrate the distance between individual offenders and our understanding of the normal. One visible defendant whose case kept the mental health issue before the public was Percy Levar Walton. Walton was convicted of the 1996 murders of Jessie and Elizabeth Kendrick, two octogenarian neighbors, and the unrelated murder of Archie Moore. These murders occurred shortly after Walton's eighteenth birthday, so *Roper* did not protect him. Walton's deteriorating mental state, however, and the problems it posed with regard to his pending execution raised, as one minister put it, "prophetic, and . . . morally just [questions that] will certainly become fodder for hot debate in the coming days."[57]

This debate featured prominently in publications and communications from abolitionist groups, as well as in the mainstream press, which covered the case extensively. Walton was described as "floridly psychotic" and displayed several symptoms of schizophrenia, such as a tendency to parrot words and a complete indifference to personal hygiene. Walton's indifference to his hygiene was so complete that prison officials would forcibly bathe him when the stench became too overpowering. His behavior in prison led the guards to dub him "Horse," short for "Crazy Horse." "Plagued by severe mental illness since adolescence," Walton was "scarcely conscious of the fate that await[ed] him."[58]

More pertinently, Walton's counsel argued, he was incapable of understanding that execution meant his death. This, they argued, rendered him incompetent to be executed. According to *Ford v. Wainwright*, it is unconstitutional to execute defendants who are insane at the time of their execution, even if they were mentally competent to stand trial. Walton understood his execution to mean any number of things, including that he, his grandfather, and his victims would rise from the dead; that he would receive a motorcycle or a nationally syndicated television show; or that he would be released from prison and either get a job at or a meal from Burger King: "After execution, I'm going to go get a Burger King." Opponents of Walton's execution pointed to the testimony of Dr. Stanton E. Samenow, a clinical psychologist and frequent expert witness in criminal trials. Samenow, a noted skeptic of the insanity defense who has frequently stated his belief that defendants use psychiatry to try to evade or lessen punishment rather than out of genuine mental health issues, examined Walton and concluded that he was decompensating, that is, that his mental state was continuously deteriorating.[59]

Adding to the problem caused by Walton's mental illness was that posed by his mental retardation; Walton's IQ was measured at 66, below the threshold guideline of 70. This made his execution problematic on two grounds simultaneously. First, opponents argued, executing Walton despite his insanity would violate Eighth Amendment case law based on *Ford*. Second, executing Walton despite his IQ, which qualified him as mentally retarded, would violate the law as established in *Atkins*. In both cases, the Court ruled that the lowered culpability of the defendants voided any valid penological purpose behind their executions. Because we cannot hold defendants in these two categories to the same standard of moral culpability as normal adults, we cannot justifiably put them to death for their crimes.[60]

In Walton's case, as in the case of Calvin Swann, another Virginia death row inmate whose sentence was commuted due to mental illness a decade earlier,[61] Governor Kaine agreed that it would be plainly unjust to allow the execution to proceed. Over the previous two years, Kaine had twice stayed Walton's execution and reviewed a number of reports and studies detailing his continued mental degradation. In his statement announcing the commutation, Kaine explicitly cited *Ford* and noted that although there was no evidence presented at trial claiming that Walton was insane or mentally retarded, his mental state since then had been one of constant deterioration consistent with his mental illness. As a result, Kaine said, "one cannot reasonably conclude that Walton is fully aware of the punishment he is about to suffer and why he is to suffer it." Kaine felt compelled to "conclude that a commutation of [Walton's] sentence to life in prison without possibility of parole is now the only constitutionally appropriate course of action."[62]

These comments echo those made by former governor Jim Gilmore, who pardoned Swann in 1999. Swann, like Walton, was schizophrenic. Gilmore stated, after issuing the pardon, that after observing that Swann's behavior on death row had been "nothing short of bizarre and totally devoid of rationality," and realizing that the jury may have been misinformed as to the extent of Swann's illness, he concluded the only just course of action was to commute Swann's sentence to life without parole. These descriptions include what we can call exile markers, signs of difference that collectively portray the defendant as *not like us*. In some cases, as with Walton, Daryl Atkins, and Thomas Wayne Akers, the differentiating factor is IQ and the ability to comprehend one's actions and their consequences, an ability that we do not recognize in those with IQs ranging from 58 to 66, as in these cases. This portrayal could be, as in Swann's case, an extensive history of commitment to mental institutions and state-provided medication designed to stabilize his mental state, coupled with recommendations that the state seek and provide more extensive treatment "before [he] injures someone, or perhaps even worse, commits a homicide."[63] It can be growing up in notoriously crime-ridden and violent neighborhoods,[64] parental drug abuse,[65] or parental suicide.[66]

In each of these cases, the abolitionist discourse posits a distinction and demands that we make an imaginative leap. This demand to imagine underscores the claim of difference, the claim that these individuals are genuinely *not like us*. These details are emphasized in the press because they make the story more attractive to consumers, though in some cases they occur awkwardly alongside descriptions of the normal. An excellent example of this is an Associated Press piece that, stupefyingly, began and ended with assertions of Walton's normality. Entitled "Court Stays Execution for Inmate Who Claims He's Insane," the article's final sentence reads: "Walton declined to be interviewed Wednesday."[67] One struggles not to read either sentence as deliberate irony, though the article gives no indication that they were so written. Rather, the article about a demonstrably insane inmate begins and ends, astoundingly, with assertions of Walton's normality, sufficient to *claim* insanity and *decline* to be interviewed.

Examples like this aside, the abolitionist discourse emphasizes these exilic elements to counteract the retentionist discourse's trope of the "normal individual." The distance posited in these cases is that between two images, between "the nine-year-old defendant tearfully pleading with his mother not to shoot the hypodermic into her tied up vein [while we were] piling into the back of the family station wagon and popping a wad of Bazooka bubble gum . . . as we set off to play a game with [our] . . . Little League team." Competing with this image of the non-normal versus the normal is the necessary element of choice, without which the discourses cannot make sense:

> He had a pretty bad childhood. The mother blew her brains out in front of him; he was a very young kid. The mom was a drug addict. She used to stay up all night and sleep all day. . . . So the sister who was just a couple of years older than he — she did all the cooking, she did all the cleaning. And I remember at one point I began crying because I had two little kids and I just, it just tore my heart out that the sister made his lunches, his first day at kindergarten, his sister, just two years older, took him to school and stood in line for him to get into kindergarten. It just tore me up. I thought he got a raw deal starting off. *But he had many, many chances, okay. . . . He chose to take that path.*[68]

We can certainly use the "poor childhood" defense as a mechanism for prodding people to realize that these offenders are sufficiently not like us that we cannot claim any motive for executing them other than base revenge. But we should move beyond that and look at how it fits in with the "social profile" of the death row offender: high rates of "childhood abuse and neglect, social and emotional dysfunction, alcohol and drug abuse. . . . Over 30 percent of juvenile death row offenders have experienced six or more distinct areas of childhood trauma." Thus the capital offense does not *create* the exile, as in the retentionist discourse; it *reveals* that the processes of exile from what we consider normal have already occurred. This revelation has the performative effect of simultaneously enacting and enforcing this distance, removing these offenders from our conceptions of the normal, of those like ourselves, and placing them sufficiently far from us and from this normal image that we cannot justly execute them, because "no truly civilized and humane society executes the most helpless among them."[69]

Both sides agree that murderers are made, not born. Where they disagree is in determining whether the decision to kill is the only necessary determinant of our response, or whether the decision to kill should be located as part of an evolving and accumulative process. Viewing it as part of an evolving process leads us to the idea of the sine qua non of humanity, per the abolitionist discourse: the ability to exercise impulse control. Once again, we see the convergence of retentionist and abolitionist ideas followed by a sharp divergence. In both cases, the decision to commit the offense is the central element around which all else revolves. Without that choice, without mens rea, we cannot claim to have established guilt. Without guilt, innocence is, as former Virginia attorney general Mary Sue Terry once quipped in a different context, "irrelevant."[70]

Moreover, we acknowledge that in order for the death penalty to be a punishment, offenders must understand that they are being punished and why. This is what prevents the death penalty from being simply "savage and inhuman," from being "only . . . an exercise in revenge." The need for offenders to understand their own guilt and the nature of their punishment is not limited to redemptive or restorative theories of justice — it is an explicit prerequisite for any exercise in retributive justice: "*If* the defendant perceives the connection between his crime and his punishment, the retributive goal of the criminal law is satisfied." Without this awareness, without this guilt, retributive justice remains unsatisfied. *With* guilt, however, we can broach the question of culpability, whether all choices made at all times, under and in all circumstances, and by all people are functionally equivalent, or whether we need to question whether this person could make a rational choice. Beyond agreeing on the necessity of the choice, however, our answers to these questions differ based on our perceptions of our power relative to the offender's and of whether our response is predetermined or whether we also have a choice to make, to kill or stay the hand.[71]

Before we continue, we should note that while the abolitionist discourse is not constructed or dependent on the offender being *not like us*, it is nevertheless more driven by this idea than the retentionist discourse is. There are three basic reasons for this. The first is culpability, which the retentionist discourse treats as irrelevant but which the abolitionist discourse takes seriously. This extends beyond issues of mental maturity and health to personal background and life experiences. Questions of procedural certainty, such as the impact of race, geography, procedural particularities, problems with evidence, and issues of the quality of counsel, are directly related to this concern, because they lead to questions over the system's ability to prevent wrongful executions. The second reason is a general rejection of the notion that the state possesses dominion over life. We can call these two reasons the "initial conditions," the questions of moral certainty and what it means to be morally certain, as discussed in chapter 2. The third reason that the abolitionist discourse is driven by the idea that the offender is *not like us* is that the abolitionist discourse turns strongly away from the offender/victim binary. As we will see, the abolitionist discourse is a multilateral discourse brought to bear on and against ourselves as well as on and against the offender.

I don't want to imply that the abolitionist discourse does not include those who are fundamentally *like us* but made a horrible, tragic decision. Nor do I claim that the abolitionist discourse relies exclusively on a posited distance between the *us* and the *they* — between the normal and the offender. Indeed, in addition to the distance imposed between the normal and the non-normal, this distance may be as slight as that indicated by pity — "I also feel a sense of pity and compassion for one who could be so twisted as to take another person's life"—or as great as that indicated by hatred, expressed ideally in the fashion of the Gospel: "We don't have to like murderers. We can tolerate them behind bars for life without parole while professional counselors work with them to change them from murderers to God-fearing people who pray for forgiveness. Their conversions are as important as any others."[72] Rather, I want to show the prevalence of this distance in the abolitionist conception of the exile. This is not the exile as created by the offense—this is the exile as revealed by the offense, which compels and allows us to look into that offender's past and see where they came from. A willingness to look "beyond the headlines" and at the offender's prior life experience accords with the individualized consideration required under current Eighth Amendment case law. It also fits much better with a detached view of life than with a derivative view.

Staying the Hand

Derivative conceptions of life and of violence hold that one can forfeit their right to life and that said forfeiture gives the state a right to take that life to mark the revocation of that right. This both cedes our autonomy to the offender and cedes the right to life to the state. Detached views, conversely, hold life to be an inherent right independent of the political state. In our context, detached views see the taking of life as God's prerogative, not mankind's: "From the protection of Cain to the conversion of Paul, Scripture testifies that God does not exact life for life."[73]

This highlights an anxiety in the abolitionist discourse—our choice. Choice, in this discourse, is not an event—the idea of staying the hand, like forgiveness and the death penalty itself, is a process-based idea. It is defined less by the decision not to act than by the process through which that decision is made and sustained. If it is sinful to respond to death with death, and if the legality of certain kinds of killing does not redeem inherently sinful acts, then punishing killing with killing is moral hypocrisy, to which we, as normal individuals operating within a system predicated on rationality, choice, and normalcy, have chosen to commit ourselves.[74]

The alternative to this is the process of nonviolence. "When we hold back our hand, rather than use it, we become strong enough to face evil down. We face down our own anger, thus demonstrating that anger and recrimination can be defeated." Staying the hand permits us to regain our agency and recover the power that the offender took from us in the retentionist conception. The process of deciding to stay the hand and then staying it also helps us heal and avoid becoming the evil to which we have to respond. It does so in several ways. First, it allows us to prevent the offender from exercising further power over the direct victim. Following the conviction and sentencing of Jeffrey Allen Thomas, Kitty Irwin, mother of Tara Munsey, Thomas's victim, said that "Tara was full of life . . . and to have her connected to someone put to death is very painful for me and my family"; "We do not wish the memory of our daughter . . . to be tainted with another person's death." Speaking in opposition to the execution of Timothy Bunch, Tong Yi, the brother of Bunch's victim, Su Cha Thomas, wrote, "[The pending execution] does not give our family any joy or satisfaction. It only leaves another death and sadness to his family."[75] Rev. John Price elaborated on this refusal to cede power in describing the murder of his son:

> Our son was our future. His untimely and senseless death obliterated our hopes and made a mockery of our dreams. . . . How can I begin to describe the pain, the grief, the loss of faith that attends the loss of the future. . . . We felt victimized and violated; someone must pay for creating this world of suffering and misery. How else were we expected to respond toward the person who, with malice aforethought, brutally snuffs out the light of our life?
>
> We have struggled and learned to live without hate and the need for vengeance. With the loss of the future, we are determined to preserve the integrity of the past. Our son was a sensitive and kind and generous person. . . . Retaliation in the form of capital punishment . . . would mar and discredit his life and our memories. Vengeance would assure the destruction of the future and the past. It would in fact make our son responsible for committing an act in death that he never engaged in in life.[76]

This passage shows that the abolitionist exile can in fact be a fully normal offender, but even in this instance, it shifts the focus to the survivors and their autonomy and ability to choose how to respond. We need to reclaim our power over the offender to reclaim our sovereignty not only over our response, but also over our pasts and futures.

Proponents of nonviolence argue that nonviolence helps the victimized regain their agency in a second way: the opportunity to unlearn violence. By using violent means to redress wrongs, "we are teaching ourselves the use of violence," contrary to the Gospel, which taught "nonviolence at all levels . . . even teaching love for the enemy, should the point be missed." On this point, abolitionists point to Jesus's last words, and what they were not. Sister Helen Prejean expresses her assessment of this problem simply: "Jesus' last words were: 'Father, forgive them.' Jesus' last words weren't: 'Peter, James, John, all of my disciples, get me some justice for this.'" This is an antivendetta, pro-reconciliation message, an ethic of love that is meant to bring life, "not kill us because we sinned." The message, according to these abolitionists, is that we should respond to violent crime by engaging in the process of forgiveness. This process, they argue, necessarily leads to confronting our own sins and wrongs; Bible study participants discussing the Nickel Mines shootings arrived at the same conclusion.[77]

This is another point at which the trope of the normal individual arises in the abolitionist discourse, once again in the persons of both the offender and the survivors. This point also involves two simultaneous reclamations of power. In addition to asserting our right to our own responses—that is, our right to act as normal individuals capable of acting with intent and in light of foreseeable consequences—by forgoing vengeance, we confer upon the offender the status of a normal individual, insofar as this is possible. This conferral is less a form of interpellation and more a kind of reclamation, a restoration to the status of the normal, of more *like us* than *not*. It is no more than this: a restoration to the status of the normal. This reclamation, even in this limited form, is both an acknowledgment and an invitation. The acknowledgment is that the offender, like us, is capable of "doing the work," as Reverend Vought puts it; it is also an invitation to do that work, a concept discussed more fully in chapter 7. For now, we need to consider two elements of this idea: judgment and rehabilitation.

In expressing their detached view of life, abolitionist churches and clergy make clear that part and parcel of this is the progression "toward greater and greater protection of human life." They argue that because all humans are capable of moral growth, it is incumbent upon survivors to use the least violent means possible to protect themselves and others. We should pursue "restrained and where possible rehabilitative punishment" and reject capital punishment because it does not allow for this reform. At the same time, the idea of judgment that accompanies this urge toward restorative responses to crime and violence is an injunction against judgment, expressed most clearly by Willie Jasper Darden, executed by Florida in 1988: "One of the most profound teaching[s] of Jesus is, 'Judge not that ye be not judged.' I think that before we can hold up the lamp of understanding to others, we [must] hold it up to ourselves." The fact that the Virginia Council of Churches used Darden to make this point underscores the nature and necessity of the challenge. "We are a violent nation," Rev. Douglas Burgoyne observes, "and our death penalty, our unwillingness to commit adequate resources and energy to our prison system, our appalling lack of gun control, and our insensitivity to those who have been victimized only serve to perpetuate our violent instincts." The abolitionist discourse drives our focus away from the offender, back toward the victim and, ultimately, back to ourselves, to our own collective failings.[78]

We can see this drive in the various iterations of the "social profile" of death row inmates, in whom we can see the impact of poverty, drugs, mental illness, and "any of the other myriad problems that criminal psychologists say help create violent criminals." The violence is ours, this discourse holds, not just the offenders'; as such, we bear a share of the responsibility. The progression toward ever-greater respect for life thus begins but does not end with our response to violence. As normal individuals, we are responsible for "the painstaking creation of communities where violence does not flourish: Communities built on . . . acceptance of personal and social responsibility, and constructive response to conflict." As one activist put it, "It is *our* collective morality at stake."[79] As in the retentionist discourse, the abolitionist discourse recognizes and takes seriously the threat that the violent criminal poses to the social order and our collective responsibility for responding to that threat. Unlike the retentionist discourse, however, the abolitionist discourse looks beyond the victim/offender binary and seeks to assess responsibility across society. The difference in approaches may be expressed and fruitfully understood as the expressions of different understandings of redemptive violence.

"They're a lot like you and me. But they're different, too."

A different way of understanding the differences between the abolitionist exile—the revealed exile—and the retentionist exile—the instantiated exile—is in the differences between the tropes of redemptive violence employed in the respective discourses.[80] The corollary to this, as one Bible study participant noted, is that the execution marks the cessation of any responsibility to the offender:

> If a person is in fact killed, there's a sense in which there's a finality of our own moral responsibility as well. But if . . . that person is not killed . . . and that person is still a member of society, we continue to have a kind of moral responsibility for our action. . . . So there's a kind of irony here, that if we keep the death penalty, it changes the nature of our moral relationship in a way that's really almost less problematic and in some ways would be more difficult if they would be retained in society. There are millions of people that are in our jails and the struggle that we have is what our appropriate moral, Christian relationship is with them.[81]

The abolitionist understanding of the exile is partially driven by the question of the extent to which we have a responsibility for or relationship with the exiles; the retentionist discourse has no such component. The retentionist conception of the exile focuses on responsibility to survivors and to ourselves. Each of these exiles presents us with distinct challenges. Each challenge marks the center of our intentions and goals with regard to the use of redemptive violence, and it is incumbent upon us to recognize the operative levels and aims of the different expressions of this violence and the ties to the power exerted over us by the exile, or by us over it.

We can understand these differences by recalling Jonathan Z. Smith's observation that "difference is rarely something simply to be noted; it is, most often, something in which one has a stake." We can easily recognize the myth of redemptive violence in the retentionist exile.[82] When we do, we can see what is at stake within the retentionist discourse: absolution—not of the offender, but of society and the individual survivor. The retentionist exile, the centerpiece of this process of absolution, lies at the intersection of the myth of redemptive violence and bilateral individualism. Both divide the world starkly between good and evil, or between perpetrator and victim, and both are predicated on a need for restoration—either to a pretransgressive state or to a position of power relative to the offender, who had, via the offense, exercised power over the victim. This may seem contradictory at first, given the discourse's understanding that the offender's power over us extends to dictating our response. The power restored, however, is societal, not individual. Although the offense determines our response, we must nevertheless accept our lot and purge evil from the community lest that evil spread and further corrupt. We purge evil by purging the community of the evildoer, who is discerned by his evil deed, which must, in all instances, have been freely and fully chosen. This choice creates the difference on which the retentionist exile is based and because of which the purgative ritual can proceed.

The acute irony here is that the impetus toward societal absolution and renewal is mirrored in practice by a drive toward personal absolution and renewal. That is to say, the purgation of evil at the state level is meant to operate as well on a local level. This idea takes various expressions, such as overcoming our own "poor childhood," being deterred or otherwise consciously refraining from making the evil choice, or in variants of the idea of standing up for what we know to be right. This is at the core of David Garland's argument that the death penalty in America is above all a local institution and phenomenon, as I read it. It is also why the "civilizing process" at work in the evolution of methods of execution is so vital. Describing his uneasiness regarding lethal injection, Alex Kozinski, a federal judge on the Ninth Circuit Court of Appeals, "find[s] it creepy that we pervert the instruments of healing—the needle, the pump, the catheter, F.D.A.-approved drugs—by putting them to such antithetical use. It also bothers me that we mask the most violent act that society can inflict on one of its members with an antiseptic veneer. Isn't death by firing squad, with mutilation and bloodshed, more honest?"[83]

The answer, it turns out, is both yes and no. Shooting would certainly be more honest in terms of the representative and communicative force of the execution, but this honesty would risk both the abandonment of violence as a means to an end and the acceptance of violence as an end itself. This is something that the retentionist discourse seeks to avoid, at times almost self-consciously. The emphasis on enhanced due process, the trumpeting of procedural safeguards, the acknowledgment that we stay the hand far more often than we could or ought, the admission that we need a continual drive to improve the process to achieve as near a perfectibility of execution as we can—all of these declare the need to retain violence as the means to the end, rather than the end in itself.[84] To slide too far away from our own control mechanisms, to engage in naked violence rather than ritualized, cloaked, antiseptic violence, is to run the risk of responding to evil with evil intent, which we go to great lengths to avoid, not only discursively, but also in practice.

This at least partially explains why we hide the execution process from ourselves so thoroughly. Debates over televising executions capture this best of all: would televised executions help or harm? Partisans on both sides are divided; retentionists and abolitionists alike divide over whether televised executions would further their aims or destroy them. Would televised executions alert us to the consequences of crime and help foster a general deterrent effect, or would they merely further desensitize us to violence and death? No one can answer this question. Ronald Reagan once famously quipped that "a simple shot or tranquilizer" was the best way to execute a criminal, because it would "spare the executioner—and by extension the rest of us—anguish." This is true as far as it goes, and correlates roughly with historical justifications for shifting to more modern, humane punishments—the need to spare needless suffering.[85]

There is a second half to this, though—the need to withhold joy and schadenfreude. I was in elementary school when Florida electrocuted Ted Bundy, and I can remember hearing and repeating jokes about people swearing to stop smoking just as soon as Bundy did. There is an element of glee that too often accompanies executions, an element that retentionists recognize as dangerous to their position and generally try to distance themselves from, to say nothing of abolitionists. Hiding our violence allows us to preserve the dignity and integrity of the "just" reaction while helping us resist the temptation to revel in the "God-given," instinctual reaction. Sterility and sobriety helps keep us the mirror of the mob, cool precision and detachment rather than passion.

If we give in to passion, we destroy the element of personal absolution contained in the execution ritual. The fact that the ritual is now more medical than not is immaterial in this sense; the issue is the degree of control that we can exercise over our own violence. The retentionist discourse tries to have it both ways here—it denies that we are all potential killers, which helps amplify the offender's power and drive our predetermined response, while nevertheless acknowledging that all of us are potentially capable of lethal violence, as the question frequently posed to abolitionists—"What if it were someone you loved?"—amply demonstrates. This kind of personal vengeance, how-

(*The Exile* (115

ever, would be a crime of passion, not of calculation, and thus a spontaneous outpouring of violence rather than a controlled discharge. This spontaneous eruption is what we seek to avoid through our procedural mechanisms.

The discomfort with the artifacts of the process of civilizing executions and our need to draw the curtain on the process, metaphorically and literally, arises not only from the stark reminder of the thin line separating life from death, but also our discomfort at our own innate violence. "Curtains have prevented witnesses from seeing botched executions. . . . The curtain was drawn so that witnesses could not observe whatever problem was occurring in the chamber." Drawing the curtains to prevent witnesses from seeing botched executions is merely one of the final means of hiding our violence from ourselves. There are at least four distinct levels of secrecy attendant with the execution itself. First, the states keep lethal injection procedures confidential, shielding them even from lawyers challenging the constitutionality of lethal injection on Eighth Amendment grounds. Second, state governments delegate the development of lethal injection procedures to corrections officials, without any oversight mechanism. Third, witnesses to executions seldom see the entire process; views are deliberately obstructed even during "error-free" procedures. Fourth, "all but two states have maintained complete secrecy surrounding postexecution records and autopsies. The records kept during executions and the autopsies performed after contain data critical to evaluating the painlessness and humaneness of lethal injection executions, but states refuse to release this information." The qualifications and training of execution participants is also secret. Perhaps most tellingly, the three-drug cocktail predominantly used in lethal injections also masks the violence we inflict. Pancurium bromide, the second of the three drugs typically injected, "does not anesthetize the inmate, does not render the inmate unconscious, and does not cause death." What the drug does is paralyze inmates so that they cannot physically signal any pain, minor or excruciating. Preventing the condemned from physically signaling pain assuages us, since it spares us any unease or discomfort in witnessing the pain that we cause.[86]

In the retentionist discourse, the execution, the way in which we exercise violence in order to exorcise it, both assuages and affirms this discomfort. This is why Austin Sarat is correct to assert that in the modern era, it is the procedure by which the body is marked for execution, rather than the body suffering the execution, that is the specific focus of state violence.[87] Unless we can be sure of guilt, and thus of warrant, we run the risk of turning a redemptive, preservative act into an evil itself; unless, meanwhile, the condemned is sufficiently normal, sufficiently *like us* as to be guilty and culpable, we risk destroying the ritual's meaning and power. One could object that the self-conscious restriction of the death penalty to the "worst of the worst" contradicts this argument, which, if carried to its logical conclusion, would demand the execution of all murderers, a position that does not represent the mainstream retentionist discourse. While the narrow point is true, that the demands for the execution of all murderers represents only the retentionist fringe, I argue that this objection, like Kozinski's question, is both true and untrue. It is true that restricting executions to the "worst of the worst" does greatly lessen the number of those for whom execution is a possibility, and thus numbers of executions. At the same time, however, this discourse makes it exquisitely clear that this limitation is a protective designed to sustain and prolong the death penalty. The FBI's 2010 *Crime in the United States* report, for example, has data on nearly thirteen thousand homicides from 2010. It beggars belief that the public would tolerate executions at a rate in excess of five per day; restricting executions to the superlatives within the class, then, is a prolonging and protective measure.

At the same time, however, even the restriction to the "worst of the worst" fails to counteract the process at work. It is, in fact, a direct corollary to the exilic process as described in this chapter, if for no other reason than that the "worst of the worst" are generally defined relative to the details of the particular offense, not the particular offender, who must in all cases be legally sound of mind and thus capable of choosing to kill. He must thus be *like us* in the most meaningful sense. Particularly brutal or heinous crimes thus reinforce this mechanism rather than arguing against it—so long as legal guilt can be determined.[88]

We need guilt to verify that we are policing ourselves, but we also know that we need guilt to exorcise our violence, to displace any moral burden from the decision to execute onto the decision *not* to execute. We need the offender to have acted willfully, in full knowledge of the consequences, as we are forced to do. We need the offender to have become an expression of the very violence and evil that we need to exercise in order to exorcise it. We need the exile to have claimed and exercised the very power over their victim that we seek to recover, however backhandedly, by exercising that power over them, and we need the exile to have willfully, with malice aforethought, committed the violence that we know, and need to demonstrate, that we are so manifestly capable of. This closes the tragic circle: we cannot exile the offender, we cannot obviate our own moral responsibility, unless the offenders are sufficiently like us that we can use them as a target for our own flaws, sins, and evils—we cannot use them, in other words, unless they were like us to begin with. It is legal guilt that affirms that the offender was like us, and so it is legal guilt that gives us warrant to commit the exilic act and that converts the scapegoat into the exile. When all of this is considered and accounted for, it becomes clear that although the act of violence is meant as a means toward an end, its effect is to become an end in itself.[89]

The abolitionist discourse and abolitionist exile, meanwhile, derive from different interpretations of redemptive violence. In contrast to the bilateral individualist element within the retentionist discourse, the abolitionist exile should be thought of in terms of a *multilateral individualism*. This multilateral individualism consists of two chief elements. The first is the rejection of the simple guilty/innocent and perpetrator/victim binaries. Concerns about culpability add a multilateral dimension to each binary. Guilt remains the starting foundation of the exile, but rather than starting and stopping on guilt, this discourse digs further and looks at whether this offender was indeed normal or whether we need to consider external factors in considering our response. This leads to the second feature of this multilateral individualism, which is the onus placed on society to respond as a victimized party—to the crime, to the offender, on behalf of society as the victimized party, on behalf of ourselves, and *to* ourselves, as part of our own development.

The abolitionist discourse makes clear that we are willing to do violence to offenders regardless of their normality. That violence is deemed lesser and, where possible, directed toward the offender's redemption and rehabilitation. The basic form of violence is imprisonment, which the discourse rightfully treats as violence, acknowledging this in attempts to provide alternatives where possible and to separate children from adult populations, for example. At the same time, attempts to expand educational or vocational opportunities for inmates speak to intended target to be redeemed—the offender, not society. This need to believe in the possibility of redemption is one of the primary causes of debate within abolitionist circles over the propriety of life sentences without the possibility of parole. As Marie Deans, one of Virginia's most prominent abolitionists, stated, "I *accept* the 25 years. I would *not* accept life with no possibility of parole. . . . I think that's hand-washing." The idea that staying the hand means accepting some moral responsibility for the imprisoned offenders, who remain part of society, echoes that expressed in the Bible studies: "If . . . that person is not killed . . . and that person is still a member of society, we continue to have a kind of moral responsibility for our action. . . . There are millions of people that are in our jails and the struggle that we have is what our appropriate moral, Christian relationship is with them."[90]

This concern for the offender, arising after the fact but directed toward attempts to rectify problems and circumstances that lead to these types of crimes, is a central element of multilateral individualism, because it incorporates the willful actions of normal individuals at various levels. We should not focus, this discourse holds, solely on the offender and the victim—we also have to look at ourselves and act in accordance with our most distinguishing characteristic, impulse control. We have to take the possibility of redemption seriously and act accordingly. When we take the hit, we must choose not to prolong or fulfill the cycle of violence, but to find a different means by which to exorcise our own evil, our own violence.

The abolitionist exile at the center of this multilateral individualism is a subject capable of redemption, as we will see in chapter 7. This exile is also a call to personal and collective redemption in a fundamentally different way than its retentionist counterpart. While the retentionist exile operates within a world of top-down redemptive violence in which the violent act that redeems society also works to help redeem the individual, the abolitionist exile operates within a world of bottom-up redemptive violence. This is what the activist quoted earlier in the chapter meant when he said that "it is our collective morality at stake." This is why Karla Faye Tucker's execution became the story it did, given her accepted genuine reclamation of herself, why her conversion presented the challenge to our collective morality that her supporters maintained it did. That is why it was important to abolitionists that Lonnie Weeks and Ronald Watkins be remembered as the men they became, rather than the men who had committed the crimes that sent them to death row. That is why William S. Geimer, Ronald Watkins's attorney, wrote to Governor Gilmore seeking clemency for his client and demanding that the governor "ignore [his] lawyers, [his] political advisers, [and] get on [his] knees and seek God in this case."[91]

The basic need in this discourse is first personal, then collective. Our task is to come to terms with our faults rather than displacing them, but our collective morality depends on our willingness to forgo vengeance. Our task, as one minister implored, is to "think constantly of those in prison as if you were prisoners at their side."[92] Rather than using the exile as created by the offense in an attempt to redeem society through violence, we are to use the exile as revealed by the offense to attempt to redeem first ourselves, then society, while leaving the offender the possibility to seek redemption. The next chapters will pursue this multilateral individualistic concept of exile through the legal process by which capital punishment is imposed. The next chapter begins this by taking up the questions raised by Geimer's demand above through a consideration of the role and duties of the contemporary executive. To what extent, if any, should personal faith inform official action, and when should faith dictate inaction? Understanding the scope of the governor's legitimate moral authority will further reveal the operative processes and concepts of redemptive violence and will further inform our understanding of the concepts of exile at work in these discourses.

5)

State governors have direct roles to play in capital punishment administration: we are sworn to uphold the law in our states and we participate in the debate as well. . . . Our moral challenge as a people not only is to continue debating this subject but also to try to make us a better people. We kill too many people and we have far too much violence—far, far too much violence.

(GOV. FRANK KEATING, "The Death Penalty: What's All the Debate About?"

It is easy to support the death penalty in the abstract. . . . But until you sit where I sit [and] . . . be the executioner, you don't know just how difficult that decision can be. . . . How has my faith influenced how I have faced this difficult issue [and other questions of] justice and fairness and morality? I just try to follow my heart and my conscience.

(GOV. GEORGE H. RYAN, "Reflections on the Death Penalty and the Moratorium"

The Bloggers' Exegesis
From the Death Penalty to Taxonomies of the Executive

The ad begins with a sad-eyed elderly gentleman seated right of center against a black background. Stanley Rosenbluth tells viewers about his son Richard and daughter-in-law Becky, who were murdered by Mark Sheppard, the couple's cocaine dealer. When Stanley says that Sheppard shot Richard twice, two gunshots ring out; the unseen gun fires twice more when Stanley continues that Sheppard then shot Becky twice. Tim Kaine, then Virginia's lieutenant governor and Democratic candidate for governor, "voluntarily represented the person who murdered my son," Stanley tells us. Not only that, but Kaine "says that Adolf Hitler doesn't qualify for the death penalty." A similar ad, "Kelly," had aired several days before "Stanley." Kelly Timbrook, widow of police sergeant Rick Timbrook, tells us that Edward Bell, "a drug dealer illegally in this country," ambushed her husband and fatally shot him in the face. When Kaine calls the death penalty "murder," Kelly says, she finds it offensive. How could anyone think that anything less than death would be appropriate, would be justice?[1]

Kelly and Stanley—and Republican gubernatorial candidate and former commonwealth's attorney general Jerry Kilgore—felt that Virginia voters needed to know more about Kaine's opposition to the death penalty. "Stanley" was a haymaker, an aggressive strike with an issue meant to turn voters in the nation's second most active death penalty state against the Democratic candidate in the last weeks of an increasingly competitive race. Within minutes, Virginia's political blogosphere had begun dissecting the ad and debating what it portended for the final three-plus weeks of the campaign. Whatever the eventual outcome, the bloggers agreed that the race's complexion had changed as soon as Hitler was mentioned.

Kaine's response ad began airing quickly. Standing in his office, looking directly into the camera, Kaine says that he wants to "set the record straight" about the conjunction of his faith and his duty. Kaine says that his faith's teaching that life is sacred is the source of his opposition to the death penalty, but tells viewers that he takes his oath of office seriously and "will carry out death sentences handed down by Virginia juries—because that's the law." It was an earnest, understated piece, one that left some viewers wondering whether Kilgore's attack caught Kaine unprepared. Others wondered whether Kaine had the requisite mettle to go on the offensive. Like "Stanley," "Law" was the subject of intense conversation and debate within moments of its airing. Some bloggers commented that Kaine appeared anxious and not in control, while other bloggers lamented that the ad was anything short of a rhetorical daisy-cutter. As one prominent Democratic blogger put it, "Kaine showed up to a knife fight with a note from his mother." Politics is war, they proclaimed, and our candidate is not willing to fight it, even though we've seen this coming for a year, ever since Kilgore's campaign hired Scott Howell as its communications director. They wondered, Why are we not fighting this harder?[2]

Once the initial furor died down, the conversation underwent a remarkable change. The rancor between Kaine's partisans and Kilgore's largely subsided, and the discussion turned to the ad's merits and legitimacy as political discourse. In pondering this question, bloggers and commenters engaged in a detailed exegetical discussion of the biblical rightness of the death penalty and the proper relationship between the individual and the state, as well as, crucially, conceptions of how an individual can and should manage themselves and their duty when running for or holding public office. Is there a divide between the "private" individual and the "public"? Are two sets of morality at work? What is faith, and how does that enter the equation? What good is faith if one is unwilling to act on it?

In addressing these questions, bloggers used the exegetical discussions and their understandings of biblical conceptions of the state to formulate a more immediate question: What is the office and what are the duties of the executive in the contemporary political state? How should we understand the executive, and how should we expect individual executives to balance their "private' and "public' duties? When we parse this exegetical discourse, we can see that the bloggers were actually developing a public taxonomy of the executive. Bloggers and commenters divided over conceptions of the executive, with some favoring a *democratic/republican* or *liberal* executive[3] and others favoring a *ministerial* executive. In this chapter, I focus on the conversations at their peak intensity and peak focus on the religious questions concerning the death penalty. From there, I follow the discussions as they turn from the death penalty to the executive, the final word in the execution process in Virginia. I then show the ways these conversations developed taxonomies of the executive and contrast these taxonomies with Kaine and Kilgore's views on the subject. I conclude by showing how these conceptions of the executive help clarify questions of distance and moral scope, as well as of event- and process-based viewpoints on capital punishment.

The Burst

By 2005, Virginia's political blogosphere—the network of linked conversations focusing primarily on state and local politics—was well established and uniquely robust. As Mark Rozell, professor of public policy at George Mason University, describes it, "There are an unusually large number of pretty sophisticated bloggers in the VA political scene." Others had noticed the new medium's potential: the University of Virginia's Sorensen Institute for Political Leadership hosted seminars titled "Blogging and Democracy in the Commonwealth" in 2005 and 2006. The exegesis occasioned by "Stanley" and the accompanying debates over the ideal executive occurred within this unusually sophisticated network.[4]

Four elements combined to make Virginia's political blogosphere unusually fertile ground for "Stanley" to take root and spread. First, bloggers swiftly agreed on the nature of the story. Second, participants knew the persons involved well and had been observing them for some time. Third, there was a situation of immediate danger, since the election was just over three weeks away and the question of the death penalty was very much a live issue. Finally, all of the evidence needed to assess the ads was online: "Stanley" and "Law" could both be viewed in full online, as could the interview from which the attack at the center of "Stanley" was taken. These four elements—quick agreement, familiarity, danger, and availability of evidence—are the requisite elements for any blog story to go viral. The first flurry of posts showed the immediate agreement on the story's nature, the attack and its impact on the race, and the fact that the campaign suddenly had become far more interesting, for better or for worse. The participants all were familiar with the three principals—Kaine, Kilgore, and now Hitler—and, courtesy of the campaigns and bloggers linking to "Stanley" and Kaine's response, the conversants had the evidence literally at their fingertips.[5]

The third requisite element quickly became the center of the discussion: the element of danger. Commonsense responses in "Stanley"'s wake were that Kaine's campaign had taken a serious blow, perhaps a mortal wound. Two popular metaphors emerged in this early phase of the discussion. Old Zach, a blogger at *Sic Semper Tyrannis* (*SST*), a popular collaborative conservative blog taking its name from Virginia's state motto, proclaimed that Kaine's campaign was now on "death row." Old Zach saw "Stanley" in terms of a metaphor of conveyance, one that was now "the driving issue of the campaign." This is perfectly acceptable, Old Zach wrote, because in Virginia, the executive has unilateral power to empty death row or declare a moratorium on executions if they choose. It is thus important that voters know more about Kaine's beliefs and weigh them against his professed unwillingness to act on them. *Richmond Magazine* wondered whether "Stanley" had "put Kaine on a swift boat to defeat," employing a second metaphor of conveyance that was sure to remind readers of the attacks on 2004 Democratic presidential candidate John Kerry.[6]

Implicit in the Swift Boat analogies was the idea that Kaine was either a "New England liberal" or someone who was simply too weak to stand up for himself and take the gloves off. Kaine's supporters tended toward the latter, wanting more of a fight. The former charge, though, is intriguing because of its locative effects within the political discourse. Defending the "Stanley" ad, Scott Howell was quick to point out that Kaine was a "Harvard-educated liberal activist." The negative lineage ascribed to Kaine extended backward to Michael Dukakis, the former Massachusetts governor and 1988 Democratic presidential candidate whose campaign was fatally injured when he could not handle the death penalty issue, either during the televised presidential debates or in response to the infamous Willie Horton ad. Calling Kaine a "Harvard-educated liberal activist" accomplishes several other rhetorical effects. It reinforces Kaine's "outsider" status as someone who is not native to the state, while the geographic locator—New England—resonates with another meme quietly running through some conservative blogs, the idea of "Vermont values," shorthand for the claim that Kaine supported gay marriage or civil unions. Referring to Kaine as possessing "Vermont values," of course, also linked the candidate to the controversial then-head of the Democratic National Committee, former Vermont governor Howard Dean.[7]

Bloggers also quickly grasped that "Stanley" was potentially dangerous to Kilgore, too. They read the ad as a huge gamble, one that could provoke a backlash against the candidate from any three different directions. First, there was the reference to Hitler, which could cut either way, they wrote. Indeed, the backlash against the ad, both in the media and in popular opinion, began in part with accusations of trivializing the Holocaust and unfairly "tar[ring] a decent man adhering to the tenets of his Catholic faith." The ad also seemed desperate, in that Kilgore went for the heaviest weapon in his rhetorical arsenal at the expense of trying to make his point by taking on a local and potentially less needlessly inflammatory example, such as the 2002 Beltway Sniper killings. In October 2002, John Allen Muhammad and Lee Boyd Malvo went on a three-week killing spree in Maryland, DC, and Virginia, killing eleven and wounding six others. They were caught on October 24, 2002, and tried for capital murder in Virginia and Maryland. Malvo received six consecutive life sentences for his role in the killings; Muhammad was executed by Virginia on November 10, 2009. Commenters noted that the Kilgore campaign could have made the same point without the controversy by shifting the discussion to the snipers rather than going straight to Hitler.[8]

Conservative blogs across the country, meanwhile, bemoaned the Kilgore campaign trying to sink itself via the ad. One blog, entitled *Crush Liberalism*, pointed to the ad as the moment that the Kilgore campaign "rendered [its] own point of view impotent. No one likes or takes seriously people who gratuitously invoke Hitler's name for political points." Other conservative blogs griped that the campaign "deserved to lose" for "Godwin[ning its] own message." Godwin's Law states that as an online discussion develops, the probability of one party referencing the Nazis approaches 1. The party who does so first is generally understood to have lost the argument. Conservatives complained that by going straight to Hitler, Kilgore had set himself up to lose the argument. Perhaps coincidentally, Kilgore lost his lead in the polls for the first time in the days following the "Stanley" ad.[9]

A second element of the backlash developed over the ad's timing: it aired on Yom Kippur, the holiest day on the Jewish calendar. After a brief lull in which the holiday was celebrated, Jewish leaders began attacking "Stanley," calling the ad "demeaning and morally repugnant." Other leaders called the ad inappropriate and insensitive and criticized the Kilgore campaign for cheapening the debate over the death penalty while simultaneously trivializing the Holocaust by exaggerating the similarities between those accused of committing capital crimes in Virginia and the crimes of the Nazis, while still others claimed that the ad was more offensive because of its timing.[10]

The third element of the backlash was the ad's implication that someone who had defended those convicted of murder during the appellate processes was thereby unfit for executive office, an assertion that Kilgore repeated on several occasions.[11] Bloggers debated this point in considering whether Kaine's activities as a lawyer would reasonably affect his ability to carry out his duties as governor and while debating the legitimate extent to which personal faith can influence public policy, questions to which we will return. The question at the root of all of these matters, the question without which the rest of the discussions do not make sense, is the question of sincerity. Was/is the candidate's faith sincere, or was/is it just a part of a public persona designed to make them more palatable to voters?

The Candidate as Artful Zealot

Another campaign attack that Kilgore leveled at Kaine is a variant on a recurring theme in American political discourse: Kaine's religiosity was fake, something that he drummed up to trot out to voters because it was an election year. Kaine's opposition to the death penalty was the focal point of such attacks, particularly his position that though he personally opposed the death penalty, he would carry out the law as governor. Some read this as a warning that Kaine's faith was not sincere or that it was perhaps an attempt to curry favor with voters, to say what needed to be said in a way that would be accepted solely to win office. For these observers, Kaine's position amounted to nothing more than a cynical political inoculation in the pursuit of power. While this opinion was not universally held among the bloggers opposing Kaine, there was a general sense of unease at the prospect of a man who, as they saw it, was willing to turn his back on his faith once in office.[12]

These bloggers were concerned that Kaine was an artful zealot. As Robert Jewett and John Shelton Lawrence explain, artful zeal is motivated by the desire for power, particularly political power. The artful zealot dissembles and is overly demonstrative and ostentatious as to the depths of their convictions. These convictions can be sincere, but the artful zealot displays them calculatedly, so that no observer can miss them. The prototypical artful zealot was Jehu, the Old Testament warrior-king who sought to ensure that the shapers of public opinion saw how dedicated he was to the cause of Yahweh, so that they would then convince the people that Jehu's usurpation of the throne was somehow divinely ordered rather than a simple military coup. Questioning whether someone is an artful zealot does not necessarily mean that you question the sincerity of their belief; on the contrary, artful zeal may be the product of a sincerely held belief that the agent is working on behalf of the divine. The distinction between artful zeal pursuant to power and sincerely held belief is seen in actions: "Only the discrepancies between ideology and behavior offer a glimpse of the real grounding of the system — not in the divine will but in the will to personal power."[13]

A blog entry from October 11 — just after the "Stanley" ad was released — captures this questioning well. Old Zach begins by noting that Kaine had spent his adult life working against the death penalty and seeking its abolition in Virginia. As a candidate for governor, Zach says, Kaine admits he would prefer that the state not have the death penalty. With "Stanley" apparently fresh in mind, Old Zach continues that Kaine "has stated his personal belief that not even heinous criminals like Adolf Hitler should be executed." During the gubernatorial debate that had taken place a few days prior, Kaine protested against accusations that he was walking back from his convictions in order to be elected. Kaine, Old Zach said, would like us to believe that his lifetime of work against the death penalty should be overlooked, or at least not considered materially relevant, once he takes on his new job title. Old Zach saw two possibilities: either Kaine doesn't actually possess the faith he claims and is lying to project an ostentatious but false piety, or Kaine believes what he says and thus clearly should be called out for trying to walk away from his convictions in order to become more electable. Old Zach believed that the evidence supported the latter.[14]

This is a clear accusation of artful zeal. Old Zach was willing to believe that Kaine's faith was genuine. Where Kaine errs, he says, is in the artful zealot's dissembling for the sake of power. Kaine understands that Virginia is a solidly pro–capital punishment state; thus if he wants to be elected, he has to convince voters that his beliefs will not interfere with the death penalty. In a post the next day, Old Zach pushes the point further, noting that in Virginia, the executive enjoys what Sister Helen Prejean called the "last vestige of the 'divine right of kings,'"[15] sole power over commutations and pardons. There are four clemency processes in death penalty states. In four states — Georgia, Nebraska, Nevada, and Utah — a board or other advisory group decides clemency petitions. In nine states — Alabama, Arkansas, Indiana, Kansas, Maryland, Missouri, Montana, New Hampshire, and Ohio — a board or advisory group can send the governor a nonbinding clemency recommendation. Eight states — Arizona, Delaware, Florida, Idaho, Louisiana, Oklahoma, Pennsylvania, and Texas — require a recommendation of clemency from a board or advisory group before the governor can act. Virginia belongs to the largest group of states — California, Colorado, Kentucky, Mississippi, New Mexico, North Carolina, Oregon, South Carolina, South Dakota, Tennessee, Virginia, Washington, and Wyoming—in which the governor has sole authority in such matters. Kaine thus would have the power to single-handedly bring the death penalty machine to a halt in Virginia for the duration of his term.[16]

The question, for those pondering whether Kaine was an artful zealot, was twofold. First, would he use his constitutional authority to empty death row? If he does, then he has lied to the voters in pursuit of office. If he does not, then the second question becomes operative: does he truly hold the moral and religious convictions that he claims if he chooses not to act on them? With this question now on the table, the bloggers and commenters turned their attention to the question of whether or not the death penalty is biblically valid, as Kilgore claimed and Kaine disputed. This exegesis never strayed far from the question of the executive's legitimate exercise of authority. Indeed, parsing the exegesis helps clarify and define the question further.[17]

The Exegesis Reconciling Romans and Matthew

One of the most remarkable attributes of this exegesis was its focus. While other exegetical considerations of the death penalty can sprawl over hundreds of different biblical texts, these conversations focused primarily on three: Matthew 5, Romans 2, and Romans 13. Given the citations, it is hardly surprising that the discussion slanted heavily toward utilizing the exegesis to articulate a theory of the state and of the proper relationship of man to God via the state and via law, and that it turns toward different theories of the executive per se, that is, to different understandings of the role and obligations of the executive in a modern democratic state. We should bear in mind James Megivern's warning regarding problems of interpretation and application of biblical texts when they are turned to for literal support: "There is nothing so fruitless as wrangling over the meaning of the Bible when the real object of debate should be the presuppositions brought to its interpretation." I want to examine these presuppositions and then systematize and clarify them.[18]

To begin with a problem of language, I do not mean to approach the presuppositions brought to the debate by treating them as a problem of eisegesis, that is, committing the interpretive fallacy of reading a text, particularly a biblical text, in such a way as to find that it says exactly what you wanted it to. This kind of textual analysis for affirmation rather than information is part of what gives rise to the dictum that biblical literalism is flawed as an analytical approach because virtually any position or argument can be supported by a text carefully selected for the specific purpose of affirming a position. Both sides in these conversations did swap veiled and explicit accusations of eisegesis, but I have no interest in impugning the participants' motives. These conversations clearly convey that these participants were earnest individuals honestly defending and explaining their positions and beliefs. They were familiar with each other, they knew each other's established positions and orientations, which both made it easier for them to engage in the discussion seriously and makes it easier to read these conversations and see people less interested in convincing others than in being heard. We have to broach the language question because one of the passages the commenters discussed most intently, Romans 13, means very different things to different people, depending on how we understand a single word: *sword*.[19]

One of the biblical texts most widely cited in defense of the death penalty, Romans 13:1-4 has been freighted with a variety of meanings over the centuries, from sanctioning the punitive function of the state to demanding the use of capital punishment:[20]

> Let every person be subject to the governing authorities; for there is no authority except from God, and those authorities that exist have been instituted by God. Therefore whoever resists authority resists what God has appointed, and those who resist will incur judgment. For rulers are not a terror to good conduct, but to bad. Do you wish to have no fear of the authority? Then do what is good, and you will receive its approval; for it is God's servant for your good. But if you do what is wrong, you should be afraid, for the authority does not bear the sword in vain! It is the servant of God to execute wrath on the wrongdoer.

One problem immediately arises from this rendering of the passage (NRSV). The King James Version of Romans 13:4 has "execute" in italics, signifying that the word does not appear in the original Greek text. By rendering the verse "a revenger to *execute* wrath upon him that doeth evil," the translators have indicated that they have filled in a verb in order to make the sentence make sense in English. While some commentators, such as the Liberty Bible Commentary, argue that the word "execute" signifies a clear New Testament acceptance of capital punishment, they must reconcile this claim with the divergent meanings of *execute*. In asserting that "the hands of good government should never be so tied that they cannot execute good judgment and the wrath of God upon those who do evil," the linguistic problem is clear, and it is unreasonable to argue against the second meaning of execute as it is employed in the analysis of the verse, as meaning "to carry out," not literally to take life.[21]

The same problem arises with verse 4's sword. Retentionist theologians understand this as a sign that Paul expressed his support for capital punishment; why else would the sign of authority be a sword, a weapon used to execute? Hans Mast, a blogger and Beachy Mennonite who describes himself as "an extremely conservative Christian," raised this point early in the discussion: "I believe in the New Testament scripture of Romans 13 where it says that the 'rulers' are 'ministers of God' to 'execute wrath' on the 'evildoers' with the 'sword' which they 'don't bear in vain.'" 'Jon' takes up the same theme, asking rhetorically whether anyone could demonstrate "that the government does *not* have the responsibility of wielding the sword against wrongdoers," and wondering what manner of punishment we should understand the sword to symbolize. Though the linguistic problems associated with "sword" went unchallenged in this discussion, they are worth considering before proceeding.[22]

The Greek word in Romans 13:4 is *machaira*, a short sword worn at the belt, more properly translated as "dirk" or "dagger." Officers accompanying tax collectors on their rounds wore the *machaira*. The executioner's sword was the *rhomphaia*, a long, broad cutlass used for decapitation. Annotations suggesting that the *rhomphaia* is the sword in verse 4 do not replicate the original text faithfully and gloss over the fact that Paul was writing in the aftermath of one tax revolt amid rumors of another such revolt brewing: not for nothing does Paul continue on to remind believers that they are obliged to pay their taxes.[23]

Although he does not question the misappropriation of "sword," Jeff Baker does intuit that this passage has more to do with persecution and less with killing as judicial punishment. Baker's take on Romans 13, given the audience, he says, is that governmental persecution is to be expected. We should focus on the way the persecution and execution of Jesus helped bring about the possibility of redemption. Given the centrality of this imperial execution to the nascent faith, Baker wonders why we should conclude that Paul would be advising the young church that the government had the legitimate authority to put them to death as well. Further, if the authorities act on God's behalf, then would Mast—or Paul—suggest that "Christians being persecuted in China today are being justly persecuted by those sanctioned by God?" Baker's comments reveal that his conception of Jesus is what Mark Lewis Taylor referred to as the adversarial Jesus, who stands in opposition to state power. For Baker, the relevant question is whether there was an asterisk attached to "Thou shalt not kill" in the Ten Commandments, an exemption for legal authorities. Unless someone can show that he is misinterpreting when he says "that Christ really was against men killing men," then Baker sees no reason to differentiate between prohibitions against individual killing or against state killing.[24]

This brings us back to the question of distance, as we discussed in chapter 2. Where Baker seems to accept the idea that in a democratic state, the scope of moral action permitted the individual and the state are essentially the same, Mast and "Jon" seem to agree with Justice Scalia in differentiating between the two, according the state a scope of moral action greater than that permitted the individual. Where Baker supports his position using injunctions against judging others or taking life, Mast and "Jon" are quick to point out that these restrict individuals, not governments, which necessarily have a greater scope of morally permissible action. Above all, Mast notes, we need to keep in mind that it is a jury, not an individual, that sentences someone to death, and juries are not simply groups of individuals, but arms of the state; they are "governmental bod[ies]." This comment raises two questions, both of which operate here and in the broader conversation. The first is a question of the composition of the *state* at each stage of the capital process, and where the borders between the individual and the state are to be found. The second is the question of those on whom the state's (legitimate) judgment falls.[25]

Mast answers the first using an unlikely source, Proverbs: "In the multitude of councilors, there is safety." Mast here reasons that because the jury is not a single fallible individual but a group of individuals—each equally well-informed, having participated in the trial process, each with access to the evidence presented at trial, and each, presumably, having some idea what the law demands by way of evidentiary concerns—then their collective strengths should offset individual weaknesses. This is a problematic image of the jury, not least because evidence indicates that juries, however well-intentioned and earnest, simply are not given the tools with which to function with the level of wisdom implied here. More directly, Mast correctly views juries as appendages of the state. At some point during voir dire, the individual has ceased to be an individual and has become essentially an *office*, carrying out an obligation to the state described and circumscribed within specific legal bounds. We will see below why this recognition of the transfer of roles—and thus of obligations—does not carry over to Mast's or "Jon"'s conception of the executive.[26]

Mast's assessment of the jury raises a second question: on whom does judgment fall? On the evildoer. At first blush, this is a natural reaction; after all, few would argue that premeditated murder, the generally if incorrectly understood threshold for incurring a capital charge, is less than an evil action. Fewer still would argue that a murder committed alongside a second felony—the circumstance that differentiates capital from first-degree murder in Virginia—is less than evil. What, then, is problematic about calling one who commits evil an evildoer? An essay written by Stanley and Phyllis Rosenbluth cuts straight to this point: "Accidental Death Is Fate, Murder Is Pure Evil."[27]

We can raise two concerns here. The first, and most argumentative, is that such a characterization is a means of defining a person by an action he has committed, while admitting nothing else, not even the possibility of a future reformation or rehabilitation. One need not advocate turning killers loose on the streets at the first hint that they have "learned their lesson" in order to raise this objection. One likewise need not advocate a "kill 'em all and let God sort 'em out" approach to criminal justice to rejoin that rehabilitation is not an explicit goal of the criminal justice system, which has come to have a definitively retributive focus. Standing on this objection may well produce nothing more than accusations of missing the point, which in this case could be articulated that we cannot judge based on what the person might become, but are limited to judging them based on what they have done.[28]

The second objection to this might be the objection that Baker tried to raise by citing Pauline injunctions and the Sermon on the Mount's prohibitions against judging others. Baker's point in raising this objection is not that we are prohibited from exercising any judgment whatsoever, that we lack completely the power to condemn, as is often suggested by retentionists arguing against these ideas, but that we lack the capacity to correctly characterize individuals, even murderers, in such black-and-white terms.[29]

This argumentation recalls the strain of American Christianity known as *zealous nationalism*, the strain of the faith that "seeks to redeem the world by destroying enemies," whereas its counterpart, *prophetic realism*, "seeks to redeem the world . . . by impartial justice that claims no favored status." Zealous nationalism and prophetic realism each assume that sin is universal and that it is willful; they differ in their convictions about how to deal with it. In asserting the government's responsibility to punish the evildoer, commenters express the zealous nationalist strain of American religion, which maintains that evil people must be destroyed. At the same time, zealous nationalism holds that those so called to destroy the evildoers do not have blood on their hands, because their task was ordained. They were called to their task, invested with the responsibility for carrying it out, and are thus morally indemnified against any qualms that could be raised against their actions. The perception of the distinction between individual actions and actions undertaken by individuals or institutions possessing the divine mandate partially accounts for the distinction that Mast and "Jon" draw between Romans 2 and Romans 13.[30]

This fundamentally deontological approach to punishment typifies what linguist George Lakoff termed "Strict Father morality." This categorization of a complex of metaphors for morality makes four assumptions: that individuals cannot know what is in the best interests of themselves and their community, and thus cannot act accordingly; that those in authority act in the best interests of those subject to their authority; that those in authority do know what is in the best interest of the individual and the community; and that the community recognizes that the authorities are responsible for the well-being of the individual and of the community. Two objections need to be raised here. First, the authority in question must be perceived as legitimate; the Strict Father model takes this legitimacy as a given, but an acknowledgment of the legitimacy of the authority is necessary before the moral imperative to punish, which this model contains, can be accepted. Second, the first characteristic—that individuals cannot know what is in their own moral best interest—should be contested, both from within the framework of the model and from without. From within, the argument that individuals cannot know what is in their own moral best interest does not stand up to the concept of authority per se. If the authorities are legitimate and know what is in the best interest of the individual and the community, then the individual need only adhere to the law to know—if not to understand—what is in their best interest.[31]

From without, this criterion is subject to criticism from a natural law perspective. Where Mast and "Jon" would likely agree with Lakoff's model is in the concept of Moral Strength, which divides the world into good and evil and holds that doing good—acting morally—is strength, while doing evil is weakness. This moral strength must be exercised. It cannot be relied on to simply exist; like forgiveness, one must cultivate moral strength through self-discipline and self-denial. Paralleling the ideals of zealous nationalism, Strict Father morality sees evil as a very real force that one can fight only by seeking its destruction. Those who act immorally, according to this model, are evildoers and cannot be dealt with by any means short of destruction. While this line is seldom carried through, this argument is visible with regard to the murderer, an evildoer, our response to whom can only be to destroy them. This understanding of moral action works on a debt-payment principle and demands reciprocity. Taking the murderer's life to balance the moral books is the only legitimate response. This is what supports the idea that executing murderers is not an *option* available to the authority, but is in fact the authority's *responsibility*.[32]

We can reach this conclusion via a parallel route, one that is equally vital to the arguments being made in this discussion. If moral strength is a virtue that needs to be cultivated and practiced, then the individual is dependent on the authorities—ecclesiastical or secular—in order to have a standard toward which to aim. Within the context of an exegetical discourse, the law can be understood to have three uses: civil, theological, and educational. The civil use of the law constrains behavior with the threat of divine punishment. At some point, since it is understood that God will demand a moral accounting and "will repay according to each one's deeds," the individual is constrained to act accordingly and cultivate the moral strength necessary to do right consistently. The theological use condemns sinners for their violation, ensuring both the humility of the sinner and the integrity of the law. This condemnation avenges the law and, by balancing the moral books, restores the law's integrity. Finally, the educational use of the law serves as an exemplar, one that deters bad behavior and helps guide the development of habitual good behavior. This reinforces a unity between public and private morality and helps individuals bring their behavior more in line with the law in private—where the law's capacity to punish transgressions is low or absent—as well as in public, where law does have that capacity. The metaphoric construct thus parallels traditional Protestant understandings of natural (or moral) law.[33]

This is how the various participants reconcile the messages of Matthew 5 and Romans. Baker sees no conflict between the two because the injunctions against levying judgment in Romans 2 correspond with injunctions against the same in Matthew 5. "Jon" and Mast agree, though for a different reason. Where Baker sees a contradiction between injunctions against judgment and the symbol of the authority's sword, Mast and "Jon" demur, pointing out that as they understand it, the individual and the state have different ordained responsibilities and thus different scopes of morally permissible action. James Young, who blogged as Skeptical Observor, and I.Publius bring natural law language into the discussion. Young accuses other discussants of hypocrisy in criticizing Christians whose faith motivates them to take political action against abortion and who support the death penalty while "telling them what controlling Christian teaching is on the subject." I.Publius invokes Strict Father morality as well as natural law when he comments that "God is a just God, and demands payment for sins." Likewise, why would Paul have instructed the church to obey earthly authorities, as he did in the letter to the Romans, unless there are "proper consequences" for disobedience? The ideas of controlling teaching and of the propriety of consequences pull Strict Father and natural law approaches together, and, in the context of an increasingly acrimonious debate over the propriety of the death penalty within the campaign, form the basis for the natural law critique of the executive within a representative democracy.[34]

Models of the Executive

One of "Stanley"'s most controversial elements was its implication that capital defendants and postconviction appellants are not entitled to a defense. This implication arose from Rosenbluth's comments that voters cannot trust Kaine because he "voluntarily represented" Mark Sheppard. Kilgore disputed that this was implied, but this was not enough to satisfy even some of his supporters. Young denied that the ad implied this, saying the ad's basis was not Kaine's conduct but comments he had made about the death penalty. Nevertheless, Young took issue with the idea, saying that it was "illegitimate to attack an attorney for representing a death-row inmate." Old Zach, while elaborating on the problems he saw with Kaine's position, was also troubled by the ad's "impl[ication] that murderers are not to be defended." Old Zach was not positive that the ad made such a claim, but it came close enough for discomfort.[35]

The press was less measured in its response. Typical responses included editorials that ran in the *Washington Post*, which rejected the "loathsome" suggestion "that Mr. Kaine . . . is morally suspect for having served as a court-appointed attorney representing a death row inmate a decade ago." The *Roanoke Times* editorialized against the "reprehensible" demagoguery of the ad, which the editorial claimed "betrays a callous disregard . . . for the rule of law that as state attorney general [Kilgore] once took an oath to protect and defend."[36]

Still, the possibility that an "activist lawyer" would be elected governor had some commentators troubled, particularly because Kaine asserted that he would uphold the law despite his belief that the death penalty is wrong. These commentators generally expressed a willingness to disagree substantively over the issue but found themselves troubled by Kaine's insistence that, as they saw it, his beliefs would take a backseat to his ambitions, that his actions would not follow from his beliefs. They saw a divide between the "private" Kaine and the "public" Kaine and tried to reconcile the two. That they could not do so was disconcerting and made them mistrustful of the candidate's claims.

It would be easier to accept Kaine's position, they blogged, if it were clear that he intended to follow through on his beliefs, to act unilaterally to halt the machinery of death in Virginia. Utilizing natural law concepts to express their concern, they criticized this apparent disjunction between public and private morality. Here the bloggers followed Kilgore's lead in questioning how we could believe that an "activist" who had spent his adult life working against the death penalty would suddenly turn around and actively engage in upholding that very process. This position, they declared, is neither tenable nor credible. Rather, because he claims that his faith is the basis of his opposition, he should be willing to act on that conviction as governor and do everything in his power to prevent executions while he is in office. These commentators "would applaud him for that principled stand" or "would respect him a great deal more if he simply stood behind his beliefs and indicated that he would not execute criminals if he were Governor." The problem lay in the dissonance created by claiming that you would not act on your religious beliefs in office. Either the beliefs are insincere and the candidate is the artful zealot, cynically trying to curry favor with voters, or the candidate is too cowardly to stand up for his beliefs. Either scenario, these bloggers posit, is unacceptable in an executive, because candidates willing to divide their moral beliefs into "public" and "private" must be considered inherently immoral according to both Strict Father morality and natural law. Moreover, these bloggers claimed to have a hard time seeing him as anything more than a cipher.[37]

Kaine's supporters and others who took exception to the "Stanley" ad rejected both premises. Insisting that the governor follow his beliefs at the expense of the law, they said, is tantamount to insisting that he disregard his duty to carry out the law. Governors, after all, do not have the ability to pick and choose which laws they will follow. For Kaine to assert that he would not interfere with the legal process except in cases of questions of innocence, they said, is perfectly legitimate. This is precisely the problem, Kaine's opponents were quick to point out, in a state like Virginia, where the governor can do away with capital punishment for the duration of his term against the expressed wishes both of the populace and of the juries in those cases, and can do so perfectly in concert with the law by declaring a moratorium or by issuing either individual or blanket clemencies. This contrast in approaches to clemency and the questions of when and how the officeholder's faith is applicable in carrying out his duties reveal that the two sides are arguing from different conceptual presuppositions. Each side articulates and advocates a different type of ideal executive.[38]

The first of these is the *democratic/republican* or *liberal* executive. This executive is fundamentally limited in her capacity to act, bound by the state's laws and constitution, as interpreted by the state's judicial branch, and constrained to work with the legislature in most things, rather than apart from it. Some actions are fully within the executive's purview, such as clemency and pardoning, but for the most part this executive is considered essentially a "superlegislator" and the implementer of legislative will. This executive works with the legislature to see her legislative agenda through, exercising her bully pulpit to induce the public to pressure the legislature to overcome legislative recalcitrance, and overseeing the management of the state's government. Acting in direct contravention of the law is forbidden or immoral—tacitly in some cases, explicitly in others. Variously termed "legislating" or "imposing" their beliefs on the populace, this circumvention of or cynical manipulation of the law contrary to its apparent intent is not to be done, except perhaps in cases of extreme moral peril.

This democratic/republican executive is the model that Kaine's supporters had in mind when they defended his position on capital punishment. "Thomas Jefferson" commented that neither Kaine nor Kilgore had given any indication that they intended to ignore the laws to which they held personal objections. In a different post, he commented that there was equally little reason to believe that Kilgore would test the judiciary by trying to ban abortion or that Kaine would "usurp the legislature's authority" by abusing his clemency powers. It is incumbent upon this executive to recognize the limitations of her vision and her ability to bring that vision to fruition. The ability to do this is the mark of successful leadership: "The constant trial of leadership is being able to recognize when your most deeply-held beliefs are not universalizable or even very popular and should consequently be ignored, or when they're such a fundament[al] right that, well, damn the torpedoes — full speed ahead." Structural checks and balances dictate this as the test of leadership, as does the order of priorities against which the liberal executive must weigh decisions. The executive's first duty, one commenter argued, is to the state's constitution, followed by her constituents, and, finally, their own beliefs. When personal beliefs conflict with obligations to constituents, liberal executives should act in deference to constituent's wishes rather than taking advantage of the opportunity to impose or "legislate" their beliefs.[39]

This conception of the executive explains two curious lines of argument taken by Kaine's defenders in the aftermath of the "Stanley" ad. The first of these was that attacks on the candidate's faith are somehow out of bounds, are sufficiently illegitimate as to amount to immoral discourse when they are raised. Anyone familiar with the stereotypes of American political discourse will immediately raise an eyebrow at this claim, if only because the reverse is so often presented as taken for granted — that the Democrats are assumed to be the party hostile to faith. One blogger summed up the feelings of many when he commented that Kaine's opposition to the death penalty is rooted in his "strong Christian faith, which *should* be a non-issue." Leaving aside questions of consistency, this can be so only from within the context of the democratic/republican conception of the executive, in which the governor is expected to implement legitimate laws even when they conflict with his beliefs. Without this assumed division, the above statement has to be read as nonsensical. Because of this assumed division, Kaine supporters and other interested observers sharing this understanding of the executive were able to render the attacks against Kaine's position as aspersions cast on his faith, rather than policy, which they took to be beyond the pale.[40]

A second curious element in the discussions involved an inordinate number of Kaine's supporters seemingly backing away from his involvement in capital cases. While trying to refute "Stanley"'s implication that capital defendants and postconviction appellants are not entitled to representation, Kaine's supporters legitimized at least the effectiveness of the attack. To be sure, they took seemingly every opportunity to complain about the illegitimacy of the implication, but, curiously, responded as frequently with at least a hint of apology. In fact, few bloggers pointed out that Kaine was doing his court-appointed duty in ways that did not register as apologetic. Others defended Kaine by arguing that he would have gone to jail had he not taken the case, or by pointing out that "he was a state appointed [*sic*] lawyer, so [taking the case was] really not his choice." They used duty to shield their candidate from accusations of "activism."[41]

By qualifying their support for Kaine on that point, the commenters distanced themselves from those instances. By creating distance, they underscored the legitimacy of the attack in terms of reception. Backing away from the actions, in other words, appeared to indicate that they expected sufficient numbers of people to agree with the implication that they felt the need to rhetorically mitigate the claim. This implicitly questions the candidate's beliefs, insofar as the timbre of the comments indicates that the bloggers accepted that Kaine simultaneously held those beliefs and, absent compulsion, would refrain from acting on them in any professional capacity. Nevertheless, the implications of such defenses, though apologetic, fit within the framework of the liberal executive. The operative concept is that the candidate has demonstrated in a prior professional capacity an understanding of his obligations under the law and has acted accordingly. It follows, then, that he should be taken at his word when he claims that he will abide by the legal and constitutional constraints on his office.

This point is clearer in defenses that do not have an air of apology, all of which recapitulate the essence of "Thomas Jefferson"'s comment referenced above, that personal distaste for a law is insufficient reason to act contrary to that law. Defense attorneys, one commenter noted, defend criminal clients not on moral grounds, but in order to force the prosecution to do a better job of demonstrating guilt beyond a reasonable doubt. They are the protectors of due process, performing a public service for which they are remunerated so poorly in proportion to their effort that one blogger claimed that "most lawyers who represent these defendants [sic] consider the work to be pro-bono, the pay is so bad." One blogger declared that "even if Tim Kaine met with [Mark] Sheppard several times, was his primary attorney, and had him acquitted of all charges, Kilgore's ad would still be [reprehensible]. No one should be attacked for providing legal defense for someone charged with a crime, it is a right of the accused and somebody has to do it."[42]

This solidifies the conception of the democratic/republican executive. Characterizing the candidate's previous professional conduct in this way legitimates "activist" behavior so long as it is channeled through established, legitimate paths. There is thus little reason to question this attribute as a legitimate trait of the executive. Certainly, the above does not mean that these curiosities are explainable only in these terms, that they were solely products of a particular understanding of the executive. It would be blinking reality not to recognize the partisan territoriality, the need to defend "my candidate" against "illegitimate" attacks, when the illegitimacy in question may well be only the attack rather than the content of said attack. That said and accounted for, the particular ways these conflicts were resolved derives from the idealized conception of the liberal executive.

This was the conception of the executive that both Kaine and Kilgore articulated. Each of them spoke in terms of the three basic elements of the democratic/republican executive: that this executive has the limited capacity to act within the bounds prescribed by the judiciary and in cooperation with the legislature; that he transitions between acting as a "superlegislator" and the implementer of legislative will; and that, because the executive is constrained in the scope of his action, he cannot legitimately impose his beliefs outside accepted legitimate channels. When I contacted Kilgore in the fall of 2008, he invited me to chat with him in his Richmond law office, where we sat in an impressive conference room with a tremendous view of downtown Richmond. A gracious host, Kilgore spent some time pointing out various local and historical landmarks and making sure I was comfortable repeatedly through our long conversation, during which he clarified what he meant when he referred to Kaine as an "activist" as a way of explaining what the ideal executive should look like. The executive should be an activist, but in order to assess whether that appellation is positive or negative, "you've got to look at where the activism is taking you. . . . The desired result is what you've got to look at." With that caveat, Kilgore's ideal executive is an aggressive conservative activist—"if you can put those two together—conservative and activist"—who works with the legislature to enact his legislative vision. The distance between the executive and the legislature, for Kilgore, is fairly minimal. He believes that the executive "has become so much a part of the legislature, whether at the federal level or at the state level, that you've basically been molded into one of the chief legislators." The executive should use his bully pulpit to try to pressure the legislature to enact his legislative agenda, but this capacity to act for the most part ends with persuasion and deal making.[43]

For all of the closeness Kilgore sees between the legislature and the executive, there is a clear distance between the executive and the judiciary, which he explains using abortion and the death penalty. Kilgore describes himself as someone who is pro-life and "believe[s] in protecting innocent life." He is proud of his record in public service and of working with former governor George Allen to obtain parental notification and consent and waiting-period laws—accomplishments, Kilgore says, that were left within the executive's scope of legitimate authority and activity under operative judicial constraints. The executive who holds pro-life beliefs should maximize his ability to act within confines set by the judiciary and in concert with public opinion. "There's no real mood in this country to overturn" *Roe v. Wade*, Kilgore says, which is a further check on the ability of the executive to legitimately try to pursue his moral vision. With regard to the death penalty, Kilgore cites the number of institutions involved in the process:

> You can offer your views, but once the court rules, directing that—in the death penalty arena, for instance, we have a jury that has to impose sentence. . . . Then

it's immediately appealed to the Virginia Supreme Court. You have a variety of opportunities for the death row inmate to file—there's habeas in the federal system, going through the Court of Appeals to the US Supreme Court. . . . And I just don't think that the executive ought to . . . impose his or her will in a particular case when all of these independent bodies have looked at it and made their decision. I think it's more of a hands-off approach absent some new DNA test that's going to show somebody innocent.[44]

Kaine describes the relationship between the executive and the legislature and refers to the limitations on executive authority and action in similar terms. An equally gracious host, Kaine agreed to talk with me about the tensions between his faith and his office. We spent nearly an hour in his office—the office I was protesting outside in late June—at the height of the speculation that he was in line to be tapped as Barack Obama's running mate. Talking with each of these men, it was easy to see how they had risen to the political heights they had. Just as Kilgore thought it inappropriate for the executive to impose his will in a given case, Kaine believed that to impose his will in a given case would be a violation of the spirit of his oath of office. Clemency powers exist for particular reasons, he says,

> not just, "Hey, I'm governor, I just want to outlaw the death penalty." . . . I would not view that as being honest about taking my oath, because [clemency] was set up with a particular purpose, really to deal with innocence, or conversions or some other dramatic experience. It wasn't to let the executive just say, "I'm not going to follow the law."

Executive power, Kaine says, rests in two areas: dialoguing with the legislature and implementing the legislative will. The executive can and should make use of her bully pulpit to explain her vision, though whereas Kilgore speaks in more aggressive plebiscitary terms, Kaine speaks in more cooperative terms: "There's a legislative-executive dialogue about laws, they pass, I veto or amend, they accept or reject, but once they're in place, I've got to implement them." Once again, the liberal executive is defined by the limitations on her capacity to act, in terms of cooperation or contestation with the legislature within the legal bounds established by the judiciary.[45]

Kaine further clarified his conception of the liberal executive with regard to the perceived division of morality. Acknowledging that the discussion in "Stanley"'s wake focused on a perceived division between public and private morality—the morality of the individual versus the morality of the office—Kaine nevertheless phrases the problem in different terms. Rejecting the idea that personal morality is separate from the executive's behavior in office, Kaine broadens the concept of personal morality to include the conception of the office: "My personal morality includes—I think the rule of law is the best and most moral system of government." While he has a personal religious belief that the death penalty is wrong, Kaine says, he also believes that "the system of government we have, where the rules are set by . . . the legislature, and the job of the . . . executive is to follow those rules rather than just do whatever the hell he wants, that is part of my personal moral code, too." This belief was reinforced during the year he spent as a Catholic missionary in Honduras while attending Harvard Law School, "where the rule of law was what the military dictator did." Abiding by the rule of law and refraining from imposing one's own will, even and perhaps especially in areas where the executive has a strong moral and ethical commitment to a particular point of view, is, for the liberal executive, perfectly commensurate with personal morality and does not necessitate a division between the "private" and "public" individual.[46]

We could reasonably object here that this model may be unable to determine when we have reached a point of moral peril sufficient to permit, or compel, the executive to act in ways that may be contrary to law or convention. This is the basis for the competing conception of the executive, one advanced by some of Kaine's opponents within the blogosphere. Several prevalent features characterize this *ministerial* executive. Ministerial executives will have no discrepancies between their political and religious viewpoints and cannot act in any way contrary to their beliefs; this unity is the source of the ministerial executive's legitimacy. They are to serve as interpreters, clarifying their political vision to help the populace understand God's purposes. The ministerial executive also has a greater range of legitimate options for exercising leadership, though in some cases, while the executive still should be obedient to the law, he is not conceived of as beholden to the democratic process to the same extent that the liberal executive is.

The ministerial executive is invested, above all, with a different personal authority than that invested in the liberal executive. The liberal executive's authority derives more from the office than the person. For the ministerial executive, this is essentially reversed, with the individual needing to affirm her personal authority even in the context of the office. While this is not simply a rejection of the machinations of artful zeal, this personal authority may be seen as its dialectical counterpart. Though there is a strong spiritual component to this personal authority, it does not exist independently of the pragmatic expertise and authority necessary to successfully fulfill the duties of the office. The ministerial executive is a professional who "know[s] how to get things done," but professional competence must be supported by religious authenticity. This religious authenticity is the basis for trust and for perceptions of trustworthiness in this model and indicates that the executive or candidate has "'head and heart' together," an idea that should be understood in two ways. The unity of "head and heart" means not only a joining of the requisite practical gifts and experience — the official component of the executive — with the spiritual vision that pushes the executive into public service to try to bring that vision about — the personal component of the executive — but also a joining of the unity between beliefs and action. The ministerial executive cannot make the argument that beliefs need not dictate action, nor that every legitimate means should not be pursued in seeking to reconcile policy and action with belief, even if that means circumventing the democratic process, if not the law.[47]

This vision, and an articulation of the proposed means by which the vision is to be realized, is the foundation of the ministerial executive as interpreter. This executive is charged with communicating his vision of the corporate life of the faithful and relating that vision to his understanding of God's will. This is analogous to the educational use of the moral law, which seeks to "enhanc[e] the spiritual development of believers [and teach] those who have already been justified 'the works that please God.'" This interpretive faculty is vital to the ministerial executive. Without it, he can neither lead the people to repentance and nor stand up to the evil in their midst. This call to repentance is not the same as declaring days of fasting and humiliation to repent for corporate sins and bring the nation back into greater fellowship with God and into greater concert with the nation's covenantal obligations. The call to repentance that the ministerial executive can make is, rather, "a turn or change from relative injustice to a more expansive and inclusive justice," where justice is understood both as fairness in carrying out transactions in the public space and acting in greater harmony with God's will. Given that the latter is understood perforce to be just, all actions conforming to this will are themselves just.[48]

This conception of agency and interpretation is predicated on an understanding of leadership as a range of activities that are either impossible or vastly more difficult to pursue without the personal authority and interpretive abilities of the ministerial executive. This executive's personal authority creates the environment within which she can pursue adaptive work, the work "needed to frame or reframe a [populace's] vision . . . and explore ways of giving expression to the vision in the face of the particular challenge[s]" facing the state. With this articulation and reframing accomplished, the executive then must decide how to act, within three broad categories of leadership as action. Like the liberal executive, the ministerial executive can act as either a consultant or a consensus leader. The executive as consultant advises based on her expertise and experience, agreeing to abide by and implement the wishes of the people. The executive as consensus leader uses the tools available to her—the bully pulpit, a public relations campaign, covert and open dialogue, and so on—to build a consensus.[49]

This is a recapitulation of the executive as superlegislator, while the executive as consultant is the executive as implementer that Kilgore and Kaine discussed. Up to now, the ministerial executive has been essentially equivalent to the liberal executive. There is a third type of action, however, one available to the ministerial executive but not the liberal. In this category of action, the ministerial executive informs the people of her intent to act and does so. Although this type of action can generally be expected to fall within legal boundaries, it need not. Either way, it is a rejection of some portion of the democratic process and, by extension, their oath of office.

Most of the blog content discussed above articulates the conception of the ministerial executive by pointing out its absence. Shaun Kenney, an amateur Catholic theologian and former communications director for the Republican Party of Virginia, typified the ministerial executive in a post criticizing Kaine from a Catholic perspective. In this post Kenney uses all three characteristics of the ministerial executive in his analysis of Kaine's candidacy and his inability to reconcile faith with politics, as Kenney sees it, judging the candidate—and the democratic/republican executive—as lacking on all three counts. Kenney grants the legitimacy of Kaine's vision but, rather than seeing this legitimacy as helping the candidate develop personal authority and political legitimacy, sees it as deceptive at best, fraudulent at worst. Kenney acknowledges that Catholic teaching "in truth argues in favor of Kaine's position on the death penalty," but he laments that the faith and politics do not match. This is not necessarily an accusation of artful zeal, but in leaving the question open-ended, Kenney leaves it open to others to judge whether the character flaw revealed by the disjunction of the "professed" faith and political positions negatively impacts the candidate's legitimacy and leadership qualities. The inference is that it does, and this inference removes the candidate from the ministerial category and locates him in the liberal category.[50]

This condemnation of the liberal executive does not stop at the denial of legitimacy. The liberal executive who fails to stand up to the evil he sees in the world around him risks becoming an evildoer, even if the evil in question is legally sanctioned. This is why Kaine's attempt to divorce his beliefs from his actions is illegitimate, Kenney says. Kenney starts by discussing an article in the Fredericksburg *Free Lance Star*, which quotes Steve Neill, editor of the *Catholic Virginian*, as saying that Kaine's position did not make him less loyal to the church. Kenney disagrees, using Pope Leo XIII's *Testem Benevolentiae Nostrae* to illustrate his point. Absent the obligation to obey the church's teachings, Leo declared, the faithful would be left "to follow out more freely the leading of his own mind and the trend of his own proper activity." Church teachings are, for Kenney, as binding as sincerely held religious beliefs are for Hans Mast, Old Zach, or "Jon"—they are to be obeyed even at the expense of political beliefs or expediency. This is where the ministerial executive differs most radically from the liberal executive. Kenney states that Catholics have an obligation to stand in the way of the application of unjust laws: "At *no point in time* is a Catholic permitted to allow an unjust law to exist." Further,

> for Kaine to turn his back on those principles and say "heck, the law is the law and I'll enforce it" strikes deep at the heart of the culture of life *and* social justice. It suggests Catholics should stand idle as injustice occurs. It suggests that what is legal—agreed upon by men—trumps what is right. It suggests that Christ was ultimately wrong for coming to us and daring to challenge the Old Law.

Appropriating the adversarial Jesus to drive the point home, Kenney argues that Kaine is morally obliged to impose his will and stop executions in Virginia. If not, we should judge him insincere and lacking the requisite personal authority, and thus the legitimacy, for the office. Here, where the ministerial executive is the ideal, obedience to the law and deference to the democratic process provide no defense against accusations that "head and heart" are in either sense disconnected.[51]

Ultimately, though, neither the democratic/republican nor the ministerial ideals are fully satisfying, because of the distance between them on the scope of legitimate activity. I find it difficult to credit assertions that honoring the democratic process over enacting one's personal religious beliefs is in all cases dishonorable. I likewise don't think that the opposite claims necessarily amount to endorsements of theocracy, though calls for repudiation of parts of the democratic process should always give us pause, either over concerns about the proper relationship between church and state or over concerns about the separation of powers, or that the executive will simply jettison the democratic process and make it up as he goes along. Whether or not one supports the death penalty, Kilgore is right to point out that capital punishment is democratically legitimate. It is part of the democratic process, from the juries that decide both guilt and the sentence to the various levels of judicial review to the legislature's ability to amend the law to the executive's ability to personally intervene when innocence, mental illness, or other serious procedural concerns necessitate executive involvement. Because capital punishment is democratically legitimate, Kaine is right to view intervening beyond these circumstances as inconsistent with his oath of office. If the candidates can overcome perceptions that they are dissemblers, artful zealots telling the voters what they want to hear, and earn sufficient trust that they will abide by the rule of law despite their individual religious objections—and voters did believe

Kaine, by a 2–1 margin—then it is illegitimate within a democratic system to label that individual a "moral hypocrite" for failing to obey the dictates of his conscience, or a "political opportunist" with no regard for his conscience. Any perceived flaw here is at least plausibly systemic, not individual.[52]

At the same time, however, the liberal executive can defer too broadly to institutional inertia and may not be able to bring about needed changes quickly enough. For the executive to fail to utilize all of the weapons in her arsenal to combat correctible evils and injustices can be a dereliction of duty. This, certainly, is the argument that is made in favor of the ministerial executive, who has the right and obligation to "lead from the front" and act unilaterally when necessary. Again, however, I think caution is in order, so that conscience is not the sole legitimating argument justifying such an action. This would be problematic for a host of reasons, not least that the United States is a pluralistic, religiously disestablished society. Further, there is a genuine danger that bypassing legitimate democratic processes will turn out to be a rule rather than an exception, and thus should be opposed as a rule. Given the limitations on the two models, and given our national history, our diversity of backgrounds and experiences, and our professed adherence to our highest national ideals, the liberal executive is legitimate, whereas the ministerial is not. However attractive the ministerial model may be, this executive's inability to lose an argument with grace and his obligation to circumvent the democratic process in these situations—even to defeat or prevent evils—makes him illegitimate. I make this assessment with the caveat that the liberal executive should witness, on the basis of whatever their innermost motivation may be, and work within the legitimate democratic channels to address any rights and injustices that they can grasp, communicate, and help correct. This may be somewhat Pollyannaish, but I take it as a given that witnessing *on behalf of* the democratic process is part and parcel of witnessing *within* the democratic process, and that the capacity to lose an argument—and thus a policy battle—with grace and aplomb strengthens that process, a necessary curative, given our collective propensity to find various other ways to subjugate the democratic process that we claim to cherish.

The typologies of the liberal and ministerial executives reveal a curiosity: neither model posits a great deal of distance between the people and the government, though for different reasons and to different ends. They also further clarify the difference between event- and process-based perspectives on the death penalty. In the liberal model, the constraints to work within the democratic process renders the executive more parochially bound, while in the ministerial model, the assumed consonance of beliefs sufficient to generate the requisite personal authority binds that executive to the people more closely than the authority to act outside of the democratic process would suggest. Whereas the ministerial executive has more room to focus on result at the expense of process, the liberal executive is focused on process even at the expense of result. The liberal executive accepts and allows for conflict and privileges the democratic process as the solution to the two moral decisions involved with the conflict of personal beliefs and democratic needs and norms in the public space, as Kaine said.[53]

Religious debates over the death penalty arising in a contest between candidates who take personally abolitionist and retentionist positions speak to a great deal more than just the death penalty and its propriety. Given the twin contexts of a contest over the propriety over a method of violence in response to violent acts within a political campaign—contexts not known for being particularly pacific—it is unsurprising that a large portion of the discourse concerns violence in some way or other. Whether it is an accusation that failure to counterattack in the context of a campaign should be read as weakness and therefore inadequacy, whether it is contestation over the best way to defend the "righteous" from attacks by the unrighteous, or whether it is an indication of the continued perceived salience of the most violent portions of the Bible, the violence that fills these discussions is generative, interpellative, and locative. It reveals the ways in which we understand who we are and where we stand in relation to others, particularly those whom we would metaphorically or literally exile from us: the evildoers.[54]

These locative effects further demonstrate the way in which *action* is taken to be interchangeable with *identity*. If representing a capital defendant during the appeals portion of their trial makes one an "activist," then how are we to understand how that defendant, that appellant, has been interpellated? What is their identity? Providing this defense during the appeals process, whether of one's own initiative or as the result of a court appointment, can be deemed illegitimate only if we identify the defendant in question as someone who has committed an action that has removed them from the legitimate democratic process. They are then, perhaps, nothing more than a murderer who is wasting the courts' time and taxpayer dollars trying to save their skins and escape the judgment and justice that they have, by their actions, earned. Alternatively, if it is legitimate and necessary to provide such a defense, does that indicate that we view the defendant as a different individual, as an appellant rather than a murderer, as someone legitimately availing themselves of the system's tools?

These questions help us move from the end of the process, in a sense—the executive's hypothetical clemency decision—back into the postconviction appellate process, when the individual defendant's trial and sentence are subject to review. We can broaden our concepts of exile and embrace by analyzing the ways in which these interpellative processes work within the post-trial legal process. An examination of these processes, and the ways religious organizations and institutions participate in them, will give us another way to look at the interaction between religion and law within the capital punishment system while affording us an opportunity to see more about how the exilic processes simultaneously work and remain hidden from view.

6

The penalty of death is qualitatively different from a sentence of imprisonment, however long. Death, in its finality, differs more from life imprisonment than a 100-year prison term differs from one of only a year or two. Because of that qualitative difference, there is a corresponding difference in the need for reliability in the determination that death is the appropriate punishment in a specific case.

(*Woodson v. North Carolina*, 1976

A jury that must choose between life imprisonment and capital punishment can do little more — and must do nothing less — than express the conscience of the community on the ultimate question of life or death.

(*Witherspoon v. Illinois*, 1968

Death, Difference, and Conscience

Two prominent truisms figure prominently in the broad death penalty discourse: "death is different" and the jury is the "conscience of the community." The idea that death is fundamentally different from other punishments, articulated by Justice Potter Stewart in *Woodson* and reaffirmed by Justice Thurgood Marshall in *Ford v. Wainwright*, formed the basis for striking down mandatory death sentence laws. North Carolina had passed the statute in question following the Supreme Court's 1972 *Furman* decision, which struck down capital punishment on the grounds that it was capricious and arbitrary.

In response, North Carolina and Louisiana adopted laws mandating the death penalty for certain offenses. Finding that these new laws violated the Eighth and Fourteenth Amendments, the Court ruled that because death cannot be considered like any other form of punishment, the individual defendant cannot be treated simply as a member of a class of offenders. Rather, he must be considered a unique, discrete individual when determining whether his offense merits the state's most awesome punishment.[1]

The capital jury—the "governmental body" specifically convened to determine whether and when that most awesome punishment should be applied—is taken to be the community's conscience. Interposed "between the accused and his accuser," this "group of laymen" is responsible for deciding first guilt and then punishment. We take for granted that juries recommend appropriate punishments, punishments that represent the community's values. Though individual jurors are expected to bring their own moral judgment and life experiences to bear on their decision, once they are convened they become a "unique collegial body" that speaks for themselves and their community and on behalf of contemporary standards of decency. Their agency is not untrammeled, however, and debate continues over the extent to which capital juries truly represent the community from which they are drawn or act as its conscience.[2]

I look at two problems in this chapter: what it means to say that "death is different" and that the jury is the community's conscience. I examine post-trial briefs filed during the appeals process, especially those filed by religious organizations,[3] to work through the arguments and counterarguments and reveal the operative conceptions of the defendant and community, as well as what it means to speak of conscience in this context. In the process, I answer two questions that arise in these briefs: whom do we sentence to death, and who is the "we" that recommends the sentence? Finally, I apply a definition of *conscience* to the discussions carried out via the briefs and, by reconciling that definition with the operative concept of conscience at work in the briefs, propose a solution to a major problem posed by the conjunction between religion and law in capital cases.

The Briefs Litigant and Amicus Curiae

Two basic types of briefs are submitted to the courts during the appeals process. The first of these is the litigant brief, submitted by the petitioner, the party seeking relief, or the respondent, the party seeking to convince the appellate court to uphold the lower court's decision. These briefs clarify the issue(s) on appeal and explain the parties' positions as clearly as possible in anticipation of argument before the appellate court. These briefs are limited in scope, content, and length by the various procedural laws and guidelines of the relevant jurisdiction and court, and are generally narrowly tailored to one or several specific points of law and the application of that law to the specific facts of the particular case.

The second type, the amicus curiae brief, is filed neither by the parties nor in conjunction with their briefs. Amicus briefs are filed by "a nonparty with a strong interest in the subject matter of the case." This nonparty is "an organization or person that intervenes in a judicial proceeding to assist the court with an additional brief or conducts an investigation on appointment by the court." Originating in the Roman Empire, the first amicus brief was filed in the US Supreme Court in 1823. Originally a neutral party in keeping with its name — "friend of the court" — the amicus's traditional participation in a case was limited to referencing prior case law to remind the court of a precedent case it may have overlooked. Over time, the amicus shifted from a neutral party interested in assisting the court to a party interested in helping one of the litigants. For more than a century, amicus briefs were filed almost exclusively by lawyers. By the 1930s, however, organizations had begun to file briefs, which began to move the amicus "from neutrality to partisanship, from friendship to advocacy."[4]

Legal scholars and jurists are ambivalent about this transition from "friend" to "advocate." Critics charge that amicus briefs can set out to circumvent court-imposed restrictions on litigant briefs; they can also walk a fine line between presenting expert, informed opinion on the relevant issue(s) and simply claiming to do so, undermining their credibility and utility. Judge Richard Posner, for example, is critical of amicus briefs, regarding them as more a nuisance than a benefit since they are too often simply extensions of litigant briefs and fail to provide the court new information or a different perspective. Others, however, suggest that on balance amicus briefs do offer unique and necessary viewpoints and that their advocacy on behalf of a party benefits the court. Overall, the openness with which the Supreme Court accepts and quotes from amicus briefs indicates that it frequently considers them helpful, an impression confirmed by the ability of an amicus brief to influence the development of legal doctrine.[5]

Both governmental and private parties may file amicus briefs: a state attorney general or several attorneys general may file a brief, as may any individual, group, or organization that meets the relevant court's requirements. While each court has its own set of rules regarding who may file amicus briefs and when, there is a general consensus among legal practitioners as to what makes a good brief. Above all, although briefs are filed on behalf of a party to the dispute, they should be even in tone and temper rather than contentious or nakedly partisan. "The goal of an amicus brief is to persuade nine Justices (or maybe a decisive Justice or two) of your position. They are far more likely to be persuaded by a document that looks and reads as though it were written by a thoughtful, even-tempered, experienced appellate advocate." A good brief "gives the practical effect of a decision on the broader legal scheme at issue; . . . explains how the sought-after . . . decision would affect interests not explained by the parties' briefs; or more fully develops the legal analysis for an argument raised in a party's brief." A good brief provides the court a unique perspective not, or not only, on the narrow legal issue at stake, but also on other aspects or impacts of the court's decision.[6]

Because the amicus is not party to the dispute, it is able to argue matters related to or reasonably consequential to the decision in the present dispute. Moreover, because it has "no immediate stake in the outcome, an amicus brings a tone of credibility that a party may not." As the number of briefs filed has proliferated, so too have the instances of citation in decisions. While there does not appear to be any simple correlation between the two — for example, more briefs equals more citations — the evidence suggests that organizations submitting well-constructed briefs can have a substantial impact on decisions, and thus on the law. Most importantly, and most relevant for our analysis, "amici for disadvantaged one-time litigants [such as capital defendants] can level the playing field with repeat players [such as the state], the so-called 'haves.'" A good brief can help litigants not regularly before the appellate courts make their case more convincingly and can help put them on more equal footing with their more experienced adversaries.[7]

Dan Schweitzer argues that we can locate amicus briefs within any of nine categories, based on the way they argue the merits of their positions. Amicus briefs filed by religious organizations in capital cases tend to fall into one or more of three of Schweizer's categories: the "go farther than the party" brief, the "amplify one issue" brief, and the "different legal argument" brief. We can use examples from the briefs filed in death-qualification cases discussed in further detail below to see how they fit these categories. The appellant's brief in *Wheeler v. Kentucky*, for example, raised seventeen questions for argument before the Supreme Court of Kentucky. One of these, Argument 2, held that it was a violation of Wheeler's due process rights to "excuse [prospective jurors] from service or allow peremptory challenges to be used against them because of their religious beliefs," thus going further than claims made in the litigant briefs.[8]

Amicus briefs filed in analogous cases are explicitly supplemental and aware of the need "to avoid repeating arguments being made . . . by others." They generally focus on a single question, amplifying that issue while offering a different legal argument. The appellant's brief in *Wheeler*, for example, focused on the harm that was allegedly done to the defendant by striking particular prospective jurors. The American Friends Service Committee (AFSC), in its brief filed in *California v. Fields*, focused instead on the harm that was done to those jurors and to people who oppose the death penalty for religious reasons—"death-scrupled" persons—rather than the harm to the defendant. This amicus also argued in favor of extending the legal argument: the AFSC urged the Court to treat death-scrupled persons as a cognizable group, thus extending to them the same protections that are granted to other cognizable groups, such as groups defined by "race, religion, national origin, sex, age, education, occupation, economic condition, place of residence and political affiliation."[9] The importance of these arguments becomes clear when we understand them in their legal context, which involves two notions central to Eighth Amendment case law: the idea of evolving standards of decency and the declaration that death is different.

Is Death Different? Whom Do We Execute?

Death has been regarded as fundamentally different from imprisonment for the entire modern era. A prison sentence can be overturned and the individual serving that sentence freed if he is later found innocent; death is final. Because death is irreversible, it is all the more imperative that no mistakes be made anywhere in the process. In the attempt to prevent any innocent person from being sentenced or put to death, the courts have adopted a series of procedural safeguards known collectively and colloquially as "super due process." This "super due process" includes the bifurcated trial, the virtual lack of limitations that defense counsel are supposed to have on their presentation of mitigating evidence, and an expanded appeals route. As Justice Sandra Day O'Connor put it in *Thompson v. Oklahoma*:

> Among the most important and consistent themes in the Court's death penalty jurisprudence is the need for special care and deliberation in decisions that may lead to the imposition of [death]. The Court has accordingly imposed a series of unique substantive and procedural restrictions designed to ensure that capital punishment is not imposed without the serious and calm reflection that ought to precede any decision of such gravity and finality.[10]

Intended to make the process less capricious and arbitrary, less emotionally charged and more rational, "super due process" has been both oxymoronic and largely fictitious. It is oxymoronic because it assumes that once due process has been achieved—once the defendant has received the full extent of the protections to which he is constitutionally entitled—there can be a higher level of these selfsame protections that can and should be employed in capital trials. It has been largely fictitious due to the process of "deregulating death" by which the Supreme Court gradually withdrew from state death penalties; to various procedural bars employed by the states to limit or inhibit the ability of death row inmates to appeal their sentences; and to attacks on habeas corpus, including the 1996 Anti-Terrorism and Effective Death Penalty Act (AEDPA), which requires appellate courts to uphold the decisions of lower courts — even if they are incorrect as matters of law — as long as they are not objectively unreasonable. The strong critique of the problems and disparities in application, raised by supporters as well as opponents, further shows that we can proceed on the understanding that even were "super due process" realizable, it has not yet been realized.[11]

With this in mind, we can turn to the question of whether death is different and examine the ways in which various parties and nonparties position their arguments on either side of that question. We can look at this using the constitutionally linked issues of whether the state has the right to execute minors or the mentally retarded[12] and whether death row inmates appealing either their sentence or their conviction have the right to have counsel provided. This may seem an odd question, given that the courts have regarded death as different for decades. *Powell v. Alabama*, a case involving the famous Scottsboro Boys, held that "in a capital case, where the defendant is unable to employ counsel . . . it is the duty of the court, whether requested or not, to assign counsel for him as a necessary requisite of due process of law." This due process protection was not extended to defendants wholesale until 1963, when the right to counsel was likewise granted during direct appeals.[13]

In *Murray v. Giarratano*, however, the Court overruled a lower court's ruling that Virginia had to provide indigent death row inmates with continuous assistance of counsel through state habeas. In a vigorous dissent, Justice Stevens argued that appointed counsel should be mandatory in order to ensure that the "touchstone" right of "meaningful" access to the courts is preserved. Observing that "capital litigation . . . is extremely complex" and that "this Court's death penalty jurisprudence unquestionably is difficult even for a trained lawyer to master," Stevens made his argument for the necessity of counsel on three points. First, arguing from the perspective that death is different, he observed that the weight of the historical precedent consistently falls on the side arguing for greater protection for capital defendants. He noted that even in the colonial and immediate postrevolutionary period capital defendants had greater protections than other defendants, including greater access to counsel and the right in some cases to two attorneys "nearly a century . . . before Congress provided for appointment of counsel in other contexts." Death, he continues, has always been different. Given this difference, and given the vital importance of appeals to the integrity of the capital process, Stevens argues that appeals, and the right to counsel during appeals, constitute "an integral component of a State's 'constitutional responsibility to . . . apply its law in a manner that avoids the arbitrary and capricious infliction of the death penalty.'"[14]

Second, because Virginia's capital procedures mean that some claims cannot be raised on direct review but are relegated to postconviction review, defendants should have a right to counsel for these proceedings. For example, Stevens argues, postconviction proceedings might be the first opportunity for counsel to examine the trial record for any constitutional deficiencies, such as ineffective trial counsel or prosecutorial misconduct. Third, because those under a sentence of death are under a time constraint not faced by those under a prison sentence, they may be even less able to file their appeals in a timely fashion. In order for petitioners to have meaningful access to the courts, therefore, they must have counsel.[15]

Briefs filed by and on behalf of the respondents made these points as well. The respondents' brief, submitted by the lawyers representing Giarratano and the other prisoners, noted the problem posed by the timetable under which capital defendants operate. The brief pointed to the high rates of reversal in postconviction proceedings as proof that counsel not only is necessary, but is necessary precisely for the reason Stevens articulated in his dissent: to help correct for the systemic inadequacies. Given that "the rates of success in federal non-capital proceedings . . . rang[e] from .25 percent to 7 percent, [and] the success rate for capital federal habeas proceedings has ranged . . . from 60 to 75 percent," respondents argue, counsel during postconviction proceedings is vital to ensure that the death penalty retains any semblance of legitimacy and reasonable perception of fairness. Recent history confirmed this, they argued: in 1988, the Supreme Court decided seven of the ten capital cases it heard in the defendant's favor.[16]

Two amicus briefs filed on behalf of the respondents extended the discussion by enhancing specific issues. These two amici contested the idea of the defendant as normal. The defendant in Stevens's dissent is normal, at least implicitly. Stevens makes no mention of mental illness or diminished capacity, for example, which would make capital defendants even less capable of navigating the relevant legal processes. The briefs filed by the American Bar Association (ABA) and several state bar associations, however, focus intently on these limitations. Even if the amici were to concede that the defendants should be considered fully normal, the sheer difficulty of the proceedings would justify mandatory appointment of counsel during postconviction habeas proceedings. As Judge John C. Godbold has noted, "The body of law that exists is complex. It's difficult. It's changeable. And it's very hard to apply. . . . It is the most complex area of the law I deal with. . . . The average trial lawyer, no matter what his or her expertise, doesn't know any more about habeas than he does about atomic energy." Moreover, the fact that the would-be-litigant is locked away on death row presents a physical impediment to the collection of necessary and relevant evidence sufficient to preclude them from being able to formulate their arguments at all, let alone within the time frame demanded by the relevant court. Even if a normal individual had a reasonable chance to perform the necessary work, that ability cannot be imputed to death row inmates. Here the amici point to the huge numbers of death row inmates who are mentally impaired, illiterate, or otherwise fundamentally unable even to be presumed capable of filing briefs on their own behalf.[17]

The majority disagreed. Writing for the Court, Chief Justice Rehnquist also made a historical argument, but found that history provided no grounds to extend the right to counsel to discretionary appeals like habeas. Inmates are able to use prison law libraries and turn to institutional attorneys for help preparing those briefs; this, the Court held, is sufficient to provide meaningful access to the courts. Critically, the Court expressly "decline[d] to read either the Eighth Amendment or the Due Process Clause to require *yet another distinction* between the rights of capital case defendants and those in noncapital cases." The petitioner's brief submitted in this case had urged that no such distinction be found. This brief also claimed that while there may be individual claimants

> who cannot effectively use a law library . . . there is no evidence that the inmates on Virginia's death row are uniformly disabled from making any effort to research and develop claims using a law library. . . . There is simply no basis for an across-the-board assumption that all cases involving a death sentence are so inherently complex that no class member can present his claims without a personal attorney to represent him.[18]

In other words, Virginia argues that capital defendants must be presumed fully capable of preparing and filing their own briefs without the assistance of counsel. This is a breathtaking and perplexing extension of the trope of the normal person onto death row. It is also an affirmation of the idea that death is different, albeit a flatly inverted affirmation of that idea. Whereas O'Connor's statement above, and the general thrust of the intention of "super due process," is to provide *more* for those facing a death sentence—greater opportunity to bring evidence, greater opportunity to challenge the evidence against them, and so on—*Murray* undercuts the idea of death as different by insisting that those sentenced to death are no different from those sentenced to prison. If those sentenced to death are no different from those sentenced to prison, then the logic of the idea that "death is different," as noted above, has been inverted and refuted.

How, then, is this an affirmation of "death is different"? It is an affirmation in the way it distinguishes between two different legal persons—the defendant and the appellant. If the question is "Whom do we execute?," the answer is that we execute the condemned. We can treat this as fact without freighting it with any greater implications: we execute those *condemned* to death, not those merely *sentenced* to death. There are two differences between sentencing and condemnation. First, the appeals process must either be completed or waived by the offender. This also means that the relevant court must decline all last-minute appeals for a stay of execution. Second, the relevant clemency authority must decline to intervene. Only after such possibilities are positively declined can the offender be truly said to be *condemned*, bereft of all hope of reprieve.

What *Murray* illustrates, however, is a difference of equal magnitude between the *defendant* and the *appellant*. The defendant *faces* a sentence of death; the appellant *has been sentenced* to death. Here, death is different. Those *facing* a death sentence are entitled, at least nominally, to "super due process." Although the offender is technically an appellant during the mandatory appeals process, it is helpful to think of him as a defendant, as someone facing a death sentence, because the process by which the sentence is imposed includes all mandatory appeals and reviews. So long as this mandatory process has not run its course, the offender still *faces* a death sentence and thus remains "different."

Once this mandatory review process concludes, however, the offender ceases to be different. This undifferentiation is made possible by both a separate undifferentiation and by a differentiation. The undifferentiation is the determination that those sentenced to death are not entitled to have counsel provided to them for postconviction proceedings. The offender is also construed as the consummate normal actor. He is presumed capable of navigating undeniably complex capital habeas proceedings while utilizing the materials contained within a prison law library to help him formulate and submit his petitions. In fact, the trope of the normal is extended here, as a case following and relying on *Murray* shows. In *Coleman v. Thompson*, a Fourth Circuit case arising from Virginia, the Circuit found that because defendants have no constitutional right to counsel at habeas they are unable to raise an "ineffective counsel" claim on higher appeal.[19] In other words, defendants are responsible for their own conduct as well as that of their counsel. The differentiation comes in the interpellation of the offender and the corresponding changes in rights and responsibilities accruing to each person.

Taking the petitioner's brief to represent the retentionist argument and, *mutatis mutandis*, the respondents' brief to represent the abolitionist argument, we can see the basic pattern at work in each discourse. The retentionist argument—downplaying the difference of death and, more importantly, the difference of those under sentence of death — seeks to bring offenders in and render them more *like us*. Though some distance between us and the Neighbor remains, effacing the difference imposed by death brings them closer to us.[20] Once the court of direct appeals affirms the death sentence, those under that sentence are considered no different from other offenders and are thus closer to the rest of us.

The abolitionist argument, on the other hand, continually seeks to undercut the trope of the normal and, in so doing, move the Neighbor further away from us to highlight the ways they are *not like us*. Vitally, however, the distance is neither permanent nor impermeable. The offender is *not like us* because, consistent with the abolitionist concept of the exile, he differs from us quantitatively rather than qualitatively. We would require counsel in a capital case, given the complexity of the problem; the need of capital offenders is greater precisely because they are not normal.[21] In this case, the offender is embraced, which is to say, brought back in, via efforts to require counsel for defendants at habeas. In fact, a change to Virginia law, effective July 1, 2004, mandates provision of counsel through state habeas. In addition to bringing Virginia more in line with the national norm, the change extended the range of activities within which death is different through state habeas. Nevertheless, though Virginia has chosen to provide counsel consistent with any interpretation of the "evolving standards of decency" doctrine (as will be discussed below), the basic inversion at the heart of *Murray* remains intact. That is, while we may choose to act as though death is in fact different, we need not do so, at least after mandatory appeals are exhausted. We make the choice in the face of legal circumstances that dictate that while death may be different, the default would be that death is not different, or it is different only in its inverted form.[22]

Moreover, while it would be easy to make too much of the syntax, it is difficult to overlook the repeated characterization of the appellant as a threat, as literally *attacking* the criminal justice system in order to undermine their own sentence, which, according to the majority, must be presumed just. The petitioner's brief in *Murray* used the word "attack" nine times, each of them in asserting that the appellant was engaging in a discretionary collateral attack on their sentence, which must be considered valid as of the conclusion of direct appeals. Neither amicus brief used the word, and the respondents' brief used it only once, in the context of pointing out the petitioner's attack on the rationale employed by the district court.[23]

The difference is again one of event and creation versus revelation and process. The retentionist exile is here doubly event-instantiated. The first event is the tripartite speech act[24] that changes the defendant into the appellant: the jury's pronouncement of the guilty verdict at the conclusion of the guilt phase of the trial, the same jury's pronouncement of a death sentence at the conclusion of the sentencing phase and the trial judge's confirmation of that sentence, and the conclusion of the unsuccessful direct appeals process, which affirms both verdict and sentence. At this point, the inverted difference of death goes into effect. The *defendant* can become the *appellant* only via the second event: electing to pursue a discretionary collateral attack on the legitimacy of his sentence. In keeping with the retentionist conception of exile, we can see, once again, that it is an act willfully undertaken that renders the individual the exile in opposition to *us* and what we value—in this case, comity and finality in, and the integrity of, the criminal justice system.

The abolitionist discourse, on the other hand, tries to reincorporate the speech acts as part of the process and preserve the offender's status as "defendant"—as procedurally defined rather than event-defined—until the moment when the defendant becomes the condemned (or the exonerated, or the commuted). There are clear analogues of this process in the broader cultural debate, which we can see using broader debates over appeals as an example. The retentionist position is typified by any variant of the "death penalty costs reside mainly in appeals costs" argument, or any variant on the argument that appeals simply delay justice.[25]

This argument recognizes the huge financial cost of the death penalty, but presumes either that the appeals are the bulk of the cost and thus the legitimate target of attack, or that the appeals themselves are illegitimate and thus the legitimate target of attack. The cost-of-appeals argument can be reasonable only if the following presumptions are considered valid. First, the death penalty itself must be considered a legitimate state tool. Second, the sentence must be unimpeachably legitimate—that is, legal guilt and actual guilt must fully coincide. Otherwise, collateral attacks would be legitimate remedies to unjust convictions or sentences. Third, postconviction appeals must be conceived as fundamentally different than direct appeals. Fourth, the postconviction appellant engaging in collateral attacks must be conceived of as fundamentally different than the defendant working through his mandatory appeals.

All four of these elements must be present for the costs-of-appeals argument to be reasonable. The abolitionist argument on this point, seeking to push the speech acts back into a process rather than letting them stand as events, must presume the opposite of these. First, the broader abolitionist discourse presumes the death penalty to be per se invalid as a state tool, while the narrow abolitionist discourse, typified by counsel acting on behalf of a client, must claim that the death penalty is illegitimate in that specific case. Second, the sentence cannot be considered unimpeachable per se; it must be shown to be such. Third, collateral attacks are presumed to be a valid way for defendants to challenge the constitutional legitimacy of their incarceration. Fourth, the defendant at habeas must be understood to be engaging in a continuous rather than discontinuous process, and thus must be considered still the *defendant*. Any of the "classic" arguments against the death penalty, such as demonstrable racial bias or demonstrable cases of innocents being exonerated from on death row, contain all four of these elements, as do any arguments in favor of extending the right of counsel through habeas proceedings based on the high reversal rate at habeas.

This brings us back to the question at hand: whom do we execute? Regardless of whether we view the offender as defendant or as appellant, we cannot escape the effects of interpellation:

> Interpellation is an address that regularly misses its mark. It requires the recognition of an authority at the same time that it confers identity through successfully compelling that recognition. Identity is a function of that circuit, but does not preexist it. The mark interpellation makes is not descriptive, but inaugurative. It seeks to introduce a reality rather than report on an existing one; it accomplishes this through a citation of existing convention. Interpellation is an act of speech whose "content" is neither true nor false: it does not have description as its primary task. Its purpose is to indicate and establish a subject in subjection, to produce its social contours in space and time.[26]

This aptly describes the process by which the offender becomes an appellant. First, in an analogue of Althusser's policeman calling out "Hey, you!,"[27] a private citizen is interpellated into a defendant by virtue of criminal charges being brought against him. The private citizen now exists in this new role, subject to the rules of defined convention—in this case, the rules governing criminal proceedings in the given jurisdiction. This new identity, though it belongs to a class of such identities—"defendants"—is essentially new, subject to the circumstances of the crime of which the defendant stands accused, as well as any number of other contingencies. Not least of these is the question of whether the prosecutor elects to pursue a capital murder charge. As such, though this new identity is a function of the circuit here described, it cannot be said to preexist it; the identity of the subject is constituted by the speaker via the act of declaring that identity.

The similar, contested move from defendant to appellant has an additional contour—a division of the discourse into forms of address based on nouns versus attributes. The jury's speech act conferring guilt removes any iterations or synonyms of "alleged" as an attribute of the subject. The question then becomes how these defendants should be addressed as subjects, and the division in preferred forms does not occur strictly down the abolitionist/retentionist divide, as briefs filed in *Payne v. Tennessee* show.[28] In *Payne*, which held that VISs are admissible as evidence during the sentencing phase of a capital trial, two victims' rights and survivors groups filed briefs urging the Court to decide in Tennessee's favor and permit the VISs. They differ, however, in terms of how they frame the defendant within their argument. One group consistently referred to the defendant as such. The other group, however, also referred to the defendant as a "murderer."[29]

Both forms of address are interpellations, but there is a significant difference in their register. The defendant is recognized as part of a process, whereas the murderer is explicitly defined by the offense, by the event. The philosophical elements of the question of truth versus falsity in the form of address can be dismissed for the moment, since each is reasonably both true and false, subject to the desired scope of the interpellative process by which the speaker seeks to constitute the subject. Reconstructing the defendant as *murderer* subjects him to a clear location in space and time. His rights and responsibilities become clearly defined by the very process that establishes his status as murderer, while his position relative to the normal also becomes clear, particularly in the full context: "The majority opinion in *Gathers* [the case the amicus urges the Court to overturn] would prevent the jury from catching even a 'glimpse of the life' the *murderer* 'chose' to extinguish.'" The contest occurs over whether the proper address is "defendant," defined by process, or "murderer," defined by event. Each "simplifies the designated [subject], reducing it to a single feature . . . dismembers the [subject], destroying its organic unity, treating its parts and properties as autonomous."[30]

Returning to the defendant/appellant binary, resolving the question one way or another certainly involves a form of violence. Some forms of address do not involve this direct violence, such as the capacious term "persons" or "evil doers," the latter of which remarkably acknowledges the offender's evil deed while still distancing him from it sufficient to prevent him from being identified solely by it. Each address nevertheless corresponds with a real and implicit definition and limitation of the rights of the offender to challenge his death sentence, which certainly constitutes a "threat of injury."[31]

Nor is the question limited to forms of address and the offender's corresponding rights and obligations. The question of address is also directed outward—at the victim—and at the community called to pass judgment, and on the rights and responsibilities accruing thereto. A stark example of this is a case summary prepared by Virginians United Against Crime. These summaries are headed with the names of the "Victim" and "Murderer," forcing the reader immediately to conceive of them in terms of the attributes appropriate to each label. Moreover, attempts to remedy the perception that victims have been stripped "of their dignity and humanity by relegating them to objects of no great importance" by including statements and testimony from friends and loved ones errs in assuming that such testimony will not similarly dissect the victim and reconstruct them not as an organic whole but as an assimilation of attributes.[32]

The related constitutional question turns on the point of individualized consideration and its corollary, personal responsibility and moral guilt. Briefs filed in *Payne* and in cases dealing with executions of juveniles and the mentally retarded extensively showcase this question. The cliché that punishment should fit the offense, central to the idea of retributive justice, is at most only conditionally valid under Eighth Amendment jurisprudence, given the prohibition against mandatory death sentences. Punishment, as several states argued in a brief, should fit the *offender* as well as the offense. The offender, in other words, is to be brought in — embraced — in order to be considered in his entirety, not as an abstract idea, not as a someone accused of murder, but as *this* individual accused of *this* murder.[33]

Without such an individualized assessment, this argument continues, we cannot be sure that we are not punishing this offender disproportionately for this offense. This is also the only way we can reasonably involve the victims, without whom the extent and nature of the offense cannot be adequately determined: "Absent full definition of the harm caused by defendant's actions, his or her 'blameworthiness' cannot be assessed." Our duty in response to these murders is to judge the offender according to our "reasoned *moral* response to the defendant's crime," which entails learning more about the life that the defendant chose to extinguish, and creating what the criminal justice system supposedly abhors — subjective considerations of the definition of crime. Leaving the victim and the impact on the victim out of the discussion not only ignores the truth but also undercuts our ability to respond by reducing the idea of responsibility to mens rea and the decision to kill.[34]

According to this argument, the impact of the crime, and the degree to which it offends our collective conscience, is also relevant to our collective response process for three reasons. First, without hearing the impact, we cannot adequately gauge the extent of the crime, and we thus deprive the offender of an element of "super due process" to which he is entitled. The irony of this is readily apparent — the crime is always bad but sometimes worse. Second, failing to consider the impact of the offender's decision limits our ability to assess the offender's moral culpability, which causes us to diminish the offender's humanity insofar as we deny the need to account for their ability to foresee the consequences of their willful action. By diminishing their culpability, in other words, we affront their inherent dignity. Third, without permitting the victim to be heard from at trial, we have effectively permitted the offender to murder them a second time and so have allowed the offender to victimize us a second time as well.[35]

Perhaps the most obvious flaw in this argument is that it explicitly holds that it would be improper to construe classes of individuals per se as unfit to face the death penalty. On its face, one could perhaps see this claim as consonant with Eighth Amendment jurisprudence, namely in conjunction with the prohibition on mandatory death sentences. Carried to its logical conclusion, however, this line of argument augurs against "degrees of murder" statutes, which differentiate among classes of murders, and thus among classes of murderers, and fail to take into account the damage done by each murder. Who is to say, for instance, that a second-degree murder is less damaging to society and to the victims than a capital murder? More reasonably, however, this is a failure to recognize that the Supreme Court's "insistence on 'individualized consideration as a constitutional requirement in imposing the death sentence['] has never prevented it from declaring that certain categories of crimes and certain classes of defendants are constitutionally beyond the reach of the death penalty."[36] Here again, the retentionist and abolitionist conceptions of the offender come into conflict, and again the result is a displacement of the point of exile.

Briefs filed in *Atkins* and *Roper* use the retentionist exile to argue against prohibiting the states from executing the mentally retarded or juvenile offenders. Reminding the Court that the point of the death penalty is to protect human life, one such brief reiterates that protecting human life means treating each individual offender as presumptively normal. This means that we cannot categorically declare juveniles non-normal and thus less culpable but must respect their humanity and dignity sufficient to

> acknowledge that they are all different with respect to their experience, maturity, intelligence and moral culpability. . . . Instead of grouping juveniles together as a class and drawing a bright line rule based on age, this Court should look at juveniles individually and respect them as human beings with unique characteristics, life experiences, personal responsibility and moral blameworthiness.[37]

A brief filed in the same case by several attorneys general, which tastelessly equates life in prison to a "free pass," completes the retentionist exile:

> Amici's experience strongly indicates that a bright-line rule categorically exempting 16- and 17-year-olds from the death penalty—no matter how elaborate the plot, how sinister the killing, or how sophisticated the cover-up—would be arbitrary at best, and downright perverse at worst. . . . Despite their chronological age, *at least some* 16- and 17-year-old killers most assuredly are able to distinguish right from wrong and to appreciate fully the consequences of their murderous actions.[38]

These parties argue that we are to embrace the individual offender, presume that we have warrant to punish them to the maximum extent the law allows, and let the jury determine whether this individual offender, who is accused of committing this particular crime, should be sentenced to death. The attorneys general brief makes this point via reference to Lee Boyd Malvo, one of the Beltway Snipers. A jury sentenced Malvo, who was seventeen at the time of the killings, to life without parole rather than death. The brief hails this as an indication that juries are capable of making this individual moral assessment in response to even the most heinous crimes.[39]

The abolitionist discourse argues the converse: that we can and must presume that certain classes of individuals are sufficiently *not like us* that whatever their individual characteristics, they must be presumed insufficiently culpable to ever merit a death sentence. Detailing the circumstances under which the law presumes that children are qualitatively different from adults in their capabilities, these briefs raise two additional, and persuasive, points. First, mentally retarded individuals and juveniles are far more likely to confess to crimes that they did not commit than are other offenders. As various churches argued in a brief filed in *Atkins*, if the death penalty is to be reserved for the worst of the worst, then these two groups cannot be so considered.[40]

Second, and directly contrary to the states' argument in favor of juveniles' presumptive normality, is the fact that no state permits minors to sit on juries. Missouri, the state in which *Roper* originated, was one of two that set the minimum age for jury service at twenty-one.[41] If juveniles can be reasonably said to be mentally and emotionally competent to choose to murder in full foreknowledge of the consequences of their actions, then they should be deemed competent to determine guilt or innocence in a criminal setting. That no state is willing to seat minors as jurors in any case, let alone a capital murder trial, is damning to the retentionist argument on this point. Nor are such restrictions limited to jury service. As we noted in chapter 4, juveniles are treated as incapable of making a mature, adult judgment in a number of different ways—juveniles cannot legally consume alcohol, vote, join the armed forces, or marry. In the last two cases, they can do so with parental permission, which only reinforces the broader point that we as a society recognize that children's diminished capacities demand both restrictions on their behavior and legal protections specific to them as a class.

Importantly, in asking the Court to make the distinction, the churches left open the possibility, in notably exilic language, that the exile could become *like us*. While juveniles as a class are different, they are also uniquely redeemable, and while they are not simply adults in smaller bodies, they can grow up to become normal adults.[42] The Court accepted the argument that juveniles and the mentally retarded should be declared ineligible as a class from facing death sentences, thus exiling those groups by declaring them *not like us*. By declaring them *not like us* according to the evolving standards of decency, they relieved the broader community of having to make that particular decision, but left the community—or at least a subset of the community—to make other death-related decisions.

Evolving Standards of Decency

The Eighth Amendment's prohibition against cruel and unusual punishment had been recognized as constantly in flux by the late 1950s. The phrase's precise meaning had been debated in different contexts for some time but was settled in *Trop v. Dulles*, which declared that although "the words of the Amendment are not precise, and ... their scope is not static," they must "draw [their] meaning from the evolving standards of decency that mark the progress of a maturing society." These evolving standards are typically found in the "instrument[s] of evolution ... [which are] the Congress of the United States and the legislatures of the fifty states." This coincides with the idea of the law as the extension of public reason. As defined by John Rawls, public reason applies in three cases in particular: in "the discourse of judges in their decisions, and especially of the judges of a supreme court; the discourse of government officials, especially chief executives and legislators; and finally, the discourse of candidates for public office." If legitimate law is defined as "the legal enactment expressing the opinion of the majority," then laws enacted by state legislatures can be seen as the most reflective of the majority's opinion. Indeed, in *Penry v. Lynaugh*, the Court pointed to the various state legislatures as providing the "clearest and most reliable objective evidence of contemporary values" in declining to find execution of the mentally retarded per se unconstitutional.[43]

Others, however, reasonably fault this method of focusing on the legislatures to the exclusion of other sources of "objective evidence." For one thing, as the United States Conference of Catholic Bishops (USCCB) argued in its brief in *Atkins*, the Eighth Amendment's prohibition of cruel and unusual punishment has historically been understood as a check against the legislatures, "hence its scope cannot depend exclusively on what legislatures do." A brief submitted in *Roper* highlights the problem posed by exclusive reliance on state legislatures. The amicus, the Missouri Ban Youth Executions (BYE) Coalition, pointed to polling conducted by the USCCB that found that Missourians favored banning juvenile executions 59–25, with 16 percent expressing no opinion. State legislators favored a ban 47–13, with 12 percent undecided and 28 percent not responding to the poll. Despite this apparent support for a ban, the legislature did not change the law accordingly.[44]

Roper drew much of its rationale from *Atkins*. In *Atkins* the Court extended both the idea of public reason and the basis from which the necessary objective evidence of the community's evolving standards should be drawn by explicitly naming the churches as "additional evidence" of the national opinion on the matter.[45] This brought the evolving standards analysis into line with what the churches have been claiming throughout the modern era, which is that they are among those uniquely positioned to provide objective evidence of the community's moral standards. The method by which this objective evidence is to be supplied, however, remains incompletely defined.

Arguing for an expansive reading of *Penry*'s observation that the Court relies on objective evidence to determine the community's standards of decency, the churches' briefs not only defend their right and their obligation to weigh in on the issue. The churches also give three reasons that they are uniquely positioned to fulfill their "responsibility . . . to provide the Court with the religious community's collective experiences and beliefs." First, they argue that "morality and decency are subjects on which religious bodies legitimately can claim a particular experience and competence," claiming that "few, if any, institutions can claim a greater tradition of working with and studying the conscience of the human person and related questions of guilt, blame and punishment than the religious community." Second, the churches point out that they have traditionally been regarded as sources of legitimate opinion regarding public policy and are thus "particularly well-suited to inform the Court of the evolving standards of decency in society." Third, the public trusts the churches to act as problem solvers and places "great stock in the contribution religion makes to the public good."[46]

The Court's inclusion of the churches in its basis for determining the broader national consensus in *Atkins* has the effect of including the doctrinal and social statements issued by the religious bodies among its evidentiary pool. The churches' brief submitted in *McCarver* and resubmitted in *Atkins* is a case in point. The brief draws on a number of sources and authorities, including the ELCA's 1991 social statement on the death penalty, the USCCB's 1999 *A Good Friday Appeal to End the Death Penalty*, the US Catholic Bishops' 1980 *Statement on Capital Punishment*, and a published collection of doctrinal and social statements against the death penalty. These statements are the "result of a long and careful process of study . . . [producing] well-considered and definitive statement[s] . . . represent[ing] a deliberate and informed consensus." Importantly, the briefs do not argue that the Court should accept the religious arguments for or against the death penalty—these are generally confined to statements and passages detailing the particular interests of the amici in the legal question.[47] The briefs instead argue for utilizing settled legal doctrines to answer the question at stake such that religion and law arrive at the same conclusions. This call for agreement between religion and law is not problematic when an outside party argues for it. It is a different matter entirely, however, when the question is phrased in terms not of standards of decency but of the conscience of the community, and when the party in question is not a denomination or coalition of religious organizations filing an amicus brief but is instead the jury.

Who Decides? Conscience and the Capital Jury

It seems no great stretch to equate the community's standards of decency with its conscience. The issue of the community's conscience is problematic, however. The issue at stake in conflicts over the community's conscience is not the question of how that conscience should be brought to bear in determining punishment. That is the question of determining evolving standards and limiting or permitting punishments in keeping with that determination. Rather, the question of the community's conscience is the question of *whose* conscience it is to be.

This question is far from idle. In 1952 Justice William O. Douglas noted, "We are a religious people whose institutions presuppose a Supreme Being." Americans continue to profess religiosity at high rates: 90 percent profess a belief in God, 28 percent claim to attend church weekly, and roughly 60 percent say that religion is "'very important' in their lives." When they are seated and called into service, jurors face the task of reconciling cultural and legal norms in the context of making a life-or-death decision. Jurors "are not expected to come into the jury box and leave behind all that their human experience has taught them. Individuals are not expected to ignore as jurors what they know as men—or women." There is an obvious conflict, however, in capital trials. Jurors charged with making a "reasoned *moral* response" to a particular crime are free to act as they believe their faith compels them to do, with two exceptions: those who believe that the death penalty is required in all instances of murder, and those who believe that the death penalty is never justified. The defendant, on the other hand, has a right to an impartial jury drawn from and representing a cross-section of the community: "Thus, courts often speak of the 'divide between' a defendant's right to an impartial jury 'and the requirement that the jury be drawn from the community as a whole.'" The defendant also has a right to be tried on the basis of facts presented and subject to challenge in open court. This cannot be done if the juror's religious beliefs, rather than the law, form the basis for the juror deciding to vote guilty or for death rather than life.[48]

How, though, can the courts reasonably prevent this from happening? The courts cannot dismiss jurors based on their religious affiliation; nor are they permitted to inquire into the juror's individual beliefs. Religious affiliations are classified as "cognizable groups," a term that has been the subject of considerable debate. One suggestion, with which the churches seem to basically agree, defines cognizable groups has having three essential features: "(1) an attribute that defines and limits the group; (2) a common attitude, idea, or experience that distinguishes the group from other segments of society; and (3) a 'community of interest' that the jury pool would not adequately reflect if it excluded members of the group."[49]

The AFSC's brief in support of the appellants in the joined cases of *California v. Alcala* and *California v. Fields* shows how this definition of cognizable groups fits with the churches' perspectives. The jurors' individual religiously opposition to the death penalty defines and limits the group. This opposition is likewise the common attitude or idea that distinguishes the group from those who favor the death penalty in all instances or are unsure whether or not they would find a death sentence justified in a particular case. The AFSC furthers this claim by pointing out that if a group can be categorically excluded, it must be cognizable as a group. The community of interests in question includes Quakers called to serve on a capital jury and, by extension, any religiously scrupled potential juror dismissed from the venire (the jury pool) on the basis of his or her beliefs. Problematically, in enumerating the groups that the courts cannot dismiss — "race, *religion*, national origin, sex, age, education, occupation, economic condition, place of residence, and *political affiliation*" — the amici liken "belief" to "viewpoint," a point to which we will return.[50]

Because the law as it stands holds that the jury should be drawn from a cross-section of the community, the solution to the dilemma in practice has been, and continues to be, excluding death-scrupled jurors from service. Death-scrupled jurors are those jurors "whose beliefs with respect to capital punishment would prevent them from voting to execute a convicted capital defendant . . . regardless of any evidence presented." They are removed from the venire, which has been pulled together from "driver's license lists, voter registration rolls, or other government records and is assembled at the courthouse" during a process called voir dire. At voir dire the potential jurors are questioned by the judge and, sometimes, by both sets of counsel to determine whether there is any legitimate reason that they should not be seated on the jury. They can be struck for cause if there is a legitimate reason that they should not be seated. In contrast to peremptory challenges, a limited number of challenges afforded to both sets of counsel to strike jurors from the venire without detailing their reasons, there is no limit on the number of venirepersons who can be struck for cause. The basis for these exclusions is the juror's perceived inability to follow the law and indicate his or her willingness to make a choice between a life and a death sentence.[51]

A group has recently organized in Louisiana to protest these kinds of exclusions. "I Want to Serve" highlights the disparities that death disqualifications, as they term them, cause: according to this "coalition of churches and church conferences, organizations and concerned citizens who oppose the government's intrusion on our right to express our religious beliefs on capital juries," as many as 50 percent of prospective jurors in some Louisiana cases are disqualified on the basis of their religious beliefs. The group uses short YouTube video statements from disqualified jurors and activists to put faces on these disqualifications while giving each person so included a chance to speak on the points most important to them. Episcopal bishop Joe Morris Doss, for example, says that his job is to teach church members how strongly the churches oppose the death penalty. He wonders whether "the American public understands how strongly the church feels about this," but notes that if he succeeds in convincing them, then they will be "excluded from the opportunity, as well as the responsibility, of judging their peers on the most important moral issue in the criminal justice system. That is a violation of religious freedom, religious liberty, in a way that goes to the heart of our system."[52]

Consider the following examples:

The State utilized it's [sic] final challenge to strike juror number 102, Ms. Curtis, who indicated that as far as the death penalty, she didn't really know, she'd have to hear evidence, that she was a "*Muller Over*," that she did not make snap decisions, that she was a Christian, that she was a Lutheran, that she was a religious person, that she loved God and she loved Jesus and that she had certain religious views toward the death penalty and that in the New Testament, Jesus said to forgive. . . . Ms. Curtis, who indicated she was very religious, was struck. This constitutes a peremptory challenge to rid the jury of someone who has strong religious views.[53]

Juror 551 [Name omitted]—He said he was not sure about considering the death penalty. He did not believe that it was an acceptable method of punishment. He "pretty much" agreed with the Catholic Church's opposition to the death penalty. . . . It would be very difficult for him to set aside his beliefs about the death penalty because he strongly felt that it was not an acceptable means of punishment.

Defense counsel wanted the court to ask Juror 551 if he could set aside his views if he were instructed to do so by the court. The court, however, responded that it would not instruct him to set aside his personal views. Counsel noted that the juror did not say unequivocally that he could not set aside his views. Over counsel's objection, Juror 551 was struck for cause.[54]

Juror 536 could consider all the penalties including the death penalty and believed that the Commonwealth was authorized to seek the death penalty. While she did say that she did not have an opinion on the death penalty, she felt that each case was different and it was in a religious context that she believed her feelings on the death penalty were irrelevant. Her belief is that the Scriptures talk about judging people, and she believed in salvation and that an individual would be saved no matter what they had done. She had no moral or religious scruples against capital punishment and specifically assured the prosecutor that she would consider all of the penalties. . . . In explaining his peremptory challenge, the prosecutor said Juror 536 believed in redemption and salvation in fixing an appropriate penalty.[55]

JUDGE: In the event that the defendant is convicted of capital murder, the jury will have only two sentencing options open to them at that point. One would be life without parole — life in the penitentiary without parole, and the other would be the death penalty. Do you have any religious, moral or philosophical beliefs which would prevent or substantially impair your ability to convict a person of a crime which potentially carries the death penalty?

M.: I don't believe anyone has the right to kill anyone else, and I would be more inclined to go with life in prison without parole. . . .[56]

JUDGE: All right. Now, if he is convicted of capital murder, do you have — are your religious, philosophical or moral beliefs such that you would or would not consider both alternatives available?

M: I could only consider one.

JUDGE: You could not under any circumstances impose the death penalty?

M: No, I couldn't. . . .

PROSECUTION: I'd ask that she be struck, Judge.

DEFENSE: Judge, I object to that, because of exactly what's happened — with what happened in *Batson*. They struck — struck all the Blacks. Now we're striking everybody who doesn't believe in the death penalty. Next time we'll strike everybody with red hair.

I object to that. I think that's improper, and she should be allowed to sit on the jury to have a cross-section of the people in Augusta County. He has a right to have a jury of his peers — a cross-section.

JUDGE: All right. Gentlemen, I believe it's my obligation to — to strike her, and that's what I'm going to do.

I'll note your objection to the ruling of the Court.[57]

We need not consider whether this process of death qualification lives up to its own ideal of fairness; the evidence convincingly suggests that it does not, if for no other reason than that the requisite mutuality in matters of this type is absent. Some excluded jurors take this as a matter of common sense. One such juror noted that the law seems inconsistent — it allows jurors to use their conscience in determining a sentence, but it "prohibit[s] those exercising their moral convictions or conscience from ever getting on such a jury." Not many people, she says, are in the middle and would give equal weight to both sentencing options, "so the jury ends up being people who favor it." This predisposition leads to a predisposition to convict; the Supreme Court has accepted the validity of studies showing that "the process of obtaining a 'death-qualified jury' . . . has the purpose and effect of obtaining a jury that is biased in favor of conviction."[58]

Our question is more basic: is the practice itself religious discrimination, as some of churches claim? As one commentator has argued, ideally, "all who are able to serve are permitted to serve." If jurors are excluded based on their religious opposition to the death penalty, are they not being discriminated against? And if so, what does this say about equal protection for defendants? The churches' briefs claim that because the jurors' beliefs are what disqualify them from service, they are being denied access to an "otherwise available public program" in direct contravention of the right to free exercise as guaranteed by the First Amendment.[59]

The two sides of the argument agree on one basic principle, which is that absent a compelling state interest, individuals cannot be forced into a situation where they are forced to choose between their civic rights and obligations and their faith — a convenient construct for the retentionist viewpoint. The courts' insistence on this very point allows us to see the idea of religion per se at work in the jurisprudence. The courts certainly do not seek to define religion in legal terms when dealing with the death penalty; in fact, a credible argument can be made that the courts deliberately seek to avoid doing so whenever possible.[60] Nevertheless, the legal understanding of religion is clear in the idea that death-scrupled jurors should be dismissed rather than forced into a situation where their civic and religious duties conflict. This idea of *religious obligations* or *duty*, evident in the judge's refusal to permit defense counsel to inquire whether the juror would be willing to set aside his beliefs, recalls James Madison's famous definition of religion: religion is the "duty we owe to our Creator." Definitions of religion proposed by legal scholars echo this idea of religious principles of duty, as in Steven Gey's definition: "(1) religious principles are derived from a source beyond human control; (2) religious principles are *immutable and absolutely authoritative*; and (3) religious principles are not based on logic or reason, and therefore, may not be proved or disproved." It may be, as Michael Sandel has suggested, that the religion clauses were necessary because religion imposes obligations, not choices, on its adherents. Softer expressions of this idea, such as the argument that religion is "far more persuasive than other forms of moral argumentation," are variations on this theme.[61]

Once we identify this functional approach to religion, it becomes clear that the courts' refusal to interrogate beliefs is in fact a refusal to interrogate the act of *believing*. Declaring an inquiry into the nature and validity of a juror's beliefs impermissible while leaving open the court's right to assess the sincerity of those beliefs insofar as they would impact the case at hand is a refusal to investigate what it means *to believe*. Declining to permit counsel to ask potential jurors whether they would be willing or able to set aside their beliefs is an endorsement of the idea that beliefs are not viewpoints but are more substantial than that—that they are obligations.[62]

This conclusion can lead to justifications of outright discrimination, however, in light of the courts' refusal to extend *Batson v. Kentucky*, which prohibits striking prospective jurors solely on the basis of race, to cover religion. If jurors can be discriminated against on the basis of their beliefs, this argument holds, they can be discriminated against on the basis of their religion, because discrimination based on religion is discrimination based on belief: "Because all members of the group share the same faith by definition, it is not unjust to attribute beliefs characteristic of the faith to all of them." A helpful analogy can be drawn to *United States v. Seeger*, the Vietnam-era case that extended conscientious objector status to those who did not object based on strictly religious rationales. If beliefs that occupy "in the life of its possessor a place parallel to that filled by the God" of the faithful, then that belief is religious. Meaningfully, the court in *Seeger* recognized this religiously analogous definition of belief as an obligation rather than a choice, and thus entitled to protection.[63]

A similar extension occurs at voir dire, where philosophical and moral beliefs are treated as equivalent to religious beliefs insofar as they would impair or prevent a juror from considering both sentencing options. In *Commonwealth v. Lenz*, for example, at voir dire Judge Thomas H. Wood asked potential jurors a variant on the following:

> In the event, and only in the event, that [the defendant] is convicted of capital murder, there are only two forms of punishment available to the jury. One would be the death sentence, and one would be life in the penitentiary.
>
> Do you have any religious, philosophical or moral beliefs which would prevent or substantially impair your ability to convict someone of a crime which potentially carried the death penalty?[64]

The refusal to interrogate the nature of believing is certainly legitimate from the perspective that sees religious freedom as a positive good.[65] The question is not the veracity of the belief and not even whether it is truly held. That is assumed. This assumption, somewhat counterintuitively, works against the idea that death-scrupled jurors constitute a cognizable group. One reason for this stems from a suggestion in *Lockhart*, which held the practice of excluding death-scrupled individuals from capital juries constitutional. If the defining feature of a cognizable group is an "immutable characteristic" that lies outside the individual's control, then the belief is a duty, and protecting jurors' right to their belief requires the state to deny them the privilege of serving on the jury. If, at the other extreme, religious discrimination based on stated belief (or affiliation) is in fact legitimate, then the death-scrupled cannot constitute a cognizable group warranting protection. Compounding the problem in either case is the fact that the courts generally do not hold that a single belief, no matter how sincerely held, amounts to a religion. In either case, then, the decision to exclude death-scrupled individuals from capital juries seems less like religious discrimination and more like an affirmation of free exercise.[66]

This being the case, can the jury truly reflect the community? Given the vital importance of measuring the community's evolving standards, can that measurement be taken if a discrete portion of the community is excluded from the ultimate decision-making process? Juries are expected to "mirror . . . the community's values and attitudes," and excluding death-scrupled individuals from juries means that the segment of the populace that opposes the death penalty cannot be represented. The full spectrum of the community's values thus cannot be brought to bear in the process, which means that we cannot "assume that a jury properly reflects community values."[67] This is a problem in at least two ways. Excluding this portion of the population loads the deck against the defendant in terms both of willingness to impose death and of willingness to convict. This undermines the trial itself as a mechanism for finding guilt beyond a reasonable doubt based on evidence presented and confronted in open court.

Having narrowed down the field with respect to whose conscience shall be reflected in the sentencing decision, the question then turns to the nature of the conscience employed. We should note that in this context, the notion of the jury acting as the conscience of the community involves an obligation, not simply because they have been tasked with deciding first guilt and then the just sentence, but because they are called specifically to make an ultimate decision, one that literally involves life or death. Because "death is different," this duty must necessarily be seen as "higher" than the same obligation in other cases, even serious felony cases. Further, this expectation placed on the jury echoes the two broad assessments of conscience: that it possesses both positive and negative qualities of judgment. Conscience is to operate in this setting both as a negative assessment of an individual offender's actions and returning the jury's—and thus the community's—positive assessment of justice in that particular case. This basic description of the duty of the conscience operative in capital trials does not change whether approached from retributivist or rehabilitationist principles. This description of conscience also echoes that proposed by Thomas Aquinas, who held that "conscience is a particular kind of judgment, the sort that one reaches in endeavoring to apply practical principles to specific situations."[68]

The procedural complexities of the situation render these basic definitions of conscience inadequate to describe the kind of conscience that the jury represents and enacts. We can draw on Lucas Swaine's definition of conscience, which presumes that conscience per se has the capacity to be free, to help clarify these issues. The courts' treatment of conscience, and of the jury, makes the same basic assumption. This is reflected in the doctrine of evolving standards, which assumes the intrinsic freedom of the community to determine for itself what punishments are just under what circumstances and allows the judiciary to compel limitations on punishment if the community chooses to reject them. The ELCA social statement and the *Evangelium Vitae* are examples of this conditional rejection, as are claims that capital punishment violates the evolving standards of decency of the community or, more specifically, that it is a relic of the past.[69]

Conscience, for Swaine, consists of three principles:

> Conscience must be free to reject lesser . . . doctrines and conceptions of the good (the principle of rejection)
> Conscience must be free to accept the good (the principle of affirmation)
> Conscience must be free to distinguish between good and bad doctrines and conceptions of the good (the principle of distinction)[70]

All three of these principles are at work in death qualification. For the purposes of this argument, it makes no difference whether a life or a death sentence is the "greater" or "lesser" good in question. A juror whose beliefs would compel her to reject the greater good cannot be said to be free to choose that good, and thus fails both the affirmation and the rejection tests. A juror whose beliefs direct that the greater good should be chosen in all instances fails both of these tests as well. Neither hypothetical juror has a problem with the principle of distinction, but neither hypothetical can be said to accept the need to distinguish and willingly accept *and* reject. Because they must be free to do so with regard to the specific defender being tried for the specific offense(s), an indication that their beliefs *compel* them to accept or reject one good categorically renders them unable to *choose* the one or the other, and thus renders them unfit for jury service.

That said, however, can we achieve the necessary goal without discriminating against death-scrupled jurors? That is, can we preserve the state's right to seek a death sentence without violating the defendant's right to a trial before a jury representing the community and without forcing the state to engage in religious discrimination? Two legitimate rights conflict here: the right to a fair and impartial jury trial and the right to not be discriminated against with regard to access to otherwise available public offices. Whatever moral, philosophical, or intellectual scruples one has against capital punishment, it is at least legally legitimate in those jurisdictions that retain it.

Several commentators have helpfully suggested viewing this as a problem not of free exercise but of establishment. We should remember that because there is a fundamental distinction in the roles played by the two sets of counsel, there is a fundamental distinction between challenges issued. Defense counsel is a private agent representing and acting on behalf of a private individual. The prosecutor, on the other hand, is a governmental agent representing and acting on behalf of the state. Their challenges to death-scrupled jurors are thus governmental actions. Viewed with regard to either the purpose-effect-entanglement test announced in *Lemon v. Kurtzman* or with regard to the endorsement test, challenges to death-scrupled jurors are constitutionally problematic, as Gary Simson and Stephen Garvey show:

> Religious-based peremptories clash with the Court's endorsement test, which bars government from sending messages of approval or disapproval of religion. Since religion-based peremptories serve to some extent the purpose of securing a fair and impartial jury, they survive [*Lemon*'s] purpose prong, which calls for invalidation only if the law under review is shown to rest entirely or almost entirely on a purpose of endorsing religion. The effect prong of the test, however, presents a hurdle that religion-based peremptories cannot overcome. That prong essentially asks whether a reasonable observer familiar with the history and context of the challenged government action is likely to view that action as sending a message of state approval or disapproval of religion. Because religion-based peremptories rather unambiguously characterize a particular religion's tenets as a threat to the fair and impartial administration of justice, a reasonable observer virtually cannot help but view the peremptories as sending a message of state disapproval of religion.[71]

We could say the same of striking jurors for cause based on their religious beliefs, because this action communicates that while *other* religions are compatible with a fair and impartial trial, *this* religion is not. Religion-based exclusions for cause thus also present an endorsement problem, though it is on its face less of a problem or, rather, more easily justified than the problem posed by religion-based peremptories. Namely, the state has a compelling interest in adjudicating criminal offenses and protecting its citizens from offenders by determining their guilt and imposing a punishment on them; this is all part of the state's police powers. If a prospective juror's beliefs prevent him from carrying out this legitimate purpose, then surely he should be struck for cause, regardless of the element of discrimination or endorsement that this striking demonstrates.

We are left, apparently, with a choice between striking otherwise qualified jurors on the basis of their religion or preventing the state from pursuing a democratically legitimate punishment. But is there a way we can avoid this false choice? Yes, there is, and the solution to the dilemma is in the basic nature of the capital trial itself — specifically, the fact that it is bifurcated into separate guilt and sentencing phases. *Lockhart* contends that these for-cause exclusions are necessary "to serve the State's concededly legitimate interest in obtaining a single jury that can properly and impartially apply the law to the facts of the case at both the guilt and sentencing phases of a capital trial."[72]

Lockhart is wrongly decided on this point. While seeking a death penalty is a *legitimate* interest within those jurisdictions, it cannot be defended as a *compelling* interest because it is not treated that way: "There is no rationale of punishment, or disposition of a convicted offender, that *requires* the death penalty." First, the Eighth Amendment, via *Woodson*, prohibits mandatory death sentences, meaning that, second, while the state can elect to bring a capital charge, the jury, third, must find the defendant both guilty and deserving of death. Fourth, the jury may consider any evidence introduced at sentencing sufficiently mitigating to vote for life; the jury, in other words, must be convinced to vote for death, rather than the reverse. Fifth, each death penalty jurisdiction allows for clemency, even in cases where a complete, full, and fully just appeals and habeas process has confirmed, to the best of human ability, that this offender does indeed deserve to die for this crime. In states like Virginia, the executive may grant clemency for any reason, or for no reason. Thus, while the death penalty may be a *legitimate* interest, the fact that the process mandates *discretion* at every stage—mandates a *choice* at every stage—coupled with the fact that the state lacks the authority to *compel* a death sentence means that capital punishment simply cannot rise to the level of a *compelling* state interest.[73]

This being the case, the question then is whether these for-cause exclusions are the least restrictive means to achieve the state's legitimate end. They are not. The solution to the dilemma is as simple as it is necessary: rather than discriminating against otherwise-qualified death-scrupled jurors and denying their right to participate in a fundamental civic procedure, these individuals should be permitted to serve during the guilt phase. If necessary, they can then be replaced by death-qualified jurors during sentencing. Beyond the legitimate interest the state may have in seeking a death sentence, it certainly has a legitimate interest in budgetary matters, and seating a second jury to hear the sentencing phase would make capital trials more expensive to prosecute. This too, however, fails to rise to the level of a compelling interest sufficient to permit the state to engage in religious discrimination, for the same reason: capital punishment is discretionary, not mandatory.[74]

This discretion mitigates against an objection that could be raised here: that the same protection should be extended to individuals who are unable to consider a life sentence. This argument is wholly unconvincing. For this argument to succeed, it would have to extend protection to a practice—mandatory death sentences—that has been deemed constitutionally prohibited. As we have noted, however, jurors may elect for a life sentence over a death sentence for any reason whatsoever. Given the untrammeled latitude given to juries in opting for life over death, and given the constitutional prohibition on mandatory death sentences, this protection can be legitimately extended to one class of excluded persons—the death-scrupled—but not the other.

Conclusion Who and by Whom?

Two ideas that guide and inform death penalty jurisprudence are the notions that "death is different" and that the jury should represent the conscience of the community. Both of these are critically limited in certain ways. Death is different from prison; it is also different relative to our perception of the offender as the exile and whether that status is revealed or created, as discussed in chapter 4. An examination of postconviction appeals has shown us the interpellative processes at work in throughout the capital trial process. This examination has also shown us how the retentionist discourse embraces offenders in order to claim warrant over them and then exile them. This embrace-to-exile rhetorical move demands that we refrain from seeing an offender as part of a class, even to the point of contesting whether the offender's culpability is more relevant to our response to their offense than the harm that they inflicted. The abolitionist discourse, on the other hand, exiles the offender as a member of a class, leaving open the door to a possible future embrace; we will see this in the next chapter. Both approaches offer an answer to the question of why we punish. Both recognize the need—and in some cases the desirability—of causing the offender harm in response to the offense. Both also deal with the question of whether and how punishment should "not just do something bad for an offender, but should also do something good for society."[75]

The "evolving standards of decency" doctrine and the idea of the jury as the community's conscience are slightly different ways of saying the same thing: punishment is our responsibility. A vital, perhaps the central, aspect of this responsibility is the need to contain our own violence. Not all serious felonies, not all violent crimes, not all murders result in potential death sentences. Death sentences cannot be mandated, and at every step of the capital process, any of the governmental parties concerned, including the jury, can choose not to seek or impose death, for whatever reason. The retentionist discourse discounts questions of culpability and selectively treats the offender as intermittently different, as intermittently *not like* either us or other offenders, in order to discharge its responsibility as it understands it. *Our* responsibility is to eliminate evildoers where appropriate, regardless of their age or mental status. If offenders are morally culpable, then they should be considered individually, not as part of a class, so that a jury can determine whether they deserve the ultimate sanction. The abolitionist discourse, meanwhile, tries to turn the question from what offenders deserve to what *we* deserve. One brief argued this explicitly: "[The defendant] should live, forever imprisoned, not because *he* deserves it, but because *we* do."[76]

The problem is in how the first-person plural is defined, as we can see in the dilemma that death qualification poses. Complicating the issue, the courts have yet to settle the definition of "community." Should, for instance, the abolitionist states be taken into account when determining whether there is a national consensus against executing juveniles, or should only the retentionist states be considered as valid members of the community for that purpose? For that matter, how relevant is world opinion on the death penalty? How relevant should it be?[77] Should death-scrupled individuals be barred from capital juries altogether, or, as I argue, only from sentencing? How do we define who *we* are in determining when we can decide to affirm or reject the judicial and societal good at stake in the capital trial?

We have made a determination that our system cannot function unless we proceed as if the community unanimously supports the death penalty. We systematically and systemically attempt to remove any qualms, doubts, or misgivings about the death penalty from the capital trial process. We should perhaps reflect on Albert Camus's take on this sort of hiddenness: "One must kill publicly or confess that one does not feel authorized to kill." As I see it, if we were collectively more serious about the jury serving as our conscience, we would need to hide less of the process. We would also need to hide ourselves from that process less. We would be able to tolerate the inclusion of otherwise-qualified jurors at the guilt phase, even if that accommodation incurred additional expense. If we were serious about death being different, and if we took seriously the awesome responsibility over life and death that we arrogate to ourselves, and if we were serious about living up to the needs of "super due process," we would provide counsel to death-sentenced offenders at all stages of the process, even discretionary appeals. The state cannot claim to take seriously the notion of evolving standards, we cannot take seriously the notions that death is different and the jury is to act as our community's conscience, while at the same time claiming the right to exclude from that community the portion that denies or questions the legitimacy of the issue in question. To do so is to derogate the ideas and ideals purportedly advanced by such exclusion. The question raised in *Clark v. New Mexico* — whether we need to discriminate in order to murder our citizens[78] — can be less contentiously but no less pointedly rephrased: in order to arrogate to ourselves the power to kill, must we systematically and pointedly exclude any voice to the contrary, even though the system by which we kill gives us an "out," gives us a choice *not* to kill at every stage of the process?

7

They are the wounded and the wounders, the criminals and the victims, the haters and the hated, and they have the power to teach us about ourselves — our denial, our hatred, our wounds and our guilt and criminality.

(REV. JOSEPH M. VOUGHT, "Pastor Visitor"

Murder is perhaps the ugliest crime, which is why it is so shocking that most murderers are so ordinary in appearance. . . . Even after all these years, some part of me expects people who commit monstrous deeds to look like monsters. I meet them, and they look like me.

(DAVID R. DOW, *The Autobiography of an Execution*

Opening the Space
From Exile to Embrace

On July 24, 1991, Albert Clozza Jr. became the twelfth person executed in Virginia in the modern era. Convicted of the murder of Patricia Bolton, Clozza was the first person executed in the state's new execution chamber at Greensville Correctional Center. Following typical practice, Clozza was transferred to Greensville several days before the execution. He spent his last days in a different sort of isolation than he had experienced on death row at Mecklenburg Correctional Center, where death row inmates were housed prior to being transferred to Greensville. In the intervening days, the possessions of the condemned are doled out to friends on the row or shipped to family members, and visits are curtailed in preparation for the execution. Chaplains, however, retain some measure of free access to the prisoner, including after-hours or weekend access in some cases.

Visits are ended three hours before the execution. The condemned then can shower and have a last meal before being bodily prepped for the execution. After the condemned is moved into the holding cell, showers, and eats, the chaplains can come back and have a last religious service or simply commune in these final hours. On the evening before his execution, Clozza, a Catholic who had developed an interest in Buddhism, received communion from Rev. Russell Ford, a Baptist minister and former volunteer death row chaplain working through the Chaplain Service Prison Ministry of Virginia. During the ceremony, when he was asked whether he had anything to say, Clozza joked that his last words should be "Anyone coming with me?" Later, Ford answered Clozza, telling him, "You asked who will join you. All will follow."[1]

Because it was the facility's first execution, the death squad's presence was perhaps more apparent than in other instances. Everything had to go according to plan. Numerous drills and rehearsals would see to this. Interactions between the squad—the cadre of prison officers and officials charged with escorting the condemned to the execution chamber and then executing him—and the condemned are typically limited. You have to understand, Ford said, that the squad usually views the condemned with contempt and tends to believe that they are acting on behalf of the victim's family. Anthony Parker, captain of the squad on the evening of Clozza's execution, was different. Two different death row chaplains described Parker as an intensely serious, meticulous man who approached his duties with focused intensity and fastidious attention to detail. Rev. Joseph Vought, a Lutheran minister and former volunteer death row chaplain, described Parker as a "committed, fervent Christian" who participated in some of these final communions. During the service Ford conducted for Clozza and all who were gathered there, when Ford asked whether anyone had anything to say, "we had a moment where each man was free to say something. And the captain of the death squad looked at Bert Clozza and said, 'There are none righteous, no, not one.'" Though corrections staff generally decline to participate in the communion itself, Parker stepped forward and partook first; Clozza went last.[2]

At several of the final services pastored by Vought, Parker did the same thing, stepping forward when the minister asked whether anyone had anything to say and offering his statement, which in context sounds like a benediction. Speaking directly to the condemned, the squad captain would remind the man of what was "given to [him] by revelation, that there are no righteous, no, not one." On another occasion, Parker prefaced his quotation of Romans 3:10 more specifically, offering "the words and insight of another man, St. Paul who once led people away to their executions." These moments, which Ford and Vought both reported occurring on several occasions, benefited and challenged the chaplains. "It increased my faith," Ford said, while Vought focuses on the message he believes Parker was offering, that "the ground is level at the foot of the cross." It is a moment, Ford says, that proclaims "There but for the grace of God go I"; it is a moment, Vought says, that reminds you, "We're all repentant sinners, we're all people."[3]

Parker's offering is more than identification with the prisoner—it is an expression of embrace. I begin this chapter by introducing and explaining Miroslav Volf's concept of embrace, focusing on the points most helpful to our exploration of the death penalty. I then revisit the discourses we considered previously to highlight the elements of embrace they contain. In order to get at embrace, however, it is necessary to work through its counterpart, which for Volf is exclusion, and differentiate *exclusion* from *exile*. From there, we will explore embrace as it arises in the context of death row chaplains performing their ministry, sermons dealing with capital punishment, and liturgies for execution vigils. Finally, this chapter shows that despite the apparent need to draw a binary between *like us* and *not like us*, exile and embrace are not binary responses to violent crime and to the creation and understanding of the other. Rather, exile and embrace are concomitant counterparts that exist alongside one another—indeed, that can only exist alongside each other. Exile and embrace are not a dialectical pair but a complementary pair forming and guided by our response to transgression.

Exclusion

Volf's concept of embrace is directly linked to his concept of exclusion. It is necessary to begin by working through his concept of exclusion and by differentiating it from exile. Although exile and exclusion share many elements, the fundamental difference between the two is the recognizability of the other as created by, existing within, and subject to the processes of identity creation that precede and announce its presence.

Exclusion is the drive to purity—of self, of society, of nation. It is a process that begins with the creation of an essentially fixed self-identity, the creation of "a situated *self*, without which exclusions . . . would be unthinkable." Exclusion begins with the processes by which the "'unitary' . . . self [is created,] which can be formed only by driving out of the self all that is nonunitary and nonidentitical." This driving out in the name of integral purity of self—or ideas of extensions of self, such as community or nation—occurs via any of three basic forms. The first is exclusion by *elimination*, by genocide or attempted genocide, broadly defined.[4] A corollary to elimination is *assimilation*, in which everything that makes the other different must be discarded in order to accept and become everything that constitutes the self. Second, exclusion via *domination* occurs when one party subjugates another and treats it as inherently inferior. Third, we can exclude via *abandonment* by closing our eyes to societal injustices and inequalities, thereby placing sufficient distance between ourselves and the unfortunate others that they can make no claim on us.[5]

Volf uses the parable of the Good Samaritan to illustrate abandonment. A man traveling the road from Jerusalem to Jericho is beaten, robbed, and left for dead. A priest and a Levite see the critically injured man alongside the road, but both cross the road and avert their eyes. A Samaritan, a foreigner, comes upon the victim and cares for him. When we consider the parable in its context, Volf's message becomes clear. The victim, "a man [who] was going down from Jerusalem to Jericho," could be anyone. The priest and the Levite represent the elite, "the highest religious leadership among the Jews" and "the designated lay-associate of the priest," respectively. Jesus told the parable to answer a man who had asked who his neighbors were. The thrust of the question was directed not at a question of physical proximity but at the question of *like me*. Who is enough *like me* that it is my duty to look out for and care for them? Who is enough *like me* that the command to "love . . . your neighbor as yourself" applies? The answering parable typifies two responses, the "real" and the ideal. The "real" response is to differentiate, to exclude, to make a determination of *insufficiently like me*—to turn our eyes away and continue as if we had not noticed. The ideal response is to bend down and help, whether or not the helper—or the victim—is a foreigner, an alien, one who we think is *not like us*.[6]

It is easy to hear correlations between these types of exclusion and the retentionist and abolitionist concepts of exile discussed in chapter 4. The recognition of exclusion demands an acknowledgment of its inherent violence. Both the retentionist and abolitionist discourses acknowledge this. This violence, as Volf points out, "stabilize[s] the power of the perpetrator," which presents a problem of which both the retentionist and abolitionist discourses are acutely aware. Inasmuch as the retentionist exile is created via transgression, it is subject to exclusion via elimination. To the extent that the exclusionary acts—imposing and executing death sentences—concur with the basic precepts of mythic redemptive violence, there is an element of both domination—the exploitation of others to reinforce our own morality—and elimination. The ties to the myth of redemptive violence are only strengthened when we reflect on the desire of both exclusion and exile to address "barbarity *within* civilization, evil *among* the good, crime against the other *right within the walls of the self.*"[7] Domination and elimination are both elements and consequences of the retentionist exile. The abolitionist exile, by contrast, focuses more on abandonment and its correlation with elimination, assimilation, and domination. To the extent that the abolitionist discourse protests prosecutorial discretion alongside the demonstrable racial inequities in the application of the death penalty, for example, the discourse protests domination and elimination. To the extent that abolitionist exiles are revealed rather than created via their transgressions, to the extent that capital murderers can be profiled, reduced discursively to markers of exile—mental issues, including illness and retardation, prior abuse, drug problems, poverty, lack of education, illiteracy, socioeconomic factors, and so on—the discourse turns on questions of abandonment leading to elimination.

Although the exile bears a strong resemblance to the excluded, there is a critical difference between the two, which we can see in the tension between the two definitions of "elimination." The idea of elimination outlined here differs from that employed by Volf, who uses Bosnia and Rwanda as his exemplary contemporary manifestations of exclusion via elimination.[8] We cannot convincingly argue that elimination in the retentionist or abolitionist discourse is equivalent to Volf's idea of exclusion. Rather, the analogous elimination as it arises in the death penalty discourse has two faces, both of which differ in both kind and degree from Volf's use of elimination. In the retentionist discourse, elimination is a penalty imposed on a specific individual in response to a specific transgression. This individual committed this transgression in full possession of his faculties and with full reasonable foreknowledge of the consequences. The discourse need not admit to having broader aims than a specific act of violence meted out in response to a specific transgression. To the extent that inequalities in the system make it appear more analogous to Volf's concept of elimination than the retentionist discourse would credit, these inequalities are the result of human failures of application, not a desire to eliminate the other wholesale. As such, they can be reasonably seen as remediable problems, and the discourse openly admits to the need to adopt whatever remedial measures can ensure more perfect application.

The abolitionist discourse essentially agrees with the retentionist's first two assertions of specific penalty as specific response. It contests the remainder, however, particularly the dismissal of issues of culpability, for the reasons discussed in chapter 4. The abolitionist exile is revealed, not created, by transgression. It thus applies more broadly than does the retentionist exile, particularly inasmuch as it admits of "types" and "profiling." While this is so, and while the paternalism inherent in the discourse somewhat echoes Volf's idea of exclusion via domination, the exile in the abolitionist religious discourse is nevertheless imagined both as possessing something sacred, something that it would be sinful to destroy—life—and as inherently redeemable. Inasmuch as they are inherently redeemable, they are fundamentally *like us*.

Moreover, if they are inherently redeemable, then there is no point of no return, no point beyond which they cannot be saved and restored, except in one specific case I will discuss below. The retentionist exile, by contrast, does admit of a point of no return—it is the transgressive act, which creates exiles and simultaneously locates them beyond the point at which we can hope to have them restored to us. Nevertheless, this discourse conceives of this point of no return in a way starkly different than Volf's concept of exclusion does. The retentionist exile is basically a taking-in in order to drive away. Once created, the other is taken in; the other is shown, at times painstakingly, to be clearly *like us* in order to establish warrant, our right and our responsibility to punish them. An extreme example of this is the states' forcibly medicating prisoners back to sanity so they can be competent to be executed. This is ironic on many levels, from the failure of the states to provide this level of mental health treatment to other prisoners to the failure of these states to provide this level of treatment for people on the outside and perhaps save lives to the use of medications designed to restore a patient's mental state with the explicit purpose of rendering them aware of the fact of and rationale behind their executions. Healing them in order to kill them is an extreme example of this kind of embrace to exile, of this taking-in in order to drive out.[9]

The abolitionist exile is a driving away in order to take in or, more specifically, a driving away—a revelation of *not like us*—in order to set in place the conditions whereby a taking-in can later occur. In both cases, we can use those located on the periphery to see the center more clearly. Like death row inmates, those in "peripheral social locations [are] consequential"; by investigating "their position on the outside, [we can] identif[y], analyz[e], and critiqu[e] the center." In other words, we can see ourselves more clearly via the other, to the point of being able to invert Paul Ricoeur's expression that "the selfhood of oneself implies otherness to such an intimate degree that one cannot be thought of without the other."[10] The various acts of exile imply, and reveal, selfhood to such an intimate degree that the other cannot be thought of apart from the self.

Exile is thus creative. It is identity-affirming. It is also emblematic of Volf's understanding of differentiation, which he defines as "separating-*and*-binding."[11] This binding operates on several levels simultaneously. First, in both cases, the differentiation binds the other irrevocably to the self. Second, again in both cases, the differentiation binds the other within defined roles within our symbolic vocabulary. This is most evident in the differentiated binding that occurs in the legal discourse and the move from defendant to executed, as discussed in the previous chapter. To see this binding to specific roles, consider the following forms of address:

> In June 1998, Robert Stacy Yarbrough was found guilty by a jury and sentenced to death for . . . capital murder. . . . Having carefully reviewed the Petition for Clemency and judicial opinions regarding this case, I find no compelling reason to set aside the sentence that was recommended by the jury, and then imposed and affirmed by the courts.
>
> We lost Robert Yarbrough tonight, or Stacy, as his friends knew him.[12]

The difference in address, and the different reception of each address, demonstrates this difference in separating-and-binding.

The third sense in which differentiation binds the other is a subset of each of the previous two, though to a different end. This is a locative binding, whereby the other is identified relative to the self and as occupying a particular *location* relative to the self. The exile's "geographic" location depends on the idea of the self at work—most directly, whether the other may be killed by, and to protect, the self—and must be considered relative to the perceived point of no return. For Volf, beyond this point of no return—the point beyond which the other is irrevocably other and no longer related to the self—is the point at which the relationship between self and other is irremediably altered:

> Exclusion can entail cutting of the bonds that connect, taking oneself out of the pattern of interdependence and placing oneself in a position of *sovereign independence*. The other then emerges either as an enemy that must be pushed away from the self and driven out of its space or as a nonentity—*a superfluous being*—that can be disregarded and abandoned.[13]

This is not what occurs via exile, however, even when the point of no return is reached, as an examination of the two italicized phrases will demonstrate. In the retentionist conception of exile, the self does not and, more to the point, *cannot* leave the "pattern of interdependence" for the very reason that the self cannot be considered either sovereign or independent: the transgression determines our response. Our reaction—our *necessary* reaction—to the other's transgression robs us of our sovereignty and independence and prevents us from acting outside the pattern of interdependence. The fact that our reaction is defended as the necessary response to a particular provocation defines its interdependence. The fact that the offender thus imposes our reaction on us undercuts any notions of sovereignty or independence. Our response is an act of total dependence, which is to say, interdependence. Arguments that we exercise our own sovereignty in responding to the murder as we *must* are unpersuasive because they hold that we respond as we *must*, not as we *choose*. The retentionist conception of exile conceives of only one normal actor: the offender. The offender is sovereign; the responding self is not. This is the amplification of the offender's power, as discussed in chapter 4. The retentionist conception of exile is thus based not on strength but rather, and exclusively, on weakness.

Further, because the exile is integral to the self, it cannot be conceived of as superfluous, for reasons that circle us back to the abolitionist exile and sovereign independence. Because the conception of justice inherent in the retentionist exile is tied to our carrying out our necessary response, the exile—the offender whose transgression provoked that response—cannot be considered superfluous. It is integral. In this context, the image of the self is interdependent on the other. So is the abolitionist exile, for the same reasons: conceptions of justice and the understanding of the self, morally and otherwise. The abolitionist exile also locates sovereignty with the offender—with the other, rather than the self—though for different reasons and to different ends than the retentionist exile, as we will see. The responding self in the abolitionist conception of exile possesses a sort of sovereign independence, inasmuch as the self is responsible for and capable of addressing the social ills that give rise to the exile as revealed via the offense. At the same time, however, this sovereignty is limited and interdependent, given the offender's ability to impose limits on it or to reveal its shortcomings. Fundamentally, however, the abolitionist exile acknowledges this interdependence by denying the point of no return, or, more accurately, by displacing it from the offender to the victim.

Within the retentionist discourse, the other does not *exist* beyond the point of no return but rather elects to venture there. The criminal offense that recreates the individual as the exile—willfully chosen, willfully perpetrated—locates him beyond this point. The abolitionist exile, because it is revealed rather than created, is closer to the idea of the excluded. Nevertheless, it remains fundamentally different because the abolitionist exile can close the distance. The point of no return is rather a point *of* return, provided the offender—here, as in the retentionist discourse, a sovereign agent—chooses to "do the work." The relative "geographic" markers underscore that the exile is also, or exclusively, normal via his sovereignty. Thus, whereas exclusion relies on this point of no return, relies on fundamental *apartness* in addition to otherness, exile posits otherness via nearness. As the following consideration of embrace shows, while the defining feature of exclusion is *opposition*, the defining feature of exile is *apposition*.

Embrace The Prodigal Son and Opening the Arms

Volf's concept of embrace consists of a four-part movement, a sequential process of opening the arms to the other, waiting, closing the arms around the other, and opening the arms again. My analysis focuses on the first act, *opening the arms*, though I will consider elements of the others as the arguments proceeds, particularly the second, *waiting*. We must proceed on the understanding that opening the arms is an ambiguous act, inasmuch as its effect on the process cannot be determined before or even at the moment of opening. In one sense, opening the arms is a determinative act, which sets the process of embrace in motion and permits it to proceed. In an equally important sense, opening the arms merely permits embrace potentially to proceed, pending the other's willingness to open his arms in return. A closer look at Volf's paradigmatic episode of embrace, the parable of the Prodigal Son, will clarify this.[14]

For Volf, this narrative highlights the two most important features of embrace, "the father's giving himself to his estranged son and his receiving that son back into his household." Coming home to himself in the pigpen, the son engages in a "strategy of return," the three movements of which — return, confession, and acceptance — will restore him to his father's household. Vitally, as Volf points out, the son seeks to be restored as a servant, not a son. The father, on the other hand, interrupts the sequence by accepting the son back before hearing the confession, confounding our expectations by inverting the son's planned order. Volf argues that the father actually interrupts the son's intentions twice. First, the father interrupts the sequence of restorative events; because transgression provoked the need for restoration, acceptance should have been preceded by confession, not the other way around. Second, offering acceptance before the (potentially) restorative speech act of the confession interrupts the process of identity and relationship negotiation that the son expected to ensue. Instead, the relationship was offered back as restored.[15]

I argue that these are elements of the same movement — closing the arms. While the parable highlights the two most salient features of embrace — giving of the self and restoration — I suggest revising the concept of embrace such that these two elements are understood to be *accompaniment* and *repentance*, both of which likewise feature prominently in the parable. What the four proposed keystone features have in common is that they mark both place and proximity. The father giving himself back to his estranged son and welcoming his son back into the household speaks of literal and metaphoric place and proximity. Accompaniment and repentance likewise speak to both place and proximity, again both literally and metaphorically. Accompaniment here refers to Volf's first movement, opening the arms, which is "a sign that I have *created space* in myself for the other to come in and that I have made a movement out of myself so as to enter the space created by the other."[16] Repentance refers to what the chaplains collectively refer to as, to borrow from one, "doing the work" of dying and then of living. As we will see, both ideas involve concepts both of proximity and of place. Recognizing proximity leads us back to the recognition that the exile is necessarily defined by apposition, by proximity. Place leads us to death row and to the volunteers who serve as prison chaplains in the state's death house.

The very idea of a volunteer death row chaplain suggests accompaniment in the sense of open arms. The free exercise and establishment paragraph of Virginia's state constitution prohibits "any tax ... for the support of any church or ministry," which has traditionally been understood to prohibit even the use of state funds to pay the salaries of prison chaplains. Prison chaplains in Virginia thus often are volunteers working for the Chaplain Service of the Churches of Virginia, an organization funded by numerous churches and denominations.[17] Others minister to those on death row because they were asked to. Death row chaplains are fully aware of the roles that place and proximity play in their work, not only in the work itself but also in the call to the work.

Entering a Security Level 5 state prison makes one acutely aware of place and proximity. In one sense, this awareness of place is generated by extrapolation from fact as much as any visual or other sensory clues. Sussex I State Prison, home to Virginia's death row, lends itself to just that sort of first impression. It lives up to the cliché of being located in the dead middle of nowhere, requiring visitors to make a deceptively long drive from virtually anywhere in the state. The guard towers, menacing obelisks poised above the countryside, command attention from every point from which they are visible. In the flat farmland of southside Virginia, the towers are visible a considerable distance from the prison. The parking lot is fairly nondescript; a visitor could be forgiven for thinking that this was any parking lot outside any administrative building. Signs reserve spots for particular individuals or for holders of particular job titles. Some spots are reserved for "Visitors." The administrative building is squat, long, and not particularly imposing; it resembles a generic administrative building from any industrial park. The chain-link fence topped with razor wire extends behind and from the building and does little either to alter or to confirm that impression.

A peculiar array of sights greets visitors just inside the door. A men's and a women's room, with a water fountain between them, in an alcove to the left. A pay phone. Signs detailing procedure — hours, banned/prohibited equipment, contact information, how to make an appointment, and so on. A low couch against one wall. And directly ahead, a reception desk, behind which a Department of Corrections official sits, fully uniformed. Behind and to the right of the official stands another guard, almost but, presumably deliberately, not quite concealed by darkly smoked glass. I assume that the glass is bulletproof, but do not ask; I likewise assume that I am better off not knowing what weaponry resides in the booth with the barely visible occupant. A visitor who has checked the Department of Corrections website to see how prisons are classified will know that Level 5 is one below "Maximum Security." One of the two state's Supermax facilities — Red Onion State Prison, in Wise County — is listed as maximum security. The other Supermax, Wallens Ridge State Prison in Big Stone Gap, is a Level 5, the only Level 5 apart from Sussex I.[18] First impressions of this place, it hardly need be said, are extremely powerful.

When our scheduled appointment time arrives, Rev. W. Eric Jackson emerges from an adjacent building. Stepping forward from behind the front desk after having passed through what appear to be three separate metal detectors in that distance, he leads me to a conference room, mere yards from the front desk, a few short feet from the nearest metal detector. There is an absurdity in the location where our interview will take place, but we sit at the conference table, talking about place and proximity over the course of the interview. Given where we are and, more to the point, where he is, a natural first question is how he made his way into prison ministry. Jackson detailed his education and training. He has a BS in business administration and an MDiv and DDiv from the Sam DeWitt Proctor School of Theology at Virginia Union University, with a focus on church growth. A Baptist minister, Jackson got to Chaplain Service because he had recently left the full-time pastorate to plant his new church and needed the income. It was not a calling at first, he said, but over the course of his prison ministry, he's learned to be a better pastor in his own church:

> It has helped me to listen, to try to understand where people are coming from a little bit more. It's also started to help me deal with my frustration that I might have in my ministry. Because you can be dealing with some difficult people, and knowing that you, as a person in ministry, you are — in order to help them, you have to know sometimes your own tendencies and issues that you deal with, and try to manage those so that you can do your best to try and help people who are in need.[19]

Father Jim Griffin, a Catholic priest, entered the prison ministry in seminary, when he began visiting prisons with other chaplains. Ordained in 1982, he worked closely with Walter Sullivan, then bishop of Richmond, a longtime, active abolitionist. Griffin accompanied Bishop Sullivan onto death row, where he met and ministered to Frank Coppola, the first person executed by Virginia in the modern era, in 1982. Griffin also met Walter Mickens, whose 2002 execution was the last that Griffin witnessed, and Joseph Giarratano, who was on death row from 1979 until his death sentence was commuted in 1991.

During one of Griffin's early visits, Giarratano asked him to conduct a death row Christmas mass. Griffin agreed, and received permission from prison officials to conduct the ceremony. That Christmas mass marked a turning point in Griffin's prison ministry: "When you do something well, they like it, you like it, it starts to snowball, you have to do it more." He was stationed in Mecklenburg, Virginia, home of the Mecklenburg Correctional Center, which housed Virginia's death row until it was moved to Sussex I in 1998. Griffin visited death row every Tuesday for the two years he was there. Putting the number of executions that he personally had witnessed at six or seven, he said, "The relationships with the men evolved into that. A guy asks you to do the last-minute rite, he could ask any of 6.5 million people and he asked you — and you can't say no."[20]

Ralph McCloud, a Catholic lay volunteer, worked with death row inmates in Texas before taking a job with the United States Conference of Catholic Bishops in Washington. He was recruited into the death row volunteer ministry by a Sister St. John, whom he describes as having an incredible passion for that ministry. McCloud initially did not share her passion or her outlook. Instead, he was glad for the prisons, which he saw as having a different function than Sister St. John envisioned: "I felt that there was a need for prisons, to warehouse and lock people up, separate them from [the] community, but she saw the whole need in terms of rehabilitating the person because of their human dignity, because they were made in the likeness of God." Evaluating his early prison ministry, McCloud admitted, "I probably didn't much help the inmates that I saw. . . . I think I would go in and just have an attitude of punishment, retribution." After what he described as his conversion experience, however, he understood the men, his work, and himself differently: "The more I went, the more I was able to see that dignity that [Sister St. John] was trying to stress personified, literally, I guess. I was able to see myself in a lot of the inmates. Listening to some of their stories, they became my stories. Oftentimes my stories became their stories." McCloud first visited an inmate on death row at the request of a colleague in the ministry, who suggested that McCloud visit this particular inmate: "He said, 'He's a good guy, he's bright, he's an inspiration to a lot of the inmates here.' He told me the name, and I recognized the name — it was the kid from across the street. . . . [So] I went."[21]

Rev. Joseph Vought's path to death row was similar to Father Griffin's. Vought, an ELCA minister, started his prison ministry in suburban Baltimore, ministering to the Community of St. Dysmas, a Lutheran congregation composed of inmates in the Maryland correctional system. The congregation took their name from the repentant thief of Luke's Passion narrative, who was crucified next to Jesus, asked to be remembered when Jesus came into the kingdom, and is the only person in the New Testament explicitly promised salvation. Like Griffin, Vought wound up on death row when he was asked to accompany an inmate. After he accepted a call to a church in a Richmond suburb, Vought was startled to receive a call from his church secretary telling him to turn on the news, asking about one of their congregants, where he was from, what he did for a living. "I said, 'Why are you asking me all of these questions?' She said, 'He's just been arrested for the murder of his family twenty years ago.' . . . They had profiled his case on *America's Most Wanted* the week before. . . . He was my member." A year after that incident,

> one of my members came to me and said, "My half-brother's just been convicted for the rape and murder of a ten-year-old girl. He's been sentenced to death. Would you go visit him?" So I went to [the county jail] and visited him. . . . When he got transferred to [death row], I started going down there. . . . I'm sure I was scared. I mean, I'd been in prisons before, and in jails, but [not death row]. . . . I guess we visited one day a month for about six or seven years. . . . He was the last guy I walked with.[22]

Two elements stand out from each of these calling narratives: place and proximity. In each case, they are related, though not interchangeable. McCloud, Griffin, and Vought arrived on death row via similar routes, each entering the prison ministry elsewhere in the system and then moving on to death row and ministering to prisoners there, even to the point of accompanying them to the execution chamber at personal request. Place is not just the pigpen, the physical location, though it is difficult to overlook the "eight steel doors, two pat-down searches and 20 minutes" that separate the outside from the inmates. Nor could they overlook the succession of rooms and corridors ending at the execution chamber, above which hangs, macabrely, an Exit sign. Place is not merely the geography of the "hell" that is the criminal justice system. It is not something that you can approximate, however incompletely, by locking yourself in your bathroom at home for an hour to get an idea of the prisoner's living space, a well-intended suggestion that one death row prisoner vehemently derided: "I remember saying to myself, 'What?' There is no freaking way you can get a feel for what the death row experience is like."[23] This place, formed by consensual structures of power operating on nearly innumerable levels, cannot be approximated; at home you can always open your own door or remove your own restraints.

More than any of these, place does two things: place shapes, and place brings people into proximity with each other and with themselves. Place shapes those subject to it, whether they are subject to it temporarily or permanently. In shaping those subject to it, it shapes proximity or, more aptly, it shapes propinquity. Approaching and entering the place begins the shaping process, whether by crossing the parking lot under the gaze of a watchtower and seeing the redundant guard stations, metal detectors, and control panels, or by traversing the two pat-downs and eight steel doors. The intended effect, the desired communication, is of danger, of the need for vigilance—of suspicion. This in turn affects the work itself; as Jackson notes, "While you're here, all of us are locked up." Death row religious services are also defined by place: "Correctional officers loo[k] coolly upon the whole scene, suspicious, aloof and questioning the sanity of the pastors as well as the worthiness of the flock." Given the controversy over death row conversions and whether we can credit them, either with acceptance of their sincerity or with mercy, and given the location, the example provided by those who have "done the work" of reforming themselves is all the more muted: "One of the inmates asked me, 'What will become of a society that kills its teachers, the people who have learned and are learning from their mistakes?' I could give no answer. We both knew the cost. The question still haunts me."[24]

Here, place brings the ministers into potential contact with the most "leprous people in our society . . . death-row inmates." This proximity, which can lead to propinquity, operates on two levels simultaneously for both minister and inmate. First, the shaping power of the place must be sufficiently broken down that some degree of trust can be possible. This is one facet of what Volf describes as opening the arms. These chaplains disdain the hellfire-and-brimstone approach preached by the "Bible notchers," whose message is "you've got to take your punishment and you're bound to the depths of hell and an eye for an eye and a tooth for a tooth":[25]

> A good example . . . one of the guys was dying, and I remember expressly being there all day, starting at three, and about six o'clock, a Baptist preacher came in from Jerry Falwell's group in Lynchburg. . . . He came in and he looked right at the guy—where my ministry is . . . more personal, just to be there, not try to change his life, just walk with him—the other guy says, looked at him and says, "You have two hours to live, and unless you give your life to Jesus Christ, you're going to hell." This was two hours before the guy is going to be executed. My ministry is not that.[26]

> It's a ministry of accompaniment . . . better than whipping a trip on them. I mean, there's nothing worse than that, you know? I remember guys, we'd go on death row, and there were always a few chaplains who would go in from the more, shall I say, evangelical, fundamentalist persuasion, who'd go in and just rail at them, wanting to give the guys their testimony, and wanting them to accept Jesus as their personal savior, and all this tripe. And one of the guys said to me and my colleague, Russ Ford, one day, "You guys are different. You guys come and you listen to us, you talk to us, you get to know us, and you let Jesus be the savior." And I think that's the spirit.[27]

Rather than haranguing, rather than entering with a message indifferent to any differences among recipients, to any need even to consider the individual toward whom the message is directed, these chaplains prefer to open their arms and wait. "My ministry is walking with them and being a spiritual adviser if they asked." "I . . . ask an open-ended question, 'How are you doing?,' and then let them talk. I don't force a relationship with anybody. . . . We don't proselytize . . . anybody; whether they want it or not is up to them."[28]

Despite its power to shape, however, place is not fixed. It can be extended both outward and inward. Both of these processes of extension occur via proximity, by building relationships and expanding the scope of those recognized as *like us*. A communion service held on December 3, 1996, the night of Gregory Beaver's execution, is an example of extending place outward. While Ford was ministering to Beaver and hosting the communion on death row, Vought sat in a nearby hotel room with Beaver's wife and family listening to the final service via telephone. When Ford administered the Eucharist to Beaver, Vought did the same for his family. Extending place outwardly, in this case by hosting simultaneous services connected over a telephone line, involves other people in the event. This expansion brought the service outward to encompass the offender's family, who are among those silenced by the capital punishment process.[29]

The Troy Davis case gives us multiple examples of extending place outwardly. Davis was executed on September 21, 2011, for the 1991 murder of officer Mark MacPhail, an off-duty police officer killed in a Savannah, Georgia, parking lot. In some ways, this was the perfect capital crime: two black suspects accused of killing an off-duty white police officer — a young man with a young family, a son, husband, and father moonlighting as a security guard for the extra income for his family, who was killed, off-duty, trying to protect a stranger from two assailants. The problem is that the case against Davis was not "ironclad," as Judge William T. Moore Jr. of the US District Court for the Southern District of Georgia, who presided over a portion of his appeals process, put it. There was no convincing moral certainty; the appellate judge admitted as much, while denying that that should impact the case because, as we noted earlier, innocence in fact is not constitutionally cognizable.[30]

Davis was convicted on eyewitness testimony — there was no physical evidence linking him to the crime, nor was a murder weapon ever found. Of the nine witnesses to name Davis as MacPhail's killer at trial, seven subsequently recanted or backed away from their testimony, including one witness who admitted that he did not know then and could not say now who actually killed MacPhail. The police gave him a statement and told him to sign it, he said; he also admitted that he had not read the statement and that he in fact could not

(*Opening the Space*

read. One of Davis's original jurors also noted that were she sitting on that jury today she would vote "not guilty."[31]

Davis's case attracted worldwide attention due to its racial overtones and, more important, questions of actual innocence. Activists delivered petitions with nearly seven hundred thousand signatures to the Georgia Board of Pardons and Paroles urging clemency in Davis's case; forty thousand were signatures of Georgians, with the overwhelming majority of signatures coming from elsewhere in the United States and around the world. Davis's list of supporters included well-known peace activists like Jimmy Carter and Pope Benedict XVI, and conservative law-and-order politicians like former prosecutor and Georgia congressman Bob Barr and former FBI director William Sessions. Over three hundred vigils were held in cities around the world, at which protestors chanted "I Am Troy Davis." These are all examples of extending space outwardly—by extending the conversation and by picturing something of the other in yourself. If this innocent man can be executed, these protestors argued, any innocent man or woman could be. This willingness to see the other in oneself was best captured by Rev. Raphael Warnock, pastor of Atlanta's Ebenezer Baptist Church: "'It's midnight in the garden of good and evil,' he said. 'But I am so glad God does his best work at midnight.'" It's midnight, and we're all in the garden together, we and the others alike; our space and their spaces are a part of the same greater space.[32]

This act of seeing the other in ourselves is a bilateral move, where we extend our space outward, toward the other, but simultaneously extend their space inward, toward us. We can read this bilateral movement in something Davis's sister Kim Davis said following his execution. Davis, who believed in her brother's innocence and continues the fight to clear his name, said that she prayed for the MacPhails because "it's sad for someone to have so much hate in their hearts." It's not difficult to assume that Davis is speaking from a position of experience, particularly given that she indicates that she forgave her brother's detractors because he had first, and it is this awareness of hate and of relinquishing hate that shows the bilaterality of the extension of place inward.[33]

Somewhat paradoxically, extending place inward is both a component of and a precursor to opening the arms. Looking at how the chaplains compare their prison and church ministries shows one such inward extension. This ministry, which the chaplains describe as ministering to the men or bringing church onto the row, works in two different ways. The first is being there and bringing ministry to anyone in the institution who wishes. As Rev. Cecil McFarland, a United Methodist minister and former executive director of the Chaplain Service, put it, "Your job is . . . being the chaplain not only to the people who are incarcerated but the staff as well."[34]

The second element is simple proximity—being there and using yourself as the conduit to bring "church" into the institution. As Vought, who describes his parish ministry as "family chaplain[cy]," puts it, "The Church is not just church; it's not the idea that people come to the church to get it. It's as much as the church goes out to meet people where they are." McFarland expresses this in similar terms: "I've been a local pastor, I've been a navy chaplain . . . and I've been with Chaplain Service, and every group has a different language. You have to learn a new language, but you're really doing the same thing. . . . You're still dealing with people." Jackson echoes Vought and McFarland in comparing prison ministry with parish ministry, though with a noteworthy difference:

> [In] a parish ministry, you know that people are going to make mistakes, and you provide some way for them to overcome those mistakes and to be able to do away with their guilt and shame. . . . [Just before our meeting] I was back there . . . doing a Bible study with a group of guys. . . . The main topic today was about guilt and shame. . . . What came out of the context . . . was the question, "Well, chaplain, . . . how do we deal with guilt and shame? Feeling like I failed God in some kind of way? How do we do that?" I deal with that, you know, from a very biblical perspective, sharing with them that God's response to guilt is grace. And that's interesting to say that in here, because that's not always the case.[35]

This is the second element of extending place inward, extending place inward bodily. Drawing on his extensive experience in the military and prison chaplaincies, McFarland states the problem simply: "That's what I tell the chaplain—be visible. Walk. Be visible. . . . That proximity makes a big difference." This proximity, the simple fact that the men will talk to you if you are there, makes a ministry of accompaniment easier. When the chaplains describe their ministry, you can hear the stress they put on the preposition: walk *with*. In Volf's articulation, the first act of embrace, opening the arms, entails creating a space within yourself for the other. This same prerequisite seems also to be at work in walking *with* someone, the willingness to accept something of the other as part of yourself. Each of the chaplains expressed some ambiguity about that. Vought talked about some of the "horrible" things he had heard while in the ministry, but immediately afterward talked about how difficult it was to see his friends, people with whom he had bonded, be marched into the execution chamber. Griffin described some of the inmates he had worked with as "skewed . . . a little off, some of them," before wondering—not rhetorically—how many on the outside are not likewise a little off; at the same time, though, "they weren't just jerks, who were monsters locked up. . . . They had hearts, too." Jackson admitted that from time to time he thinks, "I see why you're locked up," but continued that his role is to help those who want it find grace and come to terms with their situation and what they have done. McCloud explained this problem in detail, discussing what he termed his "conversion experience," which is worth quoting at length:

> Sister St. John had a particular inmate who had committed a very, very heinous crime. And I had been visiting him for several weeks, didn't know what the crime was until I saw television and him in shackles and someone on the television talking about what the crime was. Hearing that he'd been accused of killing his twelve-year-old daughter. At this point, I found it very difficult to want to go back, to talk to him, or have anything at all to do with him. And Sister St. John understood my anger, my frustration, and her response was that he's at the point where he needed me the most. And I even said something, that I didn't think he was even Catholic. And she just looked at me and said, "well, he's as Catholic as you are."
>
> So . . . I went and had an honest, very candid conversation with the guy, and said, you know, is it true? I found out what you've been accused of doing, and I said something like, "If I'd only known." And he asked me, "Well, does that mean you wouldn't have come if you had known? What if I was a bad check writer? Would you have come then? What's the level of crime that you [. . .]" — and I didn't have a good answer for him. I guess I had the vision of him being somewhat of a safe inmate. He read these big, thick software books. Blond hair, blue eyes, kind of an inmate who I found that I identified with, but I thought, you know, at some point he's going to be released, and be a responsible contributor to society, as opposed to somebody who I had a predetermined idea as to what they would be based on what kind of crime they had committed. So it was at that point — I mark that as being the point for me, personally, when I had a different way of looking at it after that.[36]

McCloud continued to visit and eventually reached the point where he could describe his death row ministry in terms of the open arms that Volf described: "I was able to see myself in a lot of the inmates. Listening to some of their stories, they became my stories. Oftentimes my stories became their stories." Griffin continued his ministry and became close enough with some of the inmates that prison officials sought to bar him from visiting. Vought speaks in terms of having watched friends die and of learning to adapt his ministry to "the old St. Francis mantra, seek first to understand, then to be understood." The sequential nature of the mantra encapsulates the bilateral nature of opening the arms and waiting, the first two acts of embrace — the person opening the arms is willing to understand, and waiting to be understood.[37]

Having arrived at the point where they could meaningfully offer to accompany the inmates — to walk *with* them — the chaplains each articulated their understanding of where they were. Following the parable of the prodigal son, the ministers found themselves in the proverbial pigpen, and their ministry had to account for where they were, and with whom. Their arrivals in the pigpen gave them a basis from which to identify with those to whom they were ministering. As they said, they had no intention of winding up on death row; it was the course of events that brought them there, at personal cost:

> I was with all these men in the chamber, seven men. . . . I've had flashbacks, not since then, I mean, I'm way over that, but I mean, I remember I went home after one execution, and—they do it at nine, you've helped me remember the time frame, because so much you just want to forget. I remember, they do it at nine, by the time all is said and done and they escort you out, you're probably driving up the road at ten-thirty. Russ [Ford] and I would always go together. We'd stop somewhere to get something to eat, I'd get home at probably [midnight], and, you know, you just can't go to bed. So I'd be up surfing channels, and I came across . . . *The Addams Family*, and the little girl's got her brother in the electric chair, and I'm just like, "Ah, shit!" . . . I'm glad I'm not doing it anymore. *I didn't ever imagine doing it, I didn't covet it, but I'm glad I was there for the men who wanted me to be there.*[38]

Once there, they learned to let go of their preconceptions, learned to be able to approach the inmates and ask them how they were, to commit to the "relationship building, and building the trust and the credibility, so when that hard stuff came up, you could go there." Coming to terms with the need to open their arms, letting go of the anger and the fear they brought into the chamber with them, is an act of repentance. We should think of it, Vought says, as "doing the work."[39]

Waiting Doing the Work of Coming Home to Yourself

One question that continues to plague the chaplains is that of their role in the process of state-sanctioned killing. The chaplains' realizations that they had landed in the pigpen and needed to take stock of their surroundings was not limited to their assessment of the inmates; they had to come home to what their new situation meant for themselves. The chaplains also had to come to terms with their role in a process that culminated in a man being put to death. Were they, as Vought wondered, speaking truth to power by coming in and visiting with the men, showing them that they had worth, that they had dignity? Or, by comforting the men and helping those who wished come to terms with their deaths, were they making it easier for the state to kill them? In other words, were they comforting the afflicted without adequately afflicting the comfortable?

Were they sinning, Jackson wondered, by participating in a process that would culminate in the destruction of life, in contravention of what Griffin termed the basic justification for their ministry, the belief that God created life and saw that it was good? How should they respond, McCloud wondered, when they received a letter from one of two inmate brothers saying that his brother has vowed to fight the guards all the way to the execution chamber and that corrections officers have asked him to counsel his brother against fighting, to convince him to submit and go quietly to his death? These questions continue to frustrate the chaplains. They have no answers. Working through these questions is part of "doing the work," of coming to terms with themselves and their actions. The chance to "do the work" to do the work of dying and then of living—is what the chaplains offer the inmates and what *waiting*, the second act of embrace, symbolizes.

"Doing the work," accepting your situation in order to take stock of and repair your life, begins with two assumptions. First, there is no essential point of no return; exile in this sense is, if not voluntary, then remediable to a degree. Second, it is up to the offender to choose to walk back from his exile as best he can; the exile, again, is the normal actor. These two assumptions—that the exilic distance can be overcome if the exile wishes to repair the breach to the extent that he can—together lead to the essential goal of the process, which lies somewhere along a continuum between taking responsibility and repentance. Here the distinction between the two is not relevant. There is a real difference between acknowledging guilt and repentance, which Volf defines as a "turnabout of a profound moral and religious import." Volf characterizes repentance as a reaction to the knowledge that one has made more than a mistake, that one has *sinned*. This process, he says, is one of renaming and remaking. During a discussion of the story of the adulterous woman from John 8, one Bible study participant described these processes in her own experience:

> I think in that sense she's punished, because she has to live with that knowledge. ... She's confronted with what she did ... and [Jesus is] the one that's able to remove that, and how many times are there things that we feel so bad about, but until someone can—I love my grandchildren, of course. My kids are pastors, so they teach their kids the right things to say, but my three grandsons fight all the time ... and the first time I heard them say this I thought it was such a powerful thing. They go up to their sibling that they've done something to and they say, "I'm sorry, please forgive me." And the other one has time to think about it. And then the words when they come back are not, "It's okay." They'll say, "I forgive you." And there's such power in that, it's so much different than just "It's okay." She was confronted with what she did, and he very kindly forgave her. So she was punished, of her own.[40]

These interrelated processes correspond with the basic question of human living, variously phrased as *Who are we to be?* and *What am I to do?* They also encapsulate the process of "doing the work" such that we can treat repentance as the goal of that process. Equally importantly, this correspondence permits, and perhaps demands, that we approach the process from what may be an unnatural position: we must take seriously the idea of the offender as victim.

Given the dominance of the trope of the normal individual at all levels of the discourse, seeing the offender as victim can indeed be difficult. It is more difficult the more strongly we believe that legal guilt corresponds with actual guilt. Nevertheless, there are three reasons that we need to approach embrace by treating the offender as a victim. First, this provides a necessary counterpoint in contextualizing what would otherwise be an incidental relationship between the chaplains and the inmates. Second, both the retentionist and abolitionist exilic discourses demand that the offender be understood as a victim, whether of his own choice or of the circumstances that prevented him from making that choice. Third, understanding the offender as victim is central to any attempt to reclaim some of the offender's power over us.

This means different things within the two discourses, however. In the retentionist discourse, the offender as victim is an affirmation of warrant, of our duty to punish transgression. To the extent that the execution is an attempt to restore a measure of power and control that the offender had taken from us, this reclamation depends on the offender also being a victim. The abolitionist discourse, meanwhile, takes our capacity to choose how to react as perhaps the sine qua non of our humanity and demands that the offender also be a victim. Viewing the offender as victim offers the capacity to choose our response, to not respond evilly to evil. Viewing the offender as victim allows the offender the possibility of repentance and the profound moral change that entails.

It is not entirely accurate to say that the chaplains do not admit of a point of no return. They do—in fact, they admit of two, one of which we will discuss later—but the point of no return that they acknowledge is the one that stands in opposition to the two basic assumptions of "doing the work." In other words, one must refuse or be unable to make the choice to try to walk back from his exile, thus remaining beyond the point of no return. There are certainly those who are unable to make the choice, including the mentally retarded and mentally ill. Others will not make the choice: "People who may be sentenced to death, or even incarcerated, can *settle with* [that] . . . We have not taken away . . . their free will . . . they still have the free will to be reconciled within themselves." Speaking of one of these, Andrew Chabrol, who reportedly went to his death believing that he had been right to kill his victim, Ford said, "There was no humanity there."[41]

Others, however, do make that choice, and they do so in a particular location: the cell, which functions as two places simultaneously. Literally, the cell is the place of confinement, the pigpen to which their decisions have led them. This place should be understood in terms of the normal, which the parable of the prodigal son depicts. Not everyone in that situation goes there, as Vought says. "The person who commits that crime that lands them on death row, they have a choice," as Jackson says. Recalling comments made by one of the Bible study participants, it is the offender's choice not to "say . . . 'It's my responsibility to change that.'" The prodigal himself arrives where he does via "stupidity ('squandering,' v. 13) and bad luck ('severe famine,' v. 14)."[42] Even affirmations that the exile is *like us* rely on this pairing of circumstance and choice:

> I don't really want to say that under the right circumstances that all of us could be killers. I don't really think that. . . . I just think that it's easy for you to get caught up, and it's easy for you to go down that road real quick, a road that you never really intended to go down.[43]
>
> From time to time I would see people who were locked up and who may have come from my old neighborhood, who recognized me and called my name out. I would see and hear stories of despair, lack of hope, desperation. And clearly, obviously, we responded in different ways. They responded to the situation differently, and I think that I had a different support system that helped me to respond in different ways. But I feel a similarity between where I was and what I was doing, and where they were and what they were doing.[44]

Like the monk in the cell, the exile has the opportunity to take stock and assess, to reflect on how he arrived in that place and see what he can do about repairing the damage he has caused. This is the cell as place in the second sense, the cell as hospice, as a part of the process of dying: "I think in the death and dying process, there is an inevitable point — and I see this a lot of times in hospice ministry, which is what death row ministry was — where people have to make sense of their lives in a narrative way."[45]

Michael Ross was one of those who did the work in the cell. Ross was executed in 2005 for the murders of eight women, the first such sentence carried out in Connecticut in forty-five years. In a short essay, Ross, who dropped his appeals because, as he explained, he "wanted to spare the families of his victims . . . further torment," reflected on his path to Connecticut's death row. "When most people think of death row inmates," he wrote, "I'm the one that they think of. I'm the worst of the worst, a man who has raped and murdered eight women, assaulted several others, and stalked and frightened many more." Having spent nearly nine years on death row by that point, Ross had had ample opportunity to "look at himself . . . not . . . [in] the cursory, superficial manner in which most people look at themselves, but rather a quite painful, unrelenting search of one's very soul."[46]

Ross's pigpen moment came when Dr. Fred Berlin, a psychiatrist in the

Sexual Disorders Clinic at Johns Hopkins University Hospital, diagnosed him as having a paraphiliac mental disorder and succeeded in compelling the corrections department to put Ross on a course of Depo-Lupron. The drug, Ross said, "eliminates the previously uncontrollable urges that drove me to commit the crimes that put me here on death row. That monster still lives in my head, but the medication has chained him." As a result, Ross said, "I am human once again." We need to note Ross's phrasing and his use of active verbs: his mental disorder drove him *to commit* the crimes that led him to death row; he does not say that the disorder *led him* to death row. Alone in his cell, Ross, who dropped his appeals rather than fight for his life, sought reconciliation, "something which under the circumstances seems all but impossible," but which he nevertheless hoped for before his execution. The reconciliation he sought was with "the spirit of [his] victims . . . the families and friends of [his] victims[,] and finally, reconciliation with [himself] and [his] God." What he desired most, in the end, was to complete the process of coming home to himself, seeing, finally, clearly, who and what he was, and reconciling himself both with that and trying to "complete [his] transformation into one who is worthy of redemption and forgiveness."[47]

Retentionists and abolitionists alike laud genuine transformations, genuine attempts to come to terms with one's crimes and repent for them; they differ, however, on what this signifies and should mean regarding how we deal with the condemned. As Dick Weinhold, former president of the Texas Christian Coalition, said of Karla Faye Tucker's conversion, in words that would be directly applicable to Ross, "As a Christian, I'm always excited when other people come to Christ, whether it's in a jailhouse or on Wall Street. But I think there's still consequences for our actions."[48] Abolitionists and the chaplains would likewise be pleased by the inmate's positive transformation, while perhaps differing over the ramifications of that transformation, but the chaplains would push the idea a step further, a step outward. The import of the personal reformation is not and should not be limited to the inmate; it should be our focus as well. The chaplains would urge all of us to extend place outward and then inward — from the cell to ourselves — an idea that resonates throughout the discourse, particularly in sermons and Bible studies.

Extending Place Resonances

The story of the woman caught in adultery contains an element of mystery that shows the chaplains' point of no return. The mystery is what Jesus wrote in the sand during the encounter. When the Scribes and Pharisees brought a woman caught in the act of committing adultery before Jesus, they asked him what should be done with her. In response, and for the only time in the Gospels, he wrote: "Jesus bent down and wrote with his finger on the ground." The narrative omits any indication of what it was that appeared in the sand behind Jesus's finger. There is no barrier, however, to Bible study participants wondering what he wrote. We can be reasonably sure, one participant noted, that he was not doodling, that the writing had purpose. He could have been writing out the names and sins of all of the accusers, one suggested, while another echoed this idea to a different end: he was indeed writing out the names and sins of the accusers because they had all been with the woman. Others suggested that what Jesus wrote was less important than the fact that he stepped out of the situation, distancing himself from it to force the mob to pause while they awaited his answer. This last option echoes a conclusion drawn by legal scholar Mark Osler. For Osler, as for some of the Bible study participants, the writing itself did not matter; the *act* of writing, of taking the time to step away from the situation and put some distance between himself and the mob and between the mob and the woman—that mattered. "In the end," Osler says, "this might be the example that Christ offers as we consider capital punishment, suggesting that we remove ourselves from the mob and quietly hold up the question before our consciences and faith."[49]

The point, for Osler, is that we should take the time to distance ourselves from the inflammatory situation, to separate ourselves and our passions from the proposed victim and consider whether we truly believe that we are doing right. Rocky, a Catholic deacon, expressed the same sentiment when he commented that John 8 always reminds him of Matthew 7, "where you don't look at the splinter in the other eye, rather [at] the log in your own." Rocky admits that he would "like to think that I'd never throw the rock, but in a mob scenario, who knows?" Carol said much the same when she remarked that her faith gave her something to stop her in her worst moments, not something that absolved her from her worst moments. These comments and reactions are variants on the idea of seeing oneself in the other, or the other in oneself, and as such are elements of embrace. To the extent that there is a difference between the two, we may think of "seeing oneself in the other" as analogous to opening the arms, while "seeing the other in oneself" is analogous to waiting. Whichever act of embrace the comment best approximates, these responses are all a part of denuding and moving past the one point of no return that the chaplains believe matters: "I think there's a point where the offender cannot return, but it has nothing to do with the accusers. I think it has to do with themselves. . . . *And I feel the same thing for the accusers.* If [we] wanted to [come back], we could."[50]

This is what the chaplains mean when they say that the inmates' stories became their stories and their stories became the inmates' stories. This is what Pastor Frazier means when he observes that the biblical narratives are "our stories" to the point that he can look at them and say, "There but for the grace of God go I. . . . . These are *our* stories." This is what former death row inmate Joe Giarratano meant when he wrote that "each day I spend [on death row] is an experience in Life," that "where there is life there is hope . . . through the recognition of humanity—both [ours] and [the offender's]." When the chaplains assert that those on death row are *like us*, that they "have done bad things but aren't bad people," when they turn the conversation and extend place outward to admonish the broader society that "sin is crouching at the door, but you can master it,"[51] they are asking the question that recurs continually throughout the religious discourse on the death penalty at all levels: what are we *for?*

This question cycles the discourse back to the exile and is the strongest indication that *exile* and *embrace* are not binary opposites but rather parts of the same continuum of response; these two apparently conflicting notions are part of the same whole. The most divergent interpretations of John 8 that arose during the Bible studies illustrate this. Beatrice, who repeatedly expressed a belief that anything that can be done to stop the spread of evil is appropriate and who rhetorically linked freedom to the fulfillment of consequences, interprets the story less as a call to self-reflection and self-criticism and more as an enhancement of the offender's power. The woman was not just an adulterer but also someone who had been with the community at large. Her sin, in other words, was not simply adultery, but adultery compounded by scale. This interpretation shows the exile at work. There is a real crisis that must be resolved, and in order to resolve it, a specific victim is chosen to bear a real act of violence. Moreover, in addition to acknowledging that the story provides no indication that the woman has been falsely accused, this interpretation goes further. We know, she said, that the woman was guilty. The mob knew it, too, because she had committed the same sin with each of them (though not, in her telling, vice versa).[52]

The other response sees the importance of the writing as directly contributing to the narrative's takeaway: Jesus lists the mob's sins to underscore the idea of letting those without sin cast the first stone. This interpretation understands the story as a call for the accusers to do the work that is demanded of the accused. As with the previous response, there is a recognition of mutuality, that the accusers and victim are fundamentally alike, that they are insufficiently unlike each other to carry out the planned act of restorative violence. By itself, the fact that the accusers and victim are sufficiently alike gives rise to warrant, to the claimed authority to punish. Insufficient difference, though, short-circuits the exilic mechanism via mutual extension of place outward. The accusers, so the narrative suggests, and so our interpretations of it confirm, had to face themselves in recognition of and by comparison with the woman. The command to do the work short-circuits the exilic mechanism by forcibly closing the distance that mechanism relies on. The woman, meanwhile, cognizant of her own transgression, was likewise commanded to do the work.[53]

These sequential but simultaneous commands can be seen anew via two questions asked at one study: who is the hero of the story, and with whom do you identify? The two heroes, for this group, were Jesus, for defusing the situation, and the first person to put down the stone. Like Rocky, we may wish to believe that we would not be part of the mob, but we cannot foreclose that possibility any more than he can. At the same time, we recognize that the mob's violence is at best problematic and at worst fundamentally unjust, as reflected in the conferring of hero status on the person who either defused the situation so as to prevent violence or was the first to give warrant to the others to drop their rocks. A similar conversation occurred when these questions arose in discussions about the Cain and Abel narrative. This is our story, not just theirs, one participant noted, while another summed up discussion about where we see ourselves in the narrative by stating that we are both Cain and Abel, that "that could have been any of us."[54]

If we could be either Cain or Abel, either the mob or the woman, the question again arises: what are we for? "Are you for compassion, or are you for violence? Are you for mercy, or are you for vengeance? Are you for love, or are you for hate? Are you for life, or are you for death?" These questions help distill the abolitionist discourse to its basic elements, particularly as they arise in vigils, sermons, and liturgies performed on the occasion of an execution. The pervading theme of these, in keeping with the concept of the exile, is the idea of our responsibility, our choice—our selves. We, "like the people of Israel, [are] challenged to choose the way of life" rather than death. Death is equated to justice, life with mercy, a formulation most apparent when it is put in terms of self-interest. "If we are totally honest we may . . . imagine ourselves on the judgment seat," and though we claim justice as our goal, "there's not a person here, and not one out there who's demanding the death of people—whether they be Christian or otherwise—who is going to say . . . 'Lord, have *justice* on me.' No one's that crazy. So if it's mercy that we want at the end of our lives, why not give mercy today?" If we are Cain as well as Abel, should we not view the mark of Cain as demanding that we act "with mercy and not revenge"?[55]

Are we for mercy, or are we for vengeance? If we are for vengeance, then we must admit that we kill out of fear, not for any other reason or for any pretense at justice, retributive or otherwise. In grieving "the loss of lives . . . the loss of our own security," we naturally will feel anger and fear but are called to go beyond that, because giving in to those emotions will lead us toward vengeance, and "revenge turns us into thugs." The death penalty is an indication "that we have lost our struggle with violence, that we have been seduced by violence"—that having become "convinced that the evil that is destroying us is the very power that can save us," we have arrogated to ourselves the power to destroy, perhaps not reflecting on our lack of capacity to perform the opposite: to create. We have, in other words, sinned by presuming ourselves equal partners with God in the care of ourselves and each other: "While God calls us to be partners, we have to know what each partner is capable of doing.... The only thing we can do is put somebody to death. But we can't reverse it.... Much of our killing is really only vengeful, and I don't think it's ever really justified." We are to do justice, but also to "love mercy, and wal[k] *humbly* with God." Loving mercy, however, demands that we do the work, that we look inside ourselves and understand the reasons we need to be merciful. This means confronting what we see in others, "the parts of ourselves that we would like to avoid."[56]

If we are to be merciful, to be "agents of grace," we need to reject the idea that only evil can come from without and only good from within. We need to reject retentionist retributive violence by recognizing evil in ourselves as well as in others. We are warned to avoid giving in to vengeance, to violence, lest we lose sight of the fact that legality may not absolve an action of its evil and of the call to overcome evil with good, rather than with another evil. We are to begin by "acknowledg[ing] the violence we perpetuate ... within our country ... [and] within our communities and homes." Lacking the capacity to adequately separate the wheat from the chaff, we should begin our work by acknowledging our sins rather than others'. Rather than settling for a response to evil and transgression that allows us not to acknowledge or "blocks us from coming to terms with our own personal demons" and that invites "good people to forget that they too are sinners," we are to recall that "we are all capable of committing the most evil of sins" and engage in "the spiritual journey [that] is finding our own sinfulness, our dark side."[57]

This self-reconciliation is vital to the concept of *grace*. If we are called to be agents of grace, then we need likewise to live up to that calling. "Living into God's grace is a lifetime process of conversion," a lifetime process of practicing grace. We are to practice forgiveness for the same reasons the chaplains have to lay the foundation with the offenders—to make ourselves ready. We need to practice grace and forgiveness so that in our hardest moments, we can behave as did the families in Bart Township, Pennsylvania, the confounding exemplars of forgiveness that repeatedly arose during the Bible studies. Participants recognized that the capacity to forgive the man who had killed their children was not an innate gift but a skill that had been tended and cultivated by people who sought to learn how to forgive so that they could. We also, these voices tell us, need to practice grace to receive it: "A requirement for receiving God's forgiveness is our willingness to forgive others."[58]

(*Opening the Space*

Sermons on the death penalty frequently focus on our need to do the work and to bear in mind that we are insufficiently different from the offenders. We should not evaluate them based on their worst moments any more than we would wish to be judged on ours; we and they are "transcendent of an action." We need to "come home to that," to learn to open our arms to the knowledge that "we are the offenders. . . . It's logs and splinters." We need to do this, we are told, not for others, but for ourselves: "We don't finally feel welcome at this table [of grace] because we cannot find it in ourselves to welcome all others who might come here. We cannot quite bring ourselves to the role of Ananias." We cannot soften our hardened hearts long enough to recognize that "their" problems are "our" problems. We cannot become Ananias—who obeyed God's command to lay his hands on Saul and cure his blindness, despite the fact that Saul was a persecutor and killer of Christians—because we lack the capacity to understand the need to do the work, to prepare to open our arms and wait.[59]

Reverend Vought likes to tell a particular story concerning our need to come home to ourselves, to do our own work:

> I remember one day we walked [on] row, there was a reporter from the *Richmond Times-Dispatch* who came along with us because she was doing a story on us and the ministry. . . . And she got up against the bars—and of course all the guys are making all these untoward comments and stuff. . . . But she was tough, and was giving it right back at them, and she asked this one guy, "What's it feel like to know you're going to die?" And he shot back and said, "What's it feel like to know *you're* going to die?" He said, "I *know* when I'm going to die, bitch, but you don't know, and you're running scared. I can get my life together." . . . There was a kind of wisdom [in that].[60]

As counterintuitive as it may seem, the prisoners on death row frequently express a conflicted gratitude for having wound up there. They have to contend with their crimes, and those of them best able to do the work did so as best they could, but they also have the possibility of becoming different people. Some offenders learn to read on death row; others get off drugs or alcohol; some can achieve some reconciliation with their family or their victims' families, provided the latter are willing. Speaking about the men he'd helped do the work, Vought said that they learned that "you have to . . . give thanks, even though you've been through some hellacious, horrific things, you have to . . . make sense of it."[61]

In a way, the execution date can help the offender do the work. Reverend Sherbon and Jesse both said as much, as we saw in previous chapters. As Karla Faye Tucker noted before her execution, however, echoing Vought's anecdote above, "We all have an execution date. I just have a better idea when." Tucker may be the paradigmatic prodigal. Having come home to herself in the pigpen, she did the work, rebuilt her life, and was deemed so sincere in her conversion and reformation that the prosecutor who brought a capital charge against her, several of the jurors who voted to send her to death row, and longtime Religious Right icon and Christian broadcaster Pat Robertson all endorsed clemency for her. Robertson went so far as to proclaim that executing Tucker would be an act of simple vengeance, shorn of all pretense of justice.[62]

Although Tucker provides an example of those who successfully did the work and came home to themselves, the abolitionist discourse balks at using that as a rationale to support the death penalty. The opposite is the case — successful conversions demonstrate the need to reject death as a punishment, because we lack the right to cut off another's chance to come to grace. Religious abolitionists argue that the death penalty pulls two rights into conflict, our right to punish to protect ourselves and the murderer's right to repent. The abolitionist discourse implores us to remember that "no human being is beyond the reach of God's infinite love" and that the most unlikely person may yet repent. Some ministers sermonizing against the death penalty seem to do so as an act of repentance. Likening capital punishment to slavery, these unlikely penitents proclaim that it yet lives because it is preached and inadequately opposed from the pulpit. This facet of the discourse points to the iconic symbol of the Christian faith and asks not only that we consider whether we could as easily replace the cross with an electric chair or lethal injection table, but also to remember the other two crosses and ask ourselves which thief we should seek to be: the one with the capacity to seek forgiveness, or the one without.[63]

This need to seek forgiveness is the need to learn to offer it, to do the work and lay a foundation that will permit us to open our arms and offer embrace to the other. Because embrace is a process rather than an event, it cannot be the binary counterpart of exile but, instead, exists alongside and with exile. There is a form of embrace at work in the demand for the death penalty, however limited. The recognition of the other as *like us*, as normal, is an act of embrace leading to an act of exile, an act of exile that is possible only because of the preceding embrace. The act of opening the arms to the offender and waiting is also a process wholly dependent on a revelation of exile. Because we cannot reasonably argue that our willingness to open our arms is anything other than contingent, we cannot see even this first act of embrace as an event. Embrace is always an interdependent process that effectively counters any claims we have to sovereign independence. We retain measures of both, certainly; the process that leads us to elect or decline to open our arms is self-driven and thus sovereign and independent to a degree. Because it is a reaction, however, it is neither fully. Although we can choose to act as though we believe ourselves fully sovereign and independent, we cannot do so without belying that claim. Not only do we react; we also lack sufficient power over our actions to reverse them and thus cannot reasonably claim to have sovereignty over them. Embrace, exile's counterpart, finally allows us to rephrase the question of what we are for in terms of the moral question at the root of the problem and discourse: what do we want to *be?*

8

Directions: The Greensville Correctional Center is located in Greensville County, not far from the town of Jarratt in Sussex County. Jarratt is at exit 20 off I-95, 55 miles south of Richmond, and 20 miles north of the North Carolina border. After taking exit 20, turn right at the end of the exit ramp if coming from Richmond (turn left if coming from Emporia). The first stop sign is at the intersection with US 301. There are convenience stores at the intersection, which have rest facilities (there are no rest facilities for us at the prison). Turn left (south) onto 301 and go eight-tenths of a mile. Turn right on the state road 397, Ridge Road (there is a marker for Greensville Correctional Center). Cross the railroad tracks and you'll soon see the prison gate. Park in the field on the right hand side.

    Bring a flashlight and bug repellent.

>   (VIRGINIANS FOR ALTERNATIVES
>   TO THE DEATH PENALTY (VADP),
>   "Vigil Information"

Conclusion

Over the course of my research, I made three trips to the Greensville Correctional Center in Jarratt, Virginia, each time to attend a protest vigil being held in a field within sight of, but a substantial distance from, the main prison gates. The location feels as isolated as it is, well removed both from any major cities or towns and from major thoroughfares. The swarms of insects buzzing around the protesters in the muggy, sweltering Virginia summer night validated the last instruction, while the isolation justified the penultimate. On this night, the sky above the field glittered and glinted, full of stars, an almost inappropriately beautiful sight, given why we were there. At this starkly isolated site, no light pollution encroached upon the stars. The principal source of illumination was the prison complex, situated an indeterminate distance down the road, or whatever the vigilers brought with them: flashlights or, intermittently, headlights.

That evening we protested a "milestone"—Virginia's hundredth modern execution—in the aftermath of a significant legal victory for death penalty opponents in *Kennedy*. Roughly fifty people from various groups filled the field that evening for a vigil service. Much to my surprise, en route to the field outside the prison gates where the vigil was held, I encountered a traffic jam. Nor was I the only one surprised. A line of cars, ultimately more than a dozen deep, had been held up. Engines were off, doors left open, keys in the ignition, as people walked among the cars, greeting friends and introducing themselves to people they hadn't met. Just ahead of the lead car I could see the cause of the traffic jam: the railroad crossbucks indicated that a train was coming through. The irony of the situation—the fact that a cargo train happened to be pulling through and blocking off the only road to the vigil site at the precise moment it did—was commented on down the line of cars.

When the vigilers got to the field, they lit candles and assembled themselves in a circle around a large bell. They spoke of the victim, Cyril Hugh Hamby, and they spoke of Yarbrough. One of the vigilers told the group that a woman he knew had met Yarbrough several years previous and that one of his favorite Bible passages was Luke 6:37, which was read in context:

> But to you who hear, I say, love your enemies, do good to those who hate you, bless those who curse you, pray for those who mistreat you. . . . Do to others as you would have them do to you. . . . Be merciful, just as your Father is merciful. . . . Stop judging and you will not be judged. Stop condemning and you will not be condemned. Forgive and you will be forgiven.[1]

Abe Bonowitz, the founder of Citizens United to Abolish the Death Penalty, reminded those assembled that

> just today, the US Supreme Court decided that we're not going to just take it to the extreme, we're not going to allow states to start executing people who have committed crimes that did not result in a death. It's a step forward. And as Virginia steps up its pace of execution, it's in contravention to what's happening across the country.[2]

Ordinarily, the vigil would have included a processional bell ringing, as the other vigils I attended did. Those assembled would read the name of each person executed and their victims, striking the bell for each execution in memory of both sets of victims. This time, the fifty or so of us assembled simply struck the bell twice each. No names were read. The bell tolling commenced at 9 p.m. — the time that offenders are executed in Virginia. The tolling ended at approximately 9:10, which, if executions proceed smoothly, is roughly the time that death is pronounced. We broke the circle and lined the street, our candles still lit, waiting for the hearse to pass us bearing Yarbrough's body. The running theme throughout all of the comments made by vigilers and representatives of the abolitionist groups who had traveled to Jarratt to attend the vigil was that while it was important that we were there, it was equally important what we did every other day, when there weren't any executions being conducted.

Two weeks earlier, on June 9, citing Percy Walton's deteriorated mental state and documented insanity, Governor Kaine commuted Walton's three death sentences to life in prison without the possibility of parole. It was not a universally popular decision. One e-mail sent to Jack Payden-Travers, then VADP's director, and signed "Sorry to see this liberal in office," lamented that Kaine had not taken his oath of office seriously, contrary to his campaign promise. A less inflamed e-mail, written June 6, bristled at the idea that Walton should be imprisoned for life. "As a society, we lament the lack of adequate funds for health insurance for children, education, social assistance for the poor, all innocent citizen [sic]. Why then should we spend limited funds on hopeless and guilty murderers?" This example of scapegoating via cost finds an echo in an article published in the *Virginian-Pilot* on January 16, 2003, excoriating a bill proposed by Hampton delegate Mary T. Christian that would have paid out a sizable annuitized settlement to Earl Washington Jr., who spent nine years on Virginia's death row for a crime he did not commit. The editorial described the bill as "an unspeakable affront to the roughly 2,000 law-abiding state employees who are facing layoffs due to budget shortfalls." Both pieces bear the same message: just think how much better we could make things if not for these guilty felons, these "useless eaters."[3]

These three pieces show the necessity of guilt as an accompaniment to the scapegoating impulse, as well as the concern over the political order and democratic process, however inarticulately expressed. A separate e-mail sent to Payden-Travers illustrates another common trope in the cultural debates over capital punishment. A man identifying himself as a seventeen-year law enforcement veteran wanted to ask why Payden-Travers didn't mention the victims in his column about Walton. It was a measured, even kindly worded e-mail that wondered why concern was expressed for the offender rather than the victims. Payden-Travers responded that he always thinks about the victims and tries to mention the victims in the pieces he writes, but conceded that sometimes he does not want to dedicate the space to the crime itself. There are too many such pieces around to begin with, pieces that try to depict the offender as "someone very different from how we see ourselves." Instead Payden-Travers believes "that myself and I think most of us, have the ability to do just as bad things as the killers we have on death row." Rather than focus on the differences, he chooses to see, and to write, from a perspective of trying to see the person, not the offense.[4] What the law enforcement veteran wanted to know was why the abolitionist empathized with the killer, openly, rather than with the victim. Is that the basis for abolitionism? — empathy with the guilty, rather than the innocent?

The proper response to this suggestion can only be *of course*. Of course the abolitionist discourse is predicated, at least partially, on empathy for the killers. It has to be. It strains belief to argue otherwise, given the emotional nature of the debate and the human need to *do something* in response to an affront, a transgression, to injury or to tragedy. In a more combative "culture wars" type of discourse, the accusation that abolitionists empathize with the offender is an illocutionary speech act meant to convey, "but we stand for the victims." The implication is that those who stand with the victims somehow do so while having no empathy with the offenders whatsoever. The only proper response to this suggestion, however, is *of course* they do. Of course the retentionist discourse empathizes with the offender — with the killer. That is the entire basis for retributive justice: to become what we fear, to do in response as was done in provocation but to do so while hiding the full measure of our violence. We become what we fear most in order to discharge that from us, but we disperse the authority for carrying out that violence among various different actors and agencies over a complicated, multistage process. We do this to hide the thing in plain sight, to have it just accessible enough for us to be aware of it, to know it, in a way, but remote enough that we can know it without ever seeing it, without ever knowing what it does.

At base, the death penalty is about our reaction, which is to say, it is about our own sovereignty in the face of the particular conditions of modernity. Retentionists and abolitionists alike acknowledge that the offender is *like us*. We acknowledge that we exile the offender in response to a sacrificial crisis, while trying to claim both that we *had* to and that we *chose* to. We go ahead with state-sanctioned killing and claim that though it is incumbent upon us to exact life for life, it is a regrettable necessity, all the while unaware — mercifully, in a way — of the violence in the system — in the event and in the process — and seemingly unconcerned with the fact that this same system, which carefully excises one voice from our collective conscience, nevertheless gives us the opportunity *not* to take life at every step of the process. Dr. Peabody's observation from *As I Lay Dying*, which serves as the epigraph to this book, is a perfect summation of the problem. Whether we react via exile or via embrace, or via both, whether we frame the problem and any solutions or suggestions we have to offer in terms of exile or embrace, it is we who respond, not they. It is — *always* — about us.

The death penalty is an admission of failure. Not because we can't prevent killings or violence in our society, though no plausible argument can be made that we've explored all reasonable possibilities to do just that or that we've done the collective soul-searching necessary to begin truly to understand our collective, cultural infatuation with violence. No, it is an admission of failure because it is an admission that while we *have* to act, we have to do so in a certain specified way — but to no end. We do not take seriously the prospect of deterrence, beyond "commonsense" platitudes of such. In fact, the best — and, indeed, only — basis for capital punishment is retribution, is turning ourselves — explicitly — into what we claim to despise most: the cold-blooded killer. Of course we empathize with the killer. So long as Virginia retains capital punishment, so long as the United States retains capital punishment, it makes of all of us cold-blooded killers, makes of all of us those who use death to witness to life.

Have we really thought about what that means for us?

Appendix

List of Bible Study Sessions

At the request of the participating institutions/organizers, the host institutions are identified by their denominational affiliation and rough geographic location.

Session A: September 17, 2008, Joint session involving an Evangelical Lutheran Church of America (ELCA) congregation and Roman Catholic parish in the Shenandoah Valley (L&C); Session 1 of 7

Session B: September 21, 2008, Episcopal church in western Virginia

Session C: September 24, 2008, L&C, Session 2 of 7

Session D: September 28, 2008, Lutheran Church—Missouri Synod (LCMS) church in Hampton Roads; Session 1 of 4

Session E: October 1, 2008, L&C, Session 3 of 7

Session F: October 5, 2008, LCMS, Session 2 of 4

Session G: October 8, 2008, L&C, Session 4 of 7

Session H: October 12, 2008, LCMS, Session 3 of 4

Session I: October 15, 2008, L&C, Session 5 of 7

Session J: October 22, 2008, L&C, Session 6 of 7

Session K: October 29, 2008, L&C, Session 7 of 7

Session L: November 9, 2008, United Methodist church in central Virginia, Session 1 of 2

Session M: November 16, 2008, Ibid., Session 2

Session N: November 19, 2008, Episcopal church in southwestern Virginia

Session O: November 23, 2008, Presbyterian church in central Virginia

Session P: January 18, 2009, Episcopal church in western Virginia, follow-up to Session B

Session Q: January 19, 2009, Roman Catholic parish in the Richmond area

Session R: January 20, 2009, Roman Catholic parish in the Richmond area

Session S: January 31, 2009, Roman Catholic parish in the Richmond area

Session T: January 31, 2009, LCMS, Session 4 of 4

Notes

1. Introduction

Epigraphs. Albert Camus, *The Rebel: An Essay on Man in Revolt*, trans. Anthony Bower (New York: Vintage International, 1991), 301; Kevin Crotty, "Democracy, Tragedy, and Responsibility: The Greek Case," in Winston Davis, ed., *Taking Responsibility: Comparative Perspectives* (Charlottesville: University Press of Virginia, 2001), 110.

1. Marie Deans, "Living in Babylon," in Ian Gray and Moira Stanley, eds., *A Punishment in Search of a Crime: Americans Speak Out against the Death Penalty* (New York: Avon Books, 1989), 72.

2. Quotations: Deans, "Living in Babylon," 77, 76; Todd C. Peppers and Laura Trevett Anderson, *Anatomy of an Execution: The Life and Death of Douglas Christopher Thomas* (Boston: Northeastern University Press, 2009), 152; "Executions," Death Penalty Information Center, deathpenaltyinfo.org/executions. Unless otherwise noted, all websites were accessed August 1, 2012. See Matthew 27:48, Mark 15:36, Luke 23:36, John 19:29. Unless otherwise indicated, all Bible citations are to the New Revised Standard Version (NRSV).

3. Quotations: Patricia Streeter, "A Mother Remembers," in Hunter P. Mabry, *Capital Punishment: A Faith-Based Study* (Nashville: Abingdon, 2002), 49.

4. First two quotations: Jane M. May, "A Juror's Perspective," in Mabry, *Capital Punishment*, 45. Third quotation: Cal Thomas, "'Oprah Disease' Clouded the Judgment of Jurors in Moussaoui Case," May 10, 2006, *Baltimore Sun*, articles.baltimoresun.com/2006-05-10/news/0605100219_1_justice-death-penalty-life.

5. Danny King, "A Thought for Today," Rev. Joseph M. Vought files, personal collection, Danny King Poem.

6. First quotation: Christian Boulanger and Austin Sarat, "Putting Culture into the Picture: Toward a Comparative Analysis of State Killing," in Austin Sarat and Christian Boulanger, eds., *The Cultural Lives of Capital Punishment: Comparative Perspectives* (Stanford: Stanford University Press, 2005), 1. Second quotation: David Garland, *Punishment and Modern Society: A Study in Social Theory* (Chicago: University of Chicago Press, 1990), 17. Phoebe C. Ellsworth and Samuel R. Gross, "Hardening of the Attitudes: Americans' Views on the Death Penalty," *Journal of Social Issues* 50, no. 2 (Summer 1994): 19–52. Samuel R. Gross, "Update: American Public Opinion on the Death Penalty—It's Getting Personal," *Cornell Law Review* 83 (1978): 1448.

7. *Furman v. Georgia*, 408 U.S. 238 (1972) at 296.

8. *Gregg v. Georgia*, 428 U.S. 153 (1976); *Furman* 408 U.S.

9. Quotation: Giorgio Agamben, *Homo Sacer: Sovereign Power and Bare Life*, trans. Daniel Heller-Roazan (Stanford: Stanford University Press, 1998), 147. Agamben develops this theme in *State of Exception*, trans. Kevin Attell (Chicago: University of Chicago Press, 2005). Slavoj Žižek, *Violence: Six Sideways Reflections* (New York: Picador, 2008), 13.

10. Here and throughout, "retentionist" will refer to the position holding that the death penalty should be retained, while "abolitionist" refers to the position holding that the death penalty should be abolished.

11. Austin Sarat, *When the State Kills: Capital Punishment and the American Condition* (Princeton, NJ: Princeton University Press, 2001); Susan F. Sharp, *Hidden Victims: The Effects of*

the Death Penalty on the Families of the Accused (New Brunswick, NJ: Rutgers University Press, 2005).

12. Thomas, "'Oprah Disease.'"

13. First quotation: Amnesty International (AI), "Abolitionist and Retentionist Countries," www.amnesty.org/en/death-penalty/abolitionist-and-retentionist-countries. Second quotation: Roger Hood and Carolyn Hoyle, *The Death Penalty: A Worldwide Perspective*, 4th ed. (New York: Oxford University Press, 2008), 12.

14. AI, "Death Sentences and Executions in 2010," www.amnesty.org/en/library/info/ACT50/001/2011/en, March 28, 2010, claims that the United States sentenced "110+" to death in 2010; the Death Penalty Information Center (DPIC), "Death Sentences in the United States from 1977 by State and by Year," deathpenaltyinfo.org/death-sentences-united-states-1977-2008, claims that states imposed 104 death sentences in 2010. Notably, AI's data does not include numbers of death sentences for China, Iran, or North Korea. Carsten Anckar, *Determinants of the Death Penalty: A Comparative Study of the World* (London: Routledge, 2004). See also generally Hood and Hoyle, *The Death Penalty*. Quotation: Michael J. Perry, *Constitutional Rights, Moral Controversy, and the Supreme Court* (Cambridge: Cambridge University Press, 2009), 12–14 (italics in original).

15. Quotation: Harold Hongju Koh, "Paying 'Decent Respect' to World Opinion on the Death Penalty," *University of California Davis Law Review* 35 (2002): 1085, quotation on 1104 (italics in original). Peter A. Ozanne, "Why Does America Still Have a Death Penalty?" in Manfred Berg, Stefan Kapsch, and Franz Streng, eds., *Criminal Justice in the United States and Germany—Strafrecht in den Vereinigten Staaten und Deutschland*, Publications of the Bavarian American Academy, vol. 6 (Heidelberg: Universitätsverlag Winter, 2006), 55–71; David Garland, *Peculiar Institution: America's Death Penalty in an Age of Abolition* (Cambridge, MA: Belknap Press of Harvard University Press, 2010). On abolition in Western Europe, see Hood and Hoyle, *The Death Penalty*, 40–50.

16. Peppers and Anderson, *Anatomy*, 66. See also James F. Horn, *A Land as God Made It: Jamestown and the Birth of America* (New York: Basic Books, 2005), 193–98; Laurence M. Friedman, *A History of American Law*, 3rd ed. (New York: Touchstone, 2005), 10–11.

17. Scott D. Seay, *Hanging between Heaven and Earth: Capital Crime, Execution Preaching, and Theology in Early New England* (DeKalb: Northern Illinois University Press, 2009), quotation 23. Laura Randa, *Society's Final Solution: A History and Discussion of the Death Penalty* (Lanham, MD: University Press of America, 1997).

18. First quotation: Mitchel P. Roth, *Crime and Punishment: A History of the Criminal Justice System* (Belmont, CA: Wadsworth, 2005), 66. Second quotation: Mark Colvin, *Penitentiaries, Reformatories, and Chain Gangs: Social Theory and the History of Punishment in Nineteenth-Century America* (New York: St. Martin's, 1997), 33. See also Frank Browning and John Gerassi, *The American Way of Crime* (New York: Putnam's Sons, 1980); John D. Bessler, *Cruel and Unusual: The American Death Penalty and the Founders' Eighth Amendment* (Boston: Northeastern University Press, 2012); Graeme Newman, *The Punishment Response* (New York: J. B. Lippincott, 1978).

19. Bessler, *Cruel and Unusual*; Seay, *Hanging between Heaven and Earth*. Quotation: Benjamin Franklin, *The Works of Dr. Benjamin Franklin; Consisting of Essays, Humorous, Moral, and Literary: With His Life, Written by Himself* (Boston: T. Bedlington, 1825), 225.

20. Louis P. Masur, *Rites of Execution: Capital Punishment and the Transformation of American Culture, 1776–1865* (New York: Oxford University Press, 1989), 50–93; Stuart Banner, *The Death Penalty: An American History* (Cambridge, MA: Harvard University Press, 2002), 88–111; James J. Megivern, *The Death Penalty: An Historical and Theological Survey* (New York: Paulist,

1997), 301–3; Cesare Beccaria, *On Crimes and Punishments and Other Writings*, ed. Richard Bellamy, trans. Richard Cox, with Virginia Cox and Richard Bellamy (New York: Cambridge University Press, 2003), 1–115; Benjamin Rush, *Considerations on the injustice and impolicy of punishing murder by death* . . . (Philadelphia, 1792); Benjamin Rush, *An enquiry into the effects of public punishments upon criminals and upon society. Read in the Society for Promoting Political Enquiries, convened at the house of His Excellency Benjamin Franklin, Esquire, in Philadelphia, March 9th, 1787* (Philadelphia, 1787); Benjamin Rush, *On the Punishment of Murder by Death* (London, 1793). First three quotations: Bessler, *Cruel and Unusual*, 268, 71, 74. Fourth quotation: Banner, *Death Penalty*, 97.

21. Banner, *Death Penalty*, 98, 131–43; Herbert H. Haines, *Against Capital Punishment: The Anti-Death Penalty Movement in America, 1972–1994* (New York: Oxford University Press, 1996), 8–9; Philip English Mackey, *Hanging in the Balance: The Anti-Capital Punishment Movement in New York State, 1776–1861* (New York: Garland, 1982); Philip English Mackey, *Voices against Death: American Opposition to Capital Punishment, 1787–1975* (New York: Burt Franklin, 1976); Masur, *Rites of Execution*; David J. Rothman, *The Discovery of the Asylum: Social Order and Disorder in the New Republic* (Boston: Little, Brown, 1971); Michael H. Reggio, "Readings—The History of the Death Penalty," *PBS Frontline*, www.pbs.org/wgbh/pages/frontline/shows/execution/readings/history.html, reprinted from Laura E. Randa, ed., *Society's Final Solution: A History and Discussion of the Death Penalty* (Lanham, MD: University Press of America, 1997).

22. Quotations: John F. Galliher, Larry W. Koch, David Patrick Keys, and Teresa J. Guess, *America without the Death Penalty: States Leading the Way* (Boston: Northeastern University Press, 2002), 56, 15.

23. *Glass v. Louisiana*, 471 U.S. 1080 (1985), at 1084. Quotations: Galliher et al., *America without the Death Penalty*, 93, 101; Banner, *Death Penalty*, 169–207; Haines, *Against*, 9–11; Rupert V. Barry, "*Furman* to *Gregg*: The Judicial and Legislative History," *Howard Law Journal* 22 (1979): 53; William J. Bowers, *Legal Homicide: Death as Punishment in America, 1864–1982* (Boston: Northeastern University Press, 984); Louis Filler, "Movements to Abolish the Death Penalty in the United States," *Annals of the American Academy of Political and Social Science* 284 (November 1952): 124–36; John F. Galliher, Gregory Ray, and Brent Cook, "Abolition and Reinstatement of Capital Punishment during the Progressive Era and Early 20th Century," *Journal of Criminal Law and Criminology* 83 (1983): 538; Mackey, *Voices against Death*; Roger Schwed, *Abolition and Capital Punishment: The United States' Judicial, Political, and Moral Barometer* (New York: AMS Press, 1983).

24. Mackey, *Voices against Death*, xlii.

25. Banner, *Death Penalty*, 239; Haines, *Against*, 11–13; James B. Christoph, *Capital Punishment and British Politics: The British Movement to Abolish the Death Penalty, 1945–1957* (Chicago: University of Chicago Press, 1962); Felix Frankfurter, "The Problem of Capital Punishment" (1950), in Philip Elman, ed., *Of Laws and Men: Papers and Addresses of Felix Frankfurter* (New York: Harcourt Brace, 1956), 81; Michael Meltsner, *Cruel and Unusual: The Supreme Court and Capital Punishment* (New York: Random House, 1973); Royal Commission on Capital Punishment, Report (London: Her Majesty's Stationery Office, 1953).

26. Marlin Shipman, *"The Penalty Is Death": U.S. Newspaper Coverage of Women's Executions* (Columbia: University of Missouri Press, 2002), 194–98; Tabor Rawson, *I Want to Live!: The Analysis of a Murder* (New York: American Library, 1958); Bill Walker, *The Case of Barbara Graham* (New York: Ballantine Books, 1961); *I Want to Live!*, dir. Robert Wise, 1958; Joseph E. Longstreth and Alan Bisbort, "Caryl Chessman, Writer," in Caryl Chessman, *Cell 2245, Death Row* (New York: Carroll and Graf, 2006), v–xxvi; Schwed, *Abolition and Capital Punishment*, 73–91; Theodore Hamm, *Rebel and a Cause: Caryl Chessman and the Politics of the Death Penalty*

in Postwar California, 1948-1974 (Berkeley: University of California Press, 2001), 1-2. See also Edmund G. "Pat" Brown and Dick Adler, *Public Justice, Private Mercy: A Governor's Education on Death Row* (New York: Weidenfeld and Nicholson, 1989).

27. Banner, *Death Penalty*, 246-66, quotation on 246. I am using the word "appeals" as Banner does, "in a nontechnical sense, to include all the methods by which courts can review criminal convictions and sentences" (246). In 1935, there were 199 executions in the United States, the largest number on record. For the decade of the 1930s, executions averaged 167 per year. "Timeline," PBS Frontline, "Angel on Death Row," www.pbs.org/wgbh/pages/frontline/angel/timeline.html, reprinted from *Congressional Quarterly Researcher* 5, no. 9, March 10, 1995. Robert A. Kagan, Bliss Cartwright, Lawrence M. Friedman, and Stanton Wheeler, "The Business of State Supreme Courts," *Stanford Law Review* 30 (1976): 146; Haines, *Against*, 14, 23-45; Franklin E. Zimring and Gordon Hawkins, *Capital Punishment and the American Agenda* (New York: Cambridge University Press, 1986), 33-38; *Rudolph v. Alabama*, 375 U.S. 889 (1963). *Furman*, 408 U.S.

28. First quotation: J. Gordon Melton, ed., *The Churches Speak On: Capital Punishment: Official Statements from Religious Bodies and Ecumenical Organizations* (Detroit: Gale Research, 1989). Second quotation: United Methodist Church, "Social Statement (1956)," in ibid., 135. Third quotation: Roman Catholic Church—U.S. Catholic Conference, "Resolution against Capital Punishment (1974)," in ibid., 3.

29. Banner, *Death Penalty*, 267-75; Haines, *Against*, 55-72; Robert Weisberg, "Deregulating Death," in Philip B. Kurland, Gerhard Casper, and Dennis J. Hutchinson, eds., *The Supreme Court Review, 1983* (Chicago: University of Chicago Press, 1984), 305-95, quotation on 305.

30. 463 U.S. 880 (1983).

31. 463 U.S. 992 (1983).

32. 464 U.S. 78 (1983) and 464 U.S. 874 (1983), respectively. Quotation: Haines, *Against*, 75.

33. 465 U.S. 37 (1984) and 469 U.S. 412 (1985), respectively.

34. *Tison v. Arizona*, 481 U.S. 137 (1987). Quotation: Haines, *Against*, 75.

35. *Strickland v. Washington*, 466 U.S. 668 (1984).

36. *Booth v. Maryland*, 482 U.S. 496 (1987); *South Carolina v. Gathers*, 490 U.S. 805 (1989); *Payne v. Tennessee*, 501 U.S. 808 (1991).

37. *Woodson v. North Carolina*, 428 U.S. 280 (1976), and *Blystone v. Pennsylvania*, 494 U.S. 299 (1990), respectively.

38. *Penry v. Lynaugh*, 492 U.S. 302 (1989), *Stanford v. Kentucky*, 492 U.S. 361 (1989), and *McCleskey v. Kemp*, 481 U.S. 279 (1987), respectively.

39. *Herrera v. Collins*, 506 U.S. 390 (1993).

40. For a list of capital-eligible crimes, see Virginia Code §18.2-31—Capital murder defined; punishment. Quotation: Peppers and Anderson, *Anatomy*, 64. David C. Baldus, George G. Woodworth, and Charles A. Pulaski Jr., *Equal Justice and the Death Penalty: A Legal and Empirical Analysis* (Boston: Northeastern University Press, 1990); American Civil Liberties Union (ACLU) of Virginia, *Broken Justice: The Death Penalty in Virginia* (Richmond: ACLU of Virginia, 2003), 8-16. See also ACLU, *Unequal, Unfair and Irreversible: The Death Penalty in Virginia* (Richmond: ACLU of Virginia, 2000), 8-11; Virginians for Alternatives to the Death Penalty (VADP), *Equal Justice and Fair Play: An Assessment of the Capital Justice System in Virginia* (Charlottesville: VADP, 2006), 56-60; Virginia General Assembly, Joint Legislative Audit and Review Commission (JLARC), *Review of Virginia's System of Capital Punishment*, Commission Draft, December 10, 2001. On the problem of geography generally, see for example Andrew Ditchfield, "Challenging the Intrastate Disparities in the Application of Capital Punishment Statutes," *Georgetown Law Review* 95, no. 3 (March 2005): 801-30; Michael Kroll, "Chatta-

hoochee Judicial District: Buckle of the Death Belt: The Death Penalty in Microcosm," Death Penalty Information Center, 1991, deathpenaltyinfo.org/chattahoochee-judicial-district-buckle-death-belt-death-penalty-microcosm; Michael J. Songer and Isaac Unah, "The Effect of Race, Gender, and Location on Prosecutorial Decisions to Seek the Death Penalty in South Carolina," *South Carolina Law Review* 58, no. 1 (Fall 2006): 161–209.

41. On death qualification, see Brooke Butler, "Death Qualification and Prejudice: The Effect of Implicit Racism, Sexism, and Homophobia on Capital Defendants' Right to Due Process," *Behavioral Sciences and the Law* 25, no. 6 (November 2007): 857–67; Brooke Butler, "The Role of Death Qualification in Venirepersons' Susceptibility to Victim Impact Statements," *Psychology, Crime and Law* 14, no. 2 (April 2008): 133–41; Brooke M. Butler and Gary Moran, "The Role of Death Qualification in Venirepersons' Evaluations of Aggravating and Mitigating Circumstances in Capital Trials," *Law and Human Behavior* 26, no. 2 (April 2002): 175–84; Claudia L. Cowan, William C. Thompson, and Phoebe C. Ellsworth, "The Effects of Death Qualification on Jurors' Predisposition to Convict and on the Quality of Deliberation," *Law and Human Behavior* 8, nos. 1 and 2 (June 1984): 53–79; Joseph B. Kadane, "A Note on Taking Account of the Automatic Death Penalty Jurors," *Law and Human Behavior* 8, nos. 1 and 2 (June 1984): 115–20; Marla Sandys, "Stacking the Deck for Guilt and Death: The Failure of Death Qualification to Ensure Impartiality," in James R. Acker, Robert M. Bohm, and Charles S. Lanier, eds., *America's Experiment with Capital Punishment: Reflections on the Past, Present and Future of the Ultimate Penal Sanction*, 2nd ed. (Durham, NC: Carolina Academic Press, 2003), 285–308.

42. Virginia Code §19.2-264.2—Conditions for imposition of death sentence and 19.2-264.4—Sentence proceeding.

43. Peppers and Anderson, *Anatomy*, 160–61, quotation on 161.

44. ACLU, "Broken Justice," 17–21, quotation on 21 (italics in original); ACLU, "Unequal, Unfair," 4; Virginia Code §19.2-270.4:1—Storage, preservation and retention of human biological evidence in felony cases.

45. A helpful resource is the National Center for State Courts, State Justice Institute, *Habeas Corpus in State and Federal Courts* (Williamsburg, VA: National Center for State Courts, 1994). For a short explanation of the habeas in the capital process, see Barry Latzer, *Death Penalty Cases: Leading U.S. Supreme Court Cases on Capital Punishment*, 2nd ed. (Boston: Butterworth Heinemann, 2002), 9–12; Ronald J. Tabak, "Capital Punishment: Is There Any Habeas Left in This Corpus?" *Loyola University of Chicago Law Journal* 217 (1996): 523. The definitive source on errors is James S. Liebman, *A Broken System, Part II: Why There Is So Much Error in Capital Cases, and What Can Be Done about It*, February 11, 2002, www2.law.columbia.edu/brokensystem2/. A separate, unpublished study found that Virginia has the lowest rate of reversal on direct appeal, at less than 8 percent. Texas, the only state to execute more people than Virginia, had a reversal rate of 28 percent. The national average of reversal at direct appeal was 47 percent. ACLU, "Unjust, Unfair," 28–29.

46. The definitive study on executions in the United States is M. Watt Espy and John Ortiz Smykla, "Executions in the United States, 1608–2002: The Espy File," based on statistics current as of March 10, 2011, available online at the Death Penalty Information Center (DPIC), deathpenaltyinfo.org/executions-us-1608-2002-espy-file. All subsequent citations refer to this document. The Espy File lists 1,277 known, documented executions in Virginia prior to 1972; the actual number is likely to be somewhat higher. This total also does not include the number of persons killed extralegally. The first person executed in Jamestown was Captain George Kendall; Kendall may also have the dubious distinction of being the first wrongful execution in American history. See David Thomas Konig, "Dale's Law and the Non-Common Law Ori-

gins of Criminal Justice in Virginia," *American Journal of Legal History* 26, no. 4 (October 1982): 354–75. On the question of Kendall's guilt, see Horn, *A Land as God Made It*, 40, and George Holbert Tucker, *Cavalier Sinners and Saints: Virginia History through a Keyhole* (Norfolk: Virginian Pilot and Ledger Star, 1990), 10–11. Though much of the historical record, including the Espy File, 359, claims that Kendall was executed in 1608, others claim that the execution occurred in late 1607. See Peppers and Anderson, *Anatomy*, 247 n. 62. On juvenile executions, see Espy File, 366, 368; Victor L. Streib, *Death Penalty for Juveniles* (Bloomington: Indiana University Press, 1987), 75–76. Douglas Christopher Thomas and Steven Roach were put to death on January 10 and 13, 2000, respectively. DPIC, "Execution of Juveniles in the U.S. and Other Countries," deathpenaltyinfo.org/execution-juveniles-us-and-other-countries, last updated February 23, 2011. On Virginia's "reliability," see ACLU, "Broken Justice," and ACLU, "Unjust, Unfair." On racial bias, see Paul W. Keve, *The History of Corrections in Virginia* (Charlottesville: University Press of Virginia, 1986), 193. Robert M. Bohm, *Deathquest II: An Introduction to the Theory and Practice of Capital Punishment in the United States*, 2nd ed. (Cincinnati: Anderson, 2003), 105–9. On the move to bring executions under state control, see Keve, *Corrections in Virginia*. Virginia has executed Mexican, Paraguayan, and Pakistani nationals in the modern era. VADP, "Virginia's Execution History." On actual innocence, see DPIC, "Innocence: List of Those Freed from Death Row," deathpenaltyinfo.org/innocence-list-those-freed-death-row, last updated October 1, 2012. See also Margaret Edds, *An Expendable Man: The Near-Execution of Earl Washington, Jr.* (New York: New York University Press, 2003). On cases alleging innocence, see Maria Glos and Michael D. Shear, "DNA Tests Confirm Guilt of Executed Man," *Washington Post*, January 13, 2006; John C. Tucker, *May God Have Mercy: A True Story of Crime and Punishment* (New York: W. W. Norton, 1997); DPIC, "Executed but Possibly Innocent," deathpenaltyinfo.org/executed-possibly-innocent#joseph; Joe Jackson and William F. Burke Jr., *Dead Run: The Shocking Story of Dennis Stockton and Life on Death Row in America* (New York: Walker and Company, 2000).

47. The literature on deterrence is particularly voluminous. Noteworthy contributions include William C. Bailey and Ruth D. Peterson, "Murder, Capital Punishment, and Deterrence: A Review of the Literature," in Hugo Adam Bedau, ed., *The Death Penalty in America: Current Controversies* (New York: Oxford University Press, 1997), 135–61; William J. Bowers, "The Effect of Executions Is Brutalization, Not Deterrence," in Kenneth C. Haas and James A. Inciardi, eds., *Challenging Capital Punishment: Legal and Social Sciences Approaches* (Newbury Park, CA: Sage, 1989), 49–89; William J. Bowers and Glen L. Pierce, "The Illusion of Deterrence in Isaac Ehrlich's Research on Capital Punishment," *Yale Law Journal* 85 (1975): 187; Isaac Ehrlich, "The Deterrent Effect of Capital Punishment: A Question of Life and Death," *American Economic Review* 65, no. 3 (June 1975): 397–417; Hood and Hoyle, *The Death Penalty*, 317–49; Ruth D. Peterson and William C. Bailey, "Is Capital Punishment an Effective Deterrent for Murder? An Examination of Social Science Research," in Acker, Bohm, and Lanier, *America's Experiment*, 157–82; Louis P. Pojman and Jeffrey Reiman, *The Death Penalty: For and Against* (Lanham, MD: Rowman and Littlefield, 1998); Michael L. Radelet and Ronald L. Akers, "Deterrence and the Death Penalty: The Views of Experts," *Journal of Criminal Law and Criminology* 87 (1996): 1; Franklin E. Zimring and Gordon Hawkins, *Capital Punishment and the American Agenda* (New York: Cambridge University Press, 1986), 167–86.

48. The Death Penalty Information Center's (DPIC) "Financial Facts about the Death Penalty Page" has links (live as of October 10, 2012) to numerous state reports that have concluded that the death penalty costs far more than life imprisonment, including California, Florida, Kansas, Indiana, Maryland, New Jersey, North Carolina, Tennessee, Texas, and Washington. See www.deathpenaltyinfo.org/costs-death-penalty. See also Mark Costanzo, *Just Revenge:*

Costs and Consequences of the Death Penalty (New York: St. Martin's, 1997), 59–69; Richard C. Dieter, *Millions Misspent: What Politicians Don't Say about the High Costs of the Death Penalty*, rev. ed. (Washington, DC: DPIC, 1994), www.deathpenaltyinfo.org/node/599; Richard C. Dieter, *Smart on Crime: Reconsidering the Death Penalty in a Time of Economic Crisis* (Washington, DC: DPIC, 2009), www.deathpenaltyinfo.org/documents/CostsRptFinal.pdf.

49. The Criminal Justice Project of the NAACP Legal Defense and Educational Fund (NAACP LDF), *Death Row USA: Summer 2009*, 1, deathpenaltyinfo.org/documents/DRUSA Summer2009.pdf; DPIC, "Race of Death Row Inmates Executed since 1976," deathpenalty info.org/race-death-row-inmates-executed-1976, last updated September 26, 2012; ACLU, "Broken Justice," 10–16, 54; ACLU, "Unequal, Unfair," 38–43; Richard C. Dieter, *The Death Penalty in Black and White: Who Lives, Who Dies, Who Decides* (Washington, DC: DPIC, 1998), www.deathpenaltyinfo.org/death-penalty-black-and-white-who-lives-who-dies-who-decides; Kroll, "Chattahoochee Judicial District"; *Racial Disparities in Federal Death Penalty Prosecutions, 1988–1994*, Committee on the Judiciary, Subcommittee on Civil and Constitutional Rights, Staff Report, 103rd Congress, 2nd sess., March 1994, www.deathpenaltyinfo.org/racial-disparities-federal-death-penalty-prosecutions-1988-1994; Isaac Unah and Jack Boger, *Race and the Death Penalty in North Carolina: An Empirical Analysis: 1993–1997*, April 16, 2001, www.deathpenaltyinfo.org/race-and-death-penalty-north-carolina; US Department of Justice, *Survey of the Federal Death Penalty System: A Statistical Survey (1988–2000)*, September 12, 2000, www.justice.gov/dag/pubdoc/dpsurvey.html; *McCleskey*, 481 U.S. at 312.

50. Governor George Ryan, "An Address on the Death Penalty," June 3, 2002, Pew Forum on Religion and Public Life, www.pewforum.org/Death-Penalty/Governor-George-Ryan-An-Address-on-the-Death-Penalty.aspx; George Ryan, "Reflections on the Death Penalty and the Moratorium," in Erik C. Owens, John D. Carlson, and Eric P. Elshtain, eds., *Religion and the Death Penalty: A Call for Reckoning* (Grand Rapids, MI: Wm. B. Eerdmans, 2004), 221–30; George Ryan, "I Must Act," in Hugo Adam Bedau and Paul G. Cassell, eds., *Debating the Death Penalty: Should America Have Capital Punishment? The Experts from Both Sides Make Their Case* (New York: Oxford University Press, 2004), 218–34.

51. Except where noted, the following description of conditions on Virginia's death row derives from Peppers and Anderson, *Anatomy*, 147–51.

52. Associated Press, "ACLU Sues Virginia over Prison Treatment," Newport News (VA) *Daily Press*, March 6, 1995; Randolph Goode, "Settlement of Inmates' Suit Enacts New Cell Search Rules," *Richmond Times-Dispatch*, May 24, 1995. On the inhumane conditions on death row specifically and in prison generally, and on the dehumanization of inmates, see generally Jan Arriens, ed., *Welcome to Hell: Letters and Writings from Death Row* (Boston: Northeastern University Press, 1997); James Austin, John Irwin, and Charis E. Kubrin, "It's about Time: America's Imprisonment Binge," in Thomas G. Blomberg and Stanley Cohen, eds., *Punishment and Social Control*, enlarged 2nd ed. (New York: Aldine de Gruyter, 2003); Donald A. Cabana, *Death at Midnight: The Confession of an Executioner* (Boston: Northeastern University Press, 1996); Costanzo, *Just Revenge*; Willie Jasper Darden Jr., "An Inhumane Way of Death," in Michael L. Radelet, ed., *Facing the Death Penalty: Essays on a Cruel and Unusual Punishment* (Philadelphia: Temple University Press, 1989), 203–5; Angela Y. Davis, *Are Prisons Obsolete?* (New York: Seven Stories, 2003); Joseph M. Giarratano, "The Pains of Life," in Radelet, *Facing the Death Penalty*, 193–97; Jackson and Burke, *Dead Run*; Robert Johnson, *Death Work: A Study of the Modern Execution Process* (Belmont, CA: Thomson/Wadsworth, 2006); Paul W. Keve, *Prison Life and Human Worth* (Minneapolis: University of Minnesota Press, 1974); C. Michael Lambrix, "The Isolation of Death Row," in Radelet, *Facing the Death Penalty*, 198–202; Laura Magnani and Harmon L. Wray, *Beyond Prisons: A New Interfaith Paradigm for Our Failed Prison

System (Minneapolis: Fortress, 2006); Marie Mulvey-Roberts, ed., *Writing for Their Lives: Death Row USA* (Champaign: University of Illinois Press, 2007); Christian Parenti, *Lockdown America: Police and Prisons in the Age of Crisis* (New York: Verso, 2000); Rev. Carroll Pickett, with Carlton Stowers, *Within These Walls: Memoirs of a Death House Chaplain* (New York: St. Martin's, 2002); David J. Rothman, "The Crime of Punishment," in Blomberg and Cohen, *Punishment and Social Control*, 403–16; Dennis Shere, *Cain's Redemption: A Story of Hope and Transformation in America's Bloodiest Prison* (Chicago: Northfield, 2005); David von Drehle, *Among the Lowest of the Dead: The Culture of Capital Punishment* (Ann Arbor: University of Michigan Press, 2005); Loïc Wacquant, "America's New 'Peculiar Institution': On the Prison as Surrogate Ghetto," in Blomberg and Cohen, *Punishment and Social Control*, 471–82. For a state-by-state comparison of death row conditions, see Sandra Babcock, "Death Row Conditions," updated June 2008, deathpenaltyinfo.org/documents/DeathRowConditions.xls.

53. Marie Deans, "Working against the Death Penalty," in Mulvey-Roberts, *Writing for Their Lives*, 61.

54. Peppers and Anderson, *Anatomy*, 144. This idea will be more extensively developed in chapter 4.

55. Ibid.

56. René Girard, *The Scapegoat*, trans. Yvonne Freccero (Baltimore: Johns Hopkins University Press, 1989); Rev. Joseph M. Vought, interview with author, July 2, 2008. Steve Baggarly, of the Norfolk Catholic Worker House, said the same during our interview on June 26, 2008.

57. Girard, *Scapegoat*, 24.

58. In this regard, the popular discourse on capital punishment is essentially Durkheimian in its concerns and its intended communicative effects. The death penalty, as I will show, is variously intended to enforce the morality of those who practice it, to reinforce the behavioral norms necessary for society to function, and to ensure that punishment per se is rational and communicates the morality of the people, what they will and will not accept, and what "must be done" in response to transgression. See generally Émile Durkheim, *The Division of Labor in Society*, trans. W. D. Halls (New York: Free Press, 1997), and Emile Durkheim, *Moral Education*, trans. Everett K. Wilson and Herman Schnurer (Mineola, NY: Dover, 2002). For an exemplary explication of Durkheim's theories, their shortcomings, and their continued validity, see Garland, *Punishment and Modern Society*, 23–81.

59. US Department of Justice, Bureau of Justice Statistics, "Homicide Trends in the U.S." (based on data from 1990–2005), bjs.ojp.usdoj.gov/content/homicide/tables/totalstab.cfm. See for example Frank Keating, "The Death Penalty: What's All the Debate About?," in Owens, Carlson, and Elshtain, *Religion and the Death Penalty*, 214.

60. I am referring primarily to *The Scapegoat* and to *Violence and the Sacred*, trans. Patrick Gregory (Baltimore: Johns Hopkins University Press, 1977). I wish to briefly note that I am not using Girard's theories uncritically or adopting them wholesale. Rather, I am utilizing them in full awareness of the criticisms to which they have been subject. I would like to address two such criticisms here. The first of these criticizes Girard's theory on the grounds that it is ahistorical and dislocates objects from their historical and cultural contexts, thus removing them from their original meanings and ignoring the importance of historical and cultural contingency. See for example Elizabeth Traube, "Incest and Mythology: Anthropological and Girardian Perspectives," *Berkshire Review* 14 (1979): 37–53. This criticism faults Girard's theories for being a kind of "grand unified theory of humanity," applicable to all cultures in all times and in all places, and is an important critique of these theories. Nevertheless, Girard's theories do possess significant explanatory power when applied to *this* culture in *this* time and *this* place. I thus avail myself of the scapegoat despite its broader limitations. To alleviate

problems associated with this criticism, I introduce the scapegoat only after establishing the context within which the model is applicable. Moreover, as I note, the scapegoat only gets us most of the way to an explanation of the contemporary death penalty; it has to be modified to provide a more complete picture. This modification occurs primarily in chapters 4 and 7.

A second important criticism, related to the first, is that even where Girard's theory of mimetic rivalry is helpful, it may still be unable to differentiate "real" mimicry from ascribed mimicry. See Steven Weitzman, "Mimic Jews and Jewish Mimics in Antiquity: A Non-Girardian Approach to Mimetic Rivalry," *Journal of the American Academy of Religion* 77, no. 4 (December 2009): 922-40. Again, this is a trenchant criticism, but as I will show, much of the mimetic rivalry and mimetic violence that arises within the death penalty discourse is *ascribed* mimetic rivalry, that is, one party assuming that the other party must be engaging in mimetic rivalry. The fact that much of this mimetic content is ascribed does not materially alter either the analysis or the conclusions that can be drawn from that analysis.

61. First quotation: *American Piety in the 21st Century: New Insights to the Depth and Complexity of Religion in the US*, Selected Findings from the Baylor Religion Survey, 2006, 4, www.baylor.edu/content/services/document.php/33304.pdf. See also Christopher D. Bader, Carson F. Mencken, and Paul Froese, "American Piety 2005: Content and Methods of the Baylor Religion Survey," *Journal for the Scientific Study of Religion* 46, no. 4 (December 2007): 447-63; Paul Froese and Christopher D. Bader, "God in America: Why Theology Is Not Simply the Concern of Philosophers," *Journal for the Scientific Study of Religion* 46, no. 4 (December 2007): 465-81; Kevin D. Dougherty, Byron R. Johnson, and Edward C. Polson, "Recovering the Lost: Remeasuring U.S. Religious Affiliation," *Journal for the Scientific Study of Religion* 46, no. 4 (December 2007): 483-99; Jerry Z. Park and Joseph Baker, "What Would Jesus Buy: American Consumption of Religious and Spiritual Material Goods," *Journal for the Scientific Study of Religion* 46, no. 4 (December 2007): 501-17; Rodney Stark, *What Americans Really Believe: New Findings from the Baylor Surveys of Religion* (Waco, TX: Baylor University Press, 2008). For a breakdown of church membership in Virginia, see Clifford Grammich et al., *2010 U.S. Religion Census: Religious Congregations and Membership Study* (Kansas City, MO: Nazarene, 2012), 584-607 and passim; Catherine L. Albanese, *America: Religions and Religion* (Belmont, CA: Wadsworth, 1992), 2; Bruce Lincoln, *Holy Terrors: Thinking about Religion after September 11*, 2nd ed. (Chicago: University of Chicago Press, 2006), 5-8. Second quotation: Talal Asad, *Formations of the Secular: Christianity, Islam, and Modernity* (Stanford: Stanford University Press, 2003), 14.

62. Costanzo, *Just Revenge*, 154-55.

63. Because my focus is primarily on the Christian discourse, I will throughout speak in the language of my interlocutors, which is, as Susan Harding put it, "a narrative landscape which simultaneously speaks biblical and contemporaneous dialects." Susan Friend Harding, *The Book of Jerry Falwell: Fundamentalist Language and Politics* (Princeton, NJ: Princeton University Press, 2000), 186. A good general source that provides statements from various religious traditions is DPIC, "Religion and the Death Penalty," deathpenaltyinfo.org/religion-and-death-penalty. For a source on Buddhist approaches to the death penalty, see Damien P. Horrigan, "Of Compassion and Capital Punishment: A Buddhist Perspective on the Death Penalty," *American Journal of Jurisprudence* 41 (1996): 271. On Islam and the death penalty, see for example Khaled Abou El Fadl, "The Death Penalty, Mercy, and Islam: A Call for Retrospection," in Owens, Carlson, and Elshtain, *Religion and the Death Penalty*, 73-105; Joan Fitzpatrick and Alice Miller, "International Standards on the Death Penalty: Shifting Discourse," *Brooklyn Journal of International Law* 19 (1993): 278; Terance D. Miethe and Hong Lu, *Punishment: A Comparative Historical Perspective* (Cambridge: Cambridge University Press, 2005), 153-93; Ved P. Nanda, "Islam and International Human Rights Law: Selected Aspects," *American Soci-*

ety of International Law Proceedings 87 (1993): 327; Abdulaziz Sachedina, "Civic Responsibility in Political Society: An Islamic Paradigm," in Davis, *Taking Responsibility*, 230–52. On Judaism and the death penalty, see for example Gerald J. Blidstein, "Capital Punishment—The Classic Jewish Discussion," *Judaism* 14 (1965): 150–72; Steven Davidoff, "A Comparative Study of the Jewish and the United States Constitutional Law of Capital Punishment," *ILSA Journal of International and Comparative Law* 3 (1996): 93; Rev. D. De Sola Pool, *Capital Punishment among the Jews* (New York: Bloch, 1916); Edna Erez, "Thou Shalt Not Execute: Hebrew Law Perspective on Capital Punishment," *Criminology* 19, no. 1 (May 1981): 25–43; David Novak, "Can Capital Punishment Ever Be Justified in the Jewish Tradition?," in Owens, Carlson, and Elshtain, *Religion and the Death Penalty*, 31–47; Daniel A. Rudolph, "The Misguided Reliance in American Jurisprudence on Jewish Law to Support the Moral Legitimacy of Capital Punishment," *American Criminal Law Review* 33 (1996): 437.

64. By "cultural lives," I mean "capital punishment's embeddedness in discourses and symbolic practices in specific times and places." Christian Boulanger and Austin Sarat, "Putting Culture into the Picture: Toward a Comparative Analysis of State Killing," in Austin Sarat and Christian Boulanger, eds., *The Cultural Lives of Capital Punishment: Comparative Perspectives* (Stanford: Stanford University Press, 2005), 1. I should add that I do not follow the cultural lives approach and related lines of questions fully. I do not, for example, engage with the question of the role that capital punishment plays in the nation's civil religious structures and myths, nor do I delve down to the individual level suggested by the cultural lives approach, that is, what happens when two retentionists or abolitionists meet to discuss the issue.

65. Helpful methodological sources include George E. Marcus, *Ethnography through Thick and Thin* (Princeton, NJ: Princeton University Press, 1998), and the various essays collected in James V. Spickard, J. Shawn Landers, and Meredith B. McGuire, eds., *Personal Knowledge and Beyond: Reshaping the Ethnography of Religion* (New York: New York University Press, 2002). Works on congregations and congregational study that influenced this book include Nancy Tatom Ammerman, *Congregation and Community* (New Brunswick, NJ: Rutgers University Press, 2001); Nancy Tatom Ammerman, *Pillars of Faith: American Congregations and Their Partners* (Berkeley: University of California Press, 2005); and the various essays collected in Nancy Tatom Ammerman, Jackson W. Carroll, Carl S. Dudley, and William McKinney, eds., *Studying Congregations: A New Handbook* (Nashville: Abingdon, 1998). Helpful methodological examples include Amy Johnson Frykholm, *Rapture Culture:* Left Behind *in Evangelical America* (New York: Oxford University Press, 2004), and Harding, *Book of Jerry Falwell*, as well as two trade publications, Kevin Roose, *The Unlikely Disciple: A Sinner's Semester at America's Holiest University* (New York: Grand Central, 2009), and Hannah Rosin, *God's Harvard: A Christian College on a Mission to Save America* (Orlando: Harcourt, 2007).

66. Though the context is different, see Susan Friend Harding, "Representing Fundamentalism: The Problem of the Repugnant Cultural Other," *Social Research* 58, no. 2 (Summer 1991): 373–93.

67. See Michel Foucault, *Discipline and Punish: The Birth of the Prison*, trans. Alan Sheridan (New York: Vintage Books, 1995). In referencing Foucault's theories of technologies of power, I explicitly decline to apply his analysis of capital punishment to the American context. I agree with the critiques of Foucault's theories as advanced in Colvin, *Penitentiaries*, and especially Garland, *Peculiar Institution*. Though this work is not about punishment per se, it has been informed by several notable works on and theories of punishment. See David Garland, *The Culture of Control: Crime and Social Order in Contemporary Society* (Chicago: University of Chicago Press, 2002); David Garland, "Punishment and Culture: The Symbolic Dimension of Criminal Justice," *Studies in Law, Politics and Society* 11 (1991); Matt Matravers, *Justice and Punishment:*

The Rationale of Coercion (New York: Oxford University Press, 2000); Matt Matravers, ed., *Punishment and Political Theory* (Oxford: Hart, 1999); and Franklin E. Zimring, Gordon Hawkins, and Sam Kamin, *Punishment and Democracy: Three Strikes and You're Out in California* (New York: Oxford University Press, 2001).

68. Brief of the American Baptist Churches (ABC) et al., as Amici Curiae in Support of Petitioners, in the Supreme Court of the United States, *High v. Zant/Wilkins v. Missouri*, Nos. 87-5666, 87-6026, October Term, 1988, 31–32, n. 7; AFSC archive, Amicus, High v. Zant (hereinafter ABC, *Zant*).

69. There is, of course, a rather important step between being charged with a crime and the postconviction appeals process—the capital murder trial itself. That process, however, is too large to fit within the scope of this project. I have dealt with some aspects of the problems posed by religion in the capital courtroom in Anthony Santoro, "Hermeneutical Communities in Conflict: The Bible and the Capital Jury," in Bart C. Labuschagne and Ari M. Solon, eds., *Religion and State: From Separation to Cooperation? Legal-Philosophical Reflections for a De-Secularized World*, ASRP Beiheft, no. 118 (Stuttgart: Franz Steiner Verlag, 2009), 87–109. See also John H. Blume and Sherri Lynn Johnson, "Don't Take His Eye, Don't Take His Tooth, and Don't Cast the First Stone: Limiting Religious Arguments in Capital Cases," *William and Mary Bill of Rights Journal* 9 (2000): 61; Brian H. Bornstein and Monica K. Miller, *God in the Courtroom: Religion's Role at Trial* (New York: Oxford University Press, 2009).

70. James McBride, "Capital Punishment as the Unconstitutional Establishment of Religion: A Girardian Reading of the Death Penalty," *Journal of Church and State* 37, no. 2 (Spring 1995): 263–86.

71. Miroslav Volf, *Exclusion and Embrace: A Theological Exploration of Identity, Otherness, and Reconciliation* (Nashville: Abingdon, 1996).

72. David Morgan, *The Sacred Gaze: Religious Visual Culture in Theory and Practice* (Berkeley: University of California Press, 2005).

73. DPIC, "Women and the Death Penalty," deathpenaltyinfo.org/women-and-death-penalty, last modified April 1, 2012.

2. Between Moral Certainty and Morally Certain

Epigraphs. Rev. D. De Sola Pool, *Capital Punishment among the Jews* (New York: Bloch, 1916), 15–16; James W. L. Park, www.religioustolerance.org/exeover.htm, last updated November 16, 2010.

1. Pamela Podger and Michael Sluss, "Death Penalty Debate Makes Religion an Issue," *Roanoke Times*/Roanoke.com, October 16, 2005, www.roanoke.com/news/roanoke.wb/36491. Except where noted, all websites referenced in this chapter were accessed July 21, 2012.

2. Robert Barnes, "Kilgore Ads Seek to Divide Democrats," *Washington Post*, October 13, 2005; US Conference of Catholic Bishops (USCCB), *Catholic Campaign to End the Use of the Death Penalty*, Publication No. 5-715 (Washington, DC: USCCB). See also Zogby International Poll for the USCCB, December 2004. A sampling of recent works dealing with the links between Christianity and capital punishment would include Timothy Gorringe, *God's Just Vengeance* (Cambridge: Cambridge University Press, 2002); Gardner C. Hanks, *Against the Death Penalty: Christian and Secular Arguments against Capital Punishment* (Scottdale, PA: Herald, 1997); Gardner C. Hanks, *Capital Punishment and the Bible* (Scottdale, PA: Herald, 2002); Joseph B. Ingle, *Last Rights: 13 Fatal Encounters with the State's Justice* (Nashville: Abingdon, 1990); Millard Lind, *The Sound of Sheer Silence and the Killing State: The Death Penalty and the Bible* (Telford, PA: Cascadia, 2004); Christopher D. Marshall, *Beyond Retribution: A New Testament Vision for Justice, Crime, and Punishment* (Grand Rapids, MI: Wm. B. Eerdmans, 2001);

Stephen Nathanson, *An Eye for an Eye? The Immorality of Punishing by Death*, 2nd ed. (Lanham, MD: Rowman and Littlefield, 2001); J. Milburn Thompson, *Justice and Peace: A Christian Primer* (Maryknoll, NY: Orbis Books, 1997); John Witte Jr., *God's Joust, God's Justice: Law and Religion in the Western Tradition* (Grand Rapids, MI: Wm. B. Eerdmans, 2006); Aharon W. Zorea, *In the Image of God: A Christian Response to Capital Punishment* (Lanham, MD: Rowman and Littlefield, 2000).

3. Quotation: Garland, *Punishment and Modern Society*, 203. Chester L. Britt, "Race, Religion, and Support for the Death Penalty: A Research Note," *Justice Quarterly* 15, no. 1 (March 1998): 175–91; Theodore Eisenberg, Stephen P. Garvey, and Martin T. Wells, "Forecasting Life and Death: Juror Race, Religion, and Attitude toward the Death Penalty," *Journal of Legal Studies* 30 (June 2001): 277–311; "Number of Executions by State and Region since 1976," www.deathpenaltyinfo.org/number-executions-state-and-region-1976, last updated September 26, 2012; Dr. Barrett Duke, comments made at Pew Forum on Religion and Public Life, "Religious Reflections on the Death Penalty," event transcript, June 5, 2001, pewforum.org/events/?EventID=10 (hereinafter Pew Forum); Grammich et al., *2010 U.S. Religion Census*, 9–51. The claim made here is correlative, not causal, however, because the reality is more complicated than that. In fact, in three of the top ten executing states—Texas, Florida, and Ohio—the Catholic Church is the largest reporting denomination, a position held by the SBC in the remaining seven. In many of the abolitionist states in the Midwest and Northeast, the United Methodist Church, another abolitionist denomination, also has a strong presence.

The literature on religion's influence on the death penalty is large and conflicted. Studies conducted by James Unnever and his colleagues, for example, find an ambivalent relationship between religion and support for the death penalty. See James D. Unnever, John P. Bartkowski, and Francis T. Cullen, "God Imagery and Opposition to Abortion and Capital Punishment: A Partial Test of Religious Support for the Consistent Life Ethic," *Sociology of Religion* 71, no. 3 (May 2010): 307–22; James D. Unnever and Francis T. Cullen, "Christian Fundamentalism and Support for Capital Punishment," *Journal of Research in Crime and Delinquency* 43, no. 2 (May 2006): 169–97; James D. Unnever and Francis T. Cullen, "The Social Sources of Americans' Punitiveness: A Test of Three Competing Models," *Criminology* 48, no. 1 (February 2010): 99–129; James D. Unnever, Francis T. Cullen, and John P. Barkowski, "Images of God and Public Support for Capital Punishment: Does a Close Relationship with a Loving God Matter?" *Criminology* 44, no. 4 (October 2006): 835–66. Others finding an ambivalent relationship between religion and capital punishment include Thomas C. Berg, "Religious Conservatives and the Death Penalty," *William and Mary Bill of Rights Journal* 9 (2000): 29; and Marla Sandys and Edmund F. McGarrell, "Beyond the Bible Belt: The Influence (or Lack Thereof) of Religion on Attitudes toward the Death Penalty," *Journal of Crime and Justice* 20 (1997): 79. Davison M. Douglas, "God and the Executioner: The Influence of Western Religion on the Use of the Death Penalty," *William and Mary Bill of Rights Journal* 9 (2000): 137, finds a minimal relationship between religion and support for the death penalty in the contemporary United States. Britt and Eisenberg, Garvey, and Wells, noted above, find a much stronger relationship between the two. See also generally Brandon Applegate, Francis T. Cullen, Bonnie Fisher, and Thomas Vander Ven, "Forgiveness and Fundamentalism: Reconsidering the Relationship between Correctional Attitudes and Religion," *Criminology* 38, no. 3 (March 2006): 719–51. Christopher Bader and Paul Froese, "Images of God: The Effect of Personal Theologies on Moral Attitudes, Political Affiliation, and Religious Behavior," *Interdisciplinary Journal of Research on Religion* 1 (2005), www.religjournal.com/pdf/ijrr01011.pdf; Thoroddur Bjarnason and Michael R. Welch, "Father Knows Best: Parishes, Priests, and American Catholic Parishioners' Attitudes toward Capital Punishment," *Journal for the Scientific Study of Religion* 43, no.

1 (March 2004): 103–18; Christopher G. Ellison and Marc A. Musick, "Southern Intolerance: A Fundamentalist Effect?," *Social Forces* 72, no. 2 (December 1993): 379–98; Harold G. Grasmick and Anne McGill, "Religion, Attribution Style, and Punitiveness toward Juvenile Offenders," *Criminology* 32, no. 1 (February 1994): 23–46; Harold G. Grasmick, Robert J. Bursik Jr., and Brenda Sims Blackwell, "Religious Beliefs and Public Support for the Death Penalty for Juveniles and Adults," *Journal of Crime and Justice* 16, no. 2 (1993): 59–86; Harold G. Grasmick, John K. Cochran, Robert Bursik Jr., and M'Lou Kempel, "Religion, Punitive Justice, and Support for the Death Penalty," *Justice Quarterly* 10, no. 2 (June 1993): 289–314; Rachel M. McNair and Stephen Zunes, *Consistently Opposing Killing: From Abortion to Assisted Suicide, the Death Penalty, and War* (Westport, CT: Praeger, 2008); Robert L. Young, "Religious Orientation, Race, and Support for the Death Penalty," *Journal for the Scientific Study of Religion* 31, no. 1 (March 1992): 76–87.

4. SBC, "Resolution on Capital Punishment," June 2000, www.sbc.net/resolutions/amResolution.asp?ID=299; United Church of Christ (UCC), "Resolution of the 12th General Synod of the United Church of Christ," 1979, in American Friends Service Committee (AFSC), *The Death Penalty: The Religious Community Calls for Abolition* (Philadelphia: American Friends Service Committee, 1998), 24–25. Though the Assemblies of God (AoG) take no formal position on capital punishment, the denomination's position paper deals with these issues succinctly and clearly. See AoG, "Capital Punishment," www.ag.org/top/Beliefs/contempissues_08_capital_punish.cfm.

5. Jean Bethke Elshtain, *Who Are We? Critical Reflections and Hopeful Possibilities* (Grand Rapids, MI: Wm. B. Eerdmans, 2000); Church Women United (CWU), "Capital Punishment," 1981, in AFSC, *Death Penalty*, 11. Quotation: Elshtain, foreword to Owens, Carlson, and Elshtain, *Religion and the Death Penalty*, xii.

6. See Thorsten Sellin, *The Death Penalty: A Report for the Model Penal Code Project of the American Law Institute* (Philadelphia: American Law Institute, 1959).

7. First quotation: Garland, *Punishment and Modern Society*, 17. See also generally Harold J. Berman, *Faith and Order: The Reconciliation of Law and Religion* (Grand Rapids, MI: Wm. B. Eerdmans, 1993). Second quotation: Asad, *Formations of the Secular*, 14.

8. Lincoln, *Holy Terrors*, 5–8. Given the nature of the concerns, conversations, and sources that I am dealing with, I am also mindful of David Chidester's definition of religion: "*Religion is a generic term for 'ways of being a human person in a human place.'* I define religion as discourses and practices that negotiate what it is to be a human person both in relation to the superhuman and in relation to whatever might be treated as subhuman. . . . Religion, in my definition, is the activity of being human in relation to superhuman transcendence and sacred inclusion, which inevitably involves dehumanization and exclusion. Religion, therefore, contains an inherent ambiguity." Chidester, *Authentic Fakes: Religion and American Popular Culture* (Berkeley: University of California Press, 2005), vii–viii. This combination of approaches is, I think, the best pairing of theoretical approaches to limn and understand the problems considered in this book. On ethics and morality, see for example G. Scott Davis, "Ethics," in Robert A. Segal, ed., *The Blackwell Companion to the Study of Religion* (Oxford: Blackwell, 2006), 239–54. I have no wish to define religion simply as a code or system of morality. A helpful clarification on this problem can be found in Martin Riesebrodt, *The Promise of Salvation: A Theory of Religion*, trans. Steven Rendall (Chicago: University of Chicago Press, 2010).

9. Winnifred Fallers Sullivan, *The Impossibility of Religious Freedom* (Princeton, NJ: Princeton University Press, 2005), 153. A useful source on the spectrum of procedural problems with capital punishment is Stephen P. Garvey, ed., *Beyond Repair? America's Death Penalty* (Durham, NC: Duke University Press, 2002).

10. First quotation: Barbara J. Shapiro, *"Beyond Reasonable Doubt" and "Probable Cause": Historical Perspectives on the Anglo-American Law of Evidence* (Berkeley: University of California Press, 1991), 8. As we will see in later chapters, this idea of "universal assent" is alive and well in the cultural debates over capital murder cases and trials. Second quotation: *Commonwealth v. John W. Webster*, 5 Cush. 295, 59 Mass. 295 (1850), at 319–20. Decision available at masscases.com/cases/sjc/59/59mass295.html. Third quotation: Keating, "The Death Penalty," 219.

11. There are several major religious bodies that do not have an official position on capital punishment. The Church of Jesus Christ of Latter-Day Saints (LDS) and the AoG are two such groups, neither supporting nor opposing capital punishment, leaving the decision up to the relevant political authority or to the individual believer, respectively. See AoG, "Capital Punishment," and LDS, "Capital Punishment," newsroom.lds.org/ldsnewsroom/eng/public-issues/capital-punishment.

12. First quotation: USCCB, *Catholic Campaign.* Second quotation: UCC, "Resolution," in AFSC, *Death Penalty*, 24. Third quotation: ABC, "Resolution on Capital Punishment," June 1977, in AFSC, *Death Penalty*, 6. A list of abolitionist denominations would include the American Baptist Churches (USA) (ABC), Christian Church (Disciples of Christ), Church of the Brethren, Churches of Christ in the USA, Eastern Orthodox Churches, Episcopal Church, Friends United Meeting (Quakers), Mennonite Church, Moravian Church in America, Presbyterian Church (USA) (PCUSA), Reformed Church in America, Unitarian Universalist Association, UCC, and the United Methodist Church (UMC). Reform Judaism also is abolitionist. On systemic fallibility, see Mennonite Central Committee (MCC), "Death Penalty," December 4, 1982, in AFSC, *Death Penalty*, 19; PCUSA, "Capital Punishment," PCUS 212th General Assembly, 2000, in PCUSA, *Public Policy Statements of the Presbyterian Church (USA): Capital Punishment*, PDS 72-620-02-705 (Louisville: General Assembly Council), 2; USCCB, *Statement on Capital Punishment*, Publication No. 740-5 (Washington, DC: United States Catholic Conference, 2001), 9.

13. First quotation: Episcopal Church, "Capital Punishment: Statement of the 1979 General Conference," in AFSC, *Death Penalty*, 11. Second quotation: Episcopal Church, "Capital Punishment," in AFSC, *Death Penalty*, 11. Third quotation: ELCA, "A Social Statement On: The Death Penalty," August 28–September 4, 1991, in AFSC, *Death Penalty*, 12. Fourth quotation: Friends Committee on National Legislation, "Statement of Legislative Policy," November 14, 1987, in AFSC, *Death Penalty*, 16 (italics added). Fifth quotation: USCCB, *Statement*, 7. Sixth quotation: American Ethical Union, "Resolution on Capital Punishment," September 17, 1976, in AFSC, *Death Penalty*, 6. Seventh and eighth quotations: Ronald Dworkin, *Life's Dominion: An Argument about Abortion and Euthanasia* (New York: HarperCollins, 1993), 11.

14. The SBC and the National Association of Evangelicals (NAE) are two retentionist groups. Orthodox Judaism is officially retentionist, though it advocates a moratorium on executions. First quotation: Duke, Pew Forum. Second quotation: Dworkin, *Life's Dominion*, 11. Remaining quotations: SBC, "On Capital Punishment" (italics added). This sentiment also recurs in the idea that the death penalty is necessary to protect the right of the offender to be treated as a human, fully capable of making his own choices, as will be discussed in subsequent chapters.

15. First quotation: Dworkin, *Life's Dominion*, 108. Second quotation: SBC, "On Capital Punishment." The Lutheran Church—Missouri Synod (LCMS) likewise finds that the state need not impose capital punishment, but since it believes that capital punishment remains legitimate in the here and now, a position that the Catholic Church and ELCA reject, it is correctly categorized as retentionist.

16. First quotation: ELCA, "Social Statement," 13. Second quotation: Pope John Paul II, *Evangelium Vitae (The Gospel of Life): On the Value and Inviolability of Human Life*, Publication Nos. 316–17 (Washington, DC: US Catholic Conference, undated), 99.

17. First quotation: Cardinal Joseph Ratzinger, quoted in E. Christian Brugger, *Capital Punishment and Roman Catholic Moral Tradition* (Notre Dame, IN: University of Notre Dame Press, 2003), 12. Second quotation: *Catechism of the Catholic Church*, 2nd ed., section 2267, www.usccb.org/beliefs-and-teachings/what-we-believe/catechism/catechism-of-the-catholic-church/epub/. Third quotation: Brugger, *Capital Punishment*, 12. On double effect, see Thomas Aquinas, *Summa Theologica*, Second Part of the Second Part, Question 64, Article 7, www.newadvent.org/summa/3064.htm.

18. Quotation: NAE, "Capital Punishment 1973," www.nae.net/government-relations/policy-resolutions/95-capital-punishment-1973. "Mend don't end": SBC, "On Capital Punishment"; Pew Forum.

19. NAE, "Capital Punishment 1972," nae.net/index.cfm?FUSEACTION=editor.page&pageID=187, accessed February 26, 2009, and "Capital Punishment 1973."

20. First quotation: USCCB, *Statement*, 3. Second quotation: USCCB, *Statement*, 4. For an example of a faith-based objection to the penitentiary system, and to the penal system generally, see Laura Magnani, *America's First Penitentiary: A 200-Year-Old Failure* (Philadelphia: American Friends Service Committee, 1990), and Magnani and Wray, *Beyond Prisons*, esp. 157–87. On retribution, see MCC, "Death Penalty," in AFSC, *Death Penalty*, 19; AFSC, "Statement on the Death Penalty," November 1976, in ibid., 7; UMC, "Capital Punishment," in ibid., 25.

21. LCMS, *Report on Capital Punishment* (St. Louis, MO: Concordia, 1980), 4; SBC, "Resolution"; AoG, "Capital Punishment." First quotation: Christian Church (Disciples of Christ), "Resolution Concerning Opposition to the Use of the Death Penalty," 1985, in AFSC, *Death Penalty*, 10. Second quotation: ELCA, "Social Statement," 13.

22. First quotation: LCMS, *Report*, 5. Second quotation: SBC, "On Capital Punishment."

23. First quotation: Antonin Scalia, "God's Justice and Ours: The Morality of Judicial Participation in the Death Penalty," in Owens, Carlson, and Elshtain, *Religion and the Death Penalty*, 234. Second quotation: Romans 13:4. The rhetorical similarities between legitimizations of killing in self-defense and just war extend beyond the merely analogous. The links between capital punishment and (just) war were discussed in detail in Sessions L, O, and P (see chapter 3). The body of literature on just war and just war theory is immense. Two pertinent examples that help clarify the comparison between war and capital punishment are Daniel C. Maguire, *The Horrors We Bless: Rethinking the Just-War Legacy* (Minneapolis: Fortress, 2007), and Gerald W. Schlabach, "Breaking Bread: Peace and War," in Stanley Hauerwas and Samuel Wells, eds., *The Blackwell Companion to Christian Ethics* (Oxford: Blackwell, 2006), 360–74.

24. Imago dei: Genesis 1:27. See SBC, "Resolution," and LCMS, *Report*, 10. From this perspective, the apparent contradiction held by conservative religious bodies with regard to abortion (opposed) and the death penalty (in favor) is less contradictory than it at first appears. The question, as understood by these groups, is less over the taking of life per se and the legitimacy of both that taking and the taker's right to that action. As the NAE's 1973 statement on abortion makes clear, the question is when "a human being may take the life of another." NAE, "Abortion 1973," www.nae.net/government-relations/policy-resolutions/59-abortion-1973. See also Dworkin, *Life's Dominion*, 11.

25. Compare Scalia, "God's Justice," 238–39, with Brugger, *Capital Punishment*.

26. Garland, *Peculiar Institution*, 127–82, is helpful on issues pertaining to the monopoly of violence in the context of the American death penalty. See also generally Franklin Zimring, *The Contradictions of American Capital Punishment* (New York: Oxford University Press, 2003).

27. Quotation: LCMS, *Report*, 9. Ditchfield, "Challenging the Intrastate Disparities"; Kroll, "Chattahoochee Judicial District"; Songer and Unah, "Race, Gender, and Location."

28. Quotation: USCCB, *Catholic Campaign.* See The Bruderhof Communities, "Statement on the Death Penalty," in AFSC, *Death Penalty*, 9; PCUSA, "Capital Punishment," PCUS 106th General Assembly, 1966, in PCUSA, *Public Policy Statements*, 9; USCCB, *Statement*, 4. UMC, "Capital Punishment," 25, and CWU, "Capital Punishment," 1981, in AFSC, *Death Penalty*, 11.

29. See USCCB, *Catholic Campaign*, and US Catholic Conference (USCC), *A Good Friday Appeal to End the Death Penalty*, Publication No. 5-327 (Washington, DC: US Catholic Conference); PCUSA, "Opposition to Capital Punishment," in PCUSA, *Public Policy Statements*, 3. First quotation: Pope John Paul II, Address in St. Louis. MO, January 27, 1999, quoted in USCC, *Good Friday.* Second quotation: ELCA, "Social Statement," 13.

30. First quotation: USCC, "Statement on Capital Punishment: Committee on Social Development and World Peace," March 1, 1978, in AFSC, *Death Penalty*, 26. Second quotation: ABC, "Resolution," in AFSC, *Death Penalty*, 6. See also Fellowship of Reconciliation (FoR), "An Appeal to End All Executions," in AFSC, *Death Penalty*, 15. Third quotation: UCC, "Resolution," 24. Fourth quotation: PCUSA, "Moratorium on Capital Punishment," PCUSA 212th General Assembly, 2000, in PCUSA, *Public Policy Statements*, 1. *McCleskey v. Kemp*, 481 U.S. 279 (1987). Among the retentionist denominations, the LCMS statement includes the greatest consideration of issues of moral certainty. See LCMS, *Report*, 9–10.

31. Quotation: Sister Helen Prejean, CSJ, "Would Jesus Pull the Switch?," *Salt of the Earth*, March/April 1997, 13. ABC, "Resolution," 6; FoR, "Appeal," 14; National Council of the Churches of Christ in the USA, "Resolution Opposing Capital Punishment and Racism in Sentencing," May 26, 1988, in AFSC, *Death Penalty*, 21; PCUSA, "Moratorium," in PCUSA, *Public Policy Statements*, 2; Ryan, "Reflections"; Scott Turow, *Ultimate Punishment: A Lawyer's Reflections on Dealing with the Death Penalty* (New York: Picador, 2003), details Turow's experience in dealing with the death penalty via his service on the study of the death penalty in Illinois Ryan commissioned.

32. Quotation: SBC, "Resolution on Capital Punishment." *McCleskey*, 481 U.S. On concerns about innocence, see Duke's comments, Pew Forum. On irrelevance of procedural problems, see comments made by William Otis at "The Death Penalty Today: Defend It, Mend It or End It?," event transcript available at the Pew Forum on Religion and Public Life, July 21, 2006, pewforum.org/events/?EventID=122 (hereinafter "The Death Penalty Today").

33. ELCA, "Social Statement," 13 (italics added). The ELCA cites Matthew 5:38–39 and John 8:3–11 as illustrations of restorative justice.

34. First quotation: PCUSA, "Moratorium," in PCUSA, *Public Policy Statements*, 2. Second quotation: *Witherspoon v. Illinois*, 391 U.S. 510 (1968) at 519. See also Mara Taub, *Juries: Conscience of the Community* (Berkeley: Chardon, 1998). Third quotation: PCUSA, "Resolution on a Continuing Witness to Abolish the Death Penalty, 1977," in PCUSA, *Public Policy Statements*, 6. This idea was reaffirmed in the PCUSA's 1985 "Opposition to Capital Punishment" and 2000 "Resolution," in ibid., 4 and 2. The Mennonite Church, "Statement on Capital Punishment," August 1965, in AFSC, *Death Penalty*, 20. General Conference, Mennonite Church, "Capital Punishment," July 16, 1965, in AFSC, *Death Penalty*, 17. Fourth quotation: Reformed Church in America, "Resolution on Capital Punishment," 1965, in AFSC, *Death Penalty*, 23. Fifth quotation: ELCA, "Social Statement," 13.

35. Javier Bleichmar, "Deportation as Punishment: A Historical Analysis of the British Practice of Banishment and Its Impact on Modern Constitutional Law," *Georgetown Immigration Law Journal* 14 (1999–2000): 115; A. Roger Ekrich, "Exiles in the Promised Land: Convict Labor in the Eighteenth-Century Chesapeake," *Maryland Historical Magazine* 82, no. 2 (Sum-

mer 1987): 95–122; Steven A. Hatfield, "Criminal Punishment in America: From the Colonial to the Modern Era," *United States Air Force Academy Journal of Legal Studies* 1 (1990): 139; Edith Ziegler, "The Transported Convict Women of Colonial Maryland, 1718–1776," *Maryland Historical Magazine* 97, no. 1 (Spring 2002): 5–32.

36. Edward L. Ayers, *Vengeance and Justice: Crime and Punishment in the Nineteenth-Century American South* (New York: Oxford University Press, 1994); Bessler, *Cruel and Unusual*; William A. Byrne, "Slave Crime in Savannah, Georgia," *Journal of Negro History* 79, no. 4 (Autumn 1994): 352–62; James Campbell, "'The Victim of Prejudice and Hasty Consideration': The Slave Trial System in Richmond, Virginia, 1830–61," *Slavery and Abolition* 26, no. 1 (April 2005): 71–91; Victor S. Navasky, "Deportation as Punishment," *University of Kansas City Law Review* 27 (1958–59): 213; Judith Kelleher Schafer, "'Under the Present Mode of Trial, Improper Verdicts Are Very Often Given': Criminal Procedure in the Trials of Slaves in Antebellum Louisiana," *Cardozo Law Review* 18 (1996): 635; Philip J. Schwarz, *Slave Laws in Virginia* (Athens: University of Georgia Press, 1996).

37. Quotation: Corey Rayburn Yung, "Banishment by a Thousand Laws: Residency Restrictions on Sex Offenders," *Washington University Law Review* 85 (2007–8): 101. Stephanie Smith, "Civil Banishment of Gang Members: Circumventing Criminal Due Process Requirements?" *University of Chicago Law Review* 67 (2000): 1461. Yung provides a helpful overview of the characteristics of contemporary exilic punishments, but I want to note two specific areas where I disagree with this analysis. First, Yung states that one of the defining characteristics of "every exile scheme" is that exile "is always to a non-institutional setting" (134). I disagree, and would point to popular conceptions of "prison justice" as a case in point—institutional settings are capable of creating a common community of persons subject to fundamentally different norms, as mentioned in chapter 1. Second, Yung writes that exiles are "people living only in the present" (140). As I show in later chapters, this is only conditionally true with persons under a death sentence.

38. The reasons for these moves, and their effects, are the focus of subsequent chapters.

39. SBC, "Resolution." See also Duke, Pew Forum, and LCMS, *Report*; Durkheim, *Moral Education*; Durkheim, *Division of Labor*. First quotation: Reverend Joseph Lowery, at Pew Forum. CWU, "Capital Punishment," 11. Second quotation: ELCA, "Social Statement," 13. Forfeit life: Duke, Pew Forum.

40. First two quotations: Texas Catholic Conference, "Statement by Catholic Bishops of Texas on Capital Punishment," October 20, 1997, Death Penalty Information Center, www.deathpenaltyinfo.org/statement-catholic-bishops-texas-capital-punishment. See also Raymond Paternoster et al., *An Empirical Analysis of Maryland's Death Sentencing System with Respect to the Influence of Race and Legal Jurisdiction, Final Report*, available at www.newsdesk.umd.edu/pdf/finalrep.pdf; Raymond Paternoster, Robert Brame, and Sarah Bacon, *The Death Penalty: America's Experience with Capital Punishment* (New York: Oxford University Press, 2007), 158–252. Third quotation: Texas Conference of Churches, "Resolution Opposing the Death Penalty: Adopted Unanimously by the General Assembly of the Texas Conference of Churches," February 24, 1988, www.deathpenaltyinfo.org/texas-conference-churches (italics added). Remaining quotations: Iowa Catholic Conference, "Catholic Bishops of Iowa Issue Statement on Death Penalty," February 4, 1998, www.deathpenaltyinfo.org/catholic-bishops-iowa-issue-statement-death-penalty (italics added). For the role of religion in the achievement and maintenance of abolition in Iowa, see Galliher et al., *America without the Death Penalty*, 170–89.

41. Virginia Conference of the United Methodist Church (VAUMC), "Call for a Moratorium on Executions," June 13, 2000, Vought files, Moratorium, VA UMC Resolution; Virginia Synod,

ELCA, "Resolution 5.0: A Resolution Calling for a Moratorium on Executions," June 19, 2001, Vought files, Death Penalty Moratorium, 2001 VA Synod Resolution; Abingdon Convocation, "Resolution #4B: Concerning: Capital Punishment," February 2001, Vought files, Moratorium, Episcopal Resolution; 206th Annual Council, Episcopal Church, Diocese of Virginia, "Resolution R-8," January 31, 2001, Vought files, Moratorium, Episcopal Resolution; 109th Council of the Episcopal Diocese of Southern Virginia, untitled undated resolution, ibid.; Vestry of St. Mark's Episcopal Church (Richmond), "Resolution for Moratorium on Executions in Virginia," September 19, 2000, ibid.; Manassas Church of the Brethren, "Resolution: The Sanctity of Life and Truth in Justice," October 1999, Vought files, Moratorium, Manassas Brethren; St. Pius X Catholic Church (Norfolk), "Resolution for a Moratorium on Executions in Virginia," March 25, 2000, Vought files, Moratorium, St. Pius X Resolution; Wythe and Blount Counties, Roundtable on Poverty, "Moratorium Resolution [on] the Death Penalty in Virginia," January 20, 2001, Vought files, Moratorium, Wythe and Blount Resolution. Quotations: First Unitarian Church of Richmond, "Congregational Resolution for a Moratorium on Executions," June 4, 2000, Vought files, Moratorium, Congressional Moratorium Resolution.

42. First quotation: Jefferson quoted in Forrest Church's preface to Thomas Jefferson, *The Jefferson Bible: The Life and Morals of Jesus of Nazareth* (Boston: Beacon, 1989), viii. Second quotation: Iowa Catholic Conference, "Catholic Bishops."

43. First quotation: Henry Schwarzchild quoted in Haines, *Against*, 104. Second quotation: Rev. Kathy Lancaster quoted in ibid., 106. PCUSA Survey, ibid., 104.

44. Virginia Council of Churches (VCC), "Death Penalty Study Packet," Virginia Council of Churches Files, Richmond. Quotation: VAUMC, "Call for Moving Forward with Study and Action on the Death Penalty," June 18, 2002, 2. National Death Penalty Archive (NDPA), Virginians for Alternatives to the Death Penalty Files, "VA Methodist Workshop / VADP Events 2003" (uncatalogued collection).

3. Between the Innocent Man and Osama bin Laden

1. First quotation: Session H. All names have been changed to protect the privacy of participants. For a list of sessions, see Appendix A. There, too, names and locations have been withheld to protect the privacy of participants, at the request of the participating institutions. All quotations from sessions were transcribed by author. Second quotation: Pastor Frazier, Session C. Cain and Abel: Genesis 4:1–16. First city: Genesis 4:17. Moses: Exodus 2:1–3:12. David: 2 Samuel 11:1–12:25. Saul/Paul: Acts 6:8–15, 7:51–60, 9:1–19.

2. Session L. These discussions all took place well before President Barack Obama announced on May 1, 2011, that US forces had killed Osama bin Laden during a raid on bin Laden's compound in Abbottabad, Pakistan.

3. Session G.

4. I am using the term "Bible studies" to refer to any organized event fulfilling the same purpose as the Bible study—that is, to investigate or instruct church teachings on a particular subject, or to provide a forum for congregants and parishioners to investigate their faith and their faith tradition, with reference to scripture or to church tradition and teaching. Parish/congregation roundtables, forums, both public and private, and seminar-style presentations at which local experts were invited to speak are examples of such related activities, and are all represented within this study.

5. I am using the term "reconciliatory practices" in the way Riesebrodt defined it, as well as in the more narrow sense that I explain below. On the tension between justice and mercy and its impact on legitimacy, see for example Oliver O'Donovan, "Payback: Thinking about Retribution," *Books and Culture* 6, no. 4 (July/August 2000): 16–21.

6. I do not mean to ascribe any negative connotations to the concept of "imagined worlds" in this context. The word is used not in terms of fantasy, but in terms of reconstructing and mentally vivifying on the basis of an incomplete understanding. In the context of the Bible study, it is worth recalling that "imagination is indeed a legitimate way of knowing." Walter Brueggeman, preface to the revised edition, *The Prophetic Imagination*, 2nd ed. (Minneapolis: Fortress, 2001), x.

7. Exodus 2:11–15. I will switch between "murder," "killing," and "homicide" to describe this event, for reasons that I explain below. Jim Fodor, "Reading the Scriptures: Rehearsing Identity, Practicing Character," in Hauerwas and Wells, *The Blackwell Companion to Christian Ethics*, 149. On the disruptive violence attendant with such endeavors as this textual dislocation, see Žižek, *Violence*, 61. On the practice and aims behind Bible studies, see also Frykholm, *Rapture Culture*, 114–15.

8. First quotation: Rowan Williams, "To Stand Where Christ Stands," in Ralph Waller and Benedicta Ward, eds., *An Introduction to Christian Spirituality* (London: SPCK 1999), 12. Rowan Williams, "Sacraments of the New Society," in David Brown and Ann Loades, eds., *Christ: The Sacramental Word* (London: SPCK, 1996), 89–90. Second quotation: Harding, *The Book of Jerry Falwell*, 239. Scott Bader-Saye, "Listening: Authority and Obedience," in Hauerwas and Wells, *Christian Ethics*, 156–68, and Charles Pinchers, "Proclaiming: Naming and Describing," in ibid., 169–81. Collective performances: Fodor, "Reading the Scriptures," 154. Third and fourth quotations: ibid., 149, 148. According to Fodor, the outward and inward movement and the bilateral dislocation, reconstruction, and reintegration is what defines these practices as Eucharistic.

9. John Berkman, "Being Reconciled: Penitence, Punishment, and Worship," in Hauerwas and Wells, *Christian Ethics*, 95. See also William Cavanaugh, *Torture and Eucharist: Theology, Politics and the Body of Christ* (Oxford: Blackwell, 1998), 238, and Jean-Marie Tillard, OP, "The Bread and the Cup of Reconciliation," in Edward Schillebeeckx, ed., *Sacramental Reconciliation* (New York: Herder and Herder, 1971), 41.

10. Pastor Brandon, Session M. On religion and memory, see generally Daniele Hervieu-Leger, *Religion as a Chain of Memory*, trans. Simon Lee (Cambridge: Polity, 2000).

11. Father Jim Griffin, interview with author, June 30, 2008. Death row ministry will be considered in chapter 7. Genesis 1:26–31. The more famous creation narrative, which sees Adam created first and then Eve from Adam's rib, occurs at Genesis 2:4b–25. The order of creation also differs in these two accounts.

12. Genesis 8:18–21, quotation from verse 21; Genesis 9:1–4; Genesis 6:11–13, quotation from verse 13 (emphasis added).

13. Rev. Wallace Sherbon, interview with author, July 28, 2008.

14. First quotation: VCC, "Death Penalty Study Packet," 11. Second quotation: Michigan Catholic Conference (MICC), *The Death Penalty: A Discussion Guide*, iii. NDPA, NCADP files, Series 3, Box 1, Michigan Bishops Capital Punishment Study Guide. Third quotation: VCC, "The Death Penalty: Exploring Faith Perspectives." Vought files, VCC Discussion Guide. Fourth quotation: VAUMC, "Death Penalty Workshop." NDPA, VADP files, VA UMC DP Workshop, VADP Events 2003. Fifth quotation: Byron Jackson, Belle Miller McMaster, Jackie Smith, Haydn O. White, and Kathy Young, compilers, *Capital Punishment Study Resource* (Atlanta; PCUS; New York: United Presbyterian Church, USA, n.d.), 1. NDPA, VADP, CP Study Resource (Presbyterian).

15. Candace Neenan, Minister of Justice and Peace, St. Nicholas Catholic Church, "Lesson Plan," September 2000, NDPA, VADP, Catholic Young People Lesson Plan. Ezekiel 33:11: "Say to them, As I live, says the Lord God, I have no pleasure in the death of the wicked, but that the

wicked turn from their ways and live; turn back, turn back from your evil ways; for why will you die, O house of Israel?" Joe McKernan, compiler, *God and the Death Penalty: A Biblical Perspective*; AFSC archive, CRD 2; John 16:2–3; Jackson, McMaster, Smith, White, and Young, *Capital Punishment Study Resource*; Luke 4:16–19, 6:27–36; Matthew 25:31–46; Romans 3:21–26, 5:8; Galatians 5:13–15; 1 Thessalonians 5:14–15; 1 John 4:13–21. Several of these passages deal with mercy, which I argue is necessarily a limitation on violence.

16. Oddly, though God is presented as frowning on Noah's sacrifice, it was Abel's sacrifice that earned God's favor, and, as Genesis 4 presents it, precipitated the chain of events whereby Cain slew his brother. This story will be discussed further below. On limits on violence, see also Robert Jay Lifton and Greg Mitchell, *Who Owns Death? Capital Punishment, the American Conscience, and the End of Executions* (New York: Perennial, 2002), 201.

17. McKernan, *God and the Death Penalty*, 5; Institute for Southern Studies, "The Bible and the Death Sentence," AFSC archive, CRD 1, Bible and DP, 2; Howard Zehr, *Death as a Penalty: A Moral, Practical, and Theological Discussion*, Mennonite Central Committee, 1998, AFSC archive, CRD 1, Howard Zehr; Britt Johnston, "Biblical Traditions and the Death Penalty," AFSC files, CRD 1, Bible.

18. First quotation: Babylonian Talmud: Sanhedrin 52b, www.come-and-hear.com/sanhedrin/sanhedrin_52.html. Second quotation: De Sola Pool, *Capital Punishment among the Jews*, 35. Third quotation: Babylonian Talmud: Sanhedrin 8b, www.come-and-hear.com/sanhedrin/sanhedrin_8.html#PARTb. See also Beth A. Berkowitz, *Execution and Invention: Death Penalty Discourse in Early Rabbinic and Christian Cultures* (New York: Oxford University Press, 2006).

19. First quotation: Zehr, *Death as a Penalty*, 13. See also Johnston, "Biblical Traditions." Second quotation: John Howard Yoder, "The Death Penalty: A Christian Perspective" (January 1979), 2. NDPA, VADP, Death Penalty, Christian Responses. Though we are not here concerned with the ways in which the Bible is read, it is interesting to note that these study guides dispense with any notions of a discontinuous Bible. That is, they see the New Testament as continuing and fulfilling the Old Testament, rather than representing a radical break from or repudiation of the Old.

20. Zehr, *Death as a Penalty*, 12; Our Lady of Wisdom Catholic Church, "Is the Death Penalty Consistent with Life?" (April 30, 1997), AFSC archive, CRD 2, Our Lady of Wisdom, 3, citing Matthew 18:21–35; Zehr, *Death as a Penalty*, 13. First quotation: Session P. Second, third, and fourth quotations: Ezekiel 18:21, 18:25, 18:30–31. Fifth and sixth quotations: MICC, *Discussion Guide*, 6. See also "Christian Values and the Death Penalty: 'Called to Be Healers,'" AFSC archive, CRD 1, Presbyterian; Zehr, *Death as a Penalty*, 13; Brooks Berndt, *Transformation through the Word: A Bible Study Guide for Developing a Christian Response to Crime* (Philadelphia: AFSC), AFSC archive, CRD 2, Transformation through the Word, 12; Jackson et al., *Study Resource*, 15; Yoder, "A Christian Perspective," 1, 3; Bob Gross, *The Death Penalty: A Guide for Christians* (Elgin, IL: FaithQuest, 1991), 9–12, 31–33.

21. On forgiveness and restorative justice, see for example Howard Zehr, *The Little Book of Restorative Justice* (Intercourse, PA: GoodBooks, 2002). Rachel King, *Don't Kill in Our Names: Families of Murder Victims Speak Out against the Death Penalty* (New Brunswick, NJ: Rutgers University Press, 2003) contains several stories of families of murder victims seeking to practice restorative justice with the killer of their loved one. See also "Restorative Justice (The Testimony of Sheldon McDowell)," in VAUMC, "Workshop."

22. James, Session H. The following summary of musings on the Moses narrative derives primarily from the transcripts for Sessions C, E, and H.

23. Quotation: H.

24. Code of Virginia § 18.2–31: Capital murder defined; punishment. Exodus 2:12. Sessions C, E, and H.

25. Exodus 2:11, 2:19. Sessions C, E, and H.

26. Exodus 20:13. We should note, however, that even to bring up the Commandments is to respond to the story anachronistically, since this killing happened well before the narrative turns to Moses and the Commandments during the Exodus. Sessions C, E, and H.

27. Sessions C, E and H. Quotation: H. Exodus 2:13–14. Quotation: 14.

28. Sessions C, E, and H. Quotation: H. Girard, *Violence and the Sacred*, 104–8.

29. Quotation: C. "God meant it for good": Genesis 50:20.

30. This summary of musings on the Cain and Abel narrative derives primarily from the transcripts for Sessions A, C, and F. Quotations: A, C, F, and A. Girard's analysis of mimetic rivalry spans several works, particularly *Violence and the Sacred* and *Things Hidden since the Foundation of the World*, trans. Stephen Bann and Michael Metteer (Stanford: Stanford University Press, 1987); and *The Scapegoat*. In this session, Pastor Frazier explicitly involved Girard in the discussion, working through the basics of Girard's theory of mimetic rivalry and strongly suggesting that anyone wishing to understand these processes read Girard.

31. Sessions A, C, and F.

32. Sessions A, C, and F. Quotations: F, A, and F. "Am I my brother's keeper": Genesis 4:9.

33. The Nickel Mines shooting was discussed particularly in Sessions A, D, and L. Melissa Dribben, "Five Years after Tragedy, Faith Remains Strong; Forgiveness Fuels Healing for Amish," *Pittsburgh Post-Gazette*, October 2, 2011; Donald B. Kraybill, Steven M. Nolt, and David L. Weaver-Zercher, *Amish Grace: How Forgiveness Transcended Tragedy* (San Francisco: Jossey-Bass, 2007); John L. Ruth, *Forgiveness: A Legacy of the West Nickel Mines Amish School* (Harrisonburg, VA: Herald, 2007). Quotation: Ann Rodgers, "Nickel Mines Legacy: Forgive First," *Pittsburgh Post-Gazette*, September 30, 2007.

34. "Complete Statement from Nickel Mines," *Intelligencer Journal* (Lancaster, PA), November 21, 2006; David Kocienieski and Shaila Dewan, "Police Reveal Darker Motive in Standoff; Investigators Say Evidence Suggests Gunmen Meant to Molest the Amish Schoolgirls," *Houston Chronicle*, October 4, 2006; Felix Alfonso Pena, "Amish Forgiveness of Killer Not Ploy, Scholar Asserts: Half the Mourners at the Nickel Mines School Shooter's Funeral Were Parents of His Victims, an Author of Seven Books about the Amish Tells a Reading Audience," *Eagle* (Reading, PA), March 31, 2008; Jack Brubaker, "Roses in Memory of Amish School Victims; Families Gather Quietly on 4th Anniversary of Tragedy at Nickel Mines," *Sunday News* (Lancaster, PA), October 3, 2010.

35. Jeff Jacoby, "Undeserved Forgiveness," *Boston Globe*, October 8, 2006, www.boston.com/news/globe/editorial_opinion/oped/articles/2006/10/08/undeserved_forgiveness/; John Podhoretz, "Hating a Child Killer," *National Review Online*, October 5, 2006, www.nationalreview.com/corner/129694/hating-child-killer/john-podhoretz; Dovid Gottlieb, "Not Always Divine," *Cross-Currents*, October 17, 2006, www.cross-currents.com/archives/2006/10/17/not-always-divine/, all accessed February 17, 2010.

36. Jack Brubaker, "A Clearer Picture; In Aftermath of Tragedy, Media, from Books to a Movie, Present a View into Amish Life and Beliefs That Goes beyond the Usual Stereotypes," *Sunday News* (Lancaster, PA), October 2, 2011; "Complete Statement from Nickel Mines"; Ron Devlin, "Forgiving Allows Amish to Absorb 2006 tragedy," *Eagle* (Reading, PA), September 29, 2008. First quotation: David Weaver-Zercher, "Amish Grace and the Rest of Us; When Amish Girls Were Gunned Down in Nickel Mines a Year Ago, We Marveled at the Community's Ability to Forgive Their Killer. But Did We Really Learn Anything?" *Pittsburgh Post-Gazette*, September 30, 2007. Remaining quotations: Tom Knapp, "Forgiveness: 'Way of Life'; E-Town Conference

Revisits Nickel Mines," *Intelligencer Journal/New Era* (Lancaster, PA), September 23, 2011. Matthew 18:21–22: "Then Peter came and said to Him, 'Lord, how often shall my brother sin against me and I forgive him? Up to seven times?' Jesus said to him, 'I do not say to you, up to seven times, but up to seventy times seven'" (New American Standard Bible).

37. Rodgers, "Nickel Mines Legacy." Quotation: Kocienieski and Dewan, "Police Reveal Darker Motive in Standoff."

38. "Interview with SueZann Bosler, Cofounder and Board Member Journey of Hope . . . From Violence to Healing," *Community of Sant'Egidio*, www.santegidio.org/pdm/news2002/04_12_02.htm. Journey of Hope: SueZann Bosler, *Journey of Hope . . . From Violence to Healing*, journeyofhope.org/who-we-are/murder-victim-family/suezann-bosler/. King, *Don't Kill in Our Names*, 138–62.

39. Sessions B, C, H, and P. Quotations: C, H. Matthew 6:9–13. Luke 11:2–4.

40. First and second quotations: Sessions F, M. Third quotation: Rev. Jesse L. Jackson Sr., Rep. Jesse L. Jackson Jr., and Bruce Shapiro, *Legal Lynching: The Death Penalty and America's Future* (New York: New Press, 2001), 92.

41. Quotation: H.

42. Genesis 9:6.

43. Christian Reformed Church in North America, "Statement on Capital Punishment (1981)," in Melton, *The Churches Speak*, 64–96, esp. 70–75.

44. Romans 13:3–4.

45. Note for Genesis 9:6, *Liberty Bible Commentary*, 36. See also generally William H. Baker, *On Capital Punishment* (Chicago: Moody, 1985). Unless otherwise specified, in all instances, I use "deterrence" to mean general deterrence, rather than specific deterrence. On marginal deterrence, see Steven Shavell, "A Note on Marginal Deterrence," *International Review of Law and Economics* 12 (1992): 345; Robert Weisberg, "The Death Penalty Meets Social Science: Deterrence and Jury Behavior under New Scrutiny," *Annual Review of Law and Social Science* 1 (2005): 151. Quotations: Beatrice, Sessions H and T.

46. Andrew, Session H; Jesse, Session D.

47. Jim Axelrod, "Going Back to the Murder Scene for Which Karla Faye Tucker Was Convicted and Sentenced to Die," *CBS This Morning*, February 3, 1998, Transcript, LexisNexis; "Karla Faye Tucker: Live from Death Row," *Larry King Live*, January 14, 1998, event transcript #98011400V22, available online at www.cnn.com/SPECIALS/1998/tucker.execution/transcripts/trans.1.14.html, accessed July 17, 2012; Steven D. Stewart, "Karla Faye Tucker," Office of the Clark County (IN) Prosecutor's Office, February 3, 1998, www.clarkprosecutor.org/html/death/US/tucker437.htm, accessed July 17, 2012; Linda Storm, *Karla Faye Tucker Set Free: Life and Faith on Death Row* (New York: Shaw Books, 2001).

48. Tucker Carlson, "Devil May Care," *Talk Magazine*, September 1999, 106; "Ronald Carlson and Richard Thornton, Relatives of Victims Killed by Karla Faye Tucker, Discuss Their Feelings about the Upcoming Execution," *Today*, NBC News Transcripts, February 3, 1998, LexisNexis; Donna Kelley, "Victim's Daughter Discusses the Execution of Karla Faye Tucker," *CNN Early Edition*, February 3, 1998, Transcript, LexisNexis; "Rally Held to Save Karla Faye Tucker from Death Penalty," *Agence France Presse English*, January 18, 1998, LexisNexis.

49. First quotation: Bill Hemmer, "Karla Faye Tucker Hopes for Pardon from Execution," CNN Morning News, February 2, 1998, Transcript #98020208V09, LexisNexis. Second quotation: Jerry Falwell on Sean Hannity and Alan Colmes, "Execution of Karla Faye Tucker," *Hannity and Colmes*, Fox News Network, February 3, 1998, Transcript, LexisNexis. "Texas Executes Karla Faye Tucker for Pickax Slaying; She Is the 1st Woman Executed in U.S. since '84," *St. Louis Post-Dispatch*, February 4, 1998, LexisNexis; Tony Wharton, "With Plea to Spare

Woman, Robertson Breaks Pattern; Some Pleased, Others Enraged That He Says This Killer Should Live," *Virginian-Pilot*, January 11, 1998. Third quotation: Rev. Pat Robertson, quoted in NCADP, "Karla Faye Tucker Faces Imminent Execution in Texas," January 5, 1998, NDPA, NCADP files, Series 1, Box 1, Tucker.

50. Sessions H, N, O, P, and T. First quotation: Jerry Falwell, Hannity and Colmes, "Execution of Karla Faye Tucker." Second quotation: Anna Schulte, letter to the editor, *Houston Chronicle*, January 25, 1998, LexisNexis. On the complicated nature of clemency petitions generally, see Cathleen Burnett, *Justice Denied: Clemency Appeals in Death Penalty Cases* (Boston: Northeastern University Press, 2002).

51. David R. Dow, *The Autobiography of an Execution* (New York: Twelve, 2010), 115–16.

52. See Victor Anderson, "Responsibility, Vengeance, and the Death Penalty," in Owens, Carlson, and Elshtain, *Religion and the Death Penalty*, 195–210, esp. 206–10. See also generally H. Richard Niebuhr, *The Responsible Self: An Essay in Christian Moral Philosophy* (Louisville: Westminster John Knox, 1999); Neenan, "Lesson Plan"; Our Lady of Wisdom, "Consistent with Life," MICC, *Discussion Guide*; "Christian Values and the Death Penalty"; Berndt, *Transformation*; Gross, *The Death Penalty*, 25–30.

53. First quotation: Session D. Executions in the Puritan commonwealth had a much more explicit theological focus and had some flexibility built into the system to try to allow the condemned to repent and save their souls. See Karen Halttunen, *Murder Most Foul: The Killer and the American Gothic Imagination* (Cambridge, MA: Harvard University Press, 1998), 18–19, and Seay, *Hanging between Heaven and Earth*. Second quotation: Session C. Saul's Damascus Road moment: Acts 9.

54. First quotation: Session K. Second quotation: "Christian Values and the Death Penalty." Third quotation: Anderson, "Responsibility," 207. *Eye for an Eye*, dir. John Schlessinger, 1996. Fourth quotation: Session G.

55. Quotations: K, B, and N. See Dale S. Recinella, *The Biblical Truth about America's Death Penalty* (Boston: Northeastern University Press, 2004), 320–23. This theme is prevalent in works written by survivors. See for example Antoinette Bosco, *Choosing Mercy: A Mother of Murder Victims Pleads to End the Death Penalty* (Maryknoll, NY: Orbis Books, 2001); Marietta Jaeger, *The Lost Child* (Grand Rapids, MI: Zondervan, 1983); King, *Don't Kill in Our Names*; Bill Pelke, *Journey of Hope: From Violence to Healing* (Bloomington, IN: Xlibris, 2003); ibid. This idea was discussed in Sessions B, D, G, J, K, and L. Session B. See Berndt, *Transformation*, 15, and "Marietta's Story" and "Marie's Story," both quoted in Gross, *The Death Penalty*, 15–16 and 26–29, respectively. Session K; "Christian Values and the Death Penalty"; McKernan, "God and the Death Penalty," 7; Gross, *The Death Penalty*, 26; Sessions B, N, and S. These ideas were discussed at sessions B, D, G, J, K, L, and S.

56. First quotation: Stephen, Session Q. See also Mark Osler, *Jesus on Death Row: The Trial of Jesus and American Capital Punishment* (Nashville: Abingdon, 2009), 5. Second quotation: McKernan, "God and the Death Penalty," 8 (italics in original).

57. Sessions B, G, H, L, N, O, Q, and R. First quotation: Philip Terzian, "Opinion: Texas Death Row Inmate Karla Faye Tucker Should Be Executed," *Providence Journal-Bulletin*, January 7, 1998, LexisNexis. Second quotation: Mabry, *Capital Punishment*, 31. See also Neenan, "Lesson Plan"; VAUMC, "Workshop"; Zehr, *Death as a Penalty*, 13–14; Berndt, *Transformation*, 2; and Meir Dan-Cohen, "Revising the Past: On the Metaphysics of Repentance, Forgiveness and Pardon," in Austin Sarat and Nasser Hussain, eds., *Forgiveness, Mercy and Clemency* (Stanford: Stanford University Press, 2007), 117–37.

58. Leslie Lytle, *Execution's Doorstep: True Stories of the Innocent and Near Damned* (Boston: Northeastern University Press, 2008).

59. Eric, Session B. The discussions in Sessions B, E, H, K, L, N, O, Q, R, and S, in particular, focused heavily on questions of innocence. See also MICC, *Discussion Guide*, 10–11; Zehr, *Death as a Penalty*, 13; "Sentenced to Die, Still Children of God: A Pax Christi Backgrounder on Capital Punishment," NDPA, VADP files, Pax Christi Backgrounder. On wrongful executions, see Michael Radelet and Hugo Adam Bedau, "The Execution of the Innocent," *Law and Contemporary Problems* 61 (1998): 105; Samuel R. Gross, "Lost Lives: Miscarriages of Justice in Capital Cases," *Law and Contemporary Problems* 61 (1998): 125; Sister Helen Prejean, *The Death of Innocents: An Eyewitness Account of Wrongful Executions* (New York: Random House, 2005); Michael Radelet, Hugo Adam Bedau, and Constance E. Putnam, *In Spite of Innocence: Erroneous Convictions in Capital Cases* (Boston: Northeastern University Press, 1992). For a criticism of the earlier study, including a claim that no proof exists of an innocent being executed, see Stephen J. Markman and Paul G. Cassell, "Protecting the Innocent: A Response to the Bedau-Radelet Study," *Stanford Law Review* 41 (1988): 121. Radelet and Bedau's response: "The Myth of Infallibility: A Reply to Markman and Cassell," *Stanford Law Review* 41 (1988): 161. Two recent controversial cases are those of Troy Anthony Davis, executed by Georgia on September 21, 2011, and Cameron Todd Willingham, executed by Texas on February 17, 2004. Davis was put to death despite substantial doubt about his guilt, as I discuss in chapter 7. Willingham was executed for setting the house fire that killed his three young children. Reports prepared prior to the execution, however, including one prepared by fire scientist Craig L. Beyler, former chairman of the International Association of Fire Safety Science, debunked the arson findings and declared that the evidence showed that the fire was accidental. See Craig L. Beyler, "Analysis of the Fire Investigation Methods and Procedures Used in the Criminal Arson Cases against Ernest Ray Willis and Cameron Todd Willingham," August 17, 2009, www.docstoc.com/docs/document-preview.aspx?doc_id=10401390, and David Grann, "Trial by Fire: Did Texas Execute an Innocent Man?" *New Yorker*, September 7, 2009, www.newyorker.com/reporting/2009/09/07/090907fa_fact_grann.

60. Belinda, Session S. First quotation: James, Session H. In all, Professor David Protess and his undergraduate journalism students have freed eleven wrongfully imprisoned individuals in Illinois; see the Medill Innocence Project, www.medillinnocenceproject.org. Professor Protess has since gone on to found the Chicago Innocence Project; see chicagoinnocenceproject.org. See also Barry Scheck, Peter Neufeld, and Jim Dwyer, *Actual Innocence: When Justice Goes Wrong and How to Make It Right* (New York: New American Library, 2003). Scheck and Neufeld founded the Innocence Project at the Benjamin N. Cardozo School of Law at Yeshiva University; see www.innocenceproject.org. Sessions B, D, L, O, Q, R, and S were particularly concerned with procedural problems. Second quotation: Caroline, Session Q. See also VCC, "Study Packet," 2; Our Lady of Wisdom, "Consistent with Life," 5; MICC, *Discussion Guide*, 10–11; Zehr, *Death as a Penalty*, 6–8; and Jackson et al., *Study Resource*, 26–31. Lytle, *Execution's Doorstep*; Richard C. Waites and David A. Giles, "Are Jurors Equipped to Decide the Outcome of Complex Cases?," *American Journal of Trial Advocacy* 29 (2005): 19; Donna L. Van Raaphorst, "Worst of the Worst," in Austin Sarat, ed., *Crime and Punishment: Perspectives from the Humanities*, Studies in Law, Politics and Society, vol. 37 (Amsterdam: Elsevier JAI, 2005), 199–239.

61. Deterrence was discussed in detail in Sessions A, B, D, L, N, O, Q, and R. Quotation: Derrick, Session N. See also Zehr, *Death as a Penalty*, 3–5. Bohm, *Deathquest II*, 93; Bowers and Pierce, "Deterrence or Brutalization"; VCC, "Study Packet," 2; Our Lady of Wisdom, "Consistent with Life," 2; MICC, *Discussion Guide*, 17; Zehr, *Death as a Penalty*, 2–6; "Pax Christi Backgrounder"; and Johnston, "Biblical Traditions." Richard C. Dieter, *On the Front Line: Law Enforcement Views on the Death Penalty* (Washington, DC: DPIC, February 1995); Richard C. Dieter, *Smart on Crime: Reconsidering the Death Penalty in a Time of Economic Crisis*

(Washington, DC: DPIC, October 2009); DPIC, "Murder Rates Nationally and by State," www.deathpenaltyinfo.org/murder-rates-nationally-and-state. With regard to the latter point, the chicken-and-egg aspect of that statistic—that the lower murder rates cannot be shown definitively to correlate with or explain the lack of the death penalty—also came up in discussions, especially Sessions L and N. Zehr, *Death as a Penalty*, 12–13, deals explicitly with this idea of capital punishment as a ritual sacrifice. There is no need here to explore the symbols and ritual involved in an execution, but see Cabana, *Death at Midnight*; "Witness to an Execution," abridged and included in Mabry, *Capital Punishment*, 54–59; Pickett, *Within These Walls*; Sister Helen Prejean, *Dead Man Walking: An Eyewitness Account of the Death Penalty in the United States* (New York: Vintage Books, 1994); Shere, *Cain's Redemption*; Rev. Joseph M. Vought, "Jesus, Remember Me," *Lutheran*, October 2000, 16–18. For a historical perspective, see Halttunen, *Murder Most Foul*; Masur, *Rites of Execution*; Seay, *Hanging between Heaven and Earth*.

62. Comments Session H and Sessions D and F, respectively. Discussions focusing on "the need for closure" and treating the death penalty as a governmental service, provided for victims, rather than as a criminal justice action, also engage with this dynamic, as I will discuss in chapters 4 and 7. First quotation: Martin Riesebrodt, "Religion in Global Perspective," in Mark Juergensmeyer, ed., *The Oxford Handbook of Global Religions* (New York: Oxford University Press, 2006), 602. This position also has a clear discursive element, as seen below. Second quotation: Jesse, Session F. Emphasis in original statement. This position also has a clear derivative element, namely the withholding of violent retribution in favor of permitting the processes described to continue.

63. Riesebrodt, "Religion," 602.

64. On reform rather than rejection, see for example Duke at Pew Forum. Ernest van den Haag, "Refuting Nathanson," in Glen H. Stassen, ed., *Capital Punishment: A Reader* (Cleveland: Pilgrim, 1998), 101–6. Sessions J and K dealt extensively with the idea of scapegoating sacrifice. See also Zehr, *Death as a Penalty*, 12–13.

65. Session B.

66. Ibid. Studies have come to ambivalent conclusions on the relationship between trust in government generally and support for the death penalty. See Unnever, Cullen, and Bartkowski, "Images of God," and Unnever and Cullen, "The Social Sources of Americans' Punitiveness," showing a correlation between trust for government and support for the death penalty. Franklin Zimring and David Garland argue differently, finding that the links are more complicated and depend on the ability to "degovernmentalize" or "localize" capital punishment, respectively. Zimring, *Contradictions*, esp. 111ff; Garland, *Peculiar Institution*.

67. Zimring, *Contradictions*, 89–118. On the vigilante tradition and other forms of extralegal justice from a theological perspective, see generally Robert Jewett, *Mission and Menace: Four Centuries of American Religious Zeal* (Minneapolis: Fortress, 2008); Robert Jewett and John Shelton Lawrence, *Captain America and the Crusade against Evil: The Dilemma of Zealous Nationalism* (Grand Rapids, MI: Wm. B. Eerdmans, 2003); and John Shelton Lawrence and Robert Jewett, *The Myth of the American Superhero* (Grand Rapids, MI: Wm. B. Eerdmans, 2002).

68. Session D (italics added). This summary combines some of Beatrice's comments from Sessions D, F, H, and T, which were paralleled in various forms and phrasings by participants in other sessions, particularly B, I, N, P, and Q.

69. Session H. Necessary consequences: Sessions D, F, H, N, O, P, and T. *Roe v. Wade*, 410 U.S. 113 (1973).

70. Sessions B, H, and T. On the difference between legal guilt and actual guilt, see Justice Sandra Day O'Connor's concurring opinion in *Herrera*, 506 U.S. at 420. It is interesting in this context to note that while an individual under sentence of death has the right to file his ap-

peals, he does not have the right to the assistance of counsel in this process. See *Murray v. Giarratano*, 492 U.S. 1 (1989). We will examine this case in chapter 6.

71. Caroline, Session Q. Beatrice, Session T.

72. First quotation: Session A. Second and third quotations: Session D. Jesus writing in the sand: John 8: 6, 8. This is the story of the woman caught in adultery, the genesis of "Let him without sin cast the first stone." Fourth quotation: Beatrice, Session T. See also Manfred Berg, "Criminal Justice, Law Enforcement and the End of Lynching in the South," in Berg, Kapsch, and Streng, *Criminal Justice in the United States and Germany*, 29–42; Manfred Berg, *Popular Justice: A History of Lynching in America* (Lanham, MD: Ivan R. Dee, 2011).

73. David Sarnoff Quotes, thinkexist.com/quotation/we_cannot_banish_dangers-but_we_can_banish_fears/202813.html. A good profile of the Briley brothers, with links for further sources, can be found at The Virginia Legend, June 1, 2005, thevirginialegend.blogspot.com/2005/06/briley-gang-mecklenburg-six.html. See also Reed Williams and Bill McKelway, "Rampage: The Briley Brothers Terrorized Richmond Area," *Richmond Times-Dispatch*, May 30, 2009, timesdispatch.com/ar/41925/. On Timothy Spencer, see for example "Murderer Put to Death in Virginia," April 28, 1994, www.nytimes.com/1994/04/28/us/murderer-put-to-death-in-virginia.html?pagewanted=1.

74. Peer pressure: see for instance *Santa Fe v. Doe*, 530 U.S. 290 (2000). Quotation: Session E. When to forgive: Sessions A, C, E, F, G, I, J, K, L, and R in particular. As Halttunen and Seay each note, this was historically the point of the Puritan execution sermons—to show that the offender was *like us* in the sense that they were all sinners in need of grace. Halttunen, *Murder Most Foul*; Seay, *Hanging between Heaven and Earth*.

4. The Exile

Epigraph. *Tison v. Arizona*, 481 U.S. 137 (1987) at 156.

1. Vought interview.

2. Kenneth J. Harvey, "Tucker Execution Violates Taboo," *Ottawa Citizen*, February 17, 1998, A19; Bob Ray Sanders, "Tucker Case Should Show Christians Why Death Penalty Is Irredeemable," *Saint Paul Pioneer Press*, February 6, 1998; Diane Clements, President of Justice for All, *NBC Nightly News*, February 2, 1998, NBC News Transcripts, LexisNexis.

3. *In re. Troy Anthony Davis*, 130 S. Ct. 1 (2009), Scalia, J. dissenting, 2, www.supremecourt.gov/opinions/08pdf/08-1443scalia.pdf. See also Frank Green, "Death Penalty Doubts Arise," *Richmond Times-Dispatch*, July 9, 2001, quoting Justice O'Connor: "If statistics are any indication, the system may well be allowing some innocent defendants to be executed."

4. Girard, *The Scapegoat*.

5. Session N.

6. See Otis, comments at "The Death Penalty Today."

7. Exodus 20:1–17, quotation 17. René Girard, *I See Satan Fall Like Lightning*, trans. James G. Williams (Maryknoll, NY: Orbis Books, 2001), 7–18. For a list of Schedule I and II controlled substances, see US Department of Justice, Drug Enforcement Administration, "Controlled Substance Schedules," September 2012, www.deadiversion.usdoj.gov/schedules/index.html. Virginia Code § 18.2-31.4, .9, .10, .2, and .1, respectively.

8. Virginia Code § 18.2-31.12, .11, .5, .1, .2, .9, and .10, respectively.

9. Virginia Code § 18.2-31.6, .14, .15, .3, .7, .8, and .13, respectively.

10. Matthew 12:30: "Whoever is not with me is against me, and whoever does not gather with me scatters."

11. Session D.

12. Session T.

13. Quotation: Session T. Comments made following Session R. On perceptions of ex-felons, see for example Velmer S. Burton Jr., "The Consequences of Official Labels: A Research Note on Rights Lost by the Mentally Ill, Mentally Incompetent, and Convicted Felons," *Community Mental Health Journal* 26, no. 3 (June 1990): 267–76; Cherie Dawson-Edwards, "Enfranchising Convicted Felons: Current Research on Opinions towards Felon Voting Rights," *Journal of Offender Rehabilitation* 46, nos. 3 & 4 (May 2008): 13–29; Marc Mauer and Michael Coyle, "The Social Cost of America's Race to Incarcerate," *Journal of Religion and Spirituality in Social Work* 23, nos. 1 & 2 (2004): 7–25; John R. Vile, "The Right to Vote as Applied to Ex-Felons," *Federal Probation* 45 (1981): 12.

14. Session Q.

15. Session H.

16. Quoted in Scott E. Sundby, *A Life and Death Decision: A Jury Weighs the Death Penalty* (New York: Palgrave Macmillan, 2005), 47.

17. First quotation: Session K. Second quotation: Session E. Third quotation: Session R.

18. Quotations: Session D, Session H.

19. VCC, Task Force Concerning the Death Penalty, "From Fear to Hope: Statement of Religious Leaders in Virginia on Public Safety and the Death Penalty," "Voices" study packet (January 1993), 19, Vought files VCC, Task Force Concerning the Death Penalty.

20. Retentionist discourse allows for repentance and redemption on the part of the criminal, which is another form of individual resolution. This is, however, a decidedly secondary concern.

21. Girard presents these four elements as signals that a scapegoating crisis is occurring or has occurred, rather than as constituent elements of the scapegoat itself. I believe, however, that his argument is more clearly and convincingly read — and more usefully augmented — if these elements of the crisis are read as elements as the scapegoat, hence my approach here. See Girard, *The Scapegoat*, 24–44.

22. See Paul G. Cassell, "In Defense of the Death Penalty," in Bedau and Cassell, *Debating the Death Penalty*, 203–5; Duke, Pew Forum; Joshua K. Marquis, "Truth and Consequences: The Penalty of Death," in Bedau and Cassell, *Debating the Death Penalty*, 117–51; *McCleskey*, 481 U.S.; Otis, "The Death Penalty Today"; Louis P. Pojman, "Why the Death Penalty Is Morally Permissible," in Bedau and Cassell, *Debating the Death Penalty*, 51–75; Ernest van den Haag, in Ernest van den Haag and John P. Conrad, *The Death Penalty: A Debate* (New York: Plenum, 1983), especially 203–7 and 223–26.

23. Ryan, "I Must Act"; Ronald J. Tabak, "How the Death Penalty Works: Empirical Studies of the Modern Capital Sentencing System," *Cornell Law Review* 83 (1998): 1431 at 1446. For a detailed account of a case in which the system "worked" by eventually freeing a wrongfully convicted man from Virginia's death row, see Edds, *An Expendable Man*. Edds convincingly demonstrates that the system "worked" only because it failed at each relevant stage of the process; the sum total of these sequential procedural failures was, somewhat miraculously, the correct result.

24. Girard and Gil Bailie both argue that the Crucifixion, by exposing the scapegoating mechanism, set in motion the process by which such processes could be dismantled. Girard, *Violence* and *Scapegoat*; Gil Bailie, *Violence Unveiled: Humanity at the Crossroads* (New York: Crossroad, 1995); Sarat, *When the State Kills*, 53.

25. First and second quotations: *Furman*, 408 U.S. at 308 and 303. Third quotation: *Gregg*, 428 U.S. at 185.

26. *Payne*, 501 U.S., overturning *Booth*, 482 U.S., and *Gathers*, 490 U.S.

27. *Payne*, 501 U.S. at 815 (internal citations omitted).

28. First quotation: Zimring, *Contradictions*, 55 (italics in original). See also Theodore Eisenberg, Stephen P. Garvey, and Martin T. Wells, "Victim Characteristics and Victim Impact Evidence in South Carolina Capital Cases," *Cornell Law Review* 88 (January 2003): 306, and Janice Nadler and Mary R. Rose, "Victim Impact Testimony and the Psychology of Punishment," *Cornell Law Review* 88 (January 2003): 420. Second quotation: Bessler, *Death in the Dark*, 12.

29. Peter Baker, "Emotional Death of Execution-Witness Bill," *Washington Post*, March 3, 1994. In March 1994, Governor George Allen changed Virginia policy to permit relatives of the victims to witness the execution. See Peppers and Anderson, *Anatomy*, 201.

30. Session T. The victims' rights movement is indeed roughly coincidental with the modern period of the death penalty. The first major victims' rights organization, the National Organization of Parents of Murdered Children, was founded in 1978, while a later, more impactful organization, Justice for All, was founded in 1993. For a critique of the victims' rights movement in the modern era, see Peter Hodgkinson, "Capital Punishment: Meeting the Needs of the Families of the Homicide Victim and the Condemned," in Peter Hodgkinson and William A. Schabas, eds., *Capital Punishment: Strategies for Abolition* (New York: Cambridge University Press, 2004), 332–58.

31. Unless otherwise indicated, all quotations and the following summary derive from Session M.

32. Code of Virginia, §19.2-264.2 (2004). See also Russell E. McGuire, "Capital Punishment for Multiple Murders That Occur in the Same Act or Transaction: A Guide to Define the Abstract," *Thomas M. Cooley Journal of Practical and Clinical Law* 2 (January 1999): 263.

33. Italicized words were especially emphasized during the presentation.

34. Sundby, *A Life and Death Decision*, 40–41, quotation on 40. See also Scott E. Sundby, "The Capital Jury and Empathy: The Problem of Worthy and Unworthy Victims," *Cornell Law Review* 88 (2003): 343.

35. First quotation: Sundby, *A Life and Death Decision*, 42. Second quotation: Session B (italics mine). See Michael L. Radelet and Marian J. Borg, "The Changing Nature of Death Penalty Debates," *Annual Review of Sociology* 26 (2000): 44; Hugo Adam Bedau, "Prison Homicides, Recidivist Murder, and Life Imprisonment," in Bedau, *The Death Penalty in America*, 176–82; James W. Marquart and Jonathan R. Sorensen, "A National Study of the Furman-Commuted Inmates: Assessing the Threat to Society from Capital Offenders," *Loyola of Los Angeles Law Review* 23 (1989): 5; Wendy Wolfson, "The Deterrent Effect of the Death Penalty upon Prison Murder," in Hugo Adam Bedau, ed., *The Death Penalty in America*, 3rd ed. (New York: Oxford University Press, 1982), 159–73; BBC News, "Duane Buck Spared Execution by US Supreme Court," September 16, 2011, www.bbc.co.uk/news/world-us-canada-14935191.

36. First quotation: Hugo Adam Bedau, "Background and Developments," in Bedau, *The Death Penalty in America*, 24. Second quotation: Patrick Buchanan, "Less Talk and More Action Needed with Capital Punishment," *Daily News* (Bangor, ME), February 1, 1989, NDPA, NCADP files, Series 3, Box 5.

37. First quotation: William Tucker, "If We Don't Enforce the Death Penalty, Others Will," *Peninsula Times Tribune*, October 22, 1989, NDPA, NCADP Files, Series 3, Box 5. Second quotation: Bruce L. Davis, "Lynching Justified," *Fresno Bee*, December 15, 1993. NDPA, Bill Pelke/Journey of Hope Files (uncatalogued collection). See also Tracy Stevenson, "Death Penalty Fan," *Fresno Bee*, December 14, 1993, and Jill Cardenas, "Our Society Is Sick," *Gazette-Journal* (Reno, NV), December 14, 1993, both in ibid.

38. Sharon Keller, "Don't End Capital Punishment," *Dallas Morning News*, September 25, 1994, NDPA, NCADP files, Series 3, Box 5.

39. Banner, *Death Penalty*, 282–83.

40. *Public Hearing before Senate Judiciary Committee on Senate No. 112* (NJ Senate, February 26, 1982), 4. Quoted in Banner, *Death Penalty*, 282.

41. First quotation: Walter Berns, *For Capital Punishment: Crime and the Morality of the Death Penalty* (New York: Basic Books, 1979), 173 (italics in original). Banner argues correctly that support for the death penalty satisfies essentially the same symbolic function as do actual executions. See Banner, *Death Penalty*, 283–84. Second quotation: Weisberg, "Deregulating Death," 385.

42. Garland, *Peculiar Institution*.

43. Stephen L. Carter, "When Victims Happen to Be Black," *Yale Law Journal* 97 (February 1988): 420, quotation on 421.

44. Ibid., 443.

45. Session H; Hugh Jones, "Just When Would Jury Use the Death Penalty?" *Birmingham (AL) News*, February 15, 1995, NDPA, NCADP files, Series 3, Box 1, Newspaper Clippings; Carter, "When Victims," 422. Quotation: Alex Kozinski, "Tinkering with Death," in Bedau and Cassell, *Debating the Death Penalty*, 9.

46. First quotation: Jennifer L. Culbert, "Beyond Intention: A Critique of the 'Normal' Criminal Agency, Responsibility, and Punishment in American Death Penalty Jurisprudence," in Austin Sarat, ed., *The Killing State: Capital Punishment in Law, Politics, and Culture* (New York: Oxford University Press, 2001), 206. Second quotation: H. L. A. Hart, "Prolegomenon to the Principles of Punishment," in *Punishment and Responsibility: Essays in the Philosophy of Law* (Oxford: Clarendon, 1968), 15.

47. Culbert, "Beyond Intention," 210, 211.

48. Michel Foucault, "About the Concept of the 'Dangerous Individual' in 19th-Century Legal Psychiatry," trans. Alain Baudot and Jane Couchman, *International Journal of Law and Psychiatry* 1, no. 1 (February 1978): 16.

49. Quotation: Garland, *Punishment and Modern Society*, 148. Foucault, *Discipline and Punish*, 264–71.

50. *Atkins v. Virginia*, 536 U.S. 304 (2002); *Roper v. Simmons*, 543 U.S. 551 (2005).

51. Haines, *Against*, 95. In all instances, I am using the term "mentally retarded" in the sense in which it was defined in the 1994 D*iagnostic and Statistical Manual of Mental Disorders*, 4th ed. (DSM-IV): "Mental Retardation refers to 'significantly subaverage general intellectual functioning (Criterion A) that is accompanied by significant limitations in adaptive functioning in at least two of the following skill areas: communication, self-care, home living, social/interpersonal skills, use of community resources, self-direction, functional academic skills, work, leisure, health, and safety (Criterion B). The onset must occur before age 18 years (Criterion C).'" Quoted in Brief of Amici Curiae of the United States Catholic Conference and Other Religious Organizations in Support of Petitioner, *McCarver v. North Carolina*, Supreme Court of the United States, No. 00-8727, June 8, 2001, 2001 WL 648613, 8 n. 10 (hereinafter USCC, *McCarver*). For a sampling of state definitions of mental retardation, see Brief of the States of Alabama, Mississippi, Nevada, South Carolina, and Utah as Amici Curiae in Support of Respondent, *Atkins v. Virginia*, Supreme Court of Virginia, No. 00-8452, January 14, 2002, 2002 WL 83600 (hereinafter Alabama et al., *Atkins*).

52. First and second quotations: Virginia Interfaith Center for Public Policy (VICPP), "Activity Summary, 1982–1983," VICPP archives, Richmond. Unless otherwise noted, all VICPP documents are from VICPP organizational archives. "Legislative Concerns for the 1983 Session of the Virginia General Assembly," December 2, 1982; VICPP, "1984 Legislative Agenda," December 1, 1983. Third quotation: VICPP, "1987 Legislative Agenda," undated. Fourth quotation: VICPP, "1988 Legislative Wrap-Up," April 25, 1988.

53. VICPP, 1983; VICPP, 1984; VICPP, "1985 Legislative Agenda of the Virginia Interfaith Center for Public Policy," undated; VICPP, 1988.

54. First quotation: VICPP, "1999 Legislative Agenda," undated. See also VICPP, "2000 Legislative Agenda," undated. On protections and the lack thereof for mentally ill death row prisoners, see Hood and Hoyle, *The Death Penalty*, 203–14; VICPP, "Introduction to the Legislative Agenda," August 14, 1991. Second quotation: VICPP, "2004 Legislative Agenda." Douglas Christopher Thomas (January 10, 2000) and Steven Roach (January 13, 2000) were the last two juvenile offenders executed in Virginia. See also Matthew Dolan, "Challenge of Juvenile Executions Met Warily," *Virginian-Pilot*, November 7, 2000; Virginians for Alternatives to the Death Penalty (VADP) files, Charlottesville, Chauncey Jackson; Matthew Dolan, "Va. Case Challenges Executions of Juveniles," *Virginian-Pilot*, November 6, 2000. For an overview of the legal issues surrounding juvenile executions, see for example Sheri Jackson, "Too Young to Die — Juveniles and the Death Penalty," *New England Journal on Crime and Civil Confinement* 22, no. 2 (Spring 1996): 391–437; VCC, "Resolution on the Juvenile Death Penalty," November 14, 2003; NDPA, VADP files; "Anti-Death Penalty Legislative Strategy Session, Meeting Notes," September 16, 2004; VICPP archives, Richmond.

55. VCC, "Resolution on the Juvenile Death Penalty." See also "Proposed Activities for MSW Interns re: Juvenile Death Penalty," VICPP files, Juvenile Death Penalty; "The Juvenile Death Penalty," in ibid.; "Issue Briefing Paper: The Juvenile Death Penalty in the United States," Draft, in ibid.; Streib, *Death Penalty for Juveniles*; Victor L. Streib, "Executing Juvenile Offenders: The Ultimate Denial of Juvenile Justice," *Stanford Law and Policy Review* 14 (2003): 121; Victor L. Streib, "Adolescence, Mental Retardation, and the Death Penalty: The Siren Call of Atkins v. Virginia," *New Mexico Law Review* 33 (2003): 183. Quotation: VICPP, 1989 Legislative Agenda, December 15, 1988. See also VICPP, "Ballot Sheet for 1990 Legislative Priorities," October 1989.

56. Quoted in Frank Green, "Religious Leaders Split on Executions; Both Sides Cite Biblical Evidence," *Richmond Times-Dispatch*, July 30, 2000, NDPA, VADP files, Newspaper clippings; see also Robert Blecker, "Roots," in James R. Acker, Robert M. Bohm, and Charles S. Lanier, eds., *America's Experiment with Capital Punishment: Reflections on the Past, Present, and Future of the Ultimate Penal Sanction*, 2nd ed. (Durham, NC: Carolina Academic Press, 2003), 169–231.

57. Rev. C. Douglas Smith, Executive Director, VICPP, e-mail to Christine Payden-Travers, June 8, 2008; VADP Files, "Percy Walton."

58. First quotation: Frank Green, "Inmate's Mental Capacity Debated," *Richmond Times Dispatch*, June 4, 2008, www.timesdispatch.com/servlet/Satellite?pagename=RTD/MGArticle/RTD_BasicArticle&c=MGArticle&cid=1149188227767, accessed June 5, 2008. VADP, "Virginia Sets Two Execution Dates for July," Action Alert, June 5, 2006, VADP files, Percy Walton; "Join a Public Vigil to Oppose the Death Penalty," VADP files, Percy Walton; "Crazy Horse": Kristen Gelineau, "Court Stays Execution for Inmate Who Claims He's Insane," Associated Press, article reprinted in full at www.floridasupport.us/forum/viewtopic.php?f=25&t=1905#p7242, posted June 7, 2006. Second and third quotations: John W. Whitehead, "John W. Whitehead's Weekly Commentary: Percy Walton Should Not Be Put to Death," May 23, 2006, VADP files, Percy Walton.

59. Candace Rondeaux, "Inmate's Execution Still Set for Tonight," *Washington Post*, June 8, 2006, B09; *Ford v. Wainwright*, 477 U.S. 399 (1986). Quotation: Jack Payden-Travers, "Essay on the Upcoming Execution of Percy LeVar Walton," May 31, 2006, VADP files, Percy Walton. Rev. Jonathan C. Tetherly, letter to Governor Kaine, June 1, 2006; VADP files, Percy Walton.

60. Payden-Travers, "Essay"; John W. Whitehead, President, The Rutherford Institute, letter to Governor Timothy M. Kaine, June 5, 2006, VADP files, Percy Walton.

61. In all, eight death row inmates in Virginia have had their sentences commuted to life in prison. Percy Walton and Calvin Swann's sentences were commuted due to their mental illness. Joseph Giarratano, Herbert Bassette, Earl Washington, Joseph Payne, and Robin Lovitt's sentences were commuted due to questions of actual innocence, with Washington subsequently being freed based on demonstration of innocence. The eighth, William Saunders, had his sentence commuted due to his rehabilitation in prison. See Death Penalty Information Center, "Clemency," www.deathpenaltyinfo.org/clemency, updated July 10, 2012.

62. Quotations: "Statement of Governor Kaine on the Scheduled Execution of Percy Levar Walton," June 9, 2008.

63. First quotation: Donald P. Baker, "Gilmore Stops Execution for First Time; Mental Illness of Inmate Cited," *Washington Post*, May 13, 1999. Patti Rosenberg, "Jury: Give Killer Death Sentence," *Daily Press* (Newport News, VA), August 20, 1999, VADP files, Atkins; Frank Green, "Murderer Fights Push for Stay," *Richmond Times-Dispatch*, February 19, 2001, VADP digital files, Akers. Second quotation: Donald P. Baker, "As Execution Nears, Man's Mental Illness at Issue," *Washington Post*, April 30, 1999.

64. "Please Join Leslie and Trevor Cavazos in Their Request That Governor Gilmore Spare the Life of Lonnie Weeks," NDPA, NCADP files, Series 1, Box 7, Lonnie Weeks.

65. Ibid.; NCADP, "Karla Faye Tucker Faces Imminent Execution in Texas," January 5, 1998, NDPA, NCADP files, Series 1, Box 1, Tucker; Green, "Murderer Fights"; Maria Saminiatelli, "Killer Is Put to Death," Associated Press, October 18, 2001, VADP digitized files, Beck.

66. Saminiatelli, "Killer."

67. Gelineau, "Court Stays."

68. First quotation: Sundby, *A Life and Death Decision*, 141. Second quotation: Capital case juror, quoted in ibid., 202 n. 7 (italics added).

69. Quotation: The Virginia Alliance to Abolish the Juvenile Death Penalty, "The Juvenile Death Penalty," Draft, VICPP files, Juvenile Capital Punishment. See also Byrgen Finkelman, *Child Abuse: Short- and Long-Term Effects* (New York: Routledge, 1995); Jaana Haapasalo and Elina Pokela, "Child-Rearing and Child Abuse Antecedents of Criminality," *Aggression and Violent Behavior* 4, no. 1 (Spring 1999): 107–27; Janet Reno, Eric H. Holder Jr., Raymond C. Fisher, Laurie Robinson, Noel Brennan, and Kathryn M. Turman, *Breaking the Cycle of Violence: Recommendations to Improve the Criminal Justice Response to Child Victims and Witnesses*, US Department of Justice, Office of Justice Programs, Office for Victims of Crime (OVC), OVC Monograph series, June 1999, www.ojp.usdoj.gov/ovc/publications/factshts/pdftxt/monograph.pdf; Cathy Spitz Widom, "Victims of Childhood Sexual Abuse—Later Criminal Consequences," US Department of Justice, Office of Justice Programs, National Institute of Justice, "Research in Brief," March 1995, www.ncjrs.gov/pdffiles/abuse.pdf; National Clearinghouse on Child Abuse and Neglect Information, "Long-Term Consequences of Child Abuse and Neglect," July 2005, www.childprotectionoffice.org/pdf/long_term_consequences.pdf. Second quotation: Whitehead, letter to Governor Kaine, June 5, 2006.

70. Renee Schafer Horton, "Celebrating Death," *Dallas Morning News*, February 15, 1998. *Mens rea:* Pastor Frazier and James made this point in Sessions E and D, respectively. See also Virginia Code §18.2-13; Paul H. Robinson and Markus Dirk Dubbler, "An Introduction to the Model Penal Code," March 12, 1999, www.law.upenn.edu/fac/phrobins/intromodpencode.pdf, 11–13. "Irrelevant": Quoted in Paul E. Brink, "American Friends Service Committee Condemns Execution of Roger Keith Coleman," AFSC News Release, May 21, 1992, AFSC archive, Friends 1992, Roger Coleman Release. See also Justice Blackmun's dissent from *Herrera*, 506 U.S. at 430.

71. First quotation: *Ford*, 477 U.S. at 406 (internal quotation marks omitted). Second quo-

tation: Whitehead, "Percy Walton." Third quotation: *Ford,* 477 U.S. at 422 (italics added). On culpability, see for example Green, "Murderer Fights"; Matt Chittum, "Meanwhile, 2 Lawyers Fight Equally Hard to Stop His Execution," *Roanoke Times,* February 26, 2001, VADP digitized files, Akers.

72. First quotation: Rev. Douglas G. Burgoyne, "Father of Murdered Daughter," September 1992, VCC, "Voices," 2. Second quotation: Deacon Reinhart Wessing, "Christians Need to Speak Out Loudly against Death Penalty," *Compass,* newspaper of the Catholic Diocese of Green Bay, WI, March 17, 1995, NDPA, NCADP files, Series 3, Box 1, Newspaper Clippings.

73. VCC, "A Virginia Council of Churches Statement on the Death Penalty," February 16, 2000, Vought files, VCC Materials (internal Bible citations omitted). See also Burgoyne, "Father of Murdered Daughter," 2; Bishop Walter Sullivan, "Virginia Should Say No to Capital Punishment," Vought files, VCC Materials; VICPP, "Talking Points: Day at the General Assembly for All People of Faith," VICPP files, 2003; VICPP, "A Statement on the Death Penalty," January 15, 2003, VICPP files, Statements.

74. 109th Council of the Episcopal Diocese of Southern Virginia, untitled undated resolution, Vought files, Moratorium, Episcopal Resolution; VCC, "Statement on the Death Penalty"; VICPP, "A Statement on the Death Penalty"; Steve Baggarly, "Judaism and the Death Penalty," NDPA, VADP files, Judaism and the Death Penalty Article by Steve Baggarly, 1; "Open Statement on Capital Punishment from the Most Reverend Edmond L. Browning, Presiding Bishop, the Episcopal Church," May 1990, Vought files, VCC Materials.

75. First quotation: Rev. Donna Schaper, "Why Karla Faye Tucker Should Not Be Executed," *Philadelphia Inquirer,* February 2, 1998, AFSC archive, CRD 1, Newspaper Clippings. Rev. Joseph M. Vought, "Pastor Visitor," September 1992, VCC, "Voices," 7; Rev. Russell Ford, "Chaplain," September 1992, VCC, "Voices," 10. Second and third quotations: Rex Bowman, "Killer Doesn't Receive Mercy," *Richmond Times-Dispatch,* July 10, 2001, VADP files, Jeffrey Allen Thomas. Fourth quotation: Tong Yi, "Family Member of Murdered Woman," November, 1992, VCC, "Voices," 4.

76. Rev. John Price, "Father of Murdered Son," September 1992, VCC, "Voices," 1.

77. First quotation: Schaper, "Karla Faye Tucker." Second quotation: Baggarly, "Judaism and the Death Penalty," 3. Third quotation: Sister Helen Prejean, quoted in Green, "Religious Leaders Split." Fourth quotation: Sister Connie Parcasio, quoted in Angela E. Pometto, "Virginia Bishops Advocate for Death Row Inmate," *Catholic Herald,* June 30, 2005, VADP files, Robin Lovitt. "Open Statement on Capital Punishment." "The Lesson of Karla Faye Tucker," Editorial, *Christianity Today,* April 6, 1998, 16. On the sessions dealing with Nickel Mines, see chapter 3.

78. First quotation: "From Fear to Hope," January 1993, VCC, "Voices," 20. See also VICPP, "1993 Legislative Agenda," VICPP files, Sullivan, "Virginia Should Say No"; "Open Statement on Capital Punishment"; Baggarly, "Judaism and the Death Penalty," 1; Brink, "AFSC Condemns." Second quotation: Catholic Diocese of Richmond, "Statement on Capital Punishment," Vought files, VCC Materials. See also "Join a Public Vigil"; "From Fear to Hope," 19; Sullivan, "Virginia Should Say No"; Rev. Joseph M. Vought, "Call for a Moratorium on Executions," Virginia Synod, ELCA, June 10, 2001, Vought files, Call for a Moratorium. Third quotation: Willie Jasper Darden, "Executed," in VCC, "Voices," 14. Fourth and fifth quotations: Burgoyne, "Father of Murdered Daughter," 2.

79. First quotation: Horton, "Celebrating Death." Second quotation: VCC, "Statement on the Death Penalty." Third quotation: Herbert Tucker, e-mail to Governor Timothy M. Kaine, December 4, 2008, VADP files, Percy Walton (italics added).

80. The quotation that serves as the heading for this section comes from "Death Row: 'This

Ain't Just a Bad Dream,'" *U.S. News and World Report*, "Capital Punishment: Education Program," May 1988, 2.

81. Session O.

82. First quotation: Jonathan Z. Smith, "What a Difference Difference Makes," *Relating Religion: Essays in the Study of Religion* (Chicago: University of Chicago Press, 2004), 252. See generally Walter Wink, *Engaging the Powers: Discernment and Resistance in a World of Domination* (Minneapolis: Fortress, 1992); Walter Wink, "Facing the Myth of Redemptive Violence," *Ekklesia*, November 16, 2007, www.ekklesia.co.uk/content/cpt/article_060823wink.shtml; Jewett, *Mission and Menace*, 293–94; Jewett and Lawrence, *Captain America*, 54.

83. Garland, *Peculiar Institution*; Kozinski, "Tinkering with Death," 12.

84. These ideas are dealt with at length in chapter 6.

85. See for example Paul Finkelman, "Execution as Carnival," *Baltimore Sun*, April 22, 2001, articles.baltimoresun.com/2001-04-22/topic/0104210159_1_mcveigh-ashcroft-federal-judge; Zachary M. Shemtob and David Lat, "Executions Should Be Televised," *New York Times*, July 29, 2011, www.nytimes.com/2011/07/31/opinion/sunday/executions-should-be-televised.html?_r=1. The best history of this subject is Bessler, *Death in the Dark*. Quotations: Jackson, Jackson, and Shapiro, *Legal Lynching*, 113.

86. First, second, and fourth quotations: Brief of Amicus Curiae of the American Civil Liberties Union, the ACLU of Kentucky, and the Rutherford Institute (TRI) in Support of Petitioners, *Baze v. Rees*, Supreme Court of the United States, No. 07-5439, November 8, 2007, 2007 WL 3353105, 20, 4, 18 (hereinafter TRI, *Baze*). See also Deborah W. Denno, "The Lethal Injection Quandary: How Medicine Has Dismantled the Death Penalty," *Fordham Law Review* 76 (2007): 49; Deborah W. Denno, "When Legislatures Delegate Death: The Troubling Paradox behind State Uses of Electrocution and Lethal Injection and What It Says about Us," *Ohio State Law Journal* 63 (2002): 63; Ellyde Roko, "Note: Executioner Identities: Toward Recognizing a Right to Know Who Is Hiding beneath the Hood," *Fordham Law Review* 75 (2007): 2791; Ellen Kreitzberg and David Richter, "But Can It Be Fixed? A Look at Constitutional Challenges to Lethal Injection Executions," *Santa Clara Law Review* 47 (2007): 445; David Biello, "Bad Drugs: Lethal Injection Does Not Work as Designed," April 23, 2007, ScientificAmerican.com, www.scientificamerican.com/article.cfm?id=lethal-injection-does-not-work-as-designed.

87. Sarat, *When the State Kills*, 128.

88. US Department of Justice, Federal Bureau of Investigation, *Crime in the United States 2010*, www.fbi.gov/about-us/cjis/ucr/crime-in-the-u.s/2010/crime-in-the-u.s.-2010/.

89. In a sense, there is nothing particularly new about this. As both Halttunen and Seay show, the Puritan execution sermons played this same role. See Seay, *Hanging between Heaven and Earth*. For the developments forward away from this trope, see Halttunen, *Murder Most Foul*.

90. VICPP 1983, 1984. First quotation: Haines, *Against*, 140 (italics in original). Second quotation: Session O.

91. First quotation: Tucker, e-mail to Governor Kaine. Robertson, quoted in NCADP, "Tucker Faces," 3; NCADP, "Memorandum," January 1998, NDPA, NCADP files, Series 1, Subseries 1, Box 1, Tucker; Kathy Walt, "Path Clear to Execute Female Killer," *Houston Chronicle*, December 8, 1997, in ibid.; William F. Buckley Jr., "Killer Leaves Gov. Bush a Tough Decision," *Houston Chronicle*, December 9, 1997, in ibid.; Allan Turner, "Religious Change of Heart Is Unlikely to Save Tucker," *Houston Chronicle*, December 9, 1997, in ibid.; Carol Rust, "Death Row Inmate Claims Responsibility for Crimes," *Houston Chronicle*, December 13, 1997, in ibid.; Kathy Walt, "Execution May Haunt Texas," *Houston Chronicle*, December 14, 1997, NDPA, NCADP files, Series 1, Subseries 1, Box 1, Tucker; King, *Don't Kill*, 57–81; Pat Robertson,

"Transcript of Speech on Religion's Role in the Administration of the Death Penalty," *William and Mary Bill of Rights Journal* 9, no. 215 (2000), http://scholarship.law.wm.edu/wmborj/vol9/iss1/12/. Weeks: "Lonnie Weeks," September 1, 1999, and "Please Join," both NDPA, NCADP files, Series 1, Box 7, Lonnie Weeks. See also Craig Timberg, "Comforters at the Death House Door; Ministers Make Murderers Their Flock," *Washington Post*, May 11, 1999, which profiles Weeks's spiritual advisers, Rev. Bob and Sarah West. Watkins: Jamie C. Ruff, "Murderer Is Recalled as Christian," *Richmond Times-Dispatch*, March 29, 1998, "Death Penalty News, Wed. 3-25-98"; Laura LeFay, "Danville Killer's Lawyer Urges Gilmore to Look to God for Clemency before Execution Tonight," *Virginian-Pilot*, March 25, 1998, and Frank Green, "Pleas Made to Spare Ronald Watkins, Whose Execution Is Slated Tomorrow," *Richmond Times-Dispatch*, March 24, 1998, all NDPA, NCADP files, Box 1, Series 1, Subseries 1, Watkins. Second quotation: LeFay, "Danville Killer's Lawyer."

92. "Chaplain Service of the Churches of Virginia, Inc.," VCC files, Task Force; Hebrews 13:3.

5. The Bloggers' Exegesis

Epigraphs. Frank Keating, "The Death Penalty: What's All the Debate About?," in Erik Owens, John D. Carlson, and Eric P. Elshtain, eds., *Religion and the Death Penalty: A Call for Reckoning* (Grand Rapids, MI: Wm. B. Eerdmans, 2004), 213, 215; George Ryan, "Reflections on the Death Penalty and the Moratorium," in Owens, Carlson, and Elshtain, *Religion and the Death Penalty*, 227, 229.

1. "Stanley," television spot sponsored by Kilgore for Governor. All transcriptions from television and radio advertisements by author. "Kelly," television spot sponsored by Kilgore for Governor. Paul Thomson, the prosecutor who secured a death sentence against Bell, "pointed out that it contained a glaring falsehood: Bell, in fact, was not in the country illegally at the time of the murder. Thomson was so incensed he contacted the Kaine campaign." Max Blumenthal, "Hitler in Virginia," *Nation*, October 26, 2005, www.thenation.com/article/hitler-virginia. Unless otherwise noted, all websites in this chapter accessed July 23, 2012. On Kaine calling the death penalty "murder," see comment number 26, left in response to Waldo Jaquith, "Kilgore Caught: Kaine Never Said It," October 13, 2005, waldo.jaquith.org/blog/2005/10/kilgore-invented-hitler-claim/, citing three instances of Kaine saying some variant of this phrase. All subsequent notes referring to comments left to blog posts will be referenced using the comment number, e.g., Jaquith, "Kilgore Caught," 26. In all instances when the bloggers post under a pseudonym, I will refer to them as such, e.g., Old Zach. When they use their first and last names, I will refer to them by their last name, e.g., Jaquith. When commenters post using only a first name, in the notes I will refer to them with that name in single quotation marks, e.g., 'Jon.' Likewise, when commenters post under historical monikers, in the notes I will also use single quotation marks, e.g., 'Thomas Jefferson.' In the text these names are in double quotation marks.

2. First quotation: "Law," television spot sponsored by Kaine for Governor. Tsuredzuregusa, "Anatomy of a Smear," October 14, 2005, tsuredzuregusa.blogspot.com/2005/10/anatomy-of-smear.html; Jaquith, "Hitler Unveils," 8. Second quotation: Waldo Jaquith, "Kaine's Response to the Hitler Ad," October 12, 2005, waldo.jaquith.org/blog/2005/10/kaine-response-ad. "Howell has played a critical but unheralded role in securing the Republican Party's recent domination of national politics. He was instrumental in shifting the Senate to the Republicans in 2002 by a one-member margin. In the Georgia senatorial race, he crafted the commercial for the draft-dodging Republican candidate Saxby Chambliss to vanquish Senator Max Cleland, a decorated war hero who lost three limbs in Vietnam, morphing Cleland's image with those

of Osama bin Laden and Saddam Hussein. Two years later Howell's spots contributed to the defeat of both then-Senate minority leader Tom Daschle and Oklahoma Democratic senatorial candidate Brad Carson. Howell's ads on behalf of Daschle's opponent, John Thune, highlighted Thune's opposition to gay marriage. To undermine Carson, Howell created an image of welfare checks being passed to anonymous brown hands. Howell also set the stage for President George W. Bush's re-election victory with the ad called 'Safer, Stronger,' which appropriated the iconic image of firefighters emerging from the wreckage of Ground Zero with a flag-draped body, a production that used actors and was condemned as phony by the president of the International Association of Firefighters." Blumenthal, "Hitler in Virginia."

For the best single criticism of Howell's ads, see Waldo Jaquith, "Howell and Kilgore, Crafting the Message," July 18, 2005, waldo.jaquith.org/blog/2005/07/howell-and-kilgore-crafting-the-message.

3. For the purposes of this chapter, I will use these terms interchangeably, except where otherwise noted. Lowercase "democratic" and "republican" as concepts should be distinguished from the denotations of the political parties, which are always capitalized.

4. Mark J. Rozell, e-mail to author, March 23, 2008. One of these is Waldo Jaquith, the "father of the Virginia Democratic blogosphere," whose blog hosted the most actively commented-on commentary during the campaign. Lowell Feld and Nate Wilcox, *Netroots Rising: How a Citizen Army of Bloggers and Online Activists Is Changing American Politics* (Westport, CT: Praeger, 2008), xxiii. On the 2005 summit, see "Political Blogging in Virginia," August 30, 2005, www.cvillepodcast.com/2005/08/30/political-blogging-in-virginia/. On the 2006 summit, see "Events," Sorensen Institute for Political Leadership at the University of Virginia, June 26, 2006, www.sorenseninstitute.org/newsroom/entry/blog-summit-2006-carnival-round.

5. Michael Cornfield, Jonathan Carson, Alison Kalis, and Emily Simon, *Buzz, Blogs, and Beyond: The Internet and the National Discourse in the Fall of 2004*, Preliminary Report, May 16, 2005, Pew Internet and American Life Project, www.pewtrusts.org/uploadedFiles/wwwpewtrustsorg/News/Press_Releases/Society_and_the_Internet/PIP_Blogs_051605.pdf.

6. First and second quotations: Old Zach, "Kaine's Campaign Is on Death Row," *Sic Semper Tyrannis* (*SST*), October 12, 2005, sicsempertyrannis.blogspot.com/2005/10/kaines-campaign-is-on-death-row.html. Third quotation: Janet Giampietro, The Blog Squad, *Richmond Magazine*, "Has the Death Penalty Put Kaine on a Swift Boat to Defeat?," October 12, 2005, richmondmagazine.blogspot.com/2005/10/has-death-penalty-put-kaine-on-swift.html. See also Tsured, "Anatomy of a Smear"; Waldo Jaquith, "Kilgore Unveils 'Hitler' Ad," October 11, 2005, waldo.jaquith.org/blog/2005/10/kilgore-hitler-ad; Waldo Jaquith, "Another Analysis of the 'Hitler' Ad," waldo.jaquith.org/blog/2005/10/hitler-ad-analysis/; Kenton Ngo, "Going Nuclear," October 11, 2005, www.kentonngo.com/750volts/2005/10/11/going-nuclear/, accessed June 3, 2008, and AnonymousIsAWoman, "How the Good Guys Won in Virginia," November 11, 2005, anonymousisawoman.blogspot.de/2005/11/how-good-guys-won-in-virginia.html.

7. Giampietro, "Has the Death Penalty"; Tsured, "Anatomy of a Smear"; Jaquith, "Kilgore Unveils," 8; Jaquith, "Kaine's Response." First quotation: Blumenthal, "Hitler in Virginia." Jaquith, "Kilgore Unveils," 66; Tsured, "Anatomy of a Smear"; *Inside Politics*, "Independent Ads: The National Security Political Action Committee 'Willie Horton,'" June 17, 2002, www.insidepolitics.org/ps111/independentads.html; Ngo, "Going Nuclear"; "Vermont Values"; Lighthorse Harry, "Katzen on Kaine," *SST*, December 15, 2004, sicsempertyrannis.blogspot.com/2004/12/katzen-on-kaine.html; Addison, "Tim Kaine and Gay Marriage," *SST*, February 1, 2005, sicsempertyrannis.blogspot.com/2005/02/tim-kaine-and-gay-marriage.html.

8. "Campaign Detours to the Low Road," Editorial, *Virginian-Pilot*, October 14, 2005, article reprinted in full at *Death Penalty News*, lists.washlaw.edu/pipermail/deathpenalty/2005-

October/003554.html. Mitch Cumstein, comment 1 left on Jim Bacon, "Down to the Wire: Hitler Hysteria," *Bacon's Rebellion*, October 15, 2005, www.baconsrebellion.com/2005/10/down-to-wire-hitler-hysteria.html. On the October 2002 killings, see Federal Bureau of Investigation, "A Byte out of History: The Beltway Snipers," Parts 1 (October 22, 2007) and 2 (October 24, 2007), www.fbi.gov/page2/oct07/snipers102207.html and www.fbi.gov/page2/oct07/snipers102407.html. See also Charles A. Moose and Charles Fleming, *Three Weeks in October: The Manhunt for the Serial Sniper* (New York: Signet, 2004).

9. First quotation: 'Jonathan,' "A Couple of Takes on the Election 2005 Results," *Crush Liberalism*, November 9, 2005, crushliberalism.blogspot.com/2005/11/couple-of-takes-on-election-2005.html. Second quotation: 'Lee,' "Shape of Things to Come?" *Right-Thinking from the Left Coast*, November 8, 2005, archives.right-thinking.com/index.php/weblog/comments/shape_of_things_to_come1/. RealClearPolitics, "Virginia 2005 Gubernatorial Election," November 9, 2005, www.realclearpolitics.com/Congressional/VA_Gov_05.html.

10. Rabbi Jack Moline, quoted in Lowell Feld, "Jewish Leaders Blast Kilgore 'Hitler' Ad," *Raising Kaine*, October 15, 2005, www.raisingkaine.com/showDiary.do?diaryId=993, accessed June 3, 2008; Feld, "Jewish Leaders." Timing: Michael D. Shear, "References to Hitler in Kilgore Ad Criticized," *Washington Post*, October 15, 2005. Trivializing genocide: "Campaign Detours," AnonymousIs, "How the Good Guys Won."

11. "But even before the latest ads hit the airwaves, Kilgore had persistently argued that Kaine's legal representation of three death row inmates and his public statements against capital punishment make him unfit to serve as governor." Podger and Sluss, "Death Penalty Debate."

12. Robert Barnes, "A Triumph for Warner, and a Guide for His Party," *Washington Post*, November 9, 2005; Sid Cottingham, "Lessons for Virginia and Beyond," *Cracker Squire*, November 9, 2005, crackersquire.blogspot.de/2005/11/lessons-for-virginia-and-beyond.html; Robert Enders, "Just One More Post on the Recent Elections: Hypothetical Questions for Candidates," *Blog of the Enders*, November 10, 2005, blogoftheenders.blogspot.com/2005/11/just-one-more-post-on-recent-elections.html; Mark Murray, "Test of Faith," *Washington Monthly*, October/November 2005, www.washingtonmonthly.com/features/2005/0510.murray.html.

13. Jewett and Lawrence, *Captain America*, 180–86, quotation on 185.

14. Old Zach, "Kaine's Inconsistency on the Death Penalty," *SST*, October 11, 2005, sic sempertyrannis.blogspot.com/2005/10/kaines-inconsistency-on-death-penalty.html.

15. Sister Helen Prejean, "Death in Texas," *New York Review of Books*, January 13, 2005, www.nybooks.com/articles/17670.

16. "Clemency," Death Penalty Information Center, deathpenaltyinfo.org/clemency, updated July 10, 2012. New Mexico abolished the death penalty for new crimes in 2009 but still has two prisoners on death row. Old Zach, "Kaine's Campaign"; Jaquith, "Kilgore Caught," 35.

17. Old Zach, "Kaine's Campaign."

18. For a list of verses concerning capital punishment, see Hanks, *Capital Punishment and the Bible*, 284–87. Except where otherwise noted, all references in this section pertain to comments left responding to "Kilgore Unveils 'Hitler' Ad," October 11, 2005, waldo.jaquith.org/blog/2005/10/kilgore-hitler-ad, and "Kilgore Caught: Kaine Never Said It," October 13, 2005, waldo.jaquith.org/2005/10/kilgore-invented-hitler-claim. Comments will be referenced by the date and the number, as, for example, "11c1" representing the first comment left in response to the October 11 post. While other conversations elsewhere in the blogosphere replicated much of what was discussed in these two conversations, these were selected as exemplary because of the intensity of the conversation and for the knowledgeable participation that created them. Megivern, *The Death Penalty*, 9.

19. See 13c36 and 13c42. It is worth noting that the participants demonstrate an acute awareness of the linguistic problems involved with literal interpretation—it is likely not accidental that accusations of eisegesis are traded over the interpretation of Romans 13:4.

20. Megivern, *The Death Penalty*, 17.

21. Recinella, *The Biblical Truth*, 97. Quotation: *Liberty Bible Commentary*, Romans 13:4, 2263.

22. First and second quotations: 13c10. Third quotation: 13c42 (italics in original). 13c54. On the sword as a sign of authority, see for example Kerby Anderson, *Christian Ethics in Plain Language*, Nelson's Plain Language Series (Nashville: Thomas Nelson, 2005), 149-50; Baker, *On Capital Punishment*, 64-69; John Jefferson Davis, *Evangelical Ethics*, rev./exp. 3rd ed. (Phillipsburg, NJ: Presbyterian and Reformed, 2004), 211; John S. Feinberg and Paul D. Feinberg, *Ethics for a Brave New World* (Wheaton, IL: Crossways Books, 1993), 139-40, 145; H. Wayne House, "In Favor of the Death Penalty," in H. Wayne House and John Howard Yoder, *The Death Penalty Debate* (Dallas: Word, 1991), 67-69; H. Wayne House, "The New Testament and Moral Arguments for Capital Punishment," in Bedau, *The Death Penalty in America*, 421-22; Scalia, "God's Justice," 234-35.

23. Recinella, *The Biblical Truth*, 97; Michael Westmoreland-White and Glen H. Stassen, "Biblical Perspectives on the Death Penalty," in Owens, Carlson, and Elshtain, *The Death Penalty*, 137. The gloss in the *Ryrie Study Bible*, for example, states, "This word for *sword* indicates one that was shaped like a sabre and was carried by magistrates to show that they had the power to punish, even to death." *Ryrie Study Bible*, Romans 13:4, 1716. Tax revolt: Romans 13:5-7. Westmoreland-White and Stassen, "Biblical Perspectives," 137, note that the word used in verse 7 for "pay" is the same word that Jesus used in Luke 20:25, when he counseled the Jews to "Render therefore unto Caesar the things which can be Caesar's" (KJV).

24. Quotations: 13c49. Mark Lewis Taylor, *The Executed God: The Way of the Cross in Lockdown America* (Minneapolis: Fortress, 2001), 70-98. See also John Dominic Crossan, *God and Empire: Jesus against Rome, Then and Now* (New York: HarperOne, 2007); John Dominic Crossan, *The Historical Jesus: The Life of a Mediterranean Jewish Peasant* (San Francisco: HarperSanFrancisco, 1993); Richard A. Horsley, ed., *Paul and Empire: Religion and Power in Roman Imperial Society* (Harrisburg, PA: Trinity Press International, 1997); Ched Myers, *Binding the Strong Man: A Political Reading of Mark's Story of Jesus*, 20th anniv. ed. (Maryknoll, NY: Orbis Books, 2008); Marianne Sawicki, *Crossing Galilee: Architectures of Contact in the Occupied Land of Jesus* (Harrisburg, PA: Trinity Press International, 2000); Elisabeth Schuessler Fiorenza, "The Praxis of Coequal Discipleship," in Horsley, *Paul and Empire*, 221-41; Wink, *Engaging the Powers*.

25. No taking life: 13c36, citing Romans 2:1-3 and Matthew 5:21-22. Individual restrictions: 13c37; 13c42; 13c50; 13c54; 13c37. Quotation: *Edmonson v. Leesville Concrete Co.*, 500 U.S. 614 (1991) at 626. On the jury as a governmental body, see Gary J. Simson and Stephen P. Garvey, "Knockin' on Heaven's Door: Rethinking the Role of Religion in Death Penalty Cases," *Cornell Law Review* 86 (2001): 1108.

26. Quotation: 13c39. Proverbs 11:14: "Where there is no guidance a nation falls, but in an abundance of counselors there is safety" (NRSV). Waites and Giles, *Are Jurors Equipped*.

27. Stanley and Phyllis Rosenbluth, "Accidental Death Is Fate, Murder Is Pure Evil," in James R. Acker and David R. Karp, eds., *Wounds That Do Not Bind: Victim-Based Perspectives on the Death Penalty* (Durham, NC: Carolina Academic Press, 2006), 103-9.

28. It is worth noting, however, that Virginia's criminal code asks jurors to do exactly this, to judge the defendant based on what they may become. Virginia Code §19.2-264.2.

29. 13c36; Romans 2:1-11; Matthew 5:21-22. See for instance 'Jon''s comment to Baker,

wondering whether by bringing up these passages he was questioning whether anyone, "including officers in the government, is allowed to make judgments." 13c42. Jennifer Culbert's *Dead Certainty: The Death Penalty and the Problem of Judgment* (Stanford: Stanford University Press, 2008) systematically investigates problems associated with our ability to pass judgment and assertions that we cannot. A good example of this non-decision-making is former Kansas governor Joan Finney allowing a death penalty statute to become law without either signing or vetoing it. See Bessler, *Death in the Dark*, 139.

30. Jewett and Lawrence, *Captain America*, 8 (quotations), 198–99.

31. George Lakoff, *Moral Politics: How Liberals and Conservatives Think*, 2nd ed. (Chicago: University of Chicago Press, 2002), 65–107, esp. 76–78.

32. Ibid., 47–49, 51–54, 71–76, 197–209; Jewett and Lawrence, *Captain America*, 231–37.

33. Romans 2:6. John Witte Jr., "The Three Uses of the Law: A Protestant Source of the Purposes of Criminal Punishment?," in Witte, *God's Joust*, 264–76.

34. 11c18; 11c32; 13c36; 13c49; and 13c52. 13c17; 13c37; 13c42; 13c50; and 13c54. skeptical observor.blogspot.com/. First quotation: 11c28. Second quotation: 13c66.

35. "Stanley." Tyler Whitley and Jeff E. Schapiro, "Kaine Attacked on Death Penalty," *Richmond Times-Dispatch*, October 12, 2005. First quotation: 11c11. Second quotation: Old Zach, "Kaine's Inconsistency."

36. First quotation: "Death Penalty Smear," Editorial, *Washington Post*, October 12, 2005. Second quotation: "Editorial: Death Penalty Demagoguery," *Roanoke Times*, Roanoke.com, October 13, 2005, www.roanoke.com/editorials/wb/wb/xp-36-011.

37. First quotation: 13c10. Second quotation: Old Zach, "Kaine's Campaign." Cipher: 11c11.

38. David Elliot, "'Astounding Ignorance,'" *Abolish the Death Penalty*, October 13, 2005, deathpenaltyusa.blogspot.com/2005/10/astounding-ignorance.html; Fouro, "Jerry Kilgore: Godwin's Law in Virginia," *Fouroboros*, October 17, 2005, www.alcmenysite.com/blog/2005/10/jerry-kilgore-godwins-law-in-virginia.html; 13c47. Old Zach, "Kaine's Campaign."

39. First quotation: 13c29; 13c34. Second quotation: 13c46. 13c63; 13c35.

40. See for example Murray, "Test of Faith." Quotation: Kenton Ngo, "More on Kilgore's Despicable Hitler Ad," October 12, 2005, www.kentonngo.com/750volts/2005/10/12/more-on-kilgores-despicable-hitler-ad/ (italics added). Beyond the pale: 13c5. "Campaign Detours." David Schraub, "Should Virginia Execute Hitler?" *Debate Link*, October 15, 2005, dsadevil.blogspot.com/2005/10/should-virginia-execute-hitler.html; AnonymousIs, "How the Good Guys Won"; Judson Vaughan, "Raising Kaine in Virginia," *New Testament Democrat*, November 13, 2005, romans10910.blogspot.com/2005/11/raising-kaine-in-virginia-so-tim-kaine.html.

41. Giampietro, "Has the Death Penalty"; Elliot, "'Astounding Ignorance'"; Josh Chernila, "Why Does Jerry Kilgore Hate Christianity?" *Raising Kaine*, October 12, 2005, www.raisingkaine.com/showDiary.do?diaryId=973&view=print, accessed June 3, 2008. Quotation: Estonianzulu, "Jesus Christ! He Used the H Word," *A Game of Boomerangs*, October 13, 2005, estonianzulu.blogspot.com/2005/10/jesus-christ-he-used-h-word.html. See also ManDrake, "Kilgore Attacks Kaine for Being a Christian," *Daffodil Lane*, October 12, 2005, www.daffodillane.com/movabletyp/archives/2005/10/kigore-attacks.html. Luna_k, "Shameful GOP Swiftboating of Kaine," posted in LiveJournal Community liberalrage, October 12, 2005, community.livejournal.com/liberalrage/181258.html.

42. Comment 9, posted to Carl Kilo, "What Would Tim Kaine Do?" *Spark It Up!!!* October 12, 2005, kilosparkitup.blogspot.com/2005/10/what-would-tim-kaine-do.html. First quotation: Not Guy Incognito, "This Will Be the Death of Me . . ." October 15, 2005, notguyincognito.blogspot.com/2005/10/this-will-be-death-of-me.html. See also Tsured, "Anatomy of a Smear."

Second quotation: Scofflaw, "To Live and Let Die," *Seven Hills Chronicle*, October 31, 2005, chronicleofthesevenhills.blogspot.com/2005/10/to-live-and-let-die.html.

43. All quotations in this paragraph: Jerry Kilgore, interview with author, October 30, 2008. For a useful approach to the idea of "conservative activists," see Omri Elisha, *Moral Ambition: Mobilization and Social Outreach in Evangelical Megachurches* (Berkeley: University of California Press, 2011), 24–27.

44. Ibid.

45. All quotations in this paragraph: Timothy M. Kaine, interview with author, August 19, 2008.

46. Ibid.

47. Ammerman, *Congregation and Community*, 48–54. First quotation: ibid., 52. Second quotation: Jackson W. Carroll, "Leadership and the Study of the Congregation," in Nancy Tatom Ammerman, Jackson W. Carroll, Carl S. Dudley, and William McKinney, eds., *Studying Congregations: A New Handbook* (Nashville: Abingdon, 1998), 172.

48. First quotation: Witte, "The Three Uses of the Law," 266. See also Ammerman, *Congregation and Community*, 52–53. Second quotation: Dan O. Via, *Divine Justice, Divine Judgment: Rethinking the Judgment of Nations* (Minneapolis: Fortress, 2007), 5.

49. Carroll, "Leadership," 172. See also Roland A. Heifetz, *Leadership without Easy Answers* (Cambridge, MA: Belknap Press of Harvard University Press, 1994), 103ff.

50. Shaun Kenney, "FLS Pontificates on What Catholics Should Believe," October 20, 2005, shaunkenney.com/index.php/2005/10/fls-pontificates-on-what-catholics-should-believe/, accessed May 14, 2009.

51. Laura Moyer, "Catholic Belief: Execution Wrong," October 20, 2005, www.fredericksburg.com/News/FLS/2005/102005/10202005/138977. First quotation: Pope Leo XIII, *Testem Benevolentiae Nostrae*, January 22, 1899, www.ewtn.com/library/PAPALDOC/L13TESTE.HTM. Remaining quotations: Kenney, "FLS Pontificates" (italics in original).

52. Here I am using Lucas Swaine's definition of theocracy: "*a mode of governance prioritizing a religious conception of the good that is strict and comprehensive in its range of teachings.*" See Lucas Swaine, *The Liberal Conscience: Politics and Principle in a World of Religious Pluralism* (New York: Columbia University Press, 2006), 7 (italics in original). Swaine distinguishes his definition of theocracy in particular from Josephus's classical definition, though I would caution that Josephus's definition still resonates with many both advocating and opposing "theocracy" in various forms. See Swaine, *The Liberal Conscience*, 4–6; Flavius Josephus, *Against Apion*, trans. Henry St. John Thackeray (Cambridge, MA: Harvard University Press, 1976). Robert Barnes, "Kilgore Ads Seek to Divide Democrats," *Washington Post*, October 13, 2005: "In a *Washington Post* poll last month, respondents were given Kaine's position—that he is personally opposed to the death penalty but says he will enforce it because it is state law—and 63 percent said they thought he would keep his word. Thirty percent said they thought he would not."

53. Kaine interview.

54. Mast explicitly mentioned the biblical conquest narratives in distinguishing between illegitimate and legitimate, or divinely authorized, violence. 13c50. For more on the relevance of biblical conquest narratives in American history, see for example Jewett, *Mission and Menace*; Jewett and Lawrence, *Captain America*; and Anthony Santoro, "The Prophet in His Own Words: Nat Turner's Biblical Construction," *Virginia Magazine of History and Biography* 116, no. 2 (June 2008): 114–49.

6. Death, Difference, and Conscience

Epigraphs. *Woodson v. North Carolina*, 428 U.S. 280 (1976) at 305; *Witherspoon v. Illinois*, 391 U.S. 490 (1968) at 519.

1. *Ford*, 477 U.S. 399 (1986) at 411; *Furman*, 408 U.S. 238 (1972); *Roberts v. Louisiana*, 428 U.S. 325 (1976).

2. First quotation: *Edmonson*, 500 U.S. at 626. See also the discussion in the preceding chapter. Second and third quotations: *Williams v. Florida*, 399 U.S. 78 (1970) at 100. Fourth quotation: Diane E. Courselle, "Struggling with Deliberative Secrecy, Jury Independence, and Jury Reform," *South Carolina Law Review* 57 (2005): 203 at 223, citing *Fischer v. State*, 49 So. 2d 1309 (Fla. Dist. Ct. App. 1983) at 1311.

3. I am using the term "religious organizations" to mean "any formally organized religious group, including what are typically referred to as Christian 'denominations,' Jewish groups, and representative groups of other religions active in the United States . . . (such as Buddhists and Muslims)." Andrew S. Mansfield, "Religious Arguments and the United States Supreme Court: A Review of Amicus Curiae Briefs Filed by Religious Organizations," *Cardozo Law, Policy and Ethics Journal* 7 (2009): 343.

4. First quotation: Judge Neal Nettesheim and Clare Ryan, "Friend of the Court Briefs: What the Curiae Wants in an Amicus," *Wisconsin Lawyer* 80 (2007): 11. See also Bruce J. Ennis, "Symposium on Supreme Court Advocacy: Effective Amicus Briefs," *Catholic University Law Review* 33 (1984): 603. Second quotation: Randy S. Parlee, "A Primer on Amicus Curiae Briefs," *Wisconsin Lawyer* 62 (1989): 14. Third quotation: Samuel Krislov, "The Amicus Curiae Brief: From Friendship to Advocacy," *Yale Law Journal* 72 (1963): 694, quotation on 704. See also Reagan William Simpson, "How to Be a Good Friend to the Court: Strategic Use of Amicus Briefs," *Spring Brief* 20 (1999): 38, quotation on 39 n. 3; Sarah F. Corbally, Donald C. Bross, and Victor E. Flango, "Filing of Amicus Curiae Briefs in Courts of Last Resort: 1960–2000," *Justice System Journal* 25 (2004): 39.

5. Ed R. Haden and Kelly Fitzgerald, "The Role of Amicus Briefs," *Alabama Lawyer* 70 (2009): 114, quotation on 115–16; Jonathan Alger and Marvin Krislov, "You've Got to Have Friends: Lessons Learned from the Role of Amici in the University of Michigan Cases," *Journal of College and University Law* 30 (2004): 503–6; Joseph D. Kearney and Thomas W. Merrill, "The Influence of Amicus Curiae Briefs on the Supreme Court," *University of Pennsylvania Law Review* 148 (2000): 743; Michael K. Lowman, "The Litigating Amicus Curiae: When Does the Party Begin after the Friends Leave?" *American University Law Review* 41 (1992): 1243; Ruben J. Garcia, "A Democratic Theory of Amicus Advocacy," *Florida State University Law Review* 35 (2008): 315; Simpson, *Good Friend*, 39; Michael Rustad and Thomas Koenig, "The Supreme Court and Junk Social Science: Selective Distortion in Amicus Briefs," *North Carolina Law Review* 72 (1993): 91; Alexander Wohl, "Friends with Agendas: Amicus Curiae Briefs May Be More Popular Than Persuasive," *American Bar Association Journal* 82, no. 11 (November 1996): 46–47; Parlee, *Primer*, 14; David S. Ruder, "The Development of Legal Doctrine through Amicus Participation: The SEC Experience," *Wisconsin Law Review* 1989 (November–December 1989): 1167.

6. Michael J. Harris, "Amicus Curiae: Friend or Foe? The Limits of Friendship in American Jurisprudence," *Suffolk Journal of Trial and Appellate Advocacy* 5 (2000): 1; US Supreme Court Rules 29–37. Virginia Supreme Court: Virginia Supreme Court Rules (vscr), §vscr-5:30. Fourth Circuit: Federal Rules of Appellate Procedure (FRAP): 28, 28.1, 29, 30, 32. See also Brief of Amici Curiae for Justice for All Alliance (JFAA) in Support of Petitioner, *Roper v. Simmons*, Supreme Court of the United States, No. 03-633, April 20, 2004, 2004 WL 865269, 1 n. 1 (hereinafter JFAA, *Roper*). First quotation: Dan Schweitzer, "Fundamentals of Preparing a

United States Supreme Court Amicus Brief," *Journal of Appellate Practice and Process* 5 (2003): 523, quotation on 531. Second quotation: Haden and Fitzgerald, *The Role of Amicus Briefs*, 118. See also Ruder, *Development of Legal Doctrine*; Schweitzer, *Fundamentals*, 527, 531–32; Barbara J. Van Arsdale, "Amicus Curiae," *American Jurisprudence* 4, 2nd ed., §6; Simpson, *Good Friend*, 40.

7. First quotation: Nettesheim and Ryan, *Friend of the Court*, 11. Corbally, Bross, and Flango, *Filing of Amicus Curiae Briefs*; Alger and Krislov, *Have Friends*, 506; Allison Lucas, "Friends of the Court? The Ethics of Amicus Brief Writing in First Amendment Litigation," *Fordham Urban Law Journal* 26 (1999): 1605. Second quotation: Alger and Krislov, *Have Friends*, 505–6. See also Garcia, *Democratic Theory*, 340–41.

8. Schweitzer, *Fundamentals*, 532–36. Quotation: Brief for Appellant, Supreme Court of Kentucky, *Wheeler v. Kentucky*, No. 2001-SC-444-MR (2001), March 12, 2002, 2002 WL 32508332, 29–35, quotation on 29 (hereinafter Appellant Brief, *Wheeler*). See also Brief-in-Chief, Supreme Court of New Mexico, *New Mexico v. Clark*, No. 23,832, April 3, 1998, 1998 WL 34373493, 33–49 (hereinafter Brief-in-Chief, *Clark*).

9. First quotation: Letter from Alan Reeve Hunt to Jan Marinssen, May 11, 1981. AFSC Archive, CRD Criminal Justice 1981, Death Penalty Direct Action, Jury Selection Amicus Briefs. Second and third quotations: Brief of Amicus Curiae, American Friends Service Committee, In Support of Certain Positions of Appellants, *California v. Alcala/California v. Fields*, Supreme Court of California, April 29, 1981, 5, 7. AFSC Archive, CRD Criminal Justice 1981, Death Penalty Direct Action, Jury Selection Amicus Briefs (hereinafter AFSC, *Fields*). See also Letter from Henry Schwarzchild to Rev. Kathy Young, "Memorandum: Proposed Joint Amicus Brief in U.S. v. Matthews, the First Military Death Case on Appeal," March 30, 1982, and Jane Motz, "Memorandum: Proposed Amicus Brief in Military Death Penalty Case," May 21, 1982, both of which sought to extend and amplify an element of the case by arguing that the planned execution would make the United States a contemporary of the USSR and South Africa, rather than the Western world. AFSC archive, Amicus, U.S. v. Matthews. For an example of the Supreme Court responding favorably to such an argument, see *Atkins*, 536 U.S. at 316, citing a brief filed by the European Union noting the world community's rejection of the practice of executing minors.

10. *Woodson*, 428 U.S. (1976). Quotation: *Thompson v. Oklahoma*, 487 U.S. 815 (1988), 856.

11. Margaret Jane Radin, "Cruel Punishment and Respect for Persons: Super Due Process for Death," *Southern California Law Review* 53 (1980): 1143. Peter Fitzpatrick, "'Always More to Do': Capital Punishment and the (De)Composition of Law," in Sarat, *The Killing State*, 130. See also Robert Bohm, "Capital Punishment and Globalization," in Gregg Barak, ed., *Violence, Conflict and World Order: Critical Conversations on State Power* (Lanham, MD: Rowman and Littlefield, 2007), 231–47; Weisberg, "Deregulating Death"; Franklin Zimring, "Inheriting the Wind: The Supreme Court and Capital Punishment in the 1990s," *Florida State University Law Review* 20 (1992): 7; Carol S. Steiker and Jordan M. Steiker, "Sober Second Thoughts: Reflections on Two Decades of Constitutional Regulation of Capital Punishment," *Harvard Law Review* 109 (1995): 355; Ronald J. Tabak, "The Egregiously Unfair Implementation of Capital Punishment in the United States: 'Super Due Process' or Super Lack of Due Process?" *Proceedings of the American Philosophical Society* 147, no. 1 (March 2003): 13–23. AEDPA: 28 US Code §2254: "An application for a writ of habeas corpus on behalf of a person in custody pursuant to the judgment of a State court shall not be granted with respect to any claim that was adjudicated on the merits in State court proceedings unless the adjudication of the claim (1) resulted in a decision that was contrary to, or involved an unreasonable application of clearly established Federal law, as determined by the Supreme Court of the United States; or (2) re-

sulted in a decision that was based on an unreasonable determination of the facts in light of the evidence presented in the State court proceeding." *Neal v. Puckett*, 339 F.3d 683 (5th Circuit, 2001) upheld this provision. See Liebman, *A Broken System, Part II*; Ronald J. Tabak, "Capital Punishment in the United States: Moratorium Efforts and Other Key Developments," in Hodgkinson and Schabas, *Capital Punishment*, 210; Ronald J. Tabak, "Striving to Eliminate Unjust Executions: Why the ABA's Individual Rights and Responsibilities Section Has Issued Protocols on Unfair Implementation of Capital Punishment," *Ohio State Law Journal* 63 (2002): 475. For critiques from proponents, see Duke, Pew Forum; Otis, "The Death Penalty Today"; Marquis, "Truth and Consequences"; Pojman, "Morally Permissible"; Van den Haag, *Debate*, esp. 203–7, 223–26.

12. I treat these two as linked not only because of similar rationales for their respective prohibitions, particularly the question of culpability, but also because of the reliance of *Atkins* on *Roper*.

13. 287 U.S. 45 (1932) at 71. *Gideon v. Wainwright*, 372 U.S. 335 (1963). *Douglas v. California*, 372 U.S. 353 (1963).

14. First two quotations: *Murray*, 492 U.S. 1 at 16, quoting *Bounds v. Smith*, 430 U.S. 817 (1977) at 823. Third and fourth quotations: ibid. at 27–28. See also *Powell*, 287 U.S. at 69, which noted that "even the intelligent and educated layman . . . requires the guiding hand of counsel at every step in the proceedings against him." Fifth quotation: *Murray*, 492 U.S. at 20. *Gregg*, 428 U.S. at 195, 206. Sixth quotation: *Murray*, 492 U.S. at 23, quoting *Godfrey v. Georgia*, 446 U.S. 420 (1980) at 428. As important as counsel is on appeal, it is of course vital to the trial itself. Some commentators suggest that the quality of counsel is perhaps "the single-most [*sic*] important factor in determining whether a capital defendant is sentenced to death or life in prison." Motion of the Rutherford Institute for Leave to File Amicus Curiae Brief in Support of the Petitioner and Amicus Curiae Brief of the Rutherford Institute in Support of Petitioner, *Moore v. Simpson*, Supreme Court of the United States, No. 06-6276, August 23, 2006, 2006 WL 2630744, 9. See Dieter, *With Justice for Few*, 90–91; Jeffrey Levinson, "Note: Don't Let Sleeping Lawyers Lie: Raising the Standards for Effective Assistance of Counsel," *American Criminal Law Review* 38 (2001): 147; Liebman, *A Broken System*, 41; Douglas W. Vick, "Poorhouse Justice: Underfunded Indigent Defense Services and Arbitrary Death Sentences," *Buffalo Law Review* 43 (1995): 329.

15. *Murray*, 492 U.S. at 24–29.

16. Brief for Respondents, *Murray v. Giarratano*, Supreme Court of the United States, No. 88-411, January 13, 1989, 1989 WL 1127812, quotation on 7 (hereinafter Respondents, *Murray*). Stevens also points to these statistics in making his argument: *Murray*, 492 U.S. at 24. See also Michael Mello, "Facing Death Alone: The Post-Conviction Attorney Crisis on Death Row," *American University Law Review* 37 (1988): 513, esp. 520–21. *Barefoot*, 463 U.S. at 915 (J. Marshall, dissenting).

17. Brief of the American Bar Association (ABA) as Amicus Curiae in Support of Respondents, *Murray v. Giarratano*, No. 88-411, January 13, 1989, 1989 WL 1127811, at 9 (hereinafter ABA Murray brief). Brief of the Maryland State Bar Association, State Bar of Michigan, North Carolina State Bar, South Carolina Bar Association, West Virginia State Bar as Amici Curiae in Support of Respondents, *Murray v. Giarratano*, Supreme Court of the United States, No. 88-411 January 13, 1989, 1989 WL 1127813 (hereinafter Maryland et al., Murray brief). The ABA brief does, however, briefly mention the rate of reversal of death sentences at habeas. See ABA Murray brief, 9. Quotation: John C. Godbold, "Pro Bono Representation of Death Sentenced Inmates," *Record of the Association of the Bar of the City of New York* 42 (1987): 865. Impediment: ABA Murray brief, 14; Maryland et al., Murray brief, 22–29. Mental impairments: ABA

Murray brief, 8–9, 20–29; Maryland et al., Murray brief, 16–22. See also Mello, *Facing Death Alone*, 545; Peter W. Lewis, "Killing the Killers: A Post-Furman Profile of Florida's Condemned: A Personal Account," *Crime and Delinquency* 25, no. 2 (April 1979): 200–211.

18. First quotation: *Murray*, 492 U.S. at 10 (italics added). See also Brief on Behalf of Respondent, *Coleman v. Thompson*, Supreme Court of the United States, No. 89-7662, January 14, 1991, 1991 WL 11003971, 29–30 (hereinafter Respondent, *Thompson*). Brief of Amicus Curiae, State of California et al., in Support of the State of Tennessee, Respondent, *Payne v. Tennessee*, Supreme Court of the United States, No. 90-5721, April 4, 1991, 1991 WL 11007883, 7 n. 2 (hereinafter California, *Payne*). Second quotation: Brief for the Petitioners, *Murray v. Giarratano*, Supreme Court of the United States, No. 88-411, December 15, 1988, 1988 WL 1026317, 29–30 (hereinafter Petitioner's brief, *Murray*).

19. 895 F.2d 139 (4th Cir., 1990). See also Brief for Petitioner, *Coleman v. Thompson*, Supreme Court of the United States, No. 89-7662, October Term, 1990, 1990 WL 10009006, 22–23.

20. Here I am referring to offenders as the Neighbor to highlight problems of proximity and the relationships and responsibilities people bear toward each other. See Žižek, *Violence*, 45–46; Slavoj Žižek, Eric L. Santner, and Kenneth Reinhard, *The Neighbor: Three Inquiries in Political Theology* (Chicago: University of Chicago Press, 2005).

21. This idea will be developed further in chapter 7.

22. Virginia Code §19.2-163.7. Counsel in capital cases. "Virginia is almost unique in having failed to make any movement towards a system for providing its death row inmates, through qualified counsel, with meaningful access to state post-conviction courts." ABA Murray brief, 9.

23. *Murray*, 492 U.S. at 6, 11; *Barefoot*, 463 U.S. at 887; Petitioner's brief, *Murray*, at i, 6, 8, 10, 12, 19, 20, 24, and 32; Respondents, *Murray*, 38.

24. J. L. Austin, *How to Do Things with Words: The William James Lectures*, 2nd ed. (Cambridge, MA: Harvard University Press, 1975); John R. Searle, *Speech Acts: An Essay in the Philosophy of Language* (Cambridge: Cambridge University Press, 1969).

25. "Pro-Death Penalty Page," www.wesleylowe.com/cp.html#cost, accessed January 23, 2010. This page is an excellent single text for seeing the exilic processes being discussed in great detail.

26. Judith Butler, *Excitable Speech: A Politics of the Performative* (New York: Routledge, 1997), 33–34.

27. Louis Althusser, "Ideology and Ideological State Apparatus (Notes toward an Investigation)," in *Lenin and Philosophy and Other Essays* (New York: Monthly Review Press, 2001), 85–126.

28. 501 U.S. 808 (1991).

29. Brief of Amici Curiae Justice for All (JFA) Political Committee et al., On Writ of Certiorari to the Supreme Court of Tennessee, *Payne v. Tennessee*, April 8, 1991, 1991 WL 11007890 (hereinafter JFA, *Payne*). Brief of the Washington Legal Foundation (WLF) et al., On Writ of Certiorari to the Supreme Court of Tennessee, *Payne v. Tennessee*, April 8, 1991, 1991 WL 11007888 (hereinafter WLF, *Payne*).

30. First quotation: WLF, *Payne*, 19, quoting *Gathers*, 490 U.S. at 816 (internal citation omitted; italics added). Second quotation: Žižek, *Violence*, 61.

31. First quotation: AFSC, *Fields*, 2. Second quotation: Brief of Amici Curiae the American Friends Service Committee et al., *State v. Ross*, Supreme Court of the State of Connecticut, August 1988, Appendix A. AFSC archive, Amicus, State v. Ross (hereinafter AFSC, *Ross*). Compare "evil doers" with "evildoers," as in the comments posted to "Kilgore Caught: Kaine Never Said

It" (waldo.jaquith.org/2005/10/kilgore-invented-hitler-claim), October 13, 2005, as discussed in chapter 5. The register in the former falls on the action; in the latter, the individual is defined by the action. The various English translations of Romans 13:4 also render the idea in different forms: Douay-Rheims: "him that doth evil"; KJV: "him that doeth evil"; NIV: "the wrongdoer"; NRSV: "the wrongdoer"; TEV: "those who do evil." Third quotation: Respondents, *Murray*, 1 (internal citation omitted). See also Respondent, *Thompson*, 28–29.

32. Virginians United Against Crime, "Virginia Death Penalty Case Summary," VADP files, Robin Lovitt. Quotation: California, *Payne*, 15.

33. JFAA, *Roper*, 4, citing *Lockett v. Ohio*, 438 U.S. 586 (1978), and 8, citing *Enmund v. Florida*, 458 U.S. 782 (1982); California, *Payne*, 1, 3, citing *Weems v. United States*, 217 U.S. 349 (1910), and *Williams*, 337 U.S., respectively, and 22–23. See also Warren M. Kato, "Note and Comment: The Juvenile Death Penalty," *Journal of Juvenile Law* 18 (1997): 112.

34. JFAA, *Roper*, 2. First quotation: California, *Payne*, 3. Second quotation: JFA, *Payne*, 8 (italics in original; internal citation omitted).

35. See generally California, *Payne*; JFA, *Payne*; WLF, *Payne*. It may sound as though this argument is based on an idea that being charged with a crime equals being guilty of that crime, as the third prong holds that the offender should already be seen as the murderer. This is not the case. Because VISs are introduced at sentencing, the jury has already pronounced guilt, so within the context of the retentionist exilic argument, there is no contradiction.

36. Brief Amici Curiae of the United States Conference of Catholic Bishops (USCCB) and Other Religious Organizations in Support of Respondent, *Roper v. Simmons*, July 14, 2004, 2004 WL 1617400, 27, citing *Lockett*, 438 U.S. at 605 (hereinafter USCCB, *Roper*).

37. JFAA, *Roper*, 2, 29.

38. Brief of the States of Alabama, Delaware, Oklahoma, Texas, Utah, and Virginia as Amici Curiae in Support of Petitioner, *Roper v. Simmons*, Supreme Court of the United States, No. 03-633, April 20, 2004, 2004 WL 865268, 1 (italics in original; hereinafter States, *Roper*). "Free pass": ibid., 9. See also Alabama et al., *Atkins*.

39. States, *Roper*, 1 n. 1.

40. See for example Petitioner's Statement, Brief and Argument, *Simmons v. Luebbers*, Supreme Court of Missouri, En Banc, No. SC84454, January 21, 2003, 2003 WL 24219767, 48–72 (hereinafter Petitioner's Statement, *Simmons*); Edds, *An Expendable* Man, 201–2; Gisli H. Gudjonsson, *The Psychology of Interrogations and Confessions: A Handbook* (Chichester: John Wiley and Sons, 2003); USCC, *McCarver*, 2–3. This brief was originally submitted in *McCarver v. North Carolina*. The Supreme Court dismissed this case after North Carolina changed its law to prohibit the execution of the mentally retarded. When the Supreme Court granted certiorari to Darryl Atkins, the churches moved to refile the brief in *Atkins*, which motion was granted. See Joint Motion of All Amici in *McCarver v. North Carolina*, No. 00-8727, to Have Their *McCarver* Amicus Briefs Considered in This Case in Support of Petitioner, *Atkins v. Virginia*, Supreme Court of the United States, No. 00-8452, November 19, 2001, 2001 WL 1682012, and Petitioner's Statement, *Simmons*, 86. For an example of the churches arguing against disproportionate punishment in other contexts, see Brief Amici Curiae for Religious Organizations in Support of Respondent, *Crawford v. Martinez*, Supreme Court of the United States, No. 03-878, August 2, 2004, 2004 WL 1776911.

41. Brief of Amicus Curiae Missouri Ban Youth Executions (BYE) Coalition in Support of Respondent, *Roper v. Simmons*, Supreme Court of Missouri, No. 03-633, July 13, 2004, 2004 WL 1588550, 8–9 (hereinafter BYE, *Roper*).

42. ABC, *Zant*, 20, 39–40.

43. First and second quotations: *Trop v. Dulles*, 356 U.S. 86 (1958) at 100–101. Third quota-

tion: Scalia, "God's Justice," 232. Fourth and fifth quotations: John Rawls, "The Idea of Public Reason Revisited," in Samuel Freeman, ed., *John Rawls: Collected Papers* (Cambridge, MA: Harvard University Press, 1999), 575, 578. Sixth quotation: 492 U.S. 300 (1989) at 331.

44. Quotation: USCC, *McCarver*, 3. BYE, *Roper*, 13, Appendix 4, Appendix 5.

45. 536 U.S. at 316 n. 21. This inclusion of the churches as among the sources of evidence of public opinion extends the idea of public reason beyond Rawls, whose conception explicitly omits the churches. See Rawls, "Public Reason Revisited," 576.

46. Brief of the American Baptist Churches et al., as Amici Curiae in Support of Petitioner, *Bryan v. Moore*, Supreme Court of the United States, No. 99-6723, December 20, 1999, 1999 WL 1249440, 10. First quotation: Amicus Brief of the American Baptist Churches et al., as Amici Curiae in Support of Appellant, Supreme Court of Georgia, *Davis v. Turpin*, April 28, 2000, iii. AFSC archive, Amicus, Davis v. Turpin (hereinafter ABC, *Davis*). See also ABC, *Zant*, 2. USCC, *McCarver*, 3, 12. Second and third quotations: USCCB, *Roper*, 4. Fourth quotation: ABC, *Davis*, 11–12. See A. J. Reichley, *Religion in American Public Life* (Washington, DC: Brookings Institution Press, 1985), 169; Laurence Tribe, *American Constitutional Law* (Mineola, NY: Foundation, 1978), 866–67. Fifth quotation: USCC, *McCarver*, 13 n. 13. See also *Ready, Willing and Able—Citizens Working for Change: A Survey of the Pew Partnership for Civic Change*, Pew Charitable Trusts, Philadelphia, January 31, 2001; George Gallup Jr. and D. Michael Lindsay, *Surveying the Religious Landscape: Trends in U.S. Beliefs* (Harrisburg, PA: Morehouse, 1999).

47. Quotation: ABC, *Zant*, 31–32 n 7. See also ABC, *Davis*, 11. On the amici's interests, see for example Barbara Moffett, letter to Executive Committee of the Board, in re: Request for Amicus Brief on Death Penalty Case, December 11, 1981, 3; AFSC archive, Friends 1981, Amicus, Jury Lewis; Brief of Amici Curiae, in the Supreme Court of Illinois, *Illinois v. Lewis*, No. 52338, i–x; AFSC archive, Amicus, IL v. Lewis; Brief of Amicus Curiae, Mennonite Central Committee, Presbyterian Church (USA), American Friends Service Committee, United Church of Christ, Board of Church and Society, North Arkansas Conference United Methodist Church, US Court of Appeals for the Eighth Circuit, *Mabry v. Grigsby/Housewright v. McCree*, No. 83-2113-EA, January 26, 1984, iii; AFSC archive, Amicus, Grigsby v. Arkansas (hereinafter AFSC, *Grigsby*); AFSC, *Ross*, Appendix A; ABC, *Zant*, 5–19; ABC, *Davis*, iv–7; USCC, *McCarver*, 13–20, Appendix; TRI, *Baze*, 1. On the denominational statements generally, see chapter 2 above.

48. First quotation: *Zorach v. Clauson*, 343 U.S. 306 (1952) at 313. Second quotation: Cory Spiller, "*People v. Harlan*: The Colorado Supreme Court Takes a Step toward Eliminating Religious Influence on Juries," *Denver University Law Review* 83 (2005): 613, 625. Stark, *What Americans Really Believe*; Jeffrey Abramson, "The Jury and Popular Culture," *DePaul Law Review* 50 (2000): 497, 498. Third quotation: *J.E.B. v. Alabama, ex rel. T.B.*, 511 U.S. 127 (1994) at 149 (internal citation omitted). Fourth quotation: *California v. Brown*, 479 U.S. 538 (1987) at 545 (italics in original). Fifth quotation: Dean Sanderford, "The Sixth Amendment, Rule 606(B), and the Intrusion into Jury Deliberations of Religious Principles of Decision," *Tennessee Law Review* 74 (2007): 167 at 173, quoting *Robinson v. Polk*, 444 F.3d 225 (4th Circuit, 2006) at 226. *Remmer v. U.S.*, 347 U.S. 227 (1954); *Turner v. Louisiana*, 379 U.S. 466 (1965); *Parker v. Gladden*, 385 U.S. 363 (1966); *Duncan v. Louisiana*, 391 U.S. 145 (1968). "Simply put, the trial juror, by appealing to [the Bible], sought to persuade the jury to decide Robinson's fate by reference to a dictate that is contrary to what our Constitution mandates, and that derives from what many consider to be a divinely inspired source of law." *Robinson*, 444 F.3d, J. King, dissenting, at 232. The reverse need not be the case: a juror's religious beliefs may properly compel them to vote for a life sentence. This is consistent with *Lockett* and the idea that anything can mitigate a sentence.

49. Sharon Blanchard Hawk, "*State v. Mann:* Extraneous Prejudicial Information in the Jury

Room: Beautiful Minds Allowed," *New Mexico Law Review* 34 (2004): 149, 155. On cognizable groups, see Richard C. Singer, *Criminal Procedure II: From Bail to Jail* (New York: Aspen, 2008), 166–68. Quotation: Mitchell S. Zuklie, "Rethinking the Fair Cross-Section Requirement," *California Law Review* 84 (1996): 101, 102.

50. Quotations: AFSC, *Fields*, 7–8 (italics added). See also AFSC, *Grigsby*; Brief-in-Chief, *Clark*, 5–39; Appellant Brief, *Wheeler*, 29–32.

51. *Taylor v. Louisiana*, 419 U.S. 522 (1975) at 531. First quotation. AFSC, *Fields*, 5–6, in the unnumbered footnote corresponding to the text spanning the two pages. Second quotation: Peppers and Anderson, *Anatomy*, 90. "A peremptory challenge is one that a party usually does not have to explain. It is exercised only after all cause challenges are made and is necessarily exercised against a person who is otherwise qualified to sit as a juror." Appellant Brief, *Wheeler*, 33.

52. *I Want to Serve: Seeking Just Juries*, www.iwanttoserve.org. Quotations: Bishop Joe Morris Doss, video statement, transcribed by author.

53. Brief-in-Chief, *Clark*, 37–38.

54. Appellant Brief, *Wheeler*, 25 (internal citations omitted).

55. Ibid., 33–34 (internal citations omitted).

56. Name of juror withheld.

57. *Commonwealth v. Lenz*, CR00000027(00), trial transcript, 225–30.

58. First two quotations: Sandra Taylor-Peterson, "Excluded Juror's Voices," *I Want to Serve*, www.iwanttoserve.org/excluded-jurors-voices/; *Lockhart v. McCree*, 476 U.S. 162 (1986) at 173. Third quotation: *Baze v. Rees*, 553 U.S. 35 (2008) at 84. See also Brief-in-Chief, *Clark*, 26–33; Bessler, *Death in the Dark*, 159–60.

59. Quotation: Nancy S. Marder, "Deliberations and Disclosures: A Study of Post-Verdict Interviews of Jurors," *Iowa Law Review* 82 (1997): 465, 470. AFSC, *Fields*, 22 (internal citation omitted). On these exclusions as religious discrimination and a burden on free exercise, see also Brief-in-Chief, *Clark*, 10, 14; Appellant Brief, *Wheeler*, 30.

60. "In concrete cases, courts do not ask, 'What is a religion?' They ask more case-specific questions, such as: 'Was a religious belief burdened?' 'Was a religious practice penalized?' 'Was the autonomy of a religious institution undermined?' 'Was a person's religious identity undermined?' Therefore, the questions courts must answer are smaller ones, which do not absolutely require encompassing definitions." Bette Novitt Evans, *Interpreting the Free Exercise of Religion: The Constitution and American Religion* (Chapel Hill: University of North Carolina Press, 1997), 74.

61. First quotation: James Madison, "Memorial and Remonstrance against Religious Assessments," in Saul K. Padover, ed., *The Complete Madison: His Basic Writings* (New York: Harper and Brothers, 1953), 299. Second quotation: Steven Gey, "Why Is Religion Special?: Reconsidering the Accommodation of Religion under the Religion Clauses of the First Amendment," *University of Pittsburgh Law Review* 52 (1990): 75, 167 (italics added). Michael Sandel, "Religious Liberty—Freedom of Conscience or Freedom of Choice," *Utah Law Review* 1989, no. 3 (1989): 597. See also Ben Clements, "Defining Religion in the First Amendment: A Functional Approach," *Cornell Law Review* 74 (1989): 532; *Capital Sentencing—Juror Prejudice—Colorado Supreme Court Holds Presence of Bible in Jury Room Prejudicial*—People v. Harlan, 109 P.3d 616 (Colo.), cert. denied, 126 S. Ct. 399 (2005), *Harvard Law Review* 119 (2005): 646.

62. This is in a sense a reversal of Milton Yinger's observation that the study of religion is not the study "of the nature of *belief*, but the nature of *believing*." John Milton Yinger, *The Scientific Study of Religion* (New York: Macmillan, 1970), 11. See AFSC, *Fields*, 8.

63. 476 U.S. 79 (1986). Simson and Garvey, *Knockin' on Heaven's Door*, 1093–96. First quotation: *Casarez v. State*, 913 SW2d 468 (Texas Criminal Appeals Court, 1994) at 496. Second quotation: *United States v. Seeger*, 380 U.S. 163 (1965) at 163.

64. Lenz transcript, esp. 20–21. See also Peppers and Anderson, *Anatomy*, 94.

65. "Heresy trials are foreign to our Constitution. Men may believe what they cannot prove." *Ballard*, 322 U.S. 86.

66. Sincerity is assumed in a long line of cases dealing with beliefs. See for example *United States v. Ballard*, 322 US 78 (1944); *Seeger*, 380 U.S.; and, in a different context, *Edwards v. Aguillard*, 482 U.S. 578 (1987). *Lockhart*, 476 U.S. at 176; *Malnak v. Yogi*, 592 F.2d 197 (3rd Circuit, 1979). See Brief-in-Chief, *Clark*, 15.

67. Quotations: Gregory M. Ashley, "Theology in the Jury Room: Religious Discussion as 'Extraneous Material' in the Course of Capital Punishment Deliberations," *Vanderbilt Law Review* 55 (2002): 127, 136, 137. See also Patrick E. Higginbotham, "Juries and the Death Penalty," *Case Western Law Review* 41 (1991): 1047; *Furman*, 408 U.S. at 402; *Gregg*, 428 U.S. at 181; *Lowenfield v. Phelps*, 484 U.S. 231 (1988) at 238; Zimring and Hawkins, *Capital Punishment and the American Agenda*, 67–68; *Lockhart*, 476 U.S. at 173; *Baze*, 553 U.S. at 84; Brief-in-Chief, *Clark*, 26–33.

68. Jesse H. Choper, *Securing Religious Liberty: Principles for Judicial Interpretation of the Religion Clauses* (Chicago: University of Chicago Press, 1995), 74–80. On positive and negative conscience, see Charles E. Curran, *Directions in Fundamental Moral Theology* (Notre Dame, IN: University of Notre Dame Press, 1985), 216. Quotation: Swaine, *The Liberal Conscience*, 47.

69. Swaine, *The Liberal Conscience*, 48. See for example Fred Hilger, Clerk, NYMRO Executive Committee and Bonnie Kerness, Associate Director, New Jersey Justice Program, letter to AFSC Board of Directors, April 16, 1994, in re: Death Penalty Case before New Jersey Supreme Court [*New Jersey v. Ramseur*]; AFSC archive, Amicus, NJ v. Ramseur; AFSC, *Ross*, 5–6; ABC, *Zant*, 3, 25, 30; ABC, *Davis*, 11, 15, 19; Brief-in-Chief, *Clark*, 5; USCC, *McCarver*, 3–6, 8; Petitioner's Statement, *Simmons*, 43; BYE, *Roper*, 2.

70. Swaine, *The Liberal Conscience*, 49.

71. *Lemon v. Kurtzman*, 403 U.S. 602 (1971); *Wallace v. Jaffree*, 472 U.S. 38 (1985) at 56, and n. 42. Quotation: Simson and Garvey, *Knockin' on Heaven's Door*, 1103.

72. *Gregg*, 428 U.S. In *McGautha v. California*, 402 U.S. 183 (1970), the Supreme Court had declined to find bifurcated trials mandatory. In the wake of *Furman*, though, many state legislators turned to the Model Penal Code for guidance on rewriting their capital procedures to suit *Furman*. "The code called for the very changes that the Supreme Court had later dismissed as unnecessary in *McGautha*: a bifurcated (or two-part) trial in which guilt or innocence was separated from the punishment of death or imprisonment." David M. Oshinsky, *Capital Punishment on Trial:* Furman v. Georgia *and the Death Penalty in Modern America* (Lawrence: University Press of Kansas, 2010), 63. Quotation: *Lockhart*, 476 U.S. at 175–76.

73. Quotation: Marvin E. Wolfgang, "We Do Not Deserve to Kill," *Thomas M. Cooley Law Review* 13 (1996): 977, quotation on 981. *Lockett*, 438 U.S. See also Ronald J. Bacigal, *Trial of Capital Murder Cases in Virginia*, 4th ed. (Richmond: Virginia Law Foundation, 2009), §5.3. On the need for a compelling state interest to override religious freedom, see *Wisconsin v. Yoder*, 406 U.S. 205. Recent cases have modified this doctrine. See for example *Employment Division v. Smith*, 494 U.S. 872 (1990) and *City of Boerne v. Flores*, 521 U.S. 507 (1997).

74. "A general grant of jury trial for serious offenses is a fundamental right." *Duncan*, 391 U.S. at 157–58. Brief-in-Chief, *Clark*, 14–23. This argument was made in Appellant Brief, *Wheeler*, at 40–42: "It is unconstitutional to seat a death-qualified jury or, alternatively, to fail to seat separate juries for the guilt and sentencing phases of a capital case."

75. ABC, *Zant*, 58.

76. Brief-in-Chief, *Clark*, 95 (italics added).

77. *Stanford*, 492 U.S. at 370 n. 2 and 384–85. On the relevance of world opinion to the American death penalty, see Thomas Banchoff, "Human Rights, the Catholic Church, and the Death Penalty in the United States," in Thomas Banchoff and Robert Wuthnow, eds., *Religion and the Global Politics of Human Rights* (New York: Oxford University Press, 2011), 285–311; Koh, *Paying "Decent Respect."*

78. Quotation: Albert Camus, "Reflections on the Guillotine," in *Resistance, Rebellion and Death*, trans. Justin O'Brien (New York: Vintage International, 1995), 187. Brief-in-Chief, *Clark*, 18.

7. Opening the Space

Epigraphs. Joseph M. Vought, "Pastor Visitor," September 1992, VCC, "Voices," 7; David R. Dow, *The Autobiography of an Execution* (New York: Twelve, 2010), 16.

1. Erik Brady, "Bringing God to Death Row," *USA Today*, August 25, 1995.

2. First quotation: Vought interview. Second quotation: Rev. Russell Ford, quoted in Frank Green, "He's Walked the Last Walk the Last Time," *Richmond Times-Dispatch*, May 31, 1994.

3. First and fifth quotations: Vought interview. Second and fourth quotations: Rev. Joseph Vought, e-mail to author, September 24, 2009. See also Rev. Joseph M. Vought, letter to the Rt. Rev. Frank Vest, Bishop, Episcopal Diocese of Southern Virginia, May 2, 1994, Vought files, Letters. Third quotation: Green, "He's Walked."

4. See for example Martin Shaw, *What Is Genocide?* (Cambridge: Polity, 2007), 154: "*Genocide is a form of violent social conflict, or war, between armed power organizations that aim to destroy civilian social groups and those groups and other actors who resist this destruction . . . in which armed power organizations treat civilian social groups as enemies and aim to destroy their real or putative social power, by means of killing, violence and coercion against individuals whom they regard as members of the groups*" (italics in original). See also United Nations, "Convention on the Prevention and Punishment of the Crime of Genocide," Article 2, www.hrweb.org/legal/genocide.html, last modified January 27, 1997.

5. First quotation: Volf, *Exclusion and Embrace*, 57 (italics in original). Second quotation: Ibid., 66. See also Judith Butler, *Gender Trouble: Feminism and the Subversion of Identity* (New York: Routledge, 1990). Volf, *Exclusion and Embrace*, 75.

6. Luke 10:29–37, quotations at 10:30; Note to Luke 10:31–33, in Bruce M. Metzger and Roland E. Murphy, eds., *The New Oxford Annotated Bible, with the Apocryphal/Deuterocanonical Books* (New York: Oxford University Press, 1994), NT97–98, 10:27. On the "real" response, see Žižek, *Violence*, 53.

7. Quotations: Volf, *Exclusion and Embrace*, 26, 60 (italics in original).

8. Ibid., 75.

9. Michelle L. Brunsvold, "Medicating to Execute: *Singleton v. Norris*," *University of Chicago-Kent Law Review* 79 (2004): 1291; Michaela P. Sewall, "Pushing Execution over the Constitutional Line: Forcible Medication of Condemned Inmates and the Eighth and Fourteenth Amendments," *Boston College Law Review* 51 (2010): 1279; *Singleton v. Norris*, 319 F.3d 1018 (8th Cir. 2003) (en banc); *Panetti v. Quarterman*, 127 S. Ct. 2842 (2007).

10. First two quotations: Edward E. Curtis IV, "Why Muslims Matter to U.S. History, 1730–1945," lecture given at the Heidelberg Center for American Studies, Heidelberg University, December 3, 2009. Third quotation: Paul Ricoeur, *Oneself as Another*, trans. Kathleen Blamey (Chicago: University of Chicago Press, 1995), 3.

11. Volf, *Exclusion and Embrace*, 65 (italics in original).

12. First quotation: "Statement of Governor Kaine on the Scheduled Execution of Robert Stacy Yarbrough," June 25, 2008. Second quotation: Jack Payden-Travers, remarks at a vigil protesting the execution of Robert Stacy Yarbrough, June 25, 2008.

13. Volf, *Exclusion and Embrace*, 67 (italics added).

14. Ibid., 140–47; Luke 15:11–32.

15. Volf, *Exclusion and Embrace*, 156–65, quotations on 156, 160.

16. Ibid., 141 (italics in original).

17. Constitution of Virginia, Art. 1, §16; Rev. Cecil McFarland, interview with author, August 18, 2008; Chaplain Service Prison Ministry of Virginia: www.chaplainservice.org/index.htm.

18. Virginia Department of Corrections, "Institutions by Security Levels," www.vadoc.state.va.us/facilities/security-levels.shtm.

19. Rev. W. Eric Jackson, interview with author, January 26, 2009.

20. Griffin interview.

21. Ralph McCloud, interview with author, January 22, 2009.

22. www.stdysmasmd.org; Luke 23:39–43. Quotation: Vought interview. See also Rev. Joseph M. Vought, letter to Rev. Edgar R. Trexler, May 22, 1995, Vought files, Letters.

23. First two quotations: Vought, "Jesus, Remember Me," 16, 18. Luanne Austin, *Death Row Minister*, *Daily News-Record* (Harrisonburg, VA), February 3, 2001; Rev. Joseph M. Vought, "Proclaiming the Gospel at an Execution," Vought files, Proclaiming the Gospel at an Execution; Vought, "Jesus, Remember Me"; "Ministry on Virginia's Death Row," Vought Files, Ministry on Death Row; "Hell," Rev. Jim Lewis, "Notes from under the Fig Tree: Thou Preparest a Table Before Me," in Religious Organizing against the Death Penalty Project, *Sermons, Homilies and Reflections on the Death Penalty: A Collection of Writings to Encourage Dialogue in the Religious Community about the Death Penalty Today* (Philadelphia: AFSC), 22. Final quotation: Joseph Giarratano, quoted in Peppers and Anderson, *Anatomy*, 147.

24. First quotation: Jackson interview. Second quotation: Vought, "Proclaiming." Third quotation: Vought, "Pastor Visitor," 7. See also Jeannie Lancaster, North Carolina Division of Prisons, "Prison Warden," February 1989, VCC, "Voices," 11: "When I have spoken to my home churches, they ask me, 'How do you work with "those people"?' I say, 'I work with "those people" because you raised me. I grew up believing.'"

25. First quotation: Prejean, "Would Jesus," 10. Second quotation: Peppers and Anderson, *Anatomy*, 207. Third quotation: McCloud interview.

26. Griffin interview.

27. Vought interview.

28. First quotation: Griffin interview. Second quotation: Jackson interview.

29. Austin, "Death Row Minister," 14. Julia Reed, "Witness at the Execution," *Vogue*, June 1993, 234. Though Prejean was speaking in this case of victim's families, what she says applies as well to offender's families. For the impacts of capital punishment on the families of victims and offenders, see generally Acker and Karp, *Wounds That Do Not Bind*; Rachel King, *Capital Consequences: Families of the Condemned Tell Their Stories* (New Brunswick, NJ: Rutgers University Press, 2005); King, *Don't Kill*; Sharp, *Hidden Victims*; Margaret Vandiver, "The Impact of the Death Penalty on the Families of Homicide Victims and of Condemned Prisoners," in Acker, Bohm, and Lanier, *America's Experiment with Capital Punishment*, 613–45.

30. Derek Smith, "Suspect Jailed in Police Slaying," *Savannah Evening Press*, August 24, 1989. Quotation: Amnesty International, "USA: Less Than 'Ironclad,' Less Than Safe," August 27, 2010, www.amnestyusa.org/research/reports/usa-less-than-ironclad-less-than-safe.

31. Amnesty International USA, "'Where Is the Justice for Me?' The Case of Troy Davis, Fac-

ing Execution in Georgia," February 1, 2007, www.amnestyusa.org/sites/default/files/troyrpt_whereisjusticeforme.pdf; States News Service, "Standing."

32. "663,000 Names on Petition Protesting Troy Davis' Execution," *This Just In—CNN.com Blogs*, September 15, 2011, news.blogs.cnn.com/2011/09/15/663000-names-on-petition-protesting-troy-davis-execution/; John Rudolf, "Troy Davis Execution: Former FBI Chief William S. Sessions Calls on Georgia to Stay Order," *Huffington Post*, September 15, 2001, www.huffingtonpost.com/2011/09/15/troy-davis-execution-william-sessions_n_963366.html. "I Am Troy Davis": Peter Rothberg, "'I Am Troy Davis,'" *Nation*, September 15, 2011, www.thenation.com/blog/163434/i-am-troy-davis#. Quotation: Moni Basu, "Family, Friends Celebrate Troy Davis' Life at Funeral," *CNN.com*, October 1, 2011, LexisNexis.

33. Moni Basu, "Troy Davis' Sister Keeps Promise to Continue Fighting," *CNN Wire*, April 7, 2012, LexisNexis.

34. McFarland interview.

35. First two quotations: Vought interview. Third quotation: McFarland interview. Fourth quotation: Jackson interview.

36. First quotation: McFarland interview. Second quotation: Vought interview. Third and fourth quotations: Griffin interview. Fifth quotation: Jackson interview. Sixth quotation: McCloud interview.

37. First quotation: McCloud interview. Father Jim Griffin, letter to Bishop Walter Sullivan, April 9, 1987, Griffin files, Letters. The Department of Corrections' barring of Griffin from his ministry provoked a hunger strike from the men on death row. See Marie Deans, Virginia Coalition on Jails and Prisons, letter to "Concerned Individuals, Groups, and Organizations and Churches," Re: Hunger Strike on Virginia's Death Row, May 5, 1987, Griffin files, Letters. Griffin was subsequently allowed to continue his ministry. Second quotation: Vought interview.

38. Vought interview (italics added).

39. Ibid.

40. First quotation: Volf, *Exclusion and Embrace*, 113. Second quotation: Session G.

41. Vought interview. First quotation: Jackson interview (italics reflect the emphasis in his statement). Second quotation: Brady, "Bringing God."

42. First quotation: Jackson interview. Second quotation: Session H. Third quotation: Volf, *Exclusion and Embrace*, 157.

43. Jackson interview.

44. McCloud interview.

45. Vought interview. See also Shere, *Cain's Redemption*; Grace Bonds Stapes, "The Final Hours," *Fort Worth Star Telegram*, AFSC files, CRD 1990s, Final Hours; Jeff Peck, "Capital Corruption: The Trial of Jesus," *Jubilee* (Fall 2000): 3; Rev. Joseph M. Vought, "Ministry on Virginia's Death Row," Vought files, Ministry on Death Row; Rev. Joseph M. Vought, "Words of Remembrance for the Executed, VADP Banquet October 6, 2001," Vought files, Words of Remembrance.

46. First quotation: Lynne Tuohy, "Execution Concludes Decades of Legal Limbo for Families; Ross Saga Ends," *Hartford Courant*, May 13, 2005. See also Acker and Karp, *Wounds*, 5. Remaining quotations: Michael Ross, "Seeking Reconciliation from Death Row," undated; AFSC archive, CRD 1990s, Seeking Reconciliation. See also Rev. Jimmy Creech, "The Lie of Violence; The Truth of Love," sermon given January 15, 1995, AFSC archive, CRD 1, Sermons and Prayers.

47. Ross, "Seeking Reconciliation."

48. Walt, "Execution May Haunt."

49. John 8:6. This summary derives from comments made during Sessions D, G, H, K, and T. Osler, *Jesus on Death Row*, 144.

50. First three quotations: Session G. Fourth quotation: Jackson interview (italics added).

51. McCloud interview. First two quotations: Session E. Third and fourth quotations: Joseph M. Giarratano, "An Experience in Life," Father Jim Griffin files, Joe G. Fifth quotation: McCloud interview. Sixth quotation: Vought interview. See also Genesis 4:7.

52. Session T.

53. John 8:11.

54. Session G. Quotation: Emmett, Session A.

55. First quotation: Prejean, "Would Jesus," 15. Second quotation: People of Faith against the Death Penalty (PFADP), "Liturgies at the Vigil to Protest the Execution of Ricky Lee Sanderson, January 29–30, 1998," AFSC archive, CRD 2, Liturgies at the Execution. Third quotation: Rev. Joseph M. Vought, "Christ the King," sermon delivered November 20, 2005, Vought files, Sermons. Fourth quotation: Father Emmanuel Charles McCarthy, "What Is the Gospel Truth on Capital Punishment? A Remembrance Day Sermon," delivered July 12, 1999, AFSC archive, CRD 1, Sermons and Prayers (emphasis in original). Fifth quotation: Lewis, "Notes," 23.

56. Rev. Wayne B. Arnason, with Steven Rosenfield, "An Eye for an Eye Makes the Whole World Blind," sermon delivered March 10, 1996, NDPA, VADP files, VA Faith (incl. Sermon); McCarthy, "Gospel Truth." First quotation: Rev. Dave Barber, in Religious Organizing, *Sermons*, 31. Second quotation: Rabbi Peter J. Rubenstein, "A Sermon for Kol Nidrei Evening, Yom Kippur 5760," in ibid., 30. Third and fourth quotations: Creech, "The Lie of Violence," 5. Fifth quotation: Jackson interview. Sixth quotation: Larry Reimer, "Big Issues Revisited at the Turn of the Millennium: The Death Penalty, from Cycles of Evil to Circles of Healing," April 9, 2000, www.afn.org/~ucg/pages/sermons/death.htm (italics added); Micah 6:8. Seventh quotation: PFADP, "Liturgies."

57. First quotation: Barber, in Religious Organizing, *Sermons*, 32. Rev. Allison Moore, "Overcoming Evil with Good," in Religious Organizing, *Sermons*, 19. Rev. Paul M. Washington, in Religious Organizing, *Sermons*, 8. Second quotation: "Inter-Faith Prayer Service of Hope in Memory of the Oklahoma Bombing Victims and in Opposition to Capital Punishment and the Execution of Timothy McVeigh," May 15, 2001, NDPA, VADP files, Faith Vigils and Services. Rev. Sandra Levy, "Murder Is Wrong, No Matter Who Carries It Out: Reflections on the Death Penalty," NDPA, VADP files, Reflections (Rev. Levy), 6. Third quotation: PFADP, "Liturgies." Fourth quotation: John H. Leith, "Theological Reflections on the Death Penalty," NDPA, VADP files, Theological Reflections on the Death Penalty, 4. Fifth and sixth quotations: Austin, "Death Row Minister," 15, quoting Ford and Vought.

58. First quotation: Moore, "Overcoming," 19. Session L; Weaver-Zercher, "Amish Grace and the Rest of Us"; Knapp, "Forgiveness: 'Way of Life.'" See also Barber, in Religious Organizing, *Sermons*, 31. Second quotation: Rev. John Miller, in Religious Organizing, *Sermons*, 39. See also Rev. Dr. Lee Barker, "Live Man Walking," in Religious Organizing, *Sermons*, 14.

59. First quotation: Prejean, quoted in Reed, "Witness," 193. Second and third quotations: Vought, quoted in Austin, "Death Row Minister," 15. Fourth quotation: Barber, in Religious Organizing, *Sermons*, 32. Rev. John Marsh, in Religious Organizing, *Sermons*, 26; Ellen R. Gelbin, "My Spiritual Journey," in Religious Organizing, *Sermons*, 34; Barber, in Religious Organizing, *Sermons*, 32; Acts 9:10–18. One Bible study participant declared that Ananias was the most faithful believer in the New Testament, because he was able to go forth and express forgiveness. Session I.

60. Vought interview; emphasis in interview. See also Austin, "Death Row Minister," 13.

61. Quotation: Vought interview. All of the chaplains I interviewed said this in varying language.

62. Quotation: Walt, "Execution May Haunt." NCADP, "Tucker Faces"; NCADP, "Memorandum"; Walt, "Path Clear"; Buckley, "Killer Leaves Gov. Bush a Tough Decision"; Turner, "Religious Change of Heart"; Rust, "Death Row Inmate Claims Responsibility"; King, *Don't Kill*, 57–81; Robertson, "Role of Religion and the Death Penalty."

63. Sanders, "Death Penalty is Irredeemable"; Sister Patricia Kelly, OCD, in Religious Organizing, *Sermons*, 12. Quotation: "Testimony before the Subcommittee of the House on Justice and Courts, General Assembly Building, Richmond, VA, January 30, 2001, Pr. Joe Vought," Vought files, Testimony in the House. See also Richard L. Nygaard, "Victims of Vengeance," *Lutheran* (August 1995): 22–25; The Dalai Lama, "Message Supporting a Global Moratorium on the Death Penalty," in Religious Organizing, *Sermons*, 18; Moore, "Overcoming," 19; Lewis, "Notes," 22; "Liturgy on Capital Punishment," AFSC archive, 1977, Easter Witness 1977. John Niven's novel *The Second Coming* (London: Vintage Books, 2011) ends with a new Christian sect sporting syringe-shaped pendants. Jennie Lancaster, "A Death and a Dilemma," *Congregations*, November/December 1993, 16.

8. Conclusion

Epigraph. Virginians for Alternatives to the Death Penalty (VADP), "Vigil Information" www.vadp.org/attend-a-vigil.html, accessed February 2, 2010.

1. Luke 6:27–28, 31, 36–37 (New American Bible).

2. Author's transcription of field recording, June 25, 2008. Bonowitz was referring to the decision in *Kennedy v. Louisiana*, 129 S. Ct. 1 (2008), announced that afternoon, which held that death sentences could not be imposed for any crime short of murder.

3. First quotation: Douglas Flinn, e-mail to Jack Payden-Travers, June 9, 2008, VADP files, Percy Walton. Second and fourth quotations: Warren E. Boisselle, e-mail to Jack Payden-Travers, June 6, 2008, ibid. Third quotation: Kerry Dougherty, "Hazel Weeks: Inconvenient for Foes of Death Penalty," *Virginian-Pilot*, January 16, 2003. Dougherty's article goes to great lengths to remind readers that Washington was in fact guilty of burglarizing and assaulting Hazel Weeks.

4. Dennis Haley, e-mail to Jack Payden-Travers, June 8, 2008, and Jack Payden-Travers, response to Dennis Haley, no date in file, both VADP files, Percy Walton.

Bibliography

Note: All newspapers, magazines, and blogs and other websites are referenced at the corresponding endnote.

Archives and File Collections
American Friends Service Committee (AFSC) archive. Philadelphia, PA.
Marie Deans files. Personal collection. Charlottesville, VA.
Father Jim Griffin files. Personal collection. Virginia Beach, VA.
National Death Penalty Archive (NDPA). Albany, NY.
    National Coalition to Abolish the Death Penalty (NCADP) files, NDPA.
    Bill Pelke / Journey of Hope (JoH) files. Uncatalogued collection, NDPA.
    Virginians for Alternatives to the Death Penalty (VADP) files. Uncatalogued collection, NDPA.
Virginia Council of Churches (VCC) files. Organizational archive. Richmond, VA.
Virginia Interfaith Center for Public Policy (VICPP) files. Organizational archive. Richmond, VA.
Virginians for Alternatives to the Death Penalty (VADP) files. Organizational archive. Charlottesville, VA.
Rev. Joseph M. Vought files. Personal collection. Harrisonburg, VA.

Bibles and Commentaries
The Douay-Rheims Bible. Fitzwilliam, NH: Loreto, 2004.
Holy Bible, King James Version. Grand Rapids, MI: Word, 1989.
The Liberty Bible Commentary. Edited by Jerry Falwell, Edward E. Hindson, and Woodrow Michael Kroll. Nashville: Thomas Nelson, 1983.
The New American Bible. New York: Oxford University Press, 2005.
The New American Standard Bible. Accessed via BibleGateway.com, www.biblegateway.com/versions/New-American-Standard-Bible-NASB/.
The New Oxford Annotated Bible, with the Apocryphal/Deuterocanonical Books, New Revised Standard Version (NRSV). Edited by Bruce M. Metzger and Roland E. Murphy. New York: Oxford University Press, 1994.
Ryrie Study Bible. Expanded ed. Chicago: Moody, 1994.
Today's Light Bible, New International Version (NIV). St. Louis, MO: Concordia, 1999.

Bible Study Guides
Berndt, Brooks. *Transformation through the Word: A Bible Study Guide for Developing a Christian Response to Crime.* Philadelphia: AFSC, n.d. AFSC files, CRD Criminal Justice 2 of 2, Unsorted, "Transforming through the Word."
Gross, Bob. *The Death Penalty: A Guide for Christians.* Elgin, IL: FaithQuest, 1991.
Institute for Southern Studies. "The Bible and the Death Sentence." Durham, NC: Institute for Southern Studies. AFSC files, CRD Criminal Justice 1 of 2, Unsorted, "The Bible and the Death Penalty."
Jackson, Byron, Belle Miller McMaster, Jackie Smith, Haydn O. White, and Kathy Young, compilers. *Capital Punishment Study Resource.* Atlanta: PCUS; New York: United

Presbyterian Church, USA, n.d. NDPA files, VADP collection, "Capital Punishment Study Pack Presbyterian Church."

Mabry, Hunter P. *Capital Punishment: A Faith-Based Study.* Nashville: Abingdon, 2002.

McKernan, Joe, compiler. *God and the Death Penalty: A Biblical Perspective.* AFSC files, CRD 2, "God and the Death Penalty a Biblical Perspective."

Michigan Catholic Conference. *The Death Penalty: A Discussion Guide.* Lansing: Michigan Catholic Conference, 1985. NDPA files, S3, B1, "Michigan Bishops Capital Punishment Study Guide."

Our Lady of Wisdom Catholic Church. "Is the Death Penalty Consistent with Life?" April 30, 1997. AFSC files, CRD 2, "Our Lady of Wisdom Program."

Virginia Council of Churches (VCC). "Death Penalty Study Packet." VCC archives.

———. "The Death Penalty: Exploring Faith Perspectives." 1993. Vought files, "VCC Discussion Guide."

———. Task Force Concerning the Death Penalty. *Voices.* January 1993. Vought files, "Voices Packet."

Yoder, John Howard. "The Death Penalty: A Christian Perspective." *Interpreter*, January 1979, 1–4. NDPA files, VADP collection, "The Death Penalty: A Christian Perspective."

Zehr, Howard. *Death as a Penalty: A Moral, Practical, and Theological Discussion.* Elkhart, IN: Mennonite Central Committee, n.d.

Briefs and Other Legal Documents

Federal Courts

Brief of Amicus Curiae, Mennonite Central Committee, Presbyterian Church (USA), American Friends Service Committee, United Church of Christ, Board of Church and Society, North Arkansas Conference United Methodist Church. US Court of Appeals for the Eighth Circuit. *Mabry v. Grigsby/Housewright v. McCree*, No. 83-2113-EA. January 26, 1984.

Brief of the American Baptist Churches (ABC) et al. as Amici Curiae in Support of Petitioners. In the Supreme Court of the United States. *High v. Zant / Wilkins v. Missouri.* Nos. 87-5666, 87-6026. October Term, 1988.

Brief for the Petitioners. *Murray v. Giarratano.* Supreme Court of the United States, No. 88-411. December 15, 1988. 1988 WL 1026317.

Brief of the American Bar Association as Amicus Curiae in Support of Respondents. *Murray v. Giarratano.* Supreme Court of the United States, No. 88-411. January 13, 1989. 1989 WL 1127811.

Brief of the Maryland State Bar Association, North Carolina State Bar, South Carolina Bar Association, West Virginia State Bar as Amici Curiae in Support of Respondents. *Murray v. Giarratano.* Supreme Court of the United States, No. 88-411. January 13, 1989. 1989 WL 1127813.

Brief for Respondents. *Murray v. Giarratano.* Supreme Court of the United States, No. 88-411. January 13, 1989. 1989 WL 1127812.

Brief for Petitioner. *Coleman v. Thompson.* Supreme Court of the United States, No. 89-7662. October Term, 1990. 1990 WL 10009006.

Brief on Behalf of Respondent. *Coleman v. Thompson.* Supreme Court of the United States, No. 89-7662. January 14, 1991. 1991 WL 11003971.

Brief of Amicus Curiae, State of California et al., in Support of the State of Tennessee, Respondent. *Payne v. Tennessee.* Supreme Court of the United States, No. 90-5721. April 4, 1991. 1991 WL 11007883.

Brief of the American Baptist Churches et al., as Amici Curiae in Support of Petitioner. *Bryan v. Moore.* Supreme Court of the United States, No. 99-6723. December 20, 1999. 1999 WL 1249440.

Brief of Amici Curiae of the United States Catholic Conference and Other Religious Organizations in Support of Petitioner. *McCarver v. North Carolina.* Supreme Court of the United States, No. 00-8727. June 8, 2001. 2001 WL 648613.

Joint Motion of All Amici in *McCarver v. North Carolina*, No. 00-8727, to Have Their *McCarver* Amicus Briefs Considered in This Case in Support of Petitioner. *Atkins v. Virginia.* Supreme Court of the United States, No. 00-8452. November 19, 2001. 2001 WL 1682012.

Brief of Amici Curiae for Justice for All Alliance (JFAA). In Support of Petitioner. *Roper v. Simmons.* Supreme Court of the United States. No. 03-633. April 20, 2004. 2004 WL 865269.

Brief of the States of Alabama, Delaware, Oklahoma, Texas, Utah, and Virginia as Amici Curiae in Support of Petitioner. *Roper v. Simmons.* Supreme Court of the United States, No. 03-633. April 20, 2004. 2004 WL 865268.

Brief of Amici Curiae of the United States Conference of Catholic Bishops (USCCB) and other Religious Organization in Support of Respondent. Supreme Court of the United States. *Roper v. Simmons.* July 14, 2004, 2004 WL 1617400.

Brief of Amici Curiae for Religious Organizations in Support of Respondent. *Crawford v. Martinez.* Supreme Court of the United States, No. 03-878. August 2, 2004. 2004 WL 1776911.

Motion of the Rutherford Institute for Leave to File Amicus Curiae Brief in Support of the Petitioner and Amicus Curiae Brief of the Rutherford Institute in Support of Petitioner. *Moore v. Simpson.* Supreme Court of the United States. No. 06-6276. August 23, 2006. 2006 WL 2630744.

Brief of Amicus Curiae of the American Civil Liberties Union, the ACLU of Kentucky, and the Rutherford Institute in Support of Petitioners. *Baze v. Rees.* Supreme Court of the United States, No. 07-5439. November 8, 2007. 2007 WL 3353105.

State Courts

Brief of Amici Curiae. In the Supreme Court of Illinois. *Illinois v. Lewis.* No. 52338, December 21, 1981.

Brief of Amicus Curiae, American Friends Service Committee. In Support of Certain Positions of Appellants. *California v. Alcala/California v. Fields.* Supreme Court of California, April 29, 1981.

Brief of Amici Curiae the American Friends Service Committee et al. *State v. Ross.* Supreme Court of the State of Connecticut. August 1988.

Brief of Amici Curiae Justice for All (JFA) Political Committee et al., on Writ of Certiorari to the Supreme Court of Tennessee. *Payne v. Tennessee.* April 8, 1991. 1991 WL 11007890.

Brief of the Washington Legal Foundation (WLF) et al., on Writ of Certiorari to the Supreme Court of Tennessee. *Payne v. Tennessee.* April 8, 1991. 1991 WL 11007888.

Brief-in-Chief. Supreme Court of New Mexico. *New Mexico v. Clark.* No. 23,832. April 3, 1998. 1998 WL 34373493.

Amicus Brief of the American Baptist Churches et al. as Amici Curiae in Support of Appellant. Supreme Court of Georgia. *Davis v. Turpin.* April 28, 2000.

Brief of the States of Alabama, Mississippi, Nevada, South Carolina, and Utah as Amici Curiae in Support of Respondent. *Atkins v. Virginia.* Supreme Court of Virginia, No. 00-8452. January 14, 2002. 2002 WL 83600.

Brief for Appellant. Supreme Court of Kentucky. *Wheeler v. Kentucky.* No. 2001-SC-444-MR (2001). March 12, 2002. 2002 WL 32508332.

Petitioner's Statement, Brief, and Argument. *Simmons v. Luebbers*. Supreme Court of Missouri, En Banc, No. SC84454. January 21, 2003. 2003 WL 24219767.

Brief of Amicus Curiae Missouri Ban Youth Executions (BYE) Coalition in Support of Respondent. *Roper v. Simmons*. Supreme Court of Missouri, No. 03-633. July 13, 2004. 2004 WL 1588550.

Commonwealth v. Lenz, CR00000027(00), trial transcript. Circuit Court of Augusta County, Commonwealth of Virginia, July 26–27, 2000.

Campaign Ads

"Kelly." Sponsored by Kilgore for Governor, 2005.
"Law." Sponsored by Kaine for Governor, 2005.
"Stanley." Sponsored by Kilgore for Governor, 2005.

Cases

Atkins v. Virginia, 536 U.S. 304 (2002)
Barclay v. Florida, 464 U.S. 874 (1983)
Barefoot v. Estelle, 463 U.S. 880 (1983)
Batson v. Kentucky, 476 U.S. 79 (1986)
Baze v. Rees, 553 U.S. 35 (2008)
Blystone v. Pennsylvania, 494 U.S. 299 (1990)
Booth v. Maryland, 482 U.S. 496 (1987)
Bounds v. Smith, 430 U.S. 817 (1977)
California v. Brown, 479 U.S. 538 (1987)
California v. Ramos, 463 U.S. 992 (1983)
Casarez v. State, 913 SW2d 468 (Texas Criminal Appeals Court, 1994)
City of Boerne v. Flores, 521 U.S. 507 (1997)
Coleman v. Thompson, 895 F.2d 139 (4th Circuit, 1990)
Commonwealth v. John W. Webster, 5 Cush. 295, 59 Mass. 295 (1850)
Douglas v. California, 372 U.S. 353 (1963)
Duncan v. Louisiana, 391 U.S. 145 (1968)
Edmondson v. Leesville Concrete Co., 500 U.S. 614 (1991)
Edwards v. Aguillard, 482 U.S. 578 (1987)
Employment Division v. Smith, 494 U.S. 872 (1990)
Enmund v. Florida, 458 U.S. 782 (1982)
Fischer v. State, 49 So.2d 1309 (Florida District Court of Appeals 1983)
Ford v. Wainwright, 477 U.S. 399 (1986)
Furman v. Georgia, 408 U.S. 238 (1972)
Gideon v. Wainwright, 372 U.S. 335 (1963)
Glass v. Louisiana, 471 U.S. 1080 (1985)
Godfrey v. Georgia, 446 U.S. 420 (1980)
Gregg v. Georgia, 428 U.S. 153 (1976)
Herrera v. Collins, 506 U.S. 390 (1993)
In re. Troy Anthony Davis, 130 S. Ct. 1 (2009)
J.E.B. v. Alabama, ex rel. T.B., 511 U.S. 127 (1994)
Kennedy v. Louisiana, 129 S. Ct. 1 (2008)
Lemon v. Kurtzman, 403 U.S. 602 (1971)
Lockett v. Ohio, 438 U.S. 586 (1978)

Lockhart v. McCree, 476 U.S. 162 (1986)
Lowenfield v. Phelps, 484 U.S. 231 (1988)
Malnak v. Yogi, 592 F.2d 197 (3rd Cir., 1979)
McCleskey v. Kemp, 481 U.S. 279 (1987)
McGautha v. California, 402 U.S. 183 (1970)
Murray v. Giarratano, 492 U.S. 1 (1989)
Neal v. Puckett, 339 F.3d 683 (5th Cir., 2001)
Panetti v. Quarterman, 127 S. Ct. 2842 (2007)
Parker v. Gladden, 385 U.S. 363 (1966)
Payne v. Tennessee, 501 U.S. 808 (1991)
Penry v. Lynaugh, 492 U.S. 302 (1989)
Powell v. Alabama, 287 U.S. 45 (1932)
Pulley v. Harris, 465 U.S. 37 (1984)
Remmer v. United States, 347 U.S. 227 (1954)
Roberts v. Louisiana, 428 U.S. 325 (1976)
Robinson v. Polk, 444 F.3d 225 (4th Cir., 2006)
Roe v. Wade, 410 U.S. 113 (1973)
Roper v. Simmons, 543 U.S. 551 (2005)
Rudolph v. Alabama, 375 U.S. 889 (1963)
Santa Fe v. Doe, 530 U.S. 290 (2000)
Singleton v. Norris, 319 F.3d 1018 (8th Cir. 2003) (en banc)
South Carolina v. Gathers, 490 U.S. 805 (1989)
Stanford v. Kentucky, 492 U.S. 361 (1989)
Strickland v. Washington, 467 U.S. 1267 (1984)
Taylor v. Louisiana, 419 U.S. 522 (1975)
Thompson v. Oklahoma, 487 U.S. 815 (1988)
Tison v. Arizona, 481 U.S. 137 (1987)
Trop v. Dulles, 356 U.S. 86 (1958)
Turner v. Louisiana, 379 U.S. 466 (1965)
United States v. Ballard, 322 U.S. 78 (1944)
United States v. Seeger, 380 U.S. 163 (1965)
Wainwright v. Goode, 464 U.S. 78 (1983)
Wainwright v. Witt, 469 U.S. 412 (1985)
Wallace v. Jaffree, 472 U.S. 38 (1985)
Weems v. United States, 217 U.S. 349 (1910)
Williams v. Florida, 399 U.S. 78 (1970)
Williams v. New York, 337 U.S. 241 (1949)
Wisconsin v. Yoder, 406 U.S. 205 (1972)
Witherspoon v. Illinois, 391 U.S. 510 (1968)
Woodson v. North Carolina, 428 U.S. 280 (1976)
Zorach v. Clauson, 343 U.S. 306 (1952)

Films, Radio, and Television

Eye for an Eye. Directed by John Schlessinger. 1996. Produced and distributed by Paramount Pictures.

I Want to Live! Directed by Robert Wise. 1958. Produced by Figaro Pictures; distributed by United Artists.

"Karla Faye Tucker: Live from Death Row." *Larry King Live*. January 14, 1998. Event transcript #98011400V22. www.cnn.com/SPECIALS/1998/tucker.execution/transcripts/trans.1.14.html.

"Witness to an Execution." *All Things Considered*, October 12, 2000. Produced by David Isay and Stacy Abramson. Abridged and included in Hunter P. Mabry, *Capital Punishment: A Faith-Based Study*. Nashville: Abingdon, 2002.

Institutional Publications and Statements

All pagination in this section refers to this booklet: American Friends Service Committee. The Death Penalty: The Religious Community Calls for Abolition: Statements of Opposition to Capital Punishment. *Philadelphia: AFSC, 1998.*

American Baptist Churches in the USA (ABC). "Resolution on Capital Punishment." June 1977. 6.

American Ethical Union. "Resolution on Capital Punishment." September 17, 1976. 6.

American Friends Service Committee (AFSC). "Statement on the Death Penalty." November 1976. 6–7.

Assemblies of God (AoG). "Capital Punishment." www.ag.org/top/Beliefs/contempissues_08_capital_punish.cfm.

Bruderhof Communities, The. "Statement on the Death Penalty." 9. N.d.

Catechism of the Catholic Church. 2nd ed. 1994. www.usccb.org/beliefs-and-teachings/what-we-believe/catechism/catechism-of-the-catholic-church/epub/.

Christian Church (Disciples of Christ). "Resolution Concerning Opposition to the Use of the Death Penalty." 1985. 10.

Christian Reformed Church in North America. "Statement on Capital Punishment (1981)." In *The Churches Speak On: Capital Punishment*, edited by J. Gordon Melton, 64–96. Detroit: Gale Research, 1989.

Church of Jesus Christ of Latter-Day Saints (LDS). "Capital Punishment." N.d. newsroom.lds.org/ldsnewsroom/eng/public-issues/capital-punishment.

Church Women United. "Capital Punishment." 1981. 11.

Episcopal Church. "Capital Punishment: Statement of the 1979 General Conference." 11–12.

Evangelical Lutheran Church in America (ELCA). "A Social Statement On: The Death Penalty." August 28–September 4, 1991. 12–14.

Fellowship of Reconciliation (FoR). "An Appeal to End All Executions." 14–15.

Friends Committee on National Legislation. "Statement of Legislative Policy." November 14, 1987. 15–16.

Iowa Catholic Conference. "Catholic Bishops of Iowa Issue Statement on Death Penalty." February 4, 1998. www.deathpenaltyinfo.org/catholic-bishops-iowa-issue-statement-death-penalty.

John Paul II. *Evangelium Vitae (The Gospel of Life): On the Value and Inviolability of Human Life.* Publication No. 316–17. Washington, DC: US Catholic Conference.

Lutheran Church—Missouri Synod (LCMS). *Report on Capital Punishment*. St. Louis: Concordia, 1980.

Mennonite Central Committee (MCC). "Death Penalty." December 4, 1982. 17–19.

Mennonite Church, The. "Statement on Capital Punishment." August 1965. 19–20.

Mennonite Church, General Conference. "Capital Punishment." July 16, 1965. 17.

National Association of Evangelicals (NAE). "Abortion 1973." www.nae.net/government-relations/policy-resolutions/59-abortion-1973.

———. "Capital Punishment 1972." nae.net/index.cfm?FUSEACTION=editor.page&pageID=187, accessed February 26, 2009.

———. "Capital Punishment 1973." www.nae.net/government-relations/policy-resolutions/95-capital-punishment-1973.

National Council of the Churches of Christ in the USA. "Resolution Opposing Capital Punishment and Racism in Sentencing." May 26, 1988. 21–22.

Presbyterian Church, USA (PCUSA). *Public Policy Statements of the Presbyterian Church (U.S.A.): Capital Punishment*. PDS 72-620-02-705. Louisville: General Assembly Council.

Reformed Church in America. "Resolution on Capital Punishment." 1965, p. 23.

Southern Baptist Convention (SBC). "Resolution on Capital Punishment." June 2000. www.sbc.net/resolutions/amResolution.asp?ID=299.

Texas Catholic Conference. "Statement by Catholic Bishops of Texas on Capital Punishment." October 20, 1997. www.deathpenaltyinfo.org/statement-catholic-bishops-texas-capital-punishment.

Texas Conference of Churches. "Resolution Opposing the Death Penalty: Adopted Unanimously by the General Assembly of the Texas Conference of Churches." February 24, 1988. www.deathpenaltyinfo.org/texas-conference-churches.

United Church of Christ (UCC). "Resolution of the 12th General Synod of the United Church of Christ." 1979. 24–25.

United Methodist Church (UMC). "Capital Punishment." 1980. 25–26.

United States Catholic Conference (USCC). "Statement on Capital Punishment: Committee on Social Development and World Peace." March 1, 1978. 26.

United States Conference of Catholic Bishops (USCCB). *Catholic Campaign to End the Use of the Death Penalty*. Publication No. 5-715. Washington, DC: USCCB, 2005.

———. *A Good Friday Appeal to End the Death Penalty*. Publication No. 5-327. Washington, DC: United States Catholic Conference, 1999.

———. *Statement on Capital Punishment*. Publication No. 740-5. Washington, DC: US Catholic Conference, 2001.

Virginia Annual Conference, United Methodist Church. "Call for Moving Forward with Study and Action on the Death Penalty." June 18, 2002.

Interviews

Steve Baggarly, Norfolk Catholic Worker, June 26, 2008.
Father Jim Griffin, June 30, 2008.
Rev. W. Eric Jackson, January 26, 2009.
Governor Timothy M. Kaine, August 19, 2008.
Jerry Kilgore, October 30, 2008.
Ralph McCloud, January 22, 2009.
Rev. Cecil McFarland, August 18, 2008.
Rev. Wallace Sherbon, July 28, 2008.
Rev. Joseph M. Vought, July 2, 2008.

Sermons

All pagination in this section refers to this booklet: American Friends Service Committee. Sermons, Homilies and Reflections on the Death Penalty. *Philadelphia: AFSC, n.d.*

Arnason, Rev. Wayne B., with Steven Rosenfield. "An Eye for an Eye Makes the Whole World Blind." March 10, 1996. NDPA Files, VADP collection, folder titled "VA Faith (incl. sermon)."

Barber, Rev. Dave. Untitled. 30–32. N.d.
Barker, Rev. Dr. Lee. "Live Man Walking." 13–15. N.d.
Creech, Rev. Jimmy. "The Lie of Violence; The Truth of Love." January 15, 1995. AFSC files, CRD 1, "Sermons and Prayers."
Gelbin, Ellen R. "My Spiritual Journey." 33–36. N.d.
Kelly, Sister Patricia OCD. Untitled. 12. N.d.
The Dalai Lama. "Message Supporting a Global Moratorium on the Death Penalty." August 1995. 17–18.
Lewis, Rev. Jim. "Notes from under the Fig Tree: Thou Preparest a Table before Me." 21–24. N.d.
Marsh, Rev. John. Untitled. 24–27. N.d.
McCarthy, Father Emmanuel Charles. "What Is the Gospel Truth on Capital Punishment? A Remembrance Day Sermon." July 12, 1999. AFSC, CRD 1, "Sermons and Prayers."
Miller, Rev. John. Untitled. August 1998. 38–39.
Moore, Rev. Allison. "Overcoming Evil with Good." 18–19. N.d.
Reimer, Larry. "Big Issues Revisited at the Turn of the Millennium: The Death Penalty, from Cycles of Evil to Circles of Healing." April 9, 2000. www.afn.org/~ucg/pages/sermons/death.htm.
Rubenstein, Rabbi Peter J. "A Sermon for Kol Nidrei Evening, Yom Kippur 5760." 30.
Vought, Rev. Joseph M. "Christ the King." November 20, 2005. 27–30.
Washington, Rev. Paul M. Untitled. 8. N.d.

Books, Articles, and Reports

Abramson, Jeffrey. "The Jury and Popular Culture." *DePaul Law Review* 50 (2000): 497.
Acker, James R., Robert M. Bohm, and Charles S. Lanier, eds. *America's Experiment with Capital Punishment: Reflections on the Past, Present and Future of the Ultimate Penal Sanction*. 2nd ed. Durham, NC: Carolina Academic Press, 2003.
Acker, James R., and David R. Karp, eds. *Wounds That Do Not Bind: Victim-Based Perspectives on the Death Penalty*. Durham, NC: Carolina Academic Press, 2006.
Agamben, Giorgio. *Homo Sacer: Sovereign Power and Bare Life*. Translated by Daniel Heller-Roazen. Stanford: Stanford University Press, 1998.
———. *State of Exception*. Translated by Kevin Attell. Chicago: University of Chicago Press, 2005.
Albanese, Catherine L. *America: Religions and Religion*. Belmont, CA: Wadsworth, 1992.
Alger, Jonathan, and Marvin Krislov. "You've Got to Have Friends: Lessons Learned from the Role of Amici in the University of Michigan Cases." *Journal of College and University Law* 30 (2004): 503.
Althusser, Louis. "Ideology and Ideological State Apparatus (Notes toward an Investigation)." In *Lenin and Philosophy and Other Essays*, 85–126. New York: Monthly Review Press, 2001.
American Civil Liberties Union of Virginia. *Broken Justice: The Death Penalty in Virginia*. Richmond: ACLU of Virginia, 2003.
———. *Unequal, Unfair, and Irreversible: The Death Penalty in Virginia*. Richmond: ACLU of Virginia, 2000.
American Piety in the 21st Century: New Insights to the Depth and Complexity of Religion in the US. Selected Findings from the Baylor Religion Survey, 2006. *www.baylor.edu/content/services/document.php/33304.pdf*.
Ammerman, Nancy Tatom. *Congregation and Community*. New Brunswick, NJ: Rutgers University Press, 1997.

———. *Pillars of Faith: American Congregations and Their Partners*. Berkeley: University of California Press, 2005.

Ammerman, Nancy Tatom, Jackson W. Carroll, Carl S. Dudley, and William McKinney, eds. *Studying Congregations: A New Handbook*. Nashville: Abingdon, 1998.

Anckar, Carsten. *Determinants of the Death Penalty: A Comparative Study of the World*. London: Routledge, 2004.

Anderson, Kerby. *Christian Ethics in Plain Language*. Nelson's Plain Language Series. Nashville: Thomas Nelson 2005.

Anderson, Victor. "Responsibility, Vengeance, and the Death Penalty." In *Religion and the Death Penalty: A Call for Reckoning*, edited by Eric C. Owens, John D. Carlson, and Eric P. Elshtain, 195–210. Grand Rapids, MI: Wm. B. Eerdmans, 2004.

Applegate, Brandon, Francis T. Cullen, Bonnie Fisher, and Thomas Vander Ven. "Forgiveness and Fundamentalism: Reconsidering the Relationship between Correctional Attitudes and Religion." *Criminology* 38, no. 3 (March 2006): 719–53.

Aquinas, Thomas. *Summa Theologica*. www.newadvent.org/summa/index.html.

Arriens, Jan, ed. *Welcome to Hell: Letters and Writings from Death Row*. Boston: Northeastern University Press, 1997.

Asad, Talal. *Formations of the Secular: Christianity, Islam, and Modernity*. Stanford: Stanford University Press, 2003.

Ashley, Gregory M. "Theology in the Jury Room: Religious Discussion as 'Extraneous Material' in the Course of Capital Punishment Deliberations." *Vanderbilt Law Review* 55 (2002): 127.

Austin, J. L. *How to Do Things with Words: The William James Lectures*. 2nd ed. Cambridge, MA: Harvard University Press, 1975.

Austin, James, John Irwin, and Charis E. Kubrin. "It's about Time: America's Imprisonment Binge." In *Punishment and Social Control*, enlarged 2nd ed., edited by Thomas G. Blomberg and Stanley Cohen, 433–70. New York: Aldine de Gruyter, 2003.

Ayers, Edward L. *Vengeance and Justice: Crime and Punishment in the Nineteenth-Century American South*. New York: Oxford University Press, 1994.

Babcock, Sandra. "Death Row Conditions." Updated June 2008. deathpenaltyinfo.org/documents/DeathRowConditions.xls.

Bacigal, Ronald J. *Trial of Capital Murder Cases in Virginia*. 4th ed. Richmond: Virginia Law Foundation, 2009.

Bader, Christopher D., and Paul Froese. "Images of God: The Effect of Personal Theologies on Moral Attitudes, Political Affiliation, and Religious Behavior." *Interdisciplinary Journal of Research on Religion* 1 (2005), article 11. www.religjournal.com.

Bader, Christopher D., Carson F. Mencken, and Paul Froese. "American Piety 2005: Content and Methods of the Baylor Religion Survey." *Journal for the Scientific Study of Religion* 46, no. 4 (December 2007): 447–63.

Bader-Saye, Scott. "Listening: Authority and Obedience." In *The Blackwell Companion to Christian Ethics*, edited by Stanley Hauerwas and Samuel Wells, 169–81. Oxford: Blackwell, 2006.

Bailey, William C., and Ruth D. Peterson. "Murder, Capital Punishment, and Deterrence: A Review of the Literature." In *The Death Penalty in America: Current Controversies*, edited by Hugo Adam Bedau, 135–61. New York: Oxford University Press, 1997.

Bailie, Gil. *Violence Unveiled: Humanity at the Crossroads*. New York: Crossroad, 1995.

Baker, William H. *On Capital Punishment*. Chicago: Moody, 1985.

Baldus, David C., George G. Woodworth, and Charles A. Pulaski Jr. *Equal Justice and the Death Penalty: A Legal and Empirical Analysis*. Boston: Northeastern University Press, 1990.

Banchoff, Thomas. "Human Rights, the Catholic Church, and the Death Penalty in the United States." In *Religion and the Global Politics of Human Rights*, edited by Thomas Banchoff and Robert Wuthnow, 285–311. New York: Oxford University Press, 2011.

Banner, Stuart. *The Death Penalty: An American History*. Cambridge, MA: Harvard University Press, 2002.

Barak, Gregg, ed. *Violence, Conflict and World Order: Critical Conversations on State Power*. Lanham, MD: Rowman and Littlefield, 2007.

Barry, Rupert V. "Furman to Gregg: The Judicial and Legislative History." *Howard Law Journal* 22 (1979): 53.

Beccaria, Cesare. *On Crimes and Punishments and Other Writings*. Edited by Richard Bellamy, translated by Richard Cox, with Virginia Cox and Richard Bellamy. New York: Cambridge University Press, 2003.

Bedau, Hugo Adam. "Background and Developments." In *The Death Penalty in America: Current Controversies*, edited by Hugo Adam Bedau, 3–25. New York: Oxford University Press, 1997.

———, ed. *The Death Penalty in America*. 3rd ed. New York: Oxford University Press, 1982.

———, ed. *The Death Penalty in America: Current Controversies*. New York: Oxford University Press, 1997.

———. "Prison Homicides, Recidivist Murder, and Life Imprisonment." In *The Death Penalty in America: Current Controversies*, edited by Hugo Adam Bedau, 176–82. New York: Oxford University Press, 1997.

Bedau, Hugo Adam, and Paul G. Cassell, eds. *Debating the Death Penalty: Should America Have Capital Punishment? The Experts from Both Sides Make Their Case*. New York: Oxford University Press, 2004.

Berg, Manfred. "Criminal Justice, Law Enforcement and the End of Lynching in the South." In *Criminal Justice in the United States and Germany—Strafrecht in den Vereinigten Staaten und Deutschland*. Publications of the Bavarian American Academy, vol. 6, 29–42. Heidelberg: Universitätsverlag Winter, 2006.

———. *Popular Justice: A History of Lynching in America*. Lanham, MD: Ivan R. Dee, 2011.

Berg, Manfred, Stefan Kapsch, and Franz Streng, eds. *Criminal Justice in the United States and Germany—Strafrecht in den Vereinigten Staaten und Deutschland*. Publications of the Bavarian American Academy, vol. 6. Heidelberg: Universitätsverlag Winter, 2006.

Berg, Thomas C. "Religious Conservatives and the Death Penalty." *William and Mary Bill of Rights Journal* 9 (2000): 29.

Berkman, John. "Being Reconciled: Penitence, Punishment, and Worship." In *The Blackwell Companion to Christian Ethics*, edited by Stanley Hauerwas and Samuel Wells, 95–109. Oxford: Blackwell, 2006.

Berkowitz, Beth A. *Execution and Invention: Death Penalty Discourse in Early Rabbinic and Christian Cultures*. New York: Oxford University Press, 2006.

Berman, Harold J. *Faith and Order: The Reconciliation of Law and Religion*. Grand Rapids, MI: Wm. B. Eerdmans, 1993.

Berns, Walter. *For Capital Punishment: Crime and the Morality of the Death Penalty*. New York: Basic Books, 1979.

Bessler, John D. *Cruel and Unusual: The American Death Penalty and the Founders' Eighth Amendment*. Boston: Northeastern University Press, 2012.

———. *Death in the Dark: Midnight Executions in America*. Boston: Northeastern University Press, 1997.

Beyler, Craig L. "Analysis of the Fire Investigation Methods and Procedures Used in the Criminal Arson Cases against Ernest Ray Willis and Cameron Todd Willingham." August 19, 2009, www.docstoc.com/docs/document-preview.aspx?doc_id=10401390.

Biello, David. "Bad Drugs: Lethal Injection Does Not Work as Designed." ScientificAmerican.com. April 23, 2007. www.scientificamerican.com/article.cfm?id=lethal-injection-does-not-work-as-designed.

Bisbort, Alan. *When You Read This, They Will Have Killed Me: The Life and Redemption of Caryl Chessman, Whose Execution Shook America*. New York: Carroll and Graf, 2006.

Bjarnason, Thoroddur, and Michael R. Welch. "Father Knows Best: Parishes, Priests, and American Catholic Parishioners' Attitudes toward Capital Punishment." *Journal for the Scientific Study of Religion* 43, no. 1 (March 2004): 103–18.

Blecker, Robert. "Roots." In *America's Experiment with Capital Punishment: Reflections on the Past, Present, and Future of the Ultimate Penal Sanction*, 2nd ed., edited by James R. Acker, Robert M. Bohm, and Charles S. Lanier, 169–231. Durham, NC: Carolina Academic Press, 2003.

Bleichmar, Javier. "Deportation as Punishment: A Historical Analysis of the British Practice of Banishment and Its Impact on Modern Constitutional Law." *Georgetown Immigration Law Journal* 14 (1999–2000): 115.

Blidstein, Gerald J. "Capital Punishment—The Classic Jewish Discussion." *Judaism* 14 (1965): 150–72.

Blomberg, Thomas G., and Stanley Cohen, eds. *Punishment and Social Control*. Enlarged 2nd ed. New York: Aldine de Gruyter, 2003.

Blume, John H., and Sherry Lynn Johnson. "Don't Take His Eye, Don't Take His Tooth, and Don't Cast the First Stone: Limiting Religious Arguments in Capital Cases." *William and Mary Bill of Rights Journal* 9 (2000): 61.

Blumenthal, Max. "Hitler in Virginia." *Nation*, October 26, 2005. www.thenation.com/doc/20051107/blumenthal.

Bohm, Robert M. "Capital Punishment and Globalization." In *Violence, Conflict and World Order: Critical Conversations on State Power*, edited by Gregg Barak, 231–47. Lanham, MD: Rowman and Littlefield, 2007.

———. *Deathquest II: An Introduction to the Theory and Practice of Capital Punishment in the United States.* 2nd ed. Cincinnati: Anderson, 2003.

Bornstein, Brian H., and Monica K. Miller. *God in the Courtroom: Religion's Role at Trial*. New York: Oxford University Press, 2009.

Bosco, Antoinette. *Choosing Mercy: A Mother of Murder Victims Pleads to End the Death Penalty*. Maryknoll, NY: Orbis Books, 2001.

Boulanger, Christian, and Austin Sarat. "Putting Culture into the Picture: Toward a Comparative Analysis of State Killing." In *The Cultural Lives of Capital Punishment: Comparative Perspectives*, edited by Austin Sarat and Christian Boulanger, 1–45. Stanford: Stanford University Press, 2005.

Bowers, William J. "The Effect of Executions Is Brutalization, Not Deterrence." In *Challenging Capital Punishment: Legal and Social Sciences Approaches*, edited by Kenneth C. Haas and James A. Inciardi, 49–89. Newbury Park, CA: Sage, 1989.

———. *Legal Homicide: Death as a Punishment in America, 1864–1982*. Boston: Northeastern University Press, 1984.

Bowers, William J., and Glen L. Pierce. "Deterrence or Brutalization: What Is the Effect of Executions?" *Crime and Delinquency* 26, no. 4 (1980): 453–84.
———. "The Illusion of Deterrence in Isaac Ehrlich's Research on Capital Punishment." *Yale Law Journal* 85 (1975): 187.
Britt, Chester L. "Race, Religion, and Support for the Death Penalty: A Research Note." *Justice Quarterly* 15, no. 1 (March 1998): 175–91.
Brown, David, and Ann Loades, eds. *Christ: The Sacramental Word*. London: SPCK, 1996.
Brown, Edmund G. "Pat," and Dick Adler. *Public Justice, Private Mercy: A Governor's Education on Death Row*. New York: Weidenfeld and Nicholson, 1989.
Browning, Frank, and John Gerassi. *The American Way of Crime*. New York: Putnam's Sons, 1980.
Brueggeman, Walter. *The Prophetic Imagination*. 2nd ed. Minneapolis: Fortress, 2001.
Brugger, E. Christian. *Capital Punishment and Roman Catholic Moral Tradition*. Notre Dame, IN: University of Notre Dame Press, 2003.
Brunsvold, Michelle L. "Medicating to Execute: *Singleton v. Norris*." *University of Chicago–Kent Law Review* 79 (2004): 1291.
Burnett, Cathleen. *Justice Denied: Clemency Appeals in Death Penalty Cases*. Boston: Northeastern University Press, 2002.
Burton, Velmer S., Jr. "The Consequences of Official Labels: A Research Note on Rights Lost by the Mentally Ill, Mentally Incompetent, and Convicted Felons." *Community Mental Health Journal* 26, no. 3 (June 1990): 267–76.
Butler, Brooke. "Death Qualification and Prejudice: The Effect of Implicit Racism, Sexism and Homophobia on Capital Defendants' Right to Due Process." *Behavioral Sciences and the Law* 25, no. 6 (November 2007): 857–67.
———. "The Role of Death Qualification in Venirepersons' Susceptibility to Victim Impact Statements." *Psychology, Crime and Law* 13, no. 2 (April 2008): 133–41.
Butler, Brooke M., and Gary Moran. "The Role of Death Qualification in Venirepersons' Evaluations of Aggravating and Mitigating Circumstances in Capital Trials." *Law and Human Behavior* 26, no. 2 (April 2002): 175–84.
Butler, Judith. *Excitable Speech: A Politics of the Performative*. New York: Routledge, 1997.
———. *Gender Trouble: Feminism and the Subversion of Identity*. New York: Routledge, 1990.
Byrne, William A. "Slave Crime in Savannah, Georgia." *Journal of Negro History* 79, no. 4 (Autumn 1994): 352–62.
Cabana, Donald A. *Death at Midnight: The Confession of an Executioner*. Boston: Northeastern University Press, 1996.
Campbell, James. "'The Victim of Prejudice and Hasty Consideration': The Slave Trial System in Richmond, Virginia, 1830–61." *Slavery and Abolition* 26, no. 1 (April 2005): 71–91.
Camus, Albert. *The Rebel: An Essay on Man in Revolt*. Translated by Anthony Bower. New York: Vintage International, 1991.
———. "Reflections on the Guillotine." In *Resistance, Rebellion and Death*. Translated by Justin O'Brien. New York: Vintage International, 1995.
"Capital Sentencing—Juror Prejudice—Colorado Supreme Court Holds Presence of Bible in Jury Room Prejudicial—*People v. Harlan*. 109 P3d 616 (Colo.), cert. denied, 126 S.Ct. 399 (2005), *Harvard Law Review* 119 (2005): 646.
Carlson, Tucker. "Devil May Care." *Talk Magazine*, September 1999, 106.
Carroll, Jackson W. "Leadership and the Study of the Congregation." In *Studying Congregations: A New Handbook*, edited by Nancy Tatom Ammerman, Jackson W. Carroll, Carl S. Dudley, and William McKinney, 167–95. Nashville: Abingdon, 1997.

Carter, Stephen L. "When Victims Happen to Be Black." *Yale Law Journal* 97 (1988): 420.
Cassell, Paul G. "In Defense of the Death Penalty." In *Debating the Death Penalty: Should America Have Capital Punishment? The Experts from Both Sides Make Their Case*, edited by Hugo Adam Bedau and Paul G. Cassell, 183–217. New York: Oxford University Press, 2004.
Cavanaugh, William. *Torture and Eucharist: Theology, Politics and the Body of Christ*. Oxford: Blackwell, 1998.
Chessman, Caryl. *Cell 2245, Death Row*. New York: Carroll and Graf, 2006.
Chidester, David. *Authentic Fakes: Religion and American Popular Culture*. Berkeley: University of California Press, 2005.
Choper, Jesse H. *Securing Religious Liberty: Principles for Judicial Interpretation of the Religion Clauses*. Chicago: University of Chicago Press, 1995.
Christoph, James B. *Capital Punishment and British Politics: The British Movement to Abolish the Death Penalty, 1945–1957*. Chicago: University of Chicago Press, 1962.
Church, Forrest. Preface to *The Jefferson Bible: The Life and Morals of Jesus of Nazareth*. Boston: Beacon, 1989.
Clements, Ben. "Defining Religion in the First Amendment: A Functional Approach." *Cornell Law Review* 74 (1989): 532.
Colvin, Mark. *Penitentiaries, Reformatories, and Chain Gangs: Social Theory and the History of Punishment in Nineteenth-Century America*. New York: St. Martin's, 1997.
Committee on the Judiciary, Subcommittee on Civil and Constitutional Rights. *Racial Disparities in Federal Death Penalty Prosecutions, 1988–1994*. Staff Report, 103rd Congress, 2nd sess., March 1994. www.deathpenaltyinfo.org/racial-disparities-federal-death-penalty-prosecutions-1988-1994.
Corbally, Sarah F., Donald C. Bross, and Victor E. Flango. "Filing of Amicus Curiae Briefs in Courts of Last Resort: 1960–2000." *Justice System Journal* 25 (2004): 39.
Cornfield, Michael, Jonathan Carson, Alison Kalis, and Emily Simon. *Buzz, Blogs, and Beyond: The Internet and the National Discourse in the Fall of 2004*, Preliminary Report. May 16, 2005. Pew Internet and American Life Project. www.pewtrusts.org/uploadedFiles/www pewtrustsorg/News/Press_Releases/Society_and_the_Internet/PIP_Blogs_051605.pdf.
Costanzo, Mark. *Just Revenge: Costs and Consequences of the Death Penalty*. New York: St. Martin's, 1997.
Courselle, Diane E. "Struggling with Deliberative Secrecy, Jury Independence, and Jury Reform." *South Carolina Law Review* 57 (2005): 203.
Cowan, Claudia L., William C. Thompson, and Phoebe C. Ellsworth. "The Effects of Death Qualification on Jurors' Predisposition to Convict and on the Quality of Deliberation." *Law and Human Behavior* 8, nos. 1 & 2 (June 1984): 53–79.
Criminal Justice Project of the NAACP Legal Defense and Educational Fund. *Death Row USA: Summer 2009*. deathpenaltyinfo.org/documents/DRUSASummer2009.pdf.
Crossan, John Dominic. *God and Empire: Jesus against Rome, Then and Now*. New York: HarperOne, 2007.
———. *The Historical Jesus: The Life of a Mediterranean Jewish Peasant*. San Francisco: HarperSanFrancisco, 1993.
Crotty, Kevin. "Democracy, Tragedy, and Responsibility: The Greek Case." In *Taking Responsibility: Comparative Perspectives*, edited by Winston Davis, 106–20. Charlottesville: University Press of Virginia, 2001.
Culbert, Jennifer L. "Beyond Intention: A Critique of the 'Normal' Criminal Agency, Responsibility, and Punishment in American Death Penalty Jurisprudence." In *The Killing*

State: Capital Punishment in Law, Politics, and Culture, edited by Austin Sarat, 206–25. New York: Oxford University Press, 2001.

———. *Dead Certainty: The Death Penalty and the Problem of Judgment*. Stanford: Stanford University Press, 2008.

Curran, Charles E. *Directions in Fundamental Moral Theology*. Notre Dame, IN: University of Notre Dame Press, 1985.

Curtis, Edward E., IV. "Why Muslims Matter to U.S. History, 1730–1945." Lecture given at the Heidelberg Center for American Studies, Heidelberg University, December 3, 2009.

Dan-Cohen, Meir. "Revising the Past: On the Metaphysics of Repentance, Forgiveness and Pardon." In *Forgiveness, Mercy and Clemency*, edited by Austin Sarat and Nasser Hussain, 117–37. Stanford: Stanford University Press, 2007.

Darden, Willie Jasper, Jr. "An Inhumane Way of Death." In *Facing the Death Penalty: Essays on a Cruel and Unusual Punishment*, edited by Michael L. Radelet, 203–5. Philadelphia: Temple University Press, 1989.

Davidoff, Steven. "A Comparative Study of the Jewish and the United States Constitutional Law of Capital Punishment." *ILSA Journal of International and Comparative Law* 3 (1996): 93.

Davis, Angela Y. *Are Prisons Obsolete?* New York: Seven Stories, 2003.

Davis, G. Scott. "Ethics." In *The Blackwell Companion to the Study of Religion*, edited by Robert A. Segal, 239–54. Oxford: Blackwell, 2006.

Davis, John Jefferson. *Evangelical Ethics*. Rev. and exp. 3rd ed. Phillipsburg, NJ: Presbyterian and Reformed, 2004.

Dawson-Edwards, Cherie. "Enfranchising Convicted Felons: Current Research on Opinions towards Felon Voting Rights." *Journal of Offender Rehabilitation* 46, nos. 3 & 4 (May 2008): 13–29.

De Sola Pool, Rev. D. *Capital Punishment among the Jews*. New York: Bloch, 1916.

Deans, Marie. "Living in Babylon." In *A Punishment in Search of a Crime: Americans Speak Out against the Death Penalty*, edited by Ian Gray and Moira Stanley, 71–77. New York: Avon Books, 1989.

———. "Working against the Death Penalty." In *Writing for Their Lives: Death Row USA*, edited by Marie Mulvey-Roberts, 59–62. Champaign: University of Illinois Press, 2007.

Denno, Deborah W. "The Lethal Injection Quandary: How Medicine Has Dismantled the Death Penalty." *Fordham Law Review* 76 (2007): 49.

———. "When Legislatures Delegate Death: The Troubling Paradox behind State Uses of Electrocution and Lethal Injection and What It Says about Us." *Ohio State Law Journal* 63 (2002): 63.

Dieter, Richard C. *The Death Penalty in Black and White: Who Lives, Who Dies, Who Decides*. Washington, DC: DPIC, 1998. www.deathpenaltyinfo.org/death-penalty-black-and-white-who-lives-who-dies-who-decides.

———. *Millions Misspent: What Politicians Don't Say about the High Costs of the Death Penalty*. Rev. ed. Washington, DC: DPIC, 1994. www.deathpenaltyinfo.org/node/599.

———. *On the Front Line: Law Enforcement Views on the Death Penalty*. Washington, DC: DPIC, 1995.

———. *Smart on Crime: Reconsidering the Death Penalty in a Time of Economic Crisis*. October 20, 2009. www.deathpenaltyinfo.org/documents/CostsRptFinal.pdf.

———. *With Justice for Few: The Growing Crisis in Death Penalty Representation*. Washington, DC: DPIC, 1995.

Ditchfield, Andrew. "Challenging the Intrastate Disparities in the Application of Capital Punishment Statutes." *Georgetown Law Review* 95 (2005): 801.

Dougherty, Kevin D., Byron R. Johnson, and Edward C. Polston. "Recovering the Lost: Remeasuring U.S. Religious Affiliation." *Journal for the Scientific Study of Religion* 46, no. 4 (December 2007): 483–99.

Douglas, Davison M. "God and the Executioner: The Influence of Western Religion on the Use of the Death Penalty." *William and Mary Bill of Rights Journal* 9 (2000): 137.

Dow, David R. *The Autobiography of an Execution*. New York: Twelve, 2010.

Durkheim, Emile. *The Division of Labor in Society*. Translated by W. D. Halls. New York: Free Press, 1997.

———. *Moral Education*. Translated by Everett K. Wilson and Herman Schnurer. Mineola, NY: Dover, 2002.

Dworkin, Ronald. *Life's Dominion: An Argument about Abortion and Euthanasia*. New York: HarperCollins, 1993.

Edds, Margaret. *An Expendable Man: The Near-Execution of Earl Washington, Jr.* New York: New York University Press, 2003.

Ehrlich, Isaac. "The Deterrent Effect of Capital Punishment: A Question of Life and Death." *American Economic Review* 65, no. 3 (June 1975): 397–417.

Eisenberg, Theodore, Stephen P. Garvey, and Martin T. Wells. "Forecasting Life and Death: Juror Race, Religion, and Attitude toward the Death Penalty." *Journal of Legal Studies* 30 (June 2001): 277–311.

———. "Victim Characteristics and Victim Impact Evidence in South Carolina Capital Cases." *Cornell Law Review* 83 (1998): 306.

Ekrich, A. Roger. "Exiles in the Promised Land: Convict Labor in the Eighteenth-Century Chesapeake." *Maryland Historical Magazine* 82, no. 2 (Summer 1987): 95–122.

El Fadl, Khaled Abou. "The Death Penalty, Mercy, and Islam: A Call for Retrospection." In *Religion and the Death Penalty: A Call for Reckoning*, edited by Erik C. Owens, John P. Carlson, and Eric P. Elshtain, 73–105. Grand Rapids, MI: Wm. B. Eerdmans, 2004.

Elisha, Omri. *Moral Ambition: Mobilization and Social Outreach in Evangelical Megachurches*. Berkeley: University of California Press, 2011.

Ellison, Christopher G., and Marc A. Musick. "Southern Intolerance: A Fundamentalist Effect?" *Social Forces* 72, no. 2 (December 1993): 379–98.

Ellsworth, Phoebe C., and Samuel R. Gross. "Hardening of the Attitudes: Americans' Views on the Death Penalty." *Journal of Social Issues* 50, no. 2 (Summer 1994): 19–52.

Elshtain, Jean Bethke. *Who Are We? Critical Reflections and Hopeful Possibilities*. Grand Rapids, MI: Wm. B. Eerdmans, 2000.

———. Foreword to *Religion and the Death Penalty: A Call for Reckoning*, edited by Eric C. Owens, John D. Carlson, and Eric P. Elshtain. Grand Rapids, MI: Wm. B. Eerdmans, 2004.

Ennis, Bruce J. "Symposium on Supreme Court Advocacy: Effective Amicus Briefs." *Catholic University Law Review* 33 (1984): 603.

Epstein, Rabbi Dr. I., ed. *Sanhedrin*. Translated by H. Freedman and Jacob Shachter. N.d. www.come-and-hear.com/sanhedrin/.

Erez, Edna. "Thou Shalt Not Execute: Hebrew Law Perspective on Capital Punishment." *Criminology* 19, no. 1 (May 1981): 25–43.

Espy, M. Watt, and John Ortiz Smykla. *Executions in the United States, 1608–2002*. Based on statistics current as of March 10, 2011. deathpenaltyinfo.org/executions-us-1608-2002-espy-file.

Evans, Bette Novitt. *Interpreting the Free Exercise of Religion: The Constitution and American Pluralism*. Chapel Hill: University of North Carolina Press, 1997.

Faulkner, William. *As I Lay Dying*. Corrected text. New York: Vintage International, 1990.

Feinberg, John S., and Paul D. Feinberg. *Ethics for a Brave New World*. Wheaton, IL: Crossways Books, 1993.

Feld, Lowell, and Nate Wilcox. *Netroots Rising: How a Citizen Army of Bloggers and Online Activists Is Changing American Politics*. Westport, CT: Praeger, 2008.

Filler, Louis. "Movements to Abolish the Death Penalty in the United States." *Annals of the American Academy of Political and Social Science* 284 (November 1952): 124–36.

Finkelman, Byrgen. *Child Abuse: Short- and Long-Term Effects*. New York: Routledge, 1995.

Fitzpatrick, Joan, and Alice Miller. "International Standards on the Death Penalty: Shifting Discourse." *Brooklyn Journal of International Law* 19 (1993): 278.

Fitzpatrick, Peter. "'Always More to Do': Capital Punishment and the (De)Composition of Law." In *The Killing State: Capital Punishment in Law, Politics, and Culture*, edited by Austin Sarat, 117–36. New York: Oxford University Press, 1999.

Fodor, Jim. "Reading the Scriptures: Rehearsing Identity, Practicing Character." In *The Blackwell Companion to Christian Ethics*, edited by Stanley Hauerwas and Samuel Wells, 141–55. Oxford: Blackwell, 2006.

Foucault, Michel. "About the Concept of the 'Dangerous Individual' in 19th-Century Legal Psychiatry." Translated by Alain Baudot and Jane Couchman. *International Journal of Law and Psychiatry* 1, no. 1 (February 1978): 1–18.

———. *Discipline and Punish: The Birth of the Prison*. Translated by Alan Sheridan. New York: Vintage Books, 1995.

Frankfurter, Felix. "The Problem of Capital Punishment" (1950). In *Of Laws and Men: Papers and Addresses of Felix Frankfurter*, edited by Philip Elman, 81. New York: Harcourt Brace, 1956.

Franklin, Benjamin. *The Works of Dr. Benjamin Franklin; Consisting of Essays, Humorous, Moral and Literary: With His Life, Written by Himself*. Boston: T. Bedlington, 1825.

Friedman, Lawrence M. *A History of American Law*. 3rd ed. New York: Touchstone, 2005.

Froese, Paul, and Christopher D. Bader. "God in America: Why Theology Is Not Simply the Concern of the Philosophers." *Journal for the Scientific Study of Religion* 46, no. 4 (December 2007): 465–81.

Frykholm, Amy Johnson. *Rapture Culture: Left Behind in Evangelical America*. New York: Oxford University Press, 2004.

Galliher, John F., Larry W. Koch, David Patrick Keys, and Teresa J. Guess. *America without the Death Penalty: States Leading the Way*. Boston: Northeastern University Press, 2002.

Galliher, John F., Gregory Ray, and Brent Cook. "Abolition and Reinstatement of Capital Punishment during the Progressive Era and Early 20th Century." *Journal of Criminal Law and Criminology* 83 (1983): 538.

Gallup, George, Jr., and D. Michael Lindsay. *Surveying the Religious Landscape: Trends in U.S. Beliefs*. Harrisburg, PA: Morehouse, 1999.

Garcia, Ruben J. "A Democratic Theory of Amicus Advocacy." *Florida State University Law Review* 325 (2008): 315.

Garland, David. *The Culture of Control: Crime and Social Order in Contemporary Society*. Chicago: University of Chicago Press, 2002.

———. *Peculiar Institution: America's Death Penalty in an Age of Abolition*. Cambridge, MA: Belknap Press of Harvard University Press, 2010.

———. "Punishment and Culture: The Symbolic Dimension of Criminal Justice." *Studies in Law, Politics and Society* 11 (1991): 191.

———. *Punishment and Modern Society: A Study in Social Theory*. Chicago: University of Chicago Press, 1990.

Garvey, Stephen P., ed. *Beyond Repair? America's Death Penalty*. Durham, NC: Duke University Press, 2002.

Gey, Steven. "Why Is Religion Special?: Reconsidering the Accommodation of Religion under the Religion Clauses of the First Amendment." *University of Pittsburgh Law Review* 52 (1990): 75.

Giarratano, Joseph M. "The Pains of Life." In *Facing the Death Penalty: Essays on a Cruel and Unusual Punishment*, edited by Michael L. Radelet, 193–97. Philadelphia: Temple University Press, 1989.

Girard, René. *I See Satan Fall Like Lightning*. Translated by James G. Williams. Maryknoll, NY: Orbis Books, 2001.

———. *The Scapegoat*. Translated by Yvonne Freccero. Baltimore: Johns Hopkins University Press, 1989.

———. *Things Hidden since the Foundation of the World*. Translated by Stephen Bann and Michael Metteer. Stanford: Stanford University Press, 1987.

———. *Violence and the Sacred*. Translated by Patrick Gregory. Baltimore: Johns Hopkins University Press, 1977.

Godbold, John C. "Pro Bono Representation of Death Sentenced Inmates." *Record of the Association of the Bar of the City of New York* 42 (1987): 865.

Gorringe, Timothy. *God's Just Vengeance*. Cambridge: Cambridge University Press, 2002.

Grammich, Clifford, et al. *2010 U.S. Religion Census: Religious Congregations and Membership Study*. Kansas City, MO: Nazarene, 2012.

Grann, David. "Trial by Fire: Did Texas Execute an Innocent Man?" *New Yorker*, September 7, 2009, www.newyorker.com/reporting/2009/09/07/090907fa_fact_grann.

Grasmick, Harold G., Robert J. Bursik Jr., and Brenda Sims Blackwell. "Religious Beliefs and Public Support for the Death Penalty for Juveniles and Adults." *Journal of Crime and Justice* 16, no. 2 (1993): 59–86.

Grasmick, Harold G., John K. Cochran, Robert J. Bursik Jr., and M'Lou Kempel. "Religion, Punitive Justice, and Support for the Death Penalty." *Justice Quarterly* 10, no. 2 (June 1993): 289–314.

Grasmick, Harold G., and Anne McGill. "Religion, Attribution Style, and Punitiveness toward Juvenile Offenders." *Criminology* 32, no. 1 (February 1994): 23–46.

Gray, Ian, and Moira Stanley, eds. *A Punishment in Search of a Crime: Americans Speak Out against the Death Penalty*. New York: Avon Books, 1989.

Gross, Samuel R. "Lost Lives: Miscarriages of Justice in Capital Cases." *Law and Contemporary Problems* 61 (1988): 125.

———. "Update: American Public Opinion on the Death Penalty—It's Getting Personal." *Cornell Law Review* 83 (1998): 1148.

Gudjonsson, Gisli H. *The Psychology of Interrogations and Confessions: A Handbook*. Chichester: John Wesley and Sons, 2003.

Haapasalo, Jaana, and Elina Pokela. "Child-Rearing and Child Abuse Antecedents of Criminality." *Aggression and Violent Behavior* 4, no. 1 (Spring 1999): 107–27.

Haas, Kenneth C., and James A. Inciardi, eds. *Challenging Capital Punishment: Legal and Social Sciences Approaches*. Newbury Park, CA: Sage, 1989.

Haden, Ed R., and Kelly Fitzgerald. "The Role of Amicus Briefs." *Alabama Lawyer* 70 (2009): 114.

Haines, Herbert H. *Against Capital Punishment: The Anti-Death Penalty Movement in America, 1972–1994*. New York: Oxford University Press, 1996.

Halttunen, Karen. *Murder Most Foul: The Killer and the American Gothic Imagination*. Cambridge, MA: Harvard University Press, 1998.

Hamm, Theodore. *Rebel and a Cause: Caryl Chessman and the Politics of the Death Penalty in Postwar California, 1948–1974*. Berkeley: University of California Press, 2001.

Hanks, Gardner C. *Against the Death Penalty: Christian and Secular Arguments against Capital Punishment*. Scottdale, PA: Herald, 1997.

———. *Capital Punishment and the Bible*. Scottdale, PA: Herald, 2002.

Harding, Susan Friend. *The Book of Jerry Falwell: Fundamentalist Language and Politics*. Princeton, NJ: Princeton University Press, 2000.

———. "Representing Fundamentalism: The Problem of the Repugnant Cultural Other." *Social Research* 58, no. 2 (Summer 1991): 373–93.

Harris, Michael J. "Amicus Curiae: Friend or Foe? The Limits of Friendship in American Jurisprudence." *Suffolk Journal of Trial and Appellate Advocacy* 5 (2000): 1.

Hart, H. L. A. *Punishment and Responsibility: Essays in the Philosophy of Law*. Oxford: Clarendon, 1968.

Hatfield, Steven A. "Criminal Punishment in America: From the Colonial to the Modern Era." *United States Air Force Academy Journal of Legal Studies* 1 (1990): 139.

Hauerwas, Stanley, and Samuel Wells, eds. *The Blackwell Companion to Christian Ethics*. Oxford: Blackwell, 2006.

Hawk, Sharon Blanchard. "*State v. Mann*: Extraneous Prejudicial Information in the Jury Room: Beautiful Minds Allowed." *New Mexico Law Review* 34 (2004): 149.

Heifetz, Roland A. *Leadership without Easy Answers*. Cambridge, MA: Belknap Press of Harvard University Press, 1994.

Hervieu-Leger, Daniele. *Religion as a Chain of Memory*. Translated by Simon Lee. Cambridge: Polity, 2000.

Higginbotham, Patrick E. "Juries and the Death Penalty." *Case Western Law Review* 41 (1991): 1047.

Hodgkinson, Peter. "Capital Punishment: Meeting the Needs of the Families of the Homicide Victim and the Condemned." In *Capital Punishment: Strategies for Abolition*, edited by Peter Hodgkinson and William A. Schabas, 332–58. New York: Cambridge University Press, 2004.

Hodgkinson, Peter, and William A. Schabas, eds. *Capital Punishment: Strategies for Abolition*. New York: Cambridge University Press, 2004.

Hood, Roger, and Carolyn Hoyle. *The Death Penalty: A Worldwide Perspective*. 4th ed. New York: Oxford University Press, 2008.

Horn, James F. *A Land as God Made It: Jamestown and the Birth of America*. New York: Basic Books, 2005.

Horrigan, Damien P. "Of Compassion and Capital Punishment: A Buddhist Perspective on the Death Penalty." *American Journal of Jurisprudence* 41 (1996): 271.

Horsley, Richard A., ed. *Paul and Empire: Religion and Power in Roman Imperial Society*. Harrisburg, PA: Trinity Press International, 1997.

House, H. Wayne. "The New Testament and Moral Arguments for Capital Punishment." In *The Death Penalty in America: Current Controversies*, edited by Hugo Adam Bedau, 415–28.

House, H. Wayne, and John Howard Yoder. *The Death Penalty Debate*. Dallas: Word, 1991.

Ingle, Joseph B. *Last Rights: 13 Fatal Encounters with the State's Justice*. Nashville: Abingdon, 1990.

Jackson, Rev. Jesse L., Sr., Rep. Jesse L. Jackson Jr., and Bruce Shapiro. *Legal Lynching: The Death Penalty and America's Future*. New York: New Press, 2001.

Jackson, Joe, and William F. Burke Jr. *Dead Run: The Shocking Story of Dennis Stockton and Life on Death Row in America*. New York: Walker and Company, 2000.

Jackson, Sherri. "Too Young to Die—Juveniles and the Death Penalty." *New England Journal on Crime and Civil Confinement* 22, no. 2 (Spring 1996): 391–437.

Jaeger, Marietta. *The Lost Child*. Grand Rapids, MI: Zondervan, 1983.

Jewett, Robert. *Mission and Menace: Four Centuries of American Religious Zeal*. Minneapolis: Fortress, 2008.

Jewett, Robert, and John Shelton Lawrence. *Captain America and the Crusade against Evil: The Dilemma of Zealous Nationalism*. Grand Rapids, MI: Wm. B. Eerdmans, 2003.

Johnson, Robert. *Death Work: A Study of the Modern Execution Process*. Belmont, CA: Thomson/Wadsworth, 2006.

Josephus, Flavius. *Against Apion*. Translated by Henry St. John Thackeray. Cambridge, MA: Harvard University Press, 1976.

Juergensmeyer, Mark, ed. *The Oxford Handbook of Global Religions*. New York: Oxford University Press, 2006.

Kadane, Joseph B. "A Note on Taking Account of the Automatic Death Penalty Jurors." *Law and Human Behavior* 8, nos. 1 & 2 (June 1984): 115–20.

Kagan, Robert A., Bliss Cartwright, Lawrence M. Friedman, and Stanton Wheeler. "The Business of State Supreme Courts, 1870–1970." *Stanford Law Review* 30 (1977): 121.

Kato, Robert M. "Note and Comment: The Juvenile Death Penalty." *Journal of Juvenile Law* 18 (1997): 12.

Kearney, Joseph D., and Thomas W. Merrill. "The Influence of Amicus Curiae Briefs on the Supreme Court." *University of Pennsylvania Law Review* 148 (2000): 743.

Keating, Frank. "The Death Penalty: What's All the Debate About?" In *Religion and the Death Penalty: A Call for Reckoning*, edited by Eric C. Owens, John D. Carlson, and Eric P. Elshtain, 213–20. Grand Rapids, MI: Wm. B. Eerdmans, 2004.

Keve, Paul. *The History of Corrections in Virginia*. Charlottesville: University Press of Virginia, 1986.

———. *Prison Life and Human Worth*. Minneapolis: University of Minnesota Press, 1974.

King, Rachel. *Capital Consequences: Families of the Condemned Tell Their Stories*. New Brunswick, NJ: Rutgers University Press, 2005.

———. *Don't Kill in Our Names: Families of Murder Victims Speak Out against the Death Penalty*. New Brunswick, NJ: Rutgers University Press, 2003.

Koh, Harold Hongju. "Paying 'Decent Respect' to World Opinion on the Death Penalty." *University of California Davis Law Review* 35 (2002): 1085.

Konig, David Thomas. "Dale's Law and the Non-Common Law Origins of Criminal Justice in Virginia." *American Journal of Legal History* 26, no. 4 (October 1982): 354–75.

Kozinski, Alex. "Tinkering with Death." In *Debating the Death Penalty: Should America Have Capital Punishment? The Experts from Both Sides Make Their Case*, edited by Hugo Adam Bedau and Paul G. Cassell, 1–14. New York: Oxford University Press, 2004.

Kreitzberg, Ellen, and David Richter. "But Can It Be Fixed? A Look at Constitutional Challenges to Lethal Injection Executions." *Santa Clara Law Review* 47 (2007): 445.

Krislov, Samuel. "The Amicus Curiae Brief: From Friendship to Advocacy." *Yale Law Journal* 72 (1963): 694.

Kroll, Michael. "Chattahoochee Judicial District: Buckle of the Death Belt: The Death Penalty in Microcosm." Death Penalty Information Center, 1991. deathpenaltyinfo.org/chattahoochee-judicial-district-buckle-death-belt-death-penalty-microcosm.

Kurland, Philip B., Gerhard Casper, and Dennis J. Hutchinson, eds. *The Supreme Court Review, 1983*. Chicago: University of Chicago Press, 1984.

Lakoff, George. *Moral Politics: How Liberals and Conservatives Think*. 2nd ed. Chicago: University of Chicago Press, 2002.

Lambrix, C. Michael. "The Isolation of Death Row." In *Facing the Death Penalty: Essays on a Cruel and Unusual Punishment*, edited by Michael L. Radelet, 198–202. Philadelphia: Temple University Press, 1989.

Lancaster, Jennie. "A Death and a Dilemma." *Congregations*, November/December 1993, 15–16.

Latzer, Barry. *Death Penalty Cases: Leading U.S. Supreme Court Cases on Capital Punishment*. 2nd ed. Boston: Butterworth Heinemann, 2002.

Lawrence, John Shelton, and Robert Jewett. *The Myth of the American Superhero*. Grand Rapids, MI: Wm. B. Eerdmans, 2002.

"The Lesson of Karla Faye Tucker." Editorial. *Christianity Today*, April 6, 1998, 15–16.

Levinson, Jeffrey. "Note: Don't Let Sleeping Lawyers Lie: Raising the Standards for Effective Assistance of Counsel." *American Criminal Law Review* 38 (2001): 147.

Lewis, Peter W. "Killing the Killers: A Post-*Furman* Profile of Florida's Condemned: A Personal Account." *Crime and Delinquency* 25, no. 2 (April 1979): 200–211.

Liebman, James S. *A Broken System, Part II: Why There Is So Much Error in Capital Cases, and What Can Be Done about It*. February 11, 2002. www2.law.columbia.edu/brokensystem2/.

Lifton, Robert Jay, and Greg Mitchell. *Who Owns Death? Capital Punishment, the American Conscience, and the End of Executions*. New York: Perennial, 2002.

Lincoln, Bruce. *Holy Terrors: Thinking about Religion after September 11*. 2nd ed. Chicago: University of Chicago Press, 2006.

Lind, Millard. *The Sound of Sheer Silence and the Killing State: The Death Penalty and the Bible*. Telford, PA: Cascadia, 2004.

Longstreth, Joseph E., and Alan Bisbort. "Caryl Chessman, Writer." In *Caryl Chessman, Cell 2245, Death Row*. New York: Carroll and Graf, 2006.

Lowman, Michael K. "The Litigating Amicus Curiae: When Does the Party Begin after the Friends Leave?" *American University Law Review* 41 (1992): 1243.

Lucas, Alison. "Friends of the Court? The Ethics of Amicus Brief Writing in First Amendment Litigation." *Fordham Urban Law Journal* 26 (1999): 1605.

Lytle, Leslie. *Execution's Doorstep: True Stories of the Innocent and Near Damned*. Boston: Northeastern University Press, 2008

Mackey, Philip English. *Hanging in the Balance: The Anti-Capital Punishment Movement in New York State, 1776–1861*. New York: Garland, 1982.

———. *Voices against Death: American Opposition to Capital Punishment, 1787–1975*. New York: Burt Franklin, 1976.

Madison, James. "Memorial and Remonstrance against Religious Assessments." In *The Complete Madison: His Basic Writings*, edited by Saul K. Padover, 299–306. New York: Harper and Brothers, 1953.

Magnani, Laura. *America's First Penitentiary: A 200-Year Old Failure*. Philadelphia: American Friends Service Committee, 1990.

Magnani, Laura, and Harmon L. Wray. *Beyond Prisons: A New Interfaith Paradigm for Our Failed Prison System*. Minneapolis: Fortress, 2006.

Maguire, Daniel C. *The Horrors We Bless: Rethinking the Just-War Legacy*. Minneapolis: Fortress, 2007.

Mansfield, Andrew S. "Religious Arguments and the United States Supreme Court: A Review of Amicus Curiae Briefs Filed by Religious Organizations." *Cardozo Law, Policy and Ethics Journal* 7 (2009): 343.

Marcus, George E. *Ethnography through Thick and Thin*. Princeton, NJ: Princeton University Press, 1998.

Marder, Nancy S. "Deliberations and Disclosures: A Study of Post-Verdict Interviews of Jurors." *Iowa Law Review* 82 (1997): 465.

Markman, Stephen J., and Paul G. Cassell. "Protecting the Innocent: A Response to the Bedau-Radelet Study." *Stanford Law Review* 41 (1988): 121.

Marquart, James W., and Jonathan R. Sorensen. "A National Study of the Furman-Commuted Inmates: Assessing the Threat to Society from Capital Offenders." *Loyola of Los Angeles Law Review* 23 (1989): 5.

Marquis, Joshua K. "Truth and Consequences: The Penalty of Death." In *Debating the Death Penalty: Should America Have Capital Punishment? The Experts from Both Sides Make Their Case*, edited by Hugo Adam Bedau and Paul G. Cassell, 117–51. New York: Oxford University Press, 2004.

Marshall, Christopher D. *Beyond Retribution: A New Testament Vision for Justice, Crime, and Punishment*. Grand Rapids, MI: Wm. B. Eerdmans, 2001.

Masur, Louis P. *Rites of Execution: Capital Punishment and the Transformation of American Culture, 1776–1865*. New York: Oxford University Press, 1989.

Matravers, Matt. *Justice and Punishment: The Rationale of Coercion*. New York: Oxford University Press, 2000.

———, ed. *Punishment and Political Theory*. Oxford: Hart, 1999.

Mauer, Marc, and Michael Coyle. "The Social Cost of America's Race to Incarcerate." *Journal of Religion and Spirituality in Social Work* 23, nos. 1 & 2 (2008): 7–25.

May, Jane M. "A Juror's Perspective." In Hunter P. Mabry, *Capital Punishment: A Faith-Based Study*, 45–46. Nashville: Abingdon, 2002.

McBride, James. "Capital Punishment as the Unconstitutional Establishment of Religion: A Girardian Reading of the Death Penalty." *Journal of Church and State* 37, no. 2 (Spring 1995): 263–86.

McGuire, Russell E. "Capital Punishment for Multiple Murders That Occur in the Same Act or Transaction: A Guide to Define the Abstract." *Thomas M. Cooley Journal of Practical and Clinical Law* 2 (January 1999): 263.

McNair, Rachel M., and Stephen Zunes. *Consistently Opposing Killing: From Abortion to Assisted Suicide, the Death Penalty, and War*. Westport, CT: Praeger, 2008.

Megivern, James. *The Death Penalty: An Historical and Theological Survey*. New York: Paulist, 1997.

Mello, Michael. "Facing Death Alone: The Post-Conviction Attorney Crisis on Death Row." *American University Law Review* 37 (1988): 513.

Melton, J. Gordon, ed. *The Churches Speak on: Capital Punishment*. Detroit: Gale Research, 1989.

Meltsner, Michael. *Cruel and Unusual: The Supreme Court and Capital Punishment*. New York: Random House, 1973.

Miethe, Terance D., and Hong Lu. *Punishment: A Comparative Historical Perspective*. Cambridge: Cambridge University Press, 2005.

Moose, Charles A., and Charles Fleming. *Three Weeks in October: The Manhunt for the Serial Sniper*. New York: Signet, 2004.

Morgan, David. *The Sacred Gaze: Religious Visual Culture in Theory and Practice*. Berkeley: University of California Press, 2005.

Mulvey-Roberts, Marie, ed. *Writing for Their Lives: Death Row USA*. Champaign: University of Illinois Press, 2007.

Murray, Mark. "Test of Faith." *Washington Monthly*, October/November 2005. www.washingtonmonthly.com/features/2005/0510.murray.html.

Myers, Ched. *Binding the Strong Man: A Political Reading of Mark's Story of Jesus*. 20th anniv. ed. Maryknoll, NY: Orbis Books, 2008.

Nadler, Janice, and Mary R. Rose. "Victim Impact Testimony and the Psychology of Punishment." *Cornell Law Review* 88 (2003): 420.

Nanda, Ved P. "Islam and International Human Rights Law: Selected Aspects." *American Society of International Law Proceedings* 87 (1993): 327.

Nathanson, Stephen. *An Eye for an Eye? The Immorality of Punishing by Death*. 2nd ed. Lanham, MD: Rowman and Littlefield, 2001.

National Center for State Courts. *Habeas Corpus in State and Federal Courts*. Williamsburg, VA: National Center for State Courts, 1994.

Navasky, Victor S. "Deportation as Punishment." *University of Kansas City Law Review* 27 (1958–59): 213.

Nettesheim, Hon. Neal, and Clare Ryan. "Friend of the Court Briefs: What the Curiae Wants in an Amicus." *Wisconsin Lawyer* 80 (2007): 11.

Newman, Graeme. *The Punishment Response*. New York: J. B. Lippincott, 1978.

Niebuhr, H. Richard. *The Responsible Self: An Essay in Christian Moral Theology*. Louisville: Westminster John Knox, 1999.

Niven, John. *The Second Coming*. London: Vintage Books, 2011.

"Note: Capital Punishment in Virginia." *Virginia Law Review* 58 (1972): 97.

Novak, David. "Can Capital Punishment Ever Be Justified in the Jewish Tradition?" In *Religion and the Death Penalty: A Call for Reckoning*, edited by Erik C. Owens, John P. Carlson, and Eric P. Elshtain, 31–47. Grand Rapids, MI: Wm. B. Eerdmans, 2004.

Nygaard, Richard L. "Victims of Vengeance." *Lutheran*, August 1995, 22–25.

O'Donovan, Oliver. "Payback: Thinking about Retribution." *Books and Culture* 6, no. 4 (July/August 2000): 16–21.

Oshinsky, David M. *Capital Punishment on Trial: Furman v. Georgia and the Death Penalty in Modern America*. Lawrence: University Press of Kansas, 2010.

Osler, Mark. *Jesus on Death Row: The Trial of Jesus and American Capital Punishment*. Nashville: Abingdon, 2009.

Owens, Eric C., John D. Carlson, and Eric P. Elshtain, eds. *Religion and the Death Penalty: A Call for Reckoning*. Grand Rapids, MI: Wm. B. Eerdmans, 2004.

Ozanne, Peter A. "Why Does America Still Have a Death Penalty?" In *Criminal Justice in the United States and Germany—Strafrecht in den Vereinigten Staaten und Deutschland*. Publications of the Bavarian American Academy, vol. 6, 55–71. Heidelberg: Universitätsverlag Winter, 2006.

Parenti, Christian. *Lockdown America: Police and Prisons in the Age of Crisis*. New York: Verso, 2000.

Park, Jerry Z., and Joseph Baker. "What Would Jesus Buy: American Consumption of Religious and Spiritual Material Goods." *Journal for the Scientific Study of Religion* 46, no. 4 (December 2007): 501–17.

Parlee, Randy S. "A Primer on Amicus Curiae Briefs." *Wisconsin Lawyer* 62 (1989): 14.

Paternoster, Raymond, et al. *An Empirical Analysis of Maryland's Death Sentencing System with Respect to the Influence of Race and Legal Jurisdiction, Final Report*. N.d. www.newsdesk.umd.edu/pdf/finalrep.pdf.

Paternoster, Raymond, Robert Brame, and Sarah Bacon. *The Death Penalty: America's Experience with Capital Punishment*. New York: Oxford University Press, 2007.

Peck, Jeff. "Capital Corruption: The Trial of Jesus." *Jubilee* (Fall 2000): 3.

Pelke, Bill. *Journey of Hope: From Violence to Healing*. Bloomington, IN: Xlibris, 2003.

Peppers, Todd C., and Laura Trevett Anderson. *Anatomy of an Execution: The Life and Death of Douglas Christopher Thomas*. Boston: Northeastern University Press, 2009.

Perry, Michael J. *Constitutional Rights, Moral Controversy, and the Supreme Court*. Cambridge: Cambridge University Press, 2009.

Peterson, Ruth D., and William C. Bailey. "Is Capital Punishment an Effective Deterrent for Murder? An Examination of Social Science Research." In *America's Experiment with Capital Punishment: Reflections on the Past, Present and Future of the Ultimate Penal Sanction*, 2nd ed., edited by James R. Acker, Robert M. Bohm, and Charles S. Lanier, 157–82. Durham, NC: Carolina Academic Press, 2003.

Pew Charitable Trusts, The. *Ready, Willing and Able—Citizens Working for Change: A Survey of the Pew Partnership for Civic Change*. Philadelphia: Pew Charitable Trusts, 2001.

Pickett, Rev. Carroll, with Carlton Stowers. *Within These Walls: Memoirs of a Death House Chaplain*. New York: St. Martin's, 2002.

Pinchers, Charles. "Proclaiming: Naming and Describing." In *The Blackwell Companion to Christian Ethics*, edited by Stanley Hauerwas and Samuel Wells, 169–81. Oxford: Blackwell, 2006.

Pojman, Louis P. "Why the Death Penalty Is Morally Permissible." In *Debating the Death Penalty: Should America Have Capital Punishment? The Experts from Both Sides Make Their Case*, edited by Hugo Adam Bedau and Paul G. Cassell, 51–75. New York: Oxford University Press, 2004.

Pojman, Louis P., and Jeffrey Reiman. *The Death Penalty: For and Against*. Lanham, MD: Rowman and Littlefield, 1998.

Prejean, Sister Helen. *Dead Man Walking: An Eyewitness Account of the Death Penalty in the United States*. New York: Vintage Books, 1994.

———. "Death in Texas." *New York Review of Books*, January 13, 2005, www.nybooks.com/articles/17670.

———. *The Death of Innocents: An Eyewitness Account of Wrongful Executions*. New York: Random House, 2005.

———. "Would Jesus Pull the Switch?" *Salt of the Earth*, March/April 1997, 13.

Radelet, Michael L., ed. *Facing the Death Penalty: Essays on a Cruel and Unusual Punishment*. Philadelphia: Temple University Press, 1989.

Radelet, Michael L., and Ronald L. Akers. "Deterrence and the Death Penalty: The Views of Experts." *Journal of Criminal Law and Criminology* 87 (1996): 1.

Radelet, Michael L., and Hugo Adam Bedau. "The Execution of the Innocent." *Law and Contemporary Problems* 61 (1988): 105.

———. "The Myth of Infallibility: A Reply to Markman and Cassell." *Stanford Law Review* 41 (1988): 161.

Radelet, Michael L., Hugo Adam Bedau, and Constance E. Putnam. *In Spite of Innocence: Erroneous Convictions in Capital Cases*. Boston: Northeastern University Press, 1992.

Radelet, Michael L., and Marian J. Borg. "The Changing Nature of Death Penalty Debates." *Annual Review of Sociology* 26 (2000): 43–61.

Radin, Margaret Jane. "Cruel Punishment and Respect for Persons: Super Due Process for Death." *Southern California Law Review* 53 (1980): 1143.

Randa, Laura. *Society's Final Solution: A History and Discussion of the Death Penalty*. Lanham, MD: University Press of America, 1997.

Rawls, John. "The Idea of Public Reason Revisited." In *John Rawls: Collected Papers*, edited by Samuel Freeman, 573–615. Cambridge, MA: Harvard University Press, 1999.

Rawson, Tabor. *I Want to Live!: The Analysis of a Murder*. New York: American Library, 1958.

Recinella, Dale S. *The Biblical Truth about America's Death Penalty*. Boston: Northeastern University Press, 2004.

Reed, Julia. "Witness at the Execution." *Vogue* (June 1993): 191–95, 234–35.

Reichley, A. J. *Religion in American Public Life*. Washington, DC: Brookings Institution Press, 1985.

Reno, Janet, Eric H. Holder Jr., Raymond C. Fisher, Laurie Robinson, Noel Brennan, and Kathryn M. Turman. *Breaking the Cycle of Violence: Recommendations to Improve the Criminal Justice Response to Child Victims and Witnesses*. United States Department of Justice, Office of Justice Programs, Office for Victims of Crime (OVC), OVC Monograph series, June 1999. www.ojp.usdoj.gov/ovc/publications/factshts/pdftxt/monograph.pdf.

Ricoeur, Paul. *Oneself as Other*. Translated by Kathleen Blamey. Chicago: University of Chicago Press, 1995.

Riesebrodt, Martin. *The Promise of Salvation: A Theory of Religion*. Translated by Steven Rendall. Chicago: University of Chicago Press, 2010.

———. "Religion in Global Perspective." In *The Oxford Handbook of Global Religions*, edited by Mark Juergensmeyer, 597–610. New York: Oxford University Press, 2006.

Robinson, Paul H., and Markus Dirk Dubber. "An Introduction to the Model Penal Code." March 12, 1999. www.law.upenn.edu/fac/phrobins/intromodpencode.pdf.

Roko, Ellyde. "Note: Executioner Identities: Toward Recognizing a Right to Know Who Is Hiding beneath the Hood." *Fordham Law Review* 75 (2007): 2791.

Roose, Kevin. *The Unlikely Disciple: A Sinner's Semester at America's Holiest University*. New York: Grand Central, 2009.

Rosenbluth, Stanley, and Phyllis Rosenbluth. "Accidental Death Is Fate, Murder Is Pure Evil." In *Wounds That Do Not Bind: Victim-Based Perspectives on the Death Penalty*, edited by James R. Acker and David R. Karp, 103–10. Durham, NC: Carolina Academic Press, 2006.

Rosin, Hannah. *God's Harvard: A Christian College on a Mission to Save America*. Orlando, FL: Harcourt, 2007.

Roth, Michael P. *Crime and Punishment: A History of the Criminal Justice System*. Belmont, CA: Wadsworth, 2005.

Rothman, David J. "The Crime of Punishment." In *Punishment and Social Control*, enlarged 2nd ed., edited by Thomas G. Blomberg and Stanley Cohen, 403–16. New York: Aldine de Gruyter, 2003.

———. *The Discovery of the Asylum: Social Order and Disorder in the New Republic*. Boston: Little, Brown, 1971.

Royal Commission on Capital Punishment. *Report*. London: Her Majesty's Stationery Office, 1953.

Ruder, David S. "The Development of Legal Doctrine through Amicus Participation: The SEC Experience." *Wisconsin Law Review* 1989 (November–December 1989): 1167.

Rudolph, Daniel A. "The Misguided Reliance in American Jurisprudence on Jewish Law to Support the Moral Legitimacy of Capital Punishment." *American Criminal Law Review* 33 (1996): 437.

Rush, Benjamin. *Considerations on the injustice and impolicy of punishing murder by death* . . . Philadelphia, 1792.

———. *An enquiry into the effects of public punishments upon criminals and upon society. Read in the Society for Promoting Political Enquiries, convened at the house of His Excellency Benjamin Franklin, Esquire, in Philadelphia, March 9th, 1787*. Philadelphia, 1787.
———. *On the Punishment of Murder by Death*. London, 1793.
Rustad, Michael, and Thomas Koenig. "The Supreme Court and Junk Social Science: Selective Distortion in Amicus Briefs." *North Carolina Law Review* 72 (1993): 91.
Ryan, George. "An Address on the Death Penalty." June 3, 2002. Pew Forum on Religion and Public Life. pewforum.org/events/?EventID=28.
———. "I Must Act." In *Debating the Death Penalty: Should America Have Capital Punishment? The Experts from Both Sides Make Their Case*, edited by Hugo Adam Bedau and Paul G. Cassell, 218–34. New York: Oxford University Press, 2004.
———. "Reflections on the Death Penalty and the Moratorium." In *Religion and the Death Penalty: A Call for Reckoning*, edited by Erik C. Owens, John D. Carlson, and Eric P. Elshtain, 221–30. Grand Rapids, MI: Wm. B. Eerdmans, 2004.
Sachedina, Abdulaziz. "Civic Responsibility in Political Society: An Islamic Paradigm." In *Taking Responsibility: Comparative Perspectives*, edited by Winston Davis, 230–52. Charlottesville: University Press of Virginia, 2001.
Sandel, Michael. "Religious Liberty—Freedom of Conscience or Freedom of Choice." *Utah Law Review* 1989, no. 3 (1989): 597.
Sanderford, Dean. "The Sixth Amendment, Rule 606(B), and the Intrusion into Jury Deliberations of Religious Principles of Decision." *Tennessee Law Review* 74 (2007): 167.
Sandys, Marla. "Stacking the Deck for Guilt and Death: The Failure of Death Qualification to Ensure Impartiality." In *America's Experiment with Capital Punishment: Reflections on the Past, Present and Future of the Ultimate Penal Sanction*, 2nd ed., edited by James R. Acker, Robert M. Bohm, and Charles S. Lanier, 285–308. Durham, NC: Carolina Academic Press, 2003.
Sandys, Marla, and Edmund F. Mcgarrell. "Beyond the Bible Belt: The Influence (or Lack Thereof) of Religion on Attitudes toward the Death Penalty." *Journal of Crime and Justice* 20 (1997): 79.
Santoro, Anthony. "Hermeneutical Communities in Conflict: The Bible and the Capital Jury." In *Religion and State: From Separation to Cooperation? Legal-Philosophical Reflections for a De-Secularized World*, ASRP Beiheft, No. 118, edited by Bart C. Labuschagne and Ari M. Solon, 87–109. Stuttgart: Franz Steiner Verlag, 2009.
———. "The Prophet in His Own Words: Nat Turner's Biblical Construction." *Virginia Magazine of History and Biography* 116, no. 2 (June 2008): 114–49.
Sarat, Austin. *When the State Kills: Capital Punishment and the American Condition*. Princeton, NJ: Princeton University Press, 2001.
———, ed. *Crime and Punishment: Perspectives from the Humanities*. Studies in Law, Politics and Society, vol. 37. Amsterdam: Elsevier JAI, 2005.
———, ed. *The Killing State: Capital Punishment in Law, Politics, and Culture*. New York: Oxford University Press, 2001.
Sarat, Austin, and Christian Boulanger, eds. *The Cultural Lives of Capital Punishment: Comparative Perspectives*. Stanford: Stanford University Press, 2005.
Sarat, Austin, and Nasser Hussain, eds. *Forgiveness, Mercy and Clemency*. Stanford: Stanford University Press, 2007.
Sawicki, Marianne. *Crossing Galilee: Architectures of Contact in the Occupied Land of Jesus*. Harrisburg, PA: Trinity Press International, 2000.
Scalia, Antonin. "God's Justice and Ours: The Morality of Judicial Participation in the Death

Penalty." In *Religion and the Death Penalty: A Call for Reckoning*, edited by Eric C. Owens, John D. Carlson, and Eric P. Elshtain, 231–39. Grand Rapids, MI: Wm. B. Eerdmans, 2004.

Schaefer, Judith Kelleher. "'Under the Present Mode of Trial, Improper Verdicts Are Very Often Given': Criminal Procedure in the Trials of Slaves in Antebellum Louisiana." *Cardozo Law Review* 18 (1996): 635.

Scheck, Barry, Peter Neufield, and Jim Dwyer. *Actual Innocence: Five Days to Execution and Other Dispatches from the Wrongfully Convicted*. New York: Doubleday, 2000.

Schillebeeckx, Edward, ed. *Sacramental Reconciliation*. New York: Herder and Herder, 1971.

Schlabach, Gerald W. "Breaking Bread: Peace and War." In *The Blackwell Companion to Christian Ethics*, edited by Stanley Hauerwas and Samuel Wells, 360–74. Oxford: Blackwell, 2006.

Schuessler-Fiorenza, Elisabeth. "The Praxis of Coequal Discipleship." In *Paul and Empire: Religion and Power in Roman Imperial Society*, edited by Richard A. Horsley, 221–41. Harrisburg, PA: Trinity Press International, 1997.

Schwarz, Philip J. *Slave Laws in Virginia*. Athens: University of Georgia Press, 1996.

Schwed, Roger. *Abolition and Capital Punishment: The United States' Judicial, Political, and Moral Barometer*. New York: AMS, 1983.

Schweizer, Dan. "Fundamentals of Preparing a United States Supreme Court Amicus Brief." *Journal of Appellate Practice and Process* 5 (2003): 523.

Searle, John R. *Speech Acts: An Essay in the Philosophy of Language*. Cambridge: Cambridge University Press, 1969.

Seay, Scott D. *Hanging between Heaven and Earth: Capital Crime, Execution Preaching, and Theology in Early New England*. DeKalb: Northern Illinois University Press, 2009.

Segal, Robert A., ed. *The Blackwell Companion to the Study of Religion*. Oxford: Blackwell, 2006.

Sellin, Thorsten. *The Death Penalty: A Report for the Model Penal Code Project of the American Law Institute*. Philadelphia: American Law Institute, 1959.

Sewall, Michaela P. "Pushing Execution over the Constitutional Line: Forcible Medication of Condemned Inmates and the Eighth and Fourteenth Amendments." *Boston College Law Review* 51 (2010): 1279.

Shapiro, Barbara J. *"Beyond Reasonable Doubt" and "Probable Cause": Historical Perspectives on the Anglo-American Law of Evidence*. Berkeley: University of California Press, 1991.

Sharp, Susan F. *Hidden Victims: The Effects of the Death Penalty on Families of the Accused*. New Brunswick, NJ: Rutgers University Press, 2005.

Shavell, Steven. "A Note on Marginal Deterrence." *International Review of Law and Economics* 12 (1992): 345.

Shaw, Martin. *What Is Genocide?* Cambridge: Polity, 2007.

Shere, Dennis. *Cain's Redemption: A Story of Hope and Transformation in America's Bloodiest Prison*. Chicago: Northfield, 2005.

Shipman, Marlin. *"The Penalty Is Death": U.S. Newspaper Coverage of Women's Executions*. Columbia: University of Missouri Press, 2002.

Simpson, Reagan William. "How to Be a Good Friend to the Court: Strategic Use of Amicus Briefs." *Spring Brief* 28 (1999): 38.

Simson, Gary J., and Stephen P. Garvey. "Knockin' on Heaven's Door: Rethinking the Role of Religion in Death Penalty Cases." *Cornell Law Review* 86 (2001): 1090.

Singer, Richard C. *Criminal Procedure II: From Bail to Jail*. New York: Aspen, 2008.

Smith, Jonathan Z. "What a Difference Difference Makes." In *Relating Religion: Essays in the Study of Religion*, 251–303. Chicago: University of Chicago Press, 2004.

Smith, Stephanie. "Civil Banishment of Gang Members: Circumventing Criminal Due Process Requirements?" *University of Chicago Law Review* 67 (2000): 1461.

Songer, Michael J., and Isaac Unah. "The Effect of Race, Gender, and Location on Prosecutorial Decisions to Seek the Death Penalty in South Carolina." *South Carolina Law Review* 58 (2006): 161.

Spickard, James V., J. Shawn Landers, and Meredith B. McGuire, eds. *Personal Knowledge and Beyond: Reshaping the Ethnography of Religion*. New York: New York University Press, 2002.

Spiller, Cory. "*People v. Harlan*: The Colorado Supreme Court Takes a Step toward Eliminating Religious Influence on Juries." *Denver University Law Review* 83 (2005): 613.

Stark, Rodney. *What Americans Really Believe: New Findings from the Baylor Surveys of Religion*. Waco, TX: Baylor University Press, 2008.

Stassen, Glen H., ed. *Capital Punishment: A Reader*. Cleveland: Pilgrim, 1998.

Steiker, Carol S., and Jordan M. Steiker. "Sober Second Thoughts: Reflections on Two Decades of Constitutional Regulation of Capital Punishment." *Harvard Law Review* 109 (1995): 355.

Storm, Linda. *Karla Faye Tucker Set Free: Life and Faith on Death Row*. New York: Shaw Books, 2001.

Streeter, Patricia. "A Mother Remembers." In Hunter P. Mabry, *Capital Punishment: A Faith-Based Study*, 48–50. Nashville: Abingdon, 2002.

Streib, Victor L. "Adolescence, Mental Retardation, and the Death Penalty: The Siren Call of Atkins v. Virginia." *New Mexico Law Review* 33 (2003): 183.

———. *Death Penalty for Juveniles*. Bloomington: Indiana University Press, 1987.

———. "Executing Juvenile Offenders: The Ultimate Denial of Juvenile Justice." *Stanford Law and Policy Review* 14 (2003): 121.

Sullivan, Winnifred Fallers. *The Impossibility of Religious Freedom*. Princeton, NJ: Princeton University Press, 2005.

Sundby, Scott E. "The Capital Jury and Empathy: The Problem of Worthy and Unworthy Victims." *Cornell Law Review* 88 (2003): 343.

———. *A Life and Death Decision: A Jury Weighs the Death Penalty*. New York: Palgrave Macmillan, 2005.

Swaine, Lucas. *The Liberal Conscience: Politics and Principle in a World of Religious Pluralism*. New York: Columbia University Press, 2006.

Tabak, Ronald J. "Capital Punishment: Is There Any Habeas Left in This Corpus?" *Loyola University of Chicago Law Journal* 217 (1996): 523.

———. "Capital Punishment in the United States: Moratorium Efforts and Other Key Developments." In *Capital Punishment: Strategies for Abolition*, edited by Peter Hodgkinson and William A. Schabas, 208–32. New York: Cambridge University Press, 2004.

———. "The Egregiously Unfair Implementation of Capital Punishment in the United States: 'Super Due Process' or Super Lack of Due Process?" *Proceedings of the American Philosophical Society* 147, no. 2 (December 1995): 13–23.

———. "How the Death Penalty Works: Empirical Studies of the Modern Capital Sentencing System." *Cornell Law Review* 83 (1998): 1431.

———. "Striving to Eliminate Unjust Executions: Why the ABA's Individual Rights and Responsibilities Section Has Issued Protocols on Unfair Implementation of Capital Punishment." *Ohio State Law Journal* 63 (2002): 475.

Taub, Maura. *Juries: Conscience of the Community*. Berkeley: Chardon, 1998.

Taylor, Mark Lewis. *The Executed God: The Way of the Cross in Lockdown America.* Minneapolis: Fortress, 2001.

Thompson, J. Millburn. *Justice and Peace: A Christian Primer.* Maryknoll, NY: Orbis Books, 1997.

Tillard, Jean-Marie, OP. "The Bread and the Cup of Reconciliation." In *Sacramental Reconciliation*, edited by Edward Schillebeeckx, 38–54. New York: Herder and Herder, 1971.

Traube, Elizabeth. "Incest and Mythology: Anthropological and Girardian Perspectives." *Berkshire Review* 14 (1979): 37–53.

Tribe, Laurence. *American Constitutional Law.* 1st ed. Mineola, NY: Foundation, 1978.

Tucker, George Holbert. *Cavalier Sinners and Saints: Virginia History through a Keyhole.* Norfolk, VA: Virginian Pilot and Ledger Star, 1990.

Tucker, John C. *May God Have Mercy: A True Story of Crime and Punishment.* New York: W. W. Norton, 1997.

Turow, Scott. *Ultimate Punishment: A Lawyer's Reflections on Dealing with the Death Penalty.* New York: Picador, 2003.

Unah, Isaac, and Jack Boger. *Race and the Death Penalty in North Carolina: An Empirical Analysis: 1993–1997.* April 16, 2001. www.deathpenaltyinfo.org/race-and-death-penalty-north-carolina.

United States Department of Justice. *Survey of the Federal Death Penalty System: A Statistical Survey (1988–2000).* September 12, 2000. www.justice.gov/dag/pubdoc/dpsurvey.html.

United States Department of Justice, Bureau of Justice Statistics. "Homicide Trends in the U.S." Data from 1990–2005. bjs.ojp.usdoj.gov/content/homicide/tables/totalstab.cfm.

United States Department of Justice, Federal Bureau of Investigation. *Crime in the United States 2010.* www.fbi.gov/about-us/cjis/ucr/crime-in-the.u.s/2010/crime-in-the.u.s.-2010/.

Unnever, James D., John P. Bartkowski, and Francis T. Cullen. "God Imagery and Opposition to Capital Punishment: A Partial Test of Religious Support for the Consistent Life Ethic." *Sociology of Religion* 71, no. 3 (May 2010): 307–22.

Unnever, James D., and Francis T. Cullen. "Christian Fundamentalism and Support for Capital Punishment." *Journal of Research in Crime and Delinquency* 43, no. 2 (May 2006): 169–97.

———. "The Social Sources of Americans' Punitiveness: A Test of Three Competing Models." *Criminology* 48, no. 1 (February 2010): 99–129.

Unnever, James D., Francis T. Cullen, and John P. Bartkowski. "Images of God and Public Support for Capital Punishment: Does a Close Relationship with a Loving God Matter?" *Criminology* 44, no. 4 (October 2006): 835–66.

van Arsdale, Barbara J. "Amicus Curiae." *American Jurisprudence* 4, 2nd ed. (2007): §6.

van den Haag, Ernest. "Refuting Nathanson." In *Capital Punishment: A Reader*, edited by Glen H. Stassen, 101–6. Cleveland: Pilgrim, 1998.

van den Haag, Ernest, and John P. Conrad. *The Death Penalty: A Debate.* New York: Plenum, 1983.

Vandiver, Margaret. "The Impact of the Death Penalty on the Families of Homicide Victims and of Condemned Prisoners." In *America's Experiment with Capital Punishment: Reflections on the Past, Present, and Future of the Ultimate Penal Sanction*, 2nd ed., edited by James R. Acker, Robert M. Bohm, and Charles S. Lanier, 613–45. Durham, NC: Carolina Academic Press, 2003.

van Raaphorst, Donna L. "Worst of the Worst." In *Crime and Punishment: Perspectives from the Humanities*, Studies in Law, Politics and Society, vol. 37, edited by Austin Sarat, 199–239. Amsterdam: Elsevier JAI, 2005.

Via, Dan O. *Divine Justice, Divine Judgment: Rethinking the Judgment of Nations*. Minneapolis: Fortress, 2007.

Vick, Douglas W. "Poorhouse Justice: Underfunded Indigent Defense Services and Arbitrary Death Sentences." *Buffalo Law Review* 43 (1995): 329.

Vile, John R. "The Right to Vote as Applied to Ex-Felons." *Federal Probation* 45 (1981): 12.

Virginia General Assembly, Joint Legislative Audit and Review Commission. *Review of Virginia's System of Capital Punishment*, Commission Draft. December 10, 2001.

Virginians for Alternatives to the Death Penalty. *Equal Justice and Fair Play: An Assessment of the Capital Justice System in Virginia*. Charlottesville: VADP, 2006.

Volf, Miroslav. *Exclusion or Embrace: A Theological Exploration of Identity, Otherness, and Reconciliation*. Nashville: Abingdon, 1996.

von Drehle, David. *Among the Lowest of the Dead: The Culture of Capital Punishment*. Ann Arbor: University of Michigan Press, 2005.

Vought, Rev. Joseph M. "Jesus, Remember Me." *Lutheran* (October 2000): 16–18.

Wacquant, Loïc. "America's New 'Peculiar Institution': On the Prison as Surrogate Ghetto." In *Punishment and Social Control*, enlarged 2nd ed., edited by Thomas G. Blomberg and Stanley Cohen, 471–82. New York: Aldine de Gruyter, 2003.

Waites, Richard C., and David A. Giles. "Are Jurors Equipped to Decide the Outcome of Complex Cases?" *American Journal of Trial Advocacy* 29 (2005): 19.

Walker, Bill. *The Case of Barbara Graham*. New York: Ballantine Books, 1961.

Waller, Ralph, and Benedicta Ward, eds.. *An Introduction to Christian Spirituality*. London: SPCK, 1999.

Weisberg, Robert. "The Death Penalty Meets Social Science: Deterrence and Jury Behavior under New Scrutiny." *Annual Review of Law and Social Science* 1 (2005): 151.

———. "Deregulating Death." In *The Supreme Court Review, 1983*, edited by Philip B. Kurland, Gerhard Casper, and Dennis J. Hutchinson, 305–95. Chicago: University of Chicago Press, 1984.

Weitzman, Steven. "Mimic Jews and Jewish Mimics in Antiquity: A Non-Girardian Approach to Mimetic Rivalry." *Journal of the American Academy of Religion* 77, no. 4 (December 2009): 922–40.

Westmoreland-White, Michael L., and Glen H. Stassen. "Biblical Perspectives on the Death Penalty." In *Religion and the Death Penalty: A Call for Reckoning*, edited by Eric C. Owens, John D. Carlson, and Eric P. Elshtain, 139–57. Grand Rapids, MI: Wm. B. Eerdmans, 2004.

Widom, Cathy Spitz. "Victims of Childhood Sexual Abuse—Later Criminal Consequences." US Department of Justice, Office of Justice Programs, National Institute of Justice, "Research in Brief," March 1995. www.ncjrs.gov/pdffiles/abuse.pdf.

Williams, Rowan. "Sacraments of the New Society." In *Christ: The Sacramental Word*, edited by David Brown and Ann Loades, 89–102. London: SPCK, 1996.

———. "To Stand Where Christ Stands." In *An Introduction to Christian Spirituality*, edited by Ralph Waller and Benedicta Ward, 1–13. London: SPCK, 1999.

Wink, Walter. *Engaging the Powers: Discernment and Resistance in a World of Domination*. Minneapolis: Fortress, 1992.

———. "Facing the Myth of Redemptive Violence." *Ekklesia*, November 16, 2007. www.ekklesia.co.uk/content/cpt/article_060823wink.shtml.

Witte, John, Jr. *God's Joust, God's Justice: Law and Religion in the Western Tradition*. Grand Rapids, MI: Wm. B. Eerdmans, 2006.

Wohl, Alexander. "Friends with Agendas: Amicus Curiae Briefs May Be More Popular Than Persuasive." *American Bar Association Journal* 82, no. 11 (November 1996): 16–17.

Wolfgang, Marvin E. "We Do Not Deserve to Kill." *Thomas M. Cooley Law Review* 13 (1996): 977.

Wolfson, Wendy. "The Deterrent Effect of the Death Penalty upon Prison Murder." In *The Death Penalty in America*, 3rd ed., edited by Hugo Adam Bedau, 159–73. New York: Oxford University Press, 1982.

Yinger, John Milton. *The Scientific Study of Religion*. New York: Macmillan, 1970.

Young, Robert L. "Religious Orientation, Race, and Support for the Death Penalty." *Journal for the Scientific Study of Religion* 31, no. 1 (March 1992): 76–87.

Yung, Corey Rayburn. "Banishment by a Thousand Laws: Residency Restrictions on Sex Offenders." *Washington University Law Review* 85 (2007–8): 101.

Zehr, Howard. *The Little Book of Restorative Justice*. Intercourse, PA: GoodBooks, 2002.

Ziegler, Edith. "The Transported Convict Women of Colonial Maryland, 1718–1776." *Maryland Historical Magazine* 97, no. 1 (Spring 2002): 5–32.

Zimring, Franklin E. *The Contradictions of American Capital Punishment*. New York: Oxford University Press, 2003.

———. "Inheriting the Wind: The Supreme Court and Capital Punishment in the 1990s." *Florida State University Law Review* 20 (1992): 7.

Zimring, Franklin E., and Gordon Hawkins. *Capital Punishment and the American Agenda*. New York: Cambridge University Press, 1986.

Zimring, Franklin E., Gordon Hawkins, and Sam Kamin. *Punishment and Democracy: Three Strikes and You're Out in California*. New York: Oxford University Press, 2001.

Žižek, Slavoj. *Violence: Six Sideways Reflections*. New York: Picador, 2008.

Žižek, Slavoj, Eric L. Santner, and Kenneth Reinhard. *The Neighbor: Three Inquiries in Political Theology*. Chicago: University of Chicago Press, 2005.

Zorea, Aharon W. *In the Image of God: A Christian Response to Capital Punishment*. Lanham, MD: Rowman and Littlefield, 2000.

Zuklie, Mitchell S. "Rethinking the Fair Cross-Section Requirement." *California Law Review* 84 (1996): 101.

Index

Abel, 47, 55, 59–61, 64, 202. *See also* Cain
abolitionism: abolitionist denominations/
　churches, 28, 32–46, 53–54, 75, 205;
　abolitionist discourse, agreement with
　retentionist discourse, 5–6, 19, 22, 82, 84,
　115, 180–81; abolitionist exile, 23, 82, 90,
　99–111, 113, 118–19, 175, 180–84, 197;
　abolitionists, 2, 48, 71, 87–88, 115, 118,
　187, 199, 209–10; and choice/sovereignty
　of action, 110–13, 175–76, 197, 202, 205;
　conceptions of the offender, 20, 68, 113,
　155–62, 175; and culpability, 20, 84, 109;
　and dignity, 7–8, 205; jurisdictions, 7–8,
　28, 74, 176; and moral certainty, 38–43;
　and political process in Virginia, 126,
　148; in U.S. history, 10–14
absolution, 114–15
accompaniment: as a defining component
　of embrace, 185–86; in ministry, 186, 189,
　190, 193–94
ACLU of Virginia, 14, 104; 2003 Report on
　Virginia's capital system, 14
"activist" public officials, 123, 134, 137–38,
　145
Adams, Janice, 94–95
Agamben, Giorgio, 20
aggravating circumstances/factors, 13–15,
　37
Akers, Thomas Wayne, 107
Alabama, 12, 28, 126, 152
Albanese, Catherine, 21
Allen, George, 138
Althusser, Louis, 158
American Baptist Churches (USA), 13, 39
American Bar Association (ABA), 153
American Civil Liberties Union (ACLU), 14
American Ethical Union, 13, 32
American Friends Service Committee
　(AFSC), 150–51, 166
amicus curiae briefs, 24, 148–51, 153, 156,
　159, 163, 165
Ananias, 204
Anckar, Carsten, 7

Anderson, Laura, 19
Anderson, Victor, 70
Anti-Terrorism and Effective Death Penalty
　Act (AEDPA), 152
appeals: costs, 157–58; and counsel, 145,
　152–56 (see also *Murray v. Giarratano*);
　direct/mandatory, 15–16, 155–57; dis-
　cretionary, 16, 139, 174, 176, 198–99
　(*see also* habeas corpus); incidence, 12;
　limitations on, 15–16, 44, 152; process,
　15–16, 148–56; questions of legitimacy of,
　69, 77–79, 145, 157
Aquinas, Thomas, 171
Arizona, 11, 81, 126
Arkansas, 126
artful zeal/artful zealot, 125–27, 134, 140,
　142–43
Assemblies of God (AoG), 36
Atkins, Daryl, 107
Atkins v. Virginia, 103–4, 106, 161–64
atonement, 29
Augustine, Saint, 72

"bad childhood defense," 88, 102, 108, 114.
　See also "poor childhood defense"
banishments, 9, 41–42, 61; of fears, 79;
　Transportation Act of 1718, 41
Banner, Stuart, 12, 97
Barclay v. Florida, 13
Barefoot v. Estelle, 13
Barr, Bob, 192
Bart Township, 62, 203. *See also* Nickel
　Mines school shooting
Batson v. Kentucky, 168, 170
Beaver, Gregory, 191
Beccaria, Cesare, 10
Bell, Edward, 121, 248n1
"Beltway Sniper" killings, 124, 162. *See also*
　Muhammad, John Allen; Malvo, Lee Boyd
Benedict XVI, 192
benefit of clergy, 9
Berlin, Fred, 198
Bible: on capital punishment, 11, 26, 44;

commentaries, 67, 128; hermeneutics, 28, 65, 67, 127; prose vs. poetry in, 67; on sacredness of life, 33; versions, 66-67. *See also* Bible studies

Bible studies, 71, 75, 84, 88, 93, 95, 199; and identification, 71, 82, 87, 198; and John 8, 196, 200-201; and Nickel Mines school shooting, 112, 203; as practices, 24, 49-52, 53, 193; statewide survey, 22-23, 46, 48; and understandings of responsibility, 113, 118

bilateral individualism, 99-101, 114, 118. *See also* multilateral individualism

blogs/bloggers/blogosphere, 21, 23, 140, 142; assessing Kaine's position on capital punishment, 125-27, 134-37; on Biblical validity of the death penalty, 127-33; on conceptions of the executive, 133-37, 142-43; response to "Stanley" and "Law" campaign advertisements, 121-25

"bloody code," 9

Body of Liberties, 9

Bolton, Patricia, 177

Bonhoeffer, Dietrich, 59

Bonowitz, Abe, 208

Bosler, SueZann, 64

Boulanger, Christian, 4

Brennan, William, 4, 11, 12, 91, 96

Briley, Linwood and James, 79

Broaddus, William G., 44

Brugger, Christian, 34

Buchanan, Patrick, 96

Buck, Duane, 96

Buddhism, 6, 178, 223n63

Bunch, Timothy, 111

Bundy, Ted, 115

Burgoyne, Douglas, 112

Bush, George W., 68, 86

Cain, 36, 65, 79-81, 110; and Abel, 47-48, 55, 59-61, 64-65, 202; and repentance, 59-62, 71

California, 88, 126

California v. Alcala, 166

California v. Fields, 151, 166

California v. Ramos, 13

Camus, Albert, 1, 176

capital jury. *See* juries/jurors

capital murder, defined (Virginia), 218n40

capital murder trial, 13-15, 83-84, 92, 151, 159, 162, 165, 171-76; bifurcation, 151, 173; guilt phase, 15, 79, 156-57, 174, 176; sentencing phase, 15, 79, 157, 159, 174; voir dire, 15, 130, 166-70

capital punishment, 2, 4-5, 22-26, 43, 73, 88, 146, 209; in Bible, 26, 128; Bible studies and, 48-52, 79; capriciousness of, 147, 151; churches/religious institutions and, 27-30, 31-41, 43-46, 54, 72, 164, 179, 205; conscience and, 27, 166, 168-70, 172, 200; democratic legitimacy of, 143, 172; detached and derivative views of, 31-34; and deterrence, 74-75, 84, 91; jurisdictions with, 7-8, 126-27; limits on, 41, 55-56, 94-95; and moral certainty, 38-41; and morally certain, 34-38; problems with, 40, 73, 83, 147-48; process, 14-21, 37, 92-95, 122, 130, 174-75, 191; as process vs. as event, 66-72, 76, 119, 122; as retribution, 55, 91-92, 98, 111-12, 211; right to counsel, 152-56; U.S. history of, 8-14, 41; in Virginia, 14-21, 27-28, 85-86, 126, 135

capriciousness of death penalty, 20, 76, 83-4, 97, 147, 151, 153

Carlson, Ron, 68

Carlson, Tucker, 68

Carter, Jimmy, 192

Carter, Stephen, 99-100

Catholic Church: Catechism of the Catholic Church, 13, 34, 37; Catholic Diocese of Richmond, 27; church teachings and opposition to capital punishment, 27, 124; death row chaplains, 187, 188; Iowa Catholic Conference, 44-45; opposition to the death penalty, 27-28, 33-34, 38, 45, 142-43, 167; Texas Catholic Conference, 43; United States Catholic Conference, 13; United States Conference of Catholic Bishops (USCCB), 163-64, 188

Chabrol, Andrew, 197

chaplains, 20-21, 24, 52, 178, 179; Chaplain Service Prison Ministry of Virginia, 178, 186-87, 192-93; death row services, 178-79, 187-88, 190; "doing the work," 112, 186 195-99; ministry of accompaniment,

52, 192–94; on offenders as "like us," 65, 199–201; point of no return, 197, 199–200; prison vs. parish ministry, 186, 192–94; relationships with offenders, 187–88, 190–91, 193–94, 200, 203; role in execution process, 69, 195–96

Chaplain Service Prison Ministry of Virginia, 178, 186, 187, 192, 193

Chessman, Caryl, 12

Christian Coalition, 44

Christian Church (Disciples of Christ), 36

Church Women United (CWU), 28, 43

Citizens United to Abolish the Death Penalty, 208

civil society, 66, 99

Clark v. New Mexico, 176

class, 33, 58–59, 79

clemency, 69, 119, 135, 139, 145, 155, 174, 183, 192, 205; state-by-state procedures for, 126–27

Clozza, Albert Jr., 177–78

Code of Virginia, 57, 218n40

cognizable groups, 151, 165–66, 170–71

Coleman v. Thompson, 155

Colorado, 11, 126

Commonwealth v. Lenz, 170

Community of St. Dysmas, 188. *See also* penitent thief

commutation, 15, 17–18, 39, 69, 106–7, 126, 157, 187, 209

Connecticut, 198

conscience: churches as authorities on, 164; collective, 160, 210; individual, 27, 59–60, 120, 144, 200; positive and negative attributes of, 171; Swaine defines, 172; as utilized in sentencing decisions, 165, 168, 171–72. *See also* juries/jurors

conversion: death row conversions, 69, 72, 110, 139, 190; executions and, 71, 205; as "lifetime process," 203; liturgical reading and, 51; McCloud, Ralph, 188, 194; punishment promoting, 38, 205; Saul/Paul, 36, 48, 110; temporal consequences of, 23, 71–72, 110, 139, 205; Tucker, Karla Faye, 68–69, 72, 119, 199, 205

Coppola, Frank, 187

corporate responsibility (for crime), 40–41

Costanzo, Mark, 21

"cruel and unusual punishment." *See* Eighth Amendment

Culbert, Jennifer, 101, 105

culpability: abolitionist exile and, 103, 118, 181; diminished, 102, 106, 160–61; and guilt, 6, 18, 20, 23, 97, 101, 109; as point of contestation between abolitionist and retentionist perspectives, 20, 105, 109, 175, 181; and scapegoat, 84; societal, 40

Cuomo, Mario, 96

Dale, Sir Thomas/Dale's Laws, 8

"Damascus road" moment, 3, 70

Darden, Willie Jasper, 112

David, 36, 47, 48, 80

Davis, Kim, 192

Davis, Troy Anthony, 73, 191–92

Dean, Howard, 124

Dean, Jerry, 68

Deans, Marie, xi, 1–2, 5, 18, 118

death-eligible offenders, 104

"death is different," 24, 147–48, 151–63, 171, 175–76

death penalty: and American exceptionalism, 4; arbitrariness/capriciousness, 14, 19, 20, 73, 83, 147, 151–53, 161; Bible and, 27, 54, 67, 93, 121–22; Bible studies and, 24, 46, 48–50, 53–62, 65–66, 87; Catholic catechism and, 34, 37; churches and; 23, 27–41, 43–46, 48–49, 53–54, 89, 104, 142–43, 163–68, 204–5; and class, 33, 79; classes of defendants ineligible for (*see* juvenile death penalty; mental issues, defendants); communicative effects of, 36, 43, 222n58; constitutionality of, 5, 12–14, 161; cultural resonances and salience of, 5, 21, 50; "degovernmentalization" of, 91–93; detached and derivative views of, 31–34; deterrence, 17, 67, 74–75, 84; cost, 17, 32, 103, 157–58, 209, 229n48; economic bias, 30, 32, 34, 37, 39, 44, 73, 79, 90, 151, 166, 181; event- vs. process-based views of, 22–23, 46, 66–72, 74–77, 110, 144–45; forgiveness and, 56, 110; geographic bias, 14, 28, 30, 32, 37, 73, 79, 109; Girard and, 19–21, 24, 84–85; and human rights, 7–8, 29; innocence and, 12, 17–18, 70, 84, 108, 135, 139, 143, 158,

(*Index* (299

162 (*see also* innocence); legitimacy of, 6, 19, 24, 32, 49, 153, 157–58; as a local phenomenon, 8, 114; mandatory death sentences, 14, 147–48, 174; modern era, 5–6, 15–16, 21; and moral certainty, 34–38; morality of, 4, 17, 27, 36–37, 43, 74, 91, 134; and morally certain, 38–41; opposition to, 2, 10–13, 22, 27, 32–34, 39, 43–46, 48, 54, 64, 76, 79, 103–5, 121–22, 125, 134, 136, 151, 166–69; in the rabbinic tradition, 55–56; racial bias/disparity, 12, 14, 16–17, 30, 32, 34, 37, 38–39, 44, 73, 79, 103, 158, 181; and redemption, 66; religion and, 4, 7, 8–11, 21–24, 27–28, 145, 151, 165–76, 201, 205, 226–27n3; responsibility for, 40–41, 46, 100, 113, 120, 138–39; restrictions on, 9–10, 93–95, 117, 151–52, 208; as retribution, 17, 35–36, 41, 109; as sacrifice, 24, 74–75, 91, 210; and the scapegoat, 82–84, 89–90; scope of moral action, 36, 129; as a Southern institution, 28, 167, 176; in the United States, 6, 8–21, 24, 28, 93; valuation of life, 31–34, 38, 53, 97–98, 161; in Virginia, 14–19, 21, 26–27, 121–27, 208–11; and vigilantism, 11, 76–77, 91, 96–97; women and, 25 (*see also* Tucker, Karla Faye); worldwide, 6–8, 11–16, 176; "worst of the worst," 20, 82, 117, 162

death qualification, 150, 174; as religious discrimination, 169–71; and increased likelihood of conviction, 15, 169

death row: arriving/being on, 186, 189, 198–99, 201, 210; chaplains, 20, 21, 24, 65, 69, 178–79, 186, 201; conditions on (VA), 18–19, 177; conversions/reform, 69, 119, 190, 204–5; escapes from, 79; exonerations and commutations, 17, 39, 73, 105–7, 123, 127, 158; innocents on, 39, 90–91, 158, 209, 241n23; men on, 2, 3, 17, 25, 32, 39, 73, 182, 190; as metaphor, 123; ministry, 52, 81–82, 187–91, 193–95, 198; offenders, appeals available to, 15–16, 139, 152–57; offenders, Christian obligation to, 54; offenders as "like us"/empathy for offenders, 70, 80, 89, 178–79, 194–95, 201, 210; offenders, legal representation, 133–34, 152–56;

offenders, "social profile" of, 108, 112; women on, 25

dehumanization, 6, 19, 221n52

Delaware, 126

democracies/democratic process, 7, 12, 24, 40, 133, 140–45

denominational statements, 33. *See also* doctrinal statements; resolutions; social statements

"deregulating death," 13, 151

derivative view of life/rights, 31–34, 43, 71, 74, 110

detached view of life/rights, 31–34, 43, 71, 110, 112

deterrence, 10, 17, 26, 67, 70, 73–75, 78, 83, 91, 114; double, 78, 91; general, 78, 90–91, 98, 115; marginal, 78, 90; rejections of, 84, 211

dignity: inherent/intrinsic, 7–8, 29, 33–34, 37, 44, 188, 195; protecting the dignity of offenders and victims, 30, 35, 37, 97, 102, 159, 160, 161

discrimination, 13, 17, 39, 103, 169–76

DNA, 72, 139

doctrinal statements, 23, 28, 164. *See also* social statements

doctrine of double effect, 34

Doss, Joe Morris, 167

Douglas, William O., 12, 165

Dow, David, 69, 177

Drinan, Robert F., SJ, 27

due process, 75, 77, 96–98, 114, 137, 150–52, 154

Dukakis, Michael, 123

Duke, Barrett, 28, 33

Duke's Laws, 9

Dworkin, Ronald, 32–33

Earley, Mark L., 92–93

Eighth Amendment, 106, 110, 116, 148, 151, 160–61, 163, 174

Elshtain, Jean Bethke, 28–29, 43

embrace: in biblical narratives/Bible studies, 49; defined, 6; and exile as pair, 5–6, 24, 42–43, 50, 162, 175, 179, 182, 201–6, 210–11; in legal process, 27, 145–46, 156; "like us," 80; model, 21, 23; moral responsibility and, 36; Miroslav

300) Index)

Volf, 24, 179, 184, 185-86, 193-94, 196; offenders and, 156, 160, 161, 175-76, 197, 200. *See also* accompaniment
endorsement test, 173
Episcopal Church, 32, 45, 75; Abington Convocation 44; Episcopal Diocese of Virginia, 44; Episcopal Diocese of Southern Virginia, 44
Evangelical Lutheran Church in America (ELCA), 28, 33-34, 36, 38, 40, 44, 188; 1991 Social Statement on capital punishment, 161, 172
Evangelium Vitae, 34, 172
evolving standards of decency, 151, 156, 163-65, 171-72, 175-76
exclusion (Volf), 24, 179-84
executions: ambivalence toward, 48, 79, 82, 84, 116-17; chamber, 189, 193, 196; as communication, 74, 114, 197; Davis, Troy Anthony, 191-92; and deterrence, 17, 74, 78, 84, 91; and exile, 41-42, 98, 182; Jesus, 52, 129; of juveniles, 103-5, 160, 163; of mentally ill/mentally retarded, 103, 105-7, 160, 163; methods, 55, 114; procedures/process, 40, 115-16, 134, 143, 155, 195, 209; process vs. event, 66-67, 70; propriety of, 76; racial disparity/bias, 17, 96; repentance and, 71-72, 199, 202-3; responsibility for, 41, 113; as ritual, 19, 74, 98, 99, 115; secrecy, 116; televising, 115; Tucker, Karla Faye, 68-69, 72, 82, 119, 202-3; to prevent vigilantism, 92-93, 99; in U.S. history, 9-12, 16, 20-21, 27-28, 117, 208, 219n46; vigils, 24, 179, 202, 207-9; in Virginia, 16, 21, 27-28, 44, 92-93, 103-7, 111, 122-23, 134, 143, 177-79, 187-89, 191, 195, 208-9; worldwide, 7-8; wrongful, 32, 34, 39, 48, 73, 75, 83-84, 91, 109. *See also* capital punishment; death penalty; juvenile death penalty; mental issues, defendants
execution vigils and protests, 12, 192, 202, 207-9; liturgies at/for, 24, 179
executive: democratic/republican (liberal), 122, 135-40, 141-45; duties, 119, 122-23, 126-27, 130, 174; ideal, 122, 135; ministerial, 122, 140-45; Kaine on, 122, 137, 139-40, 142, 145; Kilgore on, 122, 127, 137-39, 142; role in society, 24, 122, 127, 130, 133-34, 163
exegesis, 23, 24, 121-122, 127-133
exile: abolitionist exile (revealed exile), 14, 23, 80, 82, 99-111, 113, 118-19, 156, 161, 175, 180-82, 184; in biblical narratives/Bible studies, 49, 59-60, 65; characteristics of, 23, 82-83, 89-90, 95; and conversion, 23; defined 6, 231n37; and embrace as pair, 5-6, 24, 42-43, 50, 162, 175, 179, 182, 201-6, 210-11; and exclusion, 179; in legal process, 24, 145-46; "like us," 98; markers, 107, 181; model, 21, 23; moral responsibility and, 36, 117; and the other, 6, 46; and/ as punishment, 41-42, 59, 117, 175, 210; and point of no return, 196-97; retentionist exile (instantiated exile), 23, 80, 82, 97-102, 113-14, 116-19, 156-57, 161, 175, 180-84; and scapegoat, 19, 80, 89-90, 117-18; and sovereignty, 117, 182-84
exilic punishments. *See* banishments
Exodus, book of, 2, 47
exodus, the, 57, 59
exonerations, 17, 39, 73, 157, 158
Ezekiel, 18, 71; 33, 54, 56, 70

Falwell, Jerry, 68-69, 190
Fellowship of Reconciliation, 39
First Amendment, 169; free exercise clause, 169, 171, 173; establishment clause, 24, 173
First Unitarian Church of Richmond, 44
Florida, 28, 112, 115, 126
Ford, Russell, 178-79, 190-91, 195, 197
Ford v. Wainwright, 106, 147
foreign nationals, propriety of execution of, 16
forgiveness, 23, 26, 61, 70, 75, 79-80, 110, 199, 205; Jesus and, 28, 44; as a moral skill, 61-64, 132, 203; as a process, 54-57, 71, 111
Foucault, Michel, 102, 224n67
Fourteenth Amendment, 148, 154
Frankfurter, Felix, 12
Franklin, Benjamin, 9-10
"From Fear to Hope: Statement of Religious

Leaders in Virginia on Public Safety and the Death Penalty," 89–90
Furman v. Georgia, 5, 11, 13, 91, 97, 147

Garland, David, 4, 8, 29, 99, 114
Garrett, Danny, 68
Garvey, Stephen, 173
Genesis, 48, 60; 1–8, 52–53; 4, 47, 48; 9, 66–67, 74
geography: geographic bias, 14, 28, 30, 32, 37, 73, 79, 109; as marker of exile, 183–84
Georgia, 28, 42, 73, 126, 191–92
Gey, Steven, 169
Giarratano, Joseph, 153, 187–88, 201; *Murray v. Giarratano*, 152–56
Gilmore, Gov. Jim, 107, 119
Girard, Rene, 81–82, 222–23n60; scapegoat, 19–21, 23, 24, 82–83, 85, 90; theories of violence, 59–60, 85
Godbold, John C., 153
Godwin's Law, 124
Goldberg, Justice Arthur, 12
Good Friday Appeal to End the Death Penalty, A, 164
Good Samaritan, parable, 180
grace: forgiveness and, 36, 56, 63–64, 70, 80, 193–94, 203–5; repentance and, 68, 80, 193–94, 203–4
graduated murder statutes, 10
Graham, Barbara, 12
grand jury, 14
Greensville Correctional Center, 177, 207
Gregg v. Georgia: xii, 5, 13, 91
Griffin, Jim, 52, 187–89, 193–95
guilt, 6, 18, 33, 39, 67, 108, 109, 137, 164, 173–74; actual guilt, 6, 83, 90, 157, 197; corporate/community guilt, 41, 177; and culpability, 6, 18, 20, 23, 101, 105, 116–17; and grace/repentance, 193, 196; juries and, 143, 148, 156, 158, 162, 171, 174, 176; legal guilt, 6, 23, 76, 82, 90, 97, 117–18, 157, 197; and moral certainty, 29–31, 39–40, 75; moral guilt, 160; and the scapegoat, 6, 90–91, 97, 209
guilt phase. *See* capital murder trial

habeas corpus, post-conviction proceedings, 83, 153–58, 174; complexity of, 153–56; federal habeas, 16, 139, 154–56; right to counsel during, 152–56 (see also *Murray v. Giarratano*); state habeas, 16, 152–56
habeas corpus, right of, 12–13, 152
Hamby, Cyril Hugh, 208
Hart, H.L.A., 101, 105
Herrera v. Collins, 239n70
Hinduism, 7
Hitler, Adolf, 67, 121, 123–24, 126
Horton, Willie, 123
Howell, Scott, 121, 123, 248–49n2
Human rights, 7–8, 29

Idaho, 126
Illinois, 17, 39, 73, 90
imago dei, 37, 43
Indiana, 126
indigence/indigents, 2, 39, 152
ineffective counsel, 4, 153, 155, 256n14
innocence, 12, 17–18, 70, 84, 108, 135, 139, 143, 158, 162; actual innocence, 14, 16, 72–73, 83–84, 90, 191–92; evidence of, 16, 72, 91, 139
innocents, offenders: exonerations of, 17, 39, 73, 157, 158; fears of executions of, 32, 39, 48–49, 72–73, 75, 79, 95, 118, 151, 192; and procedural legitimacy, 18, 90–91
innocents, victims, 3, 5, 36, 88, 95, 138–39, 209–10
In re. Troy Anthony Davis, 83
Iowa, 44, 45
Irwin, Kitty, 111
Islam, 7, 223–24n63
"I Want to Serve," 166–67

Jackson, W. Eric, 187, 190, 193–95, 198
Jaquith, Waldo, 249n2, 249n4
Jefferson, Thomas, 9, 10, 44
Jesus: adversarial Jesus, 129, 143; example of, 44, 51, 56, 63–64, 68, 70, 111, 167; execution of/crucifixion, 52, 77, 79, 129, 188; forgiveness and, 56, 63–64, 68–69, 167, 196; John 8, 79, 199–02; and redemption/salvation, 54, 188, 190; teachings, 28, 53, 112, 180
Jewett, Robert, 125
Jim Crow, 77
John, 54; 8, 56, 79, 196, 199–02

John Paul II, 34
Judaism, 26, 58, 124, 180, 224n63
judicatory statements, 45, 54
juries/jurors, 77, 96, 97, 100, 107, 121, 135, 148, 159; as the conscience of the community, 24, 40, 147–48, 165, 171, 175; as cross-section/mirror of the community, 77, 148, 165–66, 168, 171; death-qualification/death-qualified, 15, 150, 169, 174; death qualification and bias in favor of conviction, 15; death-scrupled persons and, 151, 166, 169–75, 176; equipped for the task, 73, 130; as governmental body, 130, 148; imposing death sentences, 7, 14–16, 94, 95, 101, 121, 138, 156–57, 183; Karla Faye Tucker trial, 68, 192, 205; pronouncing guilt, 143, 156, 158; and religion, 27–28, 150–51, 165–76
jury nullification, 9
jury selection/voir dire, 13, 15, 130, 166–70
justice, 16, 29, 39, 95, 120–21, 202; in Bible, 26, 44; community's conceptions of, 171, 184; criminal justice system, 2, 20, 31, 41, 97–98, 103, 156–57, 160, 167, 189; desert-based, 105, 145; dispassionate/impartial, 44, 99, 131, 173; divine, understandings of, 67, 111, 141; extralegal/mob, 11, 76, 92; and mercy, tension between, 42, 50; miscarriages of, 34; and morality, 20; opposed to vengeance, 69, 205; our responsibility to exact, 4, 66, 203; process-based approach to, 179; redemptive, 109; rehabilitative, 40, 42; restorative, 20, 40, 56, 109; retributive, 20, 35, 74, 91, 93, 100, 109, 130, 160, 202, 210; social, 43, 45, 52, 143; vigilantist, 78–79, 91
juvenile death penalty/juvenile defendants, 14, 16, 108, 152, 163, 176; ineligible for death penalty, 45, 85, 103–5; lessened culpability, 103–5, 160, 162; as presumptively normal, 161–62; especially vulnerable, 104–5, 162

Kaine, Timothy M., 23, 26–27, 123–24, 134–35; as "activist" and eligibility for office, 125, 133–34, 136–38; clemency, 106–7, 139, 209; on death penalty, 27, 126, 136, 142; faith and/questions about, 27, 125–27, 136, 142–44; "Stanley" and "Law" campaign advertisements and, 120–20, 123; views of the executive, 122, 137, 139–40, 142, 145
Kansas, 11, 126
Keating, Frank H., 31, 120
Keller, Sharon, 97
"Kelly" (campaign advertisement), 121, 248n1
Kennedy v. Louisiana: xii, 208
Kenney, Shaun, 142–43
Kentucky, 10, 126, 150
Kerry, John, 123
Kilgore, Jerry, 23, 26, 123, 133–35, 138; on the death penalty, 27, 121, 143; and "Stanley" campaign advertisement, 121, 124–25, 137; views of the executive, 122, 127, 137–39, 142
King, Danny, 3
Koh, Harold Hongju, 8
Kozinski, Alex, 114, 117

Lakoff, George, 131–32
"Law" (campaign advertisement), 121, 123
law: in the Bible, 56–57, 67, 79; case law, 16, 40, 106, 110, 149, 151, 153–54; as distinct from proverbial wisdom, 67; due process of, 75, 77, 96–98, 114, 137, 150–52, 154; impartiality of, 30, 79; mimetic rivalry in, 83–86; Mosaic Law, 9, 55, 79; natural law, 132–34, 141; post-*Furman* death penalty laws, states, 13–14, 91, 147–48; religious and/vs. secular, 7, 8–9, 11, 27, 30, 72, 80, 127, 143, 146, 148, 165–76; in Virginia, 57, 92, 104–6, 156, 218n40
Lawrence, John Shelton, 125
Lemon v. Kurtzman, 173
Leo XIII, 1420143
lex talionis, 55. *See also* violence, limits
Liberty Bible Commentary, 67, 128
Lincoln, Bruce, 30
litigant briefs, 24, 148–51
liturgical reading/practices, 23, 50–54
Lockhart v. McCree, 170, 174
Louisiana, 126, 148, 166–67
Luke, 188; 6, 70, 208
Lutheran Church in America, 13. *See also* Evangelical Lutheran Church in America

Lutheran Church—Missouri Synod (LCMS), 35, 37, 70
lynching, 11, 91, 96–97, 99

MacPhail, Mark, 191
Madison, James, 9, 169
Maine, 2, 10–11
Malvo, Lee Boyd, 124, 162
mandatory death sentences, unconstitutionality of, 14, 147–48, 160–61, 174–75
Marshall, Thurgood: xiii, 147
Maryland, 124, 126, 188
Matthew, 5, 52, 70, 127, 133; 7, 200; 12, 86; 18, 63; 25, 44
May, Jane M., 3, 5
McBride, James, 24
McCarver v. North Carolina, 164, 258n40
McCleskey v. Kemp, 17, 39
McCloud, Ralph, 188–89, 194–95
McFarland, Cecil, 192–93
McGuire, Russell E. "Rusty," 93–95
Mecklenburg Correctional Center, 177, 188
Medill Innocence Project, 73
Megivern, James, 127
Mennonite Church, 41
Mennonite General Conference, 41
mens rea, 128, 160
mental issues, defendants: mental illness, 15, 60, 104–7, 112, 143, 153, 181–82, 197, 199, 209; mental retardation, 14, 16, 45, 103–7, 152, 160,–163, 181, 197; mental retardation, defined (DSM IV), 243n51
mercy, 26, 28, 42, 50, 56, 68–69, 70, 90, 202–3
Methodist Church, 13 *See also* United Methodist Church
Michigan, 11
Mickens, Walter, 187
mimesis/mimetic rivalry, 20–1, 23, 60, 82–87, 223–24n60
Minnesota, 11
Mississippi, 126
Missouri, 11, 28, 126, 162–63
Missouri Ban Youth Executions Coalition (BYE), 163
mitigating circumstance(s)/factors/evidence, 14, 15, 37, 97, 102, 151, 174
mob justice, 11, 76, 92, 200–202

modern era, defined: xii, 5
Montana, 126
Moore, William T. Jr., 191
moral certainty, 22, 29–31, 34, 38–41, 42, 73, 76–77, 90, 98, 109, 191; defined, 30–31; "moral certainty standard," 31
morality: common/shared (Durkheimian), 30, 91, 113, 119, 180; of death penalty, 17, 74, 168–70; and justice, 20, 120; public v. private, 122, 132, 134, 139–40; of punishment, 35; and religion, 29–30, 164; scope of moral action, 36–37, 40, 129, 133; "strict father," 131–33; "traditional," 96
morally certain, 22, 29, 30–31, 34–40, 42, 75, 76, 109
moral responsibility, 42, 113, 117–18
moratoria, 17, 39, 44, 90, 120, 123, 135
Morgan, David, 24
Mosaic Law, 9, 55, 79
Moses, 36, 80, 89; and calling, 58–60, 64–65, 70; killing of the Egyptian, 47–48, 51, 57–60, 65, 77
Moussaoui, Zacarias, 3, 18–19
Muhammad, John Allen, 124
multilateral individualism, 99, 118–19
Munsey, Tara, 111
Murray v. Giarratano, 152–56
myth of redemptive violence, 114, 180

NAACP, 12; Legal Defense Fund, 12–13
National Association of Evangelicals (NAE), 35
National Coalition to Abolish the Death Penalty (NCADP), 45, 103
National Council of the Churches of Christ in the USA, 39
Nebraska, 126
Neighbor, the, 55, 85, 93, 156, 180
Neill, Stephen, 27, 142
Nevada, 126
New Hampshire, 126
New Jersey, 10
New Mexico, 126, 176
New Testament, 26, 28, 36, 56, 128, 167, 188
New York, 9, 10, 96
Nickel Mines school shooting, 62–64, 68, 71, 112.
"normal person," the, 5, 83, 99–101, 118,

159, 184, 196–97, 198, 205; differentiated from the abolitionist exile, 103–13; juveniles as, 161–62; in the legal process, 153–56; mentally retarded offenders as, 161–62
North Carolina, 28, 126, 147–48
North Dakota, 11

Obama, Barack, 139
O'Connor, Sandra Day, 151, 154, 239n70
Ohio, 28, 126
Oklahoma, 28, 31, 126, 151
Old Testament, 28, 36, 55, 56, 125
On Crimes and Punishments, 10
Oregon, 126
Osler, Mark, 200
Ozanne, Peter A., 8

Parker, Anthony, 178–79
Paul of Tarsus (Saul), 131, 179, 204; conversion, 36, 48, 70, 80, 110; letter to the Romans, 36, 128–29, 133; stoning of Stephen, 47, 48, 77
Payden-Travers, Jack, 209–10
Payne v. Tennessee, 91–93, 158–59, 160
penitent thief, 80, 188, 205.
Pennsylvania, 10, 62, 126, 203
Penry v. Lynaugh, 14, 163, 164
Peppers, Todd, 19
peremptory challenges, 150, 166–68, 173
Perry, Michael J., 7
point of no return, 6, 63, 76, 182–84, 196, 197, 199, 200
"poor childhood defense," 88, 102, 108, 114.
Posner, Richard, 149
poverty, 112, 181
Powell, Lewis, 17
Powell v. Alabama, 152
Prejean, Helen, 19, 111, 126
Presbyterian Church USA (PCUSA), 38, 39, 40–41, 45, 54
procedural default, 15
process-based vs. event-based perspectives: of capital punishment, 23, 122, 144; of conversion, 69–70; of crime and punishment, 66–67; of due process, 75, 77; of evil, 78; of exile, 5; of forgiveness, 110; of scapegoat, 80; of vigilante, 76, 79

Prodigal Son, parable, 185, 194–95, 198
prophetic realism, 131
prosecutors, 13, 14–15, 73, 92, 93, 137, 168, 173, 192, 205; prosecutorial discretion, 14, 93–95, 158, 181; prosecutorial misconduct, 153
protests. *See* execution, vigils and protests
Proverbs, 130
public reason, 163
Pulley v. Harris, 13
punishment: alternatives to capital, 9, 41–42, 54, 98; communicative effects of, 19, 35–36, 40–41, 163–65; cultural understandings of, 19, 35–36, 40–41, 98, 160, 163–65, 175, 209–10; damnation, 53, 190; defined, 4, 29; morality of, 35; synergy with religion, 29–31

Quakers, 10, 41, 166

race: and cognizable groups, 151, 166; discrimination, 17, 170; and jury votes, 27; of offender, 14, 17, 32, 33, 79, 90, 96, 109; of victim, 14, 32, 43
Ramdass, Bobby Lee, 3
Rawls, John, 163
Reagan, Ronald, 115
reconciliation, 37, 42, 48, 49, 54–55, 111, 199, 203, 204
reconciliatory practices, 23, 50–54
redemption (redeem): Biblical narratives of, 26, 66, 80, 89; collective, 119; as event, 53, 68, 70; of offenders, 37, 38, 89, 199; possibility of, 66, 68, 118–19, 129; as process, 68, 70, 71, 75; punishment as redemptive, 70; redemptive love, 76; redemptive justice, 109, 168–70; redemptive violence/wrath, 76, 84, 113–14, 116, 118–19, 180; spiritual, 76
reform: of criminal justice system, 10, 34, 75; individual, 10–12, 35, 38, 56, 80, 112, 130, 190, 199, 205
Reformed Church in America, 13
rehabilitation, 12, 37, 69, 98, 112, 118, 171, 188
rehabilitative justice, 40, 42, 112, 130
Rehnquist, William, 154
religion: religious activism, 4, 8, 10–11, 20,

27, 45–46, 89, 103–4, 205; and capital punishment, 4–5, 7–11, 23–24, 27–29, 45–46, 74–75, 96, 122, 140, 226–27n3; defined, 21, 24, 29–30, 169–70, 223–24n63, 227n8; religious discourse, 21, 22–23, 181, 201; religious discrimination, 11, 169–176; establishment of, 24, 173; execution ritual akin to, 74–75; free exercise of, 169, 171, 173; and the jury, 165–76; legal definitions of, 169–70; and mimetic rivalry, 84–85; and politics, 125–27, 134, 140–46; in post-conviction process, 148, 150–51, 164–65; and punishment, 4, 29–31; religious bodies and capital punishment, categorized, 31–34; as obligation/duty, 169; services on death row, 178–79, 188, 190

religious practices, 74, 260n60

repentance, 179; Cain, 59–60, 61, 71; defined (Volf), 196–97; and embrace, 185–86; as event, 56, 68; and forgiveness, 56, 61, 75, 195, 205; as a moral skill, 61–62; opposition to capital punishment as, 205; as process, 56, 70, 72, 196; as profoundly transformative, 141, 196–97, 199; repentant thief, 188; and responsibility, 69, 196; and salvation, 53, 68; Saul/Paul, 70; and temporal consequences, 69, 71; the unrepentant, 60, 64, 71

resolutions, 44, 104. *See also* doctrinal statements; social statements

restoration/restorative justice, 20, 38, 40, 56, 91, 109, 112, 114, 185, 201

retentionism: Bible supporting, 66–67; and choice/sovereignty of action, 110, 113–17, 131, 175–76, 197; conceptions of the offender, 20, 95, 110, 113, 117, 155–62, 175, 195, 210; and culpability, 20, 84, 109, 175; and dignity, 7–8, 97; jurisdictions, 7–8, 28, 74, 126–27, 176; and legal guilt, 6, 82, 114–15, 117; and moral certainty, 38–43; and redemptive violence, 114, 203; retentionist denominations/churches, 28, 32–46, 53, 54, 75, 128; retentionist discourse, agreement with abolitionist discourse, 5–6, 19, 22, 82, 84, 115, 180–81; retentionist exile, 6, 23, 82, 90, 97–110, 113–14, 118–19, 156–57, 161,

175, 180–84, 197; retentionists, 2, 48, 87–89, 169, 115, 199, 210

retribution: and atonement, tension between, 29, 70, 80, 171; Cain and, 55, 61; in death penalty debate, 17; as illegitimate penological aim, 12, 35–36, 41–42, 99, 188; as legitimate penological aim, 2, 20, 35–36, 42, 93, 97–98, 130, 188; political climate, 23, 101; retributive justice, 74, 91, 93, 97–98, 100, 109, 160, 202, 210; retributive violence, 71, 99, 203, 211; and scapegoating, 75, 97–98

revenge, 10, 35–36, 55, 61, 91–92, 108, 109, 128, 202

Rhode Island, 11

Ricoeur, Paul, 182

right to life, detached and derivative views of, 32–34, 43, 71, 110, 112

Robertson, Marion G. "Pat," 44. 68–69, 205

Roe v. Wade, 77, 138

Romans, 133; Romans 2, 127, 131; Romans 3, 179; Romans 13, 37, 44, 67, 127–31

Roper v. Simmons, 103–5, 161–62, 163

Rosenbluth, Phyllis, 130

Rosenbluth, Stanley, 120, 130, 133

Ross, Michael, 198–99

Royal Commission on Capital Punishment Report, 1953 (UK), 11–12

Rozell, Mark, 122

Rudolph v. Alabama, 12

Runion, Donald, 27

Rush, Benjamin, 10

Ryan, George, 17–18, 39, 90, 120

sacrifice, 53, 55, 59, 66, 74–75, 91

sacrificial crisis, 83–85, 91, 210

salvation, 67–68, 70, 78, 167–68, 188–89

Samenow, Stanton E., 106

2 Samuel, 47

Sandel, Michael, 169

Sarat, Austin, 4, 6, 116

Scalia, Antonin, 36–37, 40, 83, 129

scapegoat, the, 14, 19–20, 23–24, 75, 80–84, 89–91, 97, 117, 209

Schwarzchild, Henry, 45

Schweitzer, Dan, 150

Scottsboro Boys, 152

secrecy, in executions, 116

sentencing phase. *See* capital murder trial
sermons, 24, 51, 179, 199, 202, 204; Sermon on the Mount, 70, 131; Sermon on the Plain, 70
Sessions, William, 192
Shapiro, Barbara J., 31
Sharp, Susan F., 6
Sheppard, Mark, 120, 133, 137
Sherbon, Wallace, 204
Sic Semper Tyrannis (SST), 123
Simson, Gary, 173
Smith, Jonathan Z., 113
social statements, 23, 28, 164, 172. *See also* doctrinal statements
South Carolina, 1, 2, 28, 126
South Carolina v. Gathers, 159
South Dakota, 11, 126
Southern Baptist Convention (SBC), 28, 33, 35–36; "Statement on Death Penalty," 33, 35–36; Ethics and Religious Liberty Commission, 28, 33
Southern Coalition on Jails and Prisons, 2
sovereignty of action, 24, 38, 110–113, 175–176, 183–84, 197, 202, 205–6, 210
speech act, 158, 185, 210
Spencer, Timothy, 79
Stanford v. Kentucky, 14
"Stanley" (campaign advertisement), 120–26, 133, 134, 136, 139
status (social), 33, 90
statutory aggravators, 15
Stephen, Saint, 47, 48, 77, 79
Stevens, John Paul, 152–53
Stewart, Potter, 91, 92, 147
Streeter, Patricia, 2–3, 5, 6
"strict father" morality, 131–34
Sullivan, Walter, 187
Sullivan, Winnifred Fallers, 30
"super due process," 151–52, 154–55, 160, 176
Supreme Court, U.S.: on actual innocence, 14, 83–84; amicus curiae briefs and, 149–50; appeals to, 16, 139; on the constitutionality of capital punishment, 5, 13, 91, 147, 161; on death-qualified juries predisposed to convicting, 169; "deregulation of death," 13–14, 151, 153; on juries as the conscience of the community, 40; *Kennedy v. Louisiana*, 208; on racial bias, 39, 96; on retribution as a valid penal aim, 35; *Roper v. Simmons*, 104. *See also individual justices by name*
Supreme Court of Virginia (SCVA), 15–16, 139
Sussex I state prison, 186–87, 188
Swaine, Lucas, 172
Swann, Calvin, 106–7

Taylor, Mark Lewis, 129
Televised executions, 115
Ten Commandments, 58, 74, 85, 129
Tennessee, 11, 91, 126, 158–59
Terry, Mary Sue, 108
Texas, 16, 27, 28, 69, 73, 87, 96, 97, 126, 188
Texas Conference of Churches, 44
Thomas, Cal, 3, 5, 18
Thomas, Jeffrey Allen, 110–11
Thomas, Sue Cha, 111
Thompson v. Oklahoma, 151
Thornton, Deborah, 68
Thornton, Katy, 68
Thornton, Richard, 68
"thou shalt not kill/murder," 57, 74, 85, 129
Timbrook, Kelly, 121
Timbrook, Rick, 121
Tison v. Arizona, 81
Transportation Act of 1718, 41
Trop v. Dulles, 163
"true bill," 14
Tucker, Karla Faye: conversion, 68–69, 72, 119, 199, 205; crime, 68; execution and controversy, 68, 19, 204–5; as scapegoat, 82
21-Day Rule, 16

Union of American Hebrew Congregations, 13
United Church of Christ, 13, 28, 39
United Methodist Church (UMC), 45, 48, 192
United Methodist Church Virginia Annual Conference, 44
United States v. Seeger, 170
Utah, 126

vengeance 29, 35–6, 40, 71, 115; avoiding/limiting, 36, 55–56, 67, 111–12, 119,

202–3; as legitimate goal of punishment, 91–93, 98; Tucker execution as, 69, 205. *See also* revenge

victim impact statements (VIS), 14, 91–92, 159

victims' rights movement, 93, 159, 242n30

vigilante/vigilantism, 11, 61, 75–79, 88, 91, 92, 96, 99; vigilante tradition (Zimring), 76–78

violence: address as, 159–60; in the Bible, 48, 53, 55–56, 58–59, 145; derivative conceptions of, 102; exclusion and, 180; impure vs. purifying, 83; limits on, 38, 44, 54–56, 71; lynch mob/vigilantist, 11, 202; means to an end/end in itself, 114–15; mimetic rivalry and, 60, 83–84, 86–87; at public executions, 10–11; prison and, 19, 102, 118; redemptive, 76, 78–79, 113–14, 118–19, 180, 203; as response to specific transgressions, 100, 181; restorative, 201; retributive, 71, 145; and the sacrificial crisis, 20, 83–86, 90, 99, 201; in society, 37, 78–79, 85–87, 90, 120, 211; society's violence/our violence, 22, 24, 80, 84, 100, 112–18, 119, 175, 202–3, 210–11; state and, 37; unlearning, 111

Virginia, 5, 211, 2005 gubernatorial campaign, 23, 26–27, 120–22, 125–27; banishment from, 41, 231n36; capital punishment in, 14–21, 93–95, 126–27, 138–39, 153, 209; churches and the death penalty, 44–45, 48, 89, 103–5, 112; clemency, 126–27, 135, 139, 174; death row, 18–19, 154, 186, 188, 209; execution history, 9, 16–21, 28, 124, 177, 187, 208–9; and the juvenile death penalty, 16, 104–5; laws of, 8–9, 57, 85–86, 92, 104–5, 130, 156, 186; and mentally ill offenders, 105–7; political blogosphere, 121–25, 126–27, 133–35, 142–43; provision of counsel, 152–56; Supreme Court of Virginia, 15–16, 139; wrongful convictions, 209, 241n23

Virginia Coalition on Jails and Prisons, 2

Virginia Conference of the UMC, 45

Virginia Council of Churches (VCC), 45, 54, 105, 112

Virginia General Assembly, 44, 45, 103

Virginia Interfaith Center for Public Policy (VICPP), 44, 103–5

Virginia People of Faith against the Death Penalty, 104

Virginians for Alternatives to the Death Penalty (VADP), 104, 207

Virginians United against Crime, 159

Volf, Miroslav, 24, 196; and embrace, 179, 185, 190, 193–94; and exclusion, 179–83

voir dire, 13, 15, 130, 166–70

Vought, Joseph, 20, 81, 112, 177–79, 188–91, 193–95, 198, 204

Wainwright v. Goode, 13

Wainwright v. Witt, 13

Walton, Percy Levar, 105–7, 209

"war on crime," 20

"war on terror," 86

warrant to punish, 105, 116, 117, 161, 175, 182, 197, 201, 202

Washington (state), 11, 87, 126

Washington, DC, 124

Washington, Earl Jr., 209

Watkins, Ronald, 119

Weinhold, Dick, 199

Weeks, Lonnie, 119

Weisberg, Robert, 13, 98

Wheeler v. Kentucky, 150

Whitley, Richard, 2

Willingham, Cameron Todd, 73, 238n59

Wisconsin, 11

Witherspoon v. Illinois, 147

women, the death penalty and, 12, 16, 25, 69

Wood, Thomas H., 170

Woodson v. North Carolina, 147, 174

"worst of the worst," 20, 82, 94, 117, 162, 198

wrongful convictions/executions, 11, 32, 34, 72–73, 90, 109, 219n46, 238n59, 241n23 *See also* Willingham, Cameron Todd; Washington, Earl Jr.; Davis, Troy Anthony

Wyoming, 127

Yarbrough, Robert Stacy: xii, 183, 208–9

Yi, Tong, 111

Yoder, John Howard, 56

zealous nationalism, 131–32

Zimring, Franklin, 76, 92